ENVIRONMENTAL LAW

ENVIRONMENTAL LAW
Meeting UK and EC Requirements

ALBERT MUMMA

McGRAW-HILL BOOK COMPANY

London · New York · St Louis · San Francisco · Auckland
Bogotá · Caracas · Lisbon · Madrid · Mexico · Montreal
New Delhi · Panama · Paris · San Juan · São Paulo
Singapore · Sydney · Tokyo · Toronto

Published by
McGraw-Hill Book Company Europe
Shoppenhangers Road, Maidenhead, Berkshire SL6 2QL, England
Telephone 01628 23432
Facsimile 01628 770224

British Library Cataloguing in Publication Data
Mumma, Albert
  Environmental Law: Meeting UK and EC
  Requirements
  I. Title
  344.10446

  ISBN 0-07-707952-3

Library of Congress Cataloging-in-publication Data
Mumma, Albert,
  Environmental law: meeting UK and EC requirements/Albert Mumma.
    p.   cm.
  Includes bibliographical references and index.
  ISBN 0-07-707952-3
    1. Environmental law–Great Britain. 2. Environmental law–
  European Economic Community countries. I. Title.
  KD3372.M85
  344.4′046–dc20
  [344.0446]

95-5091
CIP

1 2 3 4 5 BL 9 8 7 6 5

Typeset by Paston Press Ltd, Loddon, Norfolk
Printed and bound in Great Britain by Biddles Ltd, Guildford, Surrey
Printed on Permanent Paper in compliance with the ISO standard 9706

Contents

Foreword

The development of 'modern' environmental law over the past five years has been reflected in the number of law books arriving on the market, generally for the consumption of non-lawyers. This book will fill a discernible gap for corporate, commercial and property lawyers whose speciality is not environmental law, for recent qualifiers into environmental law departments and for environmental managers with some familiarity with the subject.

This area of legislation is complex and steadily evolving and ignorance of it can have serious implications for companies and their legal advisers. In this book, the author sets out clearly the current issues of particular significance in environmental law in the European Union and the United Kingdom. His use of language is precise and shows a clear desire not to compromise into over-simplification at the expense of explaining in appropriate detail the implications of the various pieces of statutory material.

Given the size of the book, Dr Mumma has managed, by diligence and an obvious enthusiasm for the subject, to create a remarkably broad base of information which will be useful both as an initial reference for those seeking to solve a practical environmental law problem and as a starting point for those wanting a thorough grounding in the subject. In short, it will provide much-needed guidance and advice to all those involved with the ramifications of environmental law. I thoroughly recommend it.

Sir Hugh Rossi
London
September 1994

Acknowledgements

The ideas discussed in this book were refined in discussions with my colleagues at the Environmental Law Department of Simmons & Simmons and I am grateful to them. I would like to single out for special thanks James Fitzgerald and Andrea Dalberg, who read the manuscript and made many useful comments. My editors at McGraw-Hill have been a pleasure to work with. Finally, I would like to thank Catherine for her encouragement.

Table of Statutes

Table of Cases

Acronyms

ALTENER	EC Alternative Energy Scheme
BAT	Best Available Techniques
BPM	Best Practicable Means
BPEO	Best Practicable Environmental Option
BATNEEC	Best Available Techniques Not Entailing Excessive Cost
BS	British Standard
BSI	British Standards Institution
CBI	Confederation of British Industry
CHIP	Chemicals (Hazard Information and Packaging) Regulations 1993
CIA	Chemical Industries Association
CLL	Contaminated Land and Liability Branch, DoE
COPA	Control of Pollution Act 1974
CPL	Classification, Packaging and Labelling Regulations
CSD	UN Commission on Sustainable Development
DG	Directorate General of the European Commission
DGXI	Environment DG of the European Commission
DoE	Department of the Environment
DLG	Derelict Land Grant
DSD	Duales System Deutschland (German packaging waste scheme)
DTI	Department of Trade and Industry
EA	Environmental Assessment
EC	European Community
ECJ	European Court of Justice
EINECS	European Inventory of Existing Commercial Chemical Substances
EMAS	Eco-management and Audit Scheme
EPA	Environmental Protection Act 1990
EQO	Environmental Quality Objective
EQS	Environmental Quality Standards
EWC	European Waste Catalogue
FoE	Friends of the Earth
GDO	General Development Order

GMO	Genetically Modified Organism
HMIP	Her Majesty's Inspectorate of Pollution
HMIPI	Her Majesty's Industrial Pollution Inspectorate (Scotland)
HMSO	Her Majesty's Stationery Office
HSC	Health and Safety Commission
HSE	Health and Safety Executive
ICC	International Chamber of Commerce
IPC	Integrated Pollution Control
IPPC	Integrated Pollution Prevention and Control
LAAPC	Local Authority Air Pollution Control
MAC	Maximum Admissible Concentration
MAFF	Ministry of Agriculture, Fisheries and Food
NACCB	National Accreditation Council for Certification Bodies
NFFO	Non-Fossil Fuel Obligation
NRA	National Rivers Authority
OFWAT	Office of Water Services
OJ	Official Journal of the European Communities
PPG	Planning Policy Guidance Note
RCEP	Royal Commission on Environmental Pollution
SAVE	Specific Actions for Vigorous Energy Efficiency (EC Energy Scheme)
SI	Statutory Instrument
SO	Scottish Office
UKEB	UK Eco-labelling Board
UNECE	United Nations Economic Commission for Europe
UNEP	United Nations Environment Programme
VOC	Volatile Organic Compound
WAMITAB	Waste Management Industry Training and Advisory Board
WO	Welsh Office
WRA	Waste Regulation Authority

Introduction

This book is aimed at the non-specialist. It is written as an introductory text and assumes very little knowledge of environmental law. At the same time, it provides a comprehensive treatment of the subject but in simple language, without jargon. It should appeal to lawyers and non-lawyers alike.

The scope of the book extends to the main areas of environmental law. Due to the inherent difficulties of defining the boundaries of environmental law the choice of topics covered has been guided by current environmental concerns. However, not every topic has been dealt with, in particular those which are adequately covered in standard texts on town and country planning, nature conservation, radioactive substances and marine pollution.

The focus of the book is environmental law in England and Wales but an indication of the law in Scotland is given in each chapter. In many instances the law is substantively the same north and south of the border although the statutory references differ. These statutory provisions are highlighted.

EC law is increasingly a part of UK law and, since the *Marleasing* judgment, it has become important to look beyond the UK implementing regulations to the EC directives and regulations themselves. Therefore, EC environmental law is dealt with as an integral part of the law in the United Kingdom. But incorporation of EC law into the text presented difficulties since UK and EC law do not make an exact fit; many UK laws exist independently of any EC requirements and several EC requirements have not yet been implemented in the UK. Integrating EC requirements into every chapter has led, inevitably, to some repetition.

The first chapter describes the regulatory framework for environmental control in the UK. EC law and institutions are fully introduced in this section. The book then breaks the subject down into three areas:

1   A technical section, discussing the law on water pollution control, waste management, contaminated land and liabilities, atmospheric pollution control, statutory nuisance and noise and the control of hazardous substances and genetically modified organisms;

2   A management section discussing environmental assessment and auditing, environmental information and communications and paying for pollution control; and
3   An enforcement section discussing enforcement through using both criminal and civil law.

Modern environmental law in the UK has witnessed rapid change in the last five years. Important new pieces of legislation have been enacted and seminal judicial pronouncements have clarified the scope and extent of liability for environmental pollution. These developments are the subject matter of this book. The one important piece of legislation that is currently awaited is an Act to establish an Environmental Protection Agency.

The main body of environmental law is currently contained in a few major statutes and judicial decisions. The **Environmental Protection Act 1990** (EPA) makes provisions for integrated pollution control, a comprehensive system of waste management, and statutory control over genetically modified substances. The **Water Resources Act 1991** and the **Water Industry Act 1991** contain the law on water pollution control while the **Clean Air Act 1993** deals with the law on dark smoke emissions. Principles of civil liability were dealt with in the famous *Cambridge Water Company case*.

Nevertheless, there are important and difficult issues still to be resolved. Liability for contaminated land and funding for clean-up is no nearer resolution than it was at the start of the decade. Legal mechanisms for incorporating financial instruments into the pollution control system are still lacking. Waste minimization, in contrast to pollution control, is also in need of further legal development. Whether there will be movement in these, and other areas, remains to be seen.

1

The Regulatory Framework

1.1 The Institutional Framework

Given the difficulty of delimiting the subject matter of environmental law it is no surprise that responsibility for environmental protection is not vested in a single authority. Instead responsibility is spread among a wide range of authorities, central, local and 'next steps'. The last-named bodies are one step removed from the direct administrative control of the minister, having their own administrative structure outside the civil service and controlling their own budget, an arrangement seen as useful in reducing red tape. Nevertheless, the agencies remain under the minister's policy direction for purposes, particularly, of parliamentary responsibility. The National Rivers Authority, the Office of Water Services, the Planning Inspectorate and the Health and Safety Executive are examples of 'next steps' agencies with an environmental mandate; Her Majesty's Inspectorate of Pollution and the Drinking Water Inspectorate are examples of authorities which are under the administrative control of the minister; and local authorities in their various guises (local planning authorities, litter authorities, waste regulatory authorities, local authority air pollution control authorities, statutory nuisance control authorities and noise control authorities) represent local control. There are also several non-statutory (but official) bodies with environmental functions.

1.1.1 Central Government

Within central government the Department of the Environment (DoE) has the primary responsibility for environmental matters. It therefore takes the lead in issues of environmental policy and acts as the parliamentary spokesman for the various 'next steps' agencies with environmental responsibilities. The name notwithstanding, less than 10 per cent of the DoE's staff work directly on environmental protection (DoE Annual Report, 1993)

The DoE is complemented in its role by other departments which also have responsibilities touching on environmental protection. The Ministry of Agriculture, Fisheries and Food (MAFF), for example, has important environmental responsibilities such as the control of discharges into the marine environment. The Ministry of Transport (MTp) has important environmental responsibilities relating, in particular, to road-construction programmes, the subject of so many environmental controversies over impact assessments. Increasingly, the Department of Trade and Industry (DTI) is getting involved, particularly with the growing trend towards reliance on market mechanisms in environmental protection. Significantly, to raise the profile of environmental considerations in governmental decision making each government department has nominated a minister to be in charge of environmental issues within that department (*This Common Inheritance*, 1990). The Welsh and the Scottish offices also have specific environment duties in relation to the two countries.

Although they are under the direct control of the Minister, Her Majesty's Inspectorate of Pollution (HMIP) (and Her Majesty's Industrial Pollution Inspectorate (HMIPI) in Scotland) and the Drinking Water Inspectorate (DWI) both have distinct environmental powers and responsibilites. HMIP and HMIPI were established in 1987 to implement a new system of pollution control known as integrated pollution control (IPC). Their antecedents can be traced back, however, to the once famous Alkali Inspectorate, the first centralized industrial pollution control agency in the UK, set up under the **Alkali Act 1906**. The DWI was set up under provisions of the **Water Act 1989** (now replaced by provisions in the **Water Industry Act 1991**) to check the quality of drinking water supplied by water companies in England and Wales for compliance with statutory water quality requirements. It has only a small staff within the DoE and often resorts to external consultancies to carry out some of its audit functions.

1.1.2   Next Steps Agencies

Pre-eminent among next steps agencies with environmental responsibilities is the National Rivers Authority (NRA). The NRA was established in September 1989 under provisions of the **Water Act 1989**, replacing the old regional water authorities which had until then delivered drinking water, collected sewage and regulated discharges into watercourses. The water supply and sewage collection functions were privatized at the same time as the establishment of the NRA. The NRA's responsibilities for the water environment are wide: they cover water resources management; water pollution control; flood defence and land drainage; fisheries regulation; and navigation, harbour and conservancy functions.

The privatized water and sewerage services are under the regulatory control of the Office of Water Services (OFWAT), which is headed by a Director General. OFWAT's function is limited to regulating the economic performance of the private water companies. Its mandate is to ensure that the companies have adequate capital to continue delivering water and sewerage services efficiently and to protect the interests of customers, seeing particularly that prices remain affordable. This latter role has important implications for the levels of investment into improvements in water quality and sewerage treatment: the more a company invests in these environmental services, the higher the charges to customers as it seeks to pass on the costs. OFWAT sees its role as being to keep down environmental expenditure, a view which has in recent years led to a sharp difference of views with the NRA, which would like to see increased capital investment (OFWAT, 1993; DoE, 1993).

The Nature Conservancy Council for England (English Nature), the Nature Conservancy Council for Scotland and the Countryside Council for Wales currently have responsibility under the EPA 1990 for nature conservation and for recreation, landscape and amenity respectively. The Councils have set up a Joint Nature Conservation Committee to look after common interests between the three. The Countryside Commission has the responsibility in England under the Countryside Act 1968 for designating national parks and areas of outstanding national beauty. The government is currently consulting on whether to unify it with English Nature, but any changes would need legislation. The timetable for change is therefore uncertain.

Finally, The Health and Safety Commission was set up under the **Health and Safety at Work etc. Act 1974** with power to direct investigations and inquiries into the workings of the Act (which is concerned principally with conditions in the workplace). The detailed implementation of the Act is delegated to the Health and Safety Executive, the Commission's operational arm.

1.1.3 Local Authorities

Local authorities are of two kinds: county councils and smaller district (known in London and the metropolitan areas as 'borough') councils. Both have important environmental protection duties at the local level. These cover waste management regulation, air pollution control, litter control, noise control, planning and statutory nuisance control. The two-tier structure of local authorities is currently under review with a view to the creation of one-tier structures.

In England, waste regulation is the responsibility of county councils in the shires. In London and the metropolitan areas it is under larger authorities, such as the London Waste Regulation Authority, bringing together smaller boroughs, voluntarily or by statute. The authorities license and monitor waste management activities and also take enforcement action. Air pollution control, noise control, statutory nuisance control, and litter control, on the other hand, are the responsibility of the district (or borough) council rather than the county council. Planning is shared. The district (or borough) council enforcement officer is known as the environmental health officer, a designation dating back to the nineteenth century. Their association is known as the Institution of Environmental Health Officers.

1.1.4   Non-statutory Bodies

Of the non-statutory bodies the Royal Commission on Environmental Pollution is quite influential. It was set up in 1970 'to advise on matters concerning pollution of the environment ... and the future possibilities of the danger to the environment'. It has produced sixteen significant reports on a variety of environmental issues and has announced that its next two reports, due out in 1994 and 1995, will be on transport and contaminated land, respectively.

Equally influential are the Parliamentary Select Committees whose function is to scrutinize the day-to-day activities of the government. In the House of Lords, the Select Committee on the European Communities and in the House of Commons the Select Committee on the Environment are both well regarded. The House of Lords Select Committee regularly examines proposals for environmental measures from the European Commission. Under the chairmanship of Sir Hugh Rossi (1983–92) the House of Commons Select Committee concentrated on environmental (as opposed to local government or housing) issues and had a significant influence on the government's environmental policy.

1.1.5   An Environment Agency

In 1991 the government proposed far-reaching changes in the institutional arrangements for environmental protection and regulation, involving the creation of an Environment Protection Agency (DoE, 1991). Several factors dictate change.

First, the fact that agencies currently have problems of overlap and potential conflict in their roles. Both HMIP and the NRA have responsibilities for controlling discharges to water from industrial processes, requiring close coordination. The present arrangements fall short of securing a fully integrated, effective and multi-media approach to pollution control, confuse industry and make difficult the task of delivering a high-quality public service. Similar concerns arise for waste regulation, where close liaison is needed between the waste regulation authorities and the NRA in setting licence conditions to prevent the contamination of water by leachate from landfill sites and other waste management facilities. As the standards and techniques for waste management become increasingly sophisticated, it is increasingly difficult for individual waste regulation authorities either to provide the necessary expertise or to coordinate policies and standards over a wide enough area.

Another concern was the necessity to ensure that decisions about pollution control take full account of the need to select the best practicable environmental option. As things stand, trade-offs between the different objectives of the regulatory bodies may not always be established at the point which is best suited for minimizing environmental impact. For example, the disposal of waste has the potential for polluting air, land and water, depending on the method of disposal chosen, and it is important that their environmental consequences are considered in relation to each other before the choice is made. This decision is best taken by one agency.

The government proposed therefore to combine the key regulatory pollution control responsibilities of HMIP, the NRA and the waste regulation functions of local authorities within a new independent Environment Protection Agency, for England and Wales and separately, for Scotland. In the Queen's Speech of 18 November 1993 the government promised a paving Bill in the 1993/4 session of Parliament to enable preparatory work to be undertaken so that the Agency can be up and running in October 1995 as soon as a substantive Bill, expected in the 1994/5 session, has been passed, giving it the necessary powers. Whether this timetable will be met is difficult to say, although a draft Environment Agencies Bill was published in October 1994.

1.2   The European Community

1.2.1   Historical Background

The Treaty Establishing the European Economic Community (EEC) was signed in Rome (hence, the Treaty of Rome) on 25 March 1957 by six European countries—Italy, Belgium, Germany, France, Luxembourg and The Netherlands. Its entry into force on 1 January 1958 marked the formal establishment of the European Common Market. The EEC has since been enlarged by the addition of the United Kingdom, Ireland and Denmark in 1972, Greece in 1981 and Spain and Portugal in 1986. Another three countries, Austria, Sweden and Finland are expected to join in 1995, bringing the number of member states to fifteen. Norway voted against joining. Additionally, the Community countries entered into an agreement in 1993 with member countries of the European Free Trade Area (EFTA), i.e. the three countries expected to join the Community in 1995 together with Norway, Iceland and Liechtenstein (Switzerland failed to ratify) setting up the European Economic Area, an internal market with over 370 million people.

Enlargement went alongside amendments to the EEC Treaty; first by the **Single European Act 1987** and then, more fundamentally, by the Treaty of European Union which was signed at Maastricht on 7 February 1992. The

Maastricht Treaty entered into force on 1 November 1993 following much soul searching in several countries on the question of whether the new treaty would undermine national sovereignty by transferring power to the Community head-quarters in Brussels. Opponents were only mollified after the Community developed the concept of 'subsidiarity', i.e. that action would be taken by the Community only where the relevant objectives could not be better attained at member state level. Subsidiarity has become a central plank in the argument that Community measures, including environmental ones, viewed as unecessarily prescriptive should be modified.

The Maastricht Treaty changed the name of the EEC in two respects. First, it replaced the term 'European Economic Community', which dates back to the Treaty of Rome, with 'European Community' (EC), reflecting the wider mandate of the Community. Second, it established a 'European Union' (EU) to be built upon the EC. The Union took over all EC objectives (e.g. a common market) and added several of its own: a single currency; monetary union; a common foreign and security policy; a common citizenship; and cooperation in justice and home affairs. In relation to these new activities the Community must now be referred to as the EU (Council Decision 93/591, OJ No. L 281/18). In relation to those objectives predating the Maastricht Treaty it is correct to refer to the EU either as the EU or as the EC because the EU incorporates the EC. Environmental policy predates the Maastricht Treaty and so either designation would be correct. The 'EC', as the more farmiliar term, is used here.

The Treaty of Rome did not mention environmental protection because in 1957 this was not a significant concern of governments. Between then and the early 1970s, however, environmental protection became a priority item on the international community's agenda, culminating in a UN-sponsored conference on the environment in Stockholm in 1972. The twentieth anniversary of this conference was marked in June 1992 by a follow-up conference, the UN Conference on Environment and Development, in Rio de Janeiro.

Community heads of state and government, at a meeting in Paris in 1972, reflected the mood of the times by proposing that the Community set up an Environmental Action Programme, stating its general approach and policy towards environmental protection. The proposal set in train the EC practice of periodically adopting Action Programmes: the first (OJ No. C 112 of 20 December 1973) ran to 1976; the second (OJ No. C 139 of 13 June 1977) ran to 1981; the third (OJ No. C 46 of 17 February 1983) ran to 1986; the fourth (OJ No. C 328 of 7 December 1987) ran to 1992; and the fifth (No. C 138 of 17 May 1993) runs to the year 2000, but with an interim appraisal in 1995. The fifth Action Programme marks a shift in policy by calling for the integration of environmental and other Community measures.

Action Programmes were followed up by specific pieces of legislation. Although the Treaty of Rome had made no specific provision for environmental legislation the Community relied on its general law-making powers under Articles 100 and 235 of the Treaty. The inadequacy of these provisions for environmental legislation was plain for all to see; Article 100 gives power to make laws 'as directly affect the establishment or functioning of the common market' while Article 235 states that even though the Treaty has not provided the necessary powers 'appropriate action' may be taken if that is necessary to attain the Community's objectives. Reliance on Article 235 was justified on the basis that environmental protection was one of the Community's objectives but the legal basis of Community environmental action remained hazy.

The opportunity presented by the Single European Act 1987 was used therefore to amend the Treaty of Rome and insert a new chapter on the environment, Title VII, giving clear legal powers to legislate on environmental matters. Title VII added three new Articles to the Treaty of Rome; 130r, 130s and 130t. Article 130r states explicitly that 'environmental protection requirements shall be a component of the Community's other policies'. It also specifies the three principles on which action shall be based; the need to take preventative action, rectify environmental damage at source and make the polluter pay. The objectives of the action shall be to preserve, protect and improve the quality of the environment, to contribute towards protecting human health and ensure a prudent and rational utilization of natural resources. Article 130s provides that environmental action by member states shall be taken by unanimous vote while Article 130t enables those member states who wish to take more stringent measures than those taken by the Community to do so as long as the measures are not a disguised trade restriction.

1.2.2   EC Institutions

The Community has six institutions: a Council, a Commission, a Parliament, a Court of Justice, an Economic and Social Committee (ECOSOC) and a Court of Auditors. ECOSOC's function is to advise the Council and the Commission while the Court of Auditors audits the Community's accounts. Additionally, there is a political body known as the European Council, not to be confused with the legal institution known as the Council; the latter is one of the six Community institutions, the former is not.

The Council

The Council, which is the law-making body of the Community, is made up of ministerial representatives of each member state with authority to commit their governments. The presidency of the Council rotates among member states every six months in two cycles of six years. The current cycle, which began in January 1993, runs as follows: Belgium, Denmark, Greece, Germany, Spain, France, Ireland, Italy, Luxembourg, The Netherlands, Portugal, the UK. The second cycle does not begin until 1999 and although the order is already laid in Article 146 of the Treaty, it may change to accommodate the 1995 entrants. The importance of the presidency lies in its management of the agenda of the Council, thereby influencing which proposals are taken forward and which not.

The Council's work is prepared by a Committee of Permanent Representatives of Member States (COREPER), which is itself assisted by a General Secretariat. Under the Council's Rules of Procedure (Wyatt and Dashwoods, 1993, p. 25) the agenda for each Council meeting is in two parts: A and B. Part A consists of items (known as A-points) which COREPER has laid down for adoption by the Council without debate. This procedure is used for the formal adoption of items whose texts have been agreed in principle at an earlier Council meeting but which could not be adopted formally for some reason, such as the need to give Parliament an opportunity to consider the item. Such a Council agreement is known as a 'political agreement'.

Although any minister may represent his or her government at Council meetings it is customary for the agenda items to dictate the composition of the Council. Thus, there is the Environment Council, the Transport Council and so on, holding regular meetings whose dates are set well in advance although special meetings are not unknown. A-points may be put to any Council, however composed. B-points, on the other hand, are debated by the ministers.

To mark the end of each presidency the country holding the presidency of the Council hosts a meeting of the political heads of state and government. This meeting is known as the European Council. It was provided for in the **Single European Act 1987** to give a legal basis to a common practice of the political leaders of the EC meeting periodically. The European Council is a high-profile event at which important decisions are taken. Two recent examples are the amplification of the doctrine of 'subsidiarity' and the decision to begin enlargement negotiations with the four countries (Austria, Sweden, Finland and Norway), both taken at the European Council meeting in Edinburgh in December 1992.

The Commission

The Commission is based permanently in Brussels. It has seventeen members, taking decisions by majority voting at regular meetings during which, for instance, it formally adopts proposals for legislation which it wishes to put forward. The Commission's role is pre-eminent insofar as its job is to put forward proposals for decision to the Council. Indeed, its stance once it has put forward proposals is to defend them from outside attempts to alter them. After the Council the Commission is the most powerful organ of the EC. Its role as an initiator of legislation means that it is not just a civil service. It also has responsibility for enforcing EC law by bringing proceedings in the European Court against member states who breach EC law.

Each of the member states has at least one Commissioner, with the larger countries having two. But once appointed, the Commissioners are required to be independent of national interests. The President of the Commission is appointed by the governments of the member states after consulting the European Parliament. The next appointees of both the Commissioners and the President are due to take office in January 1995 for a five-year term. The Commission is assisted by a staff of civil servants organized in Directorates General, DG XI having charge of environmental affairs.

The Commission publishes the *Official Journal of the European Comunities* (OJ), the official source of information on Community matters. The OJ is published in two series; the 'C' series contains proposals while the 'L' series contains legislation, i.e. adopted texts of directives and other legislation. Proposals are published only after they have been formally adopted by the Commission; working drafts are not published and are obtainable only informally. Each directive published is numbered according to the year and order in which it was adopted by the Council, which forms part of its reference together with the number and relevant page of the OJ in which it appears (e.g. Directive 92/75/ EEC, OJ No. L 45, p. 1). Separately the Commission occasionally publishes some documents singly, giving them a 'COM' document number reflecting once again their year and order of adoption (e.g. COM (93) 499). These do not appear in the OJ. Examples include annual reports on the implementation by member states of EC requirements.

The European Parliament

The European Parliament has an 'advisory and supervisory' function. Its seat has alternated between Brussels and Strasbourg for decades due to an inability of member states to agree a permanent base. The Parliament consists of elected members (MEPs) from EC member states who organize themselves on the basis of broad ideological affiliations. The number of seats which each country holds reflects roughly the size of the population of the member state. Like most parliaments, it is organized into committees, the Environment and Social Affairs Committee being one of the more vocal. The committees examine proposals and make detailed recommendations which are voted on by the full Parliament. Each committee appoints a rapporteur to write its report on each proposal; the report is referred to by the rapporteur's name.

The powers of the European Parliament were traditionally limited but since the Maastricht Treaty it has acquired significant new powers which are examined below under 'Law Making'. Additionally it has power to request the Commission to submit proposals for legislation to the Council.

The European Court of Justice

The European Court of Justice (ECJ) is based in Luxembourg. It has thirteen judges. There is also a lower court known as the Court of First Instance whose remit is to deal with actions delegated to it, the bulk of which relate to the implementation of EC competition law. There is provision to appeal to the Court of Justice from the decisions of the Court of First Instance. The Court of Justice is assisted by six Advocates-General who, like the judges, are appointed for six years. An Advocate-General is drawn from the Continental legal systems and has no parallel in the English legal system. The duty of the Advocate-General is to give an opinion on a case before it 'to assist the Court'; quite often, though not always, the Court follows the opinion.

The jurisdiction of the Court of Justice is to 'ensure that in the intepretation and application of the Treaty the law is observed'. Proceedings may be brought in the Court of Justice by either the Commission or another member state against a member state which fails 'to fulfil its obligations under the Treaty', the phrase used in the Treaty to refer to breaches. An individual wishing to complain against a member state must do so through the Commission. Under the Maastricht Treaty there is provision for a financial penalty to be imposed on a member state who fails to take remedial measures required by the Court. Additionally, the Court has jurisdiction to review the legality of the decisions of the Community's institutions. If addressed to an individual, then that individual, or another with a 'direct and individual concern' in the decision, may bring proceedings before the Court. Environmental decisions are not, however, the kind that get addressed to individuals.

Environment Agency

The Environment Agency is not one of the Community's institutions for which provision is made in the Treaty. Rather, it is set up under Council Regulation No. 1210/90 (OJ No. L 120/1) on the establishment of the European Environment Agency and the European environment information and observation network. The Agency's seat is in Copenhagen and it is headed by an Executive Director appointed for five years.

The tasks of the Agency are set out in the Regulation; they relate mainly to the collection, processing, analysis and dissemination of enviromnental information. Thus the Agency is required to publish a report on the state of the environment every three years. Member states are expected to designate a 'national focal point' for coordinating and transmitting the information to be supplied to the Agency. Since non-members of the EC may participate in the work of the Agency, a number of European countries, in particular the Scandinavian ones, have expressed an interest.

Significantly, it is *not* an enforcement agency at the moment although there is provision for its activities to be expanded to include:

1 Associating in the monitoring of the implementation of Community environmental legislation
2 Preparing environmental labels and criteria for the award of eco-labels
3 Promoting environmentally friendly technologies and processes
4 Establishing criteria for environmental impact assessment.

1.2.3 The EC Law-making Process

The process under which EC law is made is exceptionally complex, involving a subtle and often protracted interaction between the three EC institutions; the Council, the Commission and Parliament, which, acting together, make EC law.

Voting Procedures Generally

Article 148 of the Treaty of Rome provides that the Council shall act by a majority of its members, unless the Treaty provides otherwise. The general position therefore requires EC measures to be adopted by a majority vote of the Council. This, however, is not a simple majority of seven members out of the twelve. Rather, the majority required is a 'qualified majority' of the twelve; a simple majority would mean that a small country like Luxembourg would command the same weight in decision making as a major country such as Germany, a situation seen as unfair since the wealthier member states make larger contributions to the EC budget. Article 148(2) therefore assigns each member state a number of votes based not on their budgetary contributions but on their populations as follows: Germany, France, Italy and the UK (ten each); Spain (eight); Greece, Belgium, The Netherlands and Portugal (five each); Denmark and Ireland (three each); and Luxembourg (two). This gives a total of 76 votes of which 54 makes a qualified majority. The blocking minority of 23 will increase provisionally to 27 once the three new entrants, each holding four votes, join in 1995; the position is to be reviewed in 1996.

The general rule that measures are to be adopted by qualified majority vote can be deceptive since in reality the Treaty of Rome requires several of the more important measures to be adopted unanimously. Therefore the process for adopting a particular measure depends on the Treaty's provisions for that measure, be it environmental, agricultural, tax and so on. Cutting across all these categories, however, Article 100 of the Treaty requires all 'measures which directly affect the establishment and functioning of the common market' to be adopted unanimously. Unanimous action is inevitably slow since one member state could hold up progress for years by threatening a veto.

Therefore, when EC member states decided in 1987 that the establishment of the internal market must be completed by the end of 1992 they decided also to speed up the process for adopting the measures for doing so. A new Article 100A was introduced by the **Single European Act 1987** requiring that measures aimed at completing the establishment of the internal market by the end of 1992 be adopted by a qualified majority. But such measures could only be adopted 'in cooperation with the Parliament', hence the name 'the cooperation procedure' for the adoption of EC law.

Measures not aimed at completing the establishment of the internal market by 1992 continued to be adopted under the old procedure; i.e. the Commission makes a proposal for legislation, consults Parliament on it and then places it before the Council for adoption, either unanimously or by a qualified majority. The requirement to consult Parliament has given this procedure the name the 'consultation procedure'. A proposal cannot be adopted before Parliament has given its opinion on it or, if it is substantially amended, on the amended version. But the formal involvement of Parliament is limited to giving its opinion; it cannot veto the measure.

Under the 'cooperation procedure', the details of which are set out in Article 149(2), Parliament has enhanced powers. Again the Commission makes a proposal, consults Parliament and then places it before the Council. If the Council agrees with it, it adopts what the Treaty refers to as a 'common position' on the proposal. The Council's common position is then sent to Parliament which has a second opportunity to give its opinion, this time on the Council's common position. Parliament has three months in which to take a decision on the common position after which the Council adopts the measure. There are three possible courses of action which Parliament may take.

First, Parliament may reject the Council's common position. If so, the Council can only adopt the measure unanimously. Second, Parliament may amend the Council's common position. If it does the Commission has one month in which to examine the proposal and accept or reject all or some of Parliament's amendments. The Commission then places the proposal before the Council a second time, either amended in the light of Parliament's opinion or not amended. This time round the Council adopts the measure, by qualified majority vote if it agrees with it and unanimously if it amends it by, say, including amendments proposed by Parliament but rejected by the Commission. Third, Parliament may let three months lapse before taking a decision, in which case the Council may adopt the proposal unanimously.

Voting Procedures for Environmental Measures

The **Single European Act 1987** which made provision for the Community to take measures relating to the environment provided under Article 130s that such measures be adopted unanimously. Things did not work smoothly, however. After the introduction of Article 100A, which was intended to facilitate the completion of the internal market by 1992, the Council would adopt measures under both Article 100A and the specific Article of the Treaty dealing with that matter. Thus environmental measures were adopted under Articles 100A and 130s; the one requiring qualified majority voting, the other, unanimity. This practice deprived Parliament of a chance of a second reading under the cooperation procedure.

The dispute over the proper basis for the adoption of Community measures was taken to the European Court of Justice twice, in *Case C-300/89*, a case concerning the Titanium Dioxide Directive, and again in *Case C-155/91*, concerning the amendment to the Waste Framework Directive. The ECJ accepted that measures could have twin objectives but ruled that the Treaty made environmental protection requirements a component of the Community's other policies and so a measure could not be based on Article 130s solely by reason of the fact that it pursues, among others, aims of environmental protection. At the same time the mere fact that the establishment of the internal market was concerned was not sufficient for Article 100A to be applied if this was simply an ancilliary effect of the measure. The choice of the legal basis for a measure must be based on objective factors, including its aim and content. The ECJ held that the Titanium Dioxide measure was aimed primarily at completing the internal market whereas the amendment to the Waste Framework Directive was primarily an environmental protection measure.

The Maastricht Treaty retained the cooperation procedure for adopting Community measures and enlarged its scope. Article 130s, for instance, was rewritten so that as from 1 November 1993, environmental measures are adopted by qualified majority voting. There are three exceptions to this and in those areas action must still be unanimous: provisions primarily of a fiscal nature (e.g. the carbon/energy tax proposal); measures concerning town and country planning, land use (except waste management), and the management of water resources; and energy-related measures.

The Maastricht Treaty also introduced a third procedure for adopting certain measures (e.g. Article 100A measures) under which Parliament can veto measures. Before it does so there is provision for negotiations between it and the Council to be held, the Commission acting as conciliator. The negotiations may lead to an agreed text otherwise the measure will fail. This is referred to as the 'co-decision procedure' and, in the environmental field, will apply to the adoption of environmental action programmes and measures brought under Article 100A, such as the packaging and packaging waste directive proposal.

1.2.4 Sources of EC Law

EC treaties are the primary source of EC law while measures adopted by the law-making institutions of the EC as well as judgments of the ECJ constitute secondary sources. Article 189 provides that the Council, the Commission and Parliament shall 'make regulations and issue directives, take decisions, make recommendations or deliver opinions'. 'Regulations' are binding in their entirety and directly applicable in all member states; 'directives' are binding as to the result to be achieved but leave to the national authorities the choice of form and methods; 'decisions' are binding in their entirety upon those to whom they are addresssed, often non-state entities; and 'recommendations and opinions' have no binding force. Thus whereas member states need to take action to implement directives, regulations apply directly without the need for implementing measures.

A line of ECJ judgments (Wyatt and Dashwoods, 1993, Chap. 4) have established that directives and decisions can have a 'direct effect', i.e. bypassing the state and giving individuals rights which can be invoked before national courts, even though the member state has not acted to implement the measure or has implemented it inadequately. The directive must, however, be unambiguous, unconditional and not requiring further action by some other entity, preconditions that exclude most environmental measures. In the *Lombardia case* the ECJ ruled that Article 4 of the Waste Framework Directive, which requires waste to be disposed of without endangering health or the environment, does not have direct effect.

Nevertheless, as the court pointed out in *Wychavon DC v Secretary of State for the Environment*, a directive cannot be relied on directly against another private individual; it can only be relied on against the state and its organs. But in *Marleasing* the ECJ decided that national courts must interpret national law in a manner consistent with the requirements of relevant EC directives, whether or not they have been implemented by the state. This may result in directives having a direct effect on non-state entities since the ruling applies to private disputes and disputes with state entities alike.

1.2.5   Enforcement of EC Law

The task of supervising member states' compliance with their obligations under the Treaty belongs to the Commission. Ultimately this may involve the Commission initiating proceedings against a member state in the ECJ. Member states also have the right to initiate proceedings against each other but they have demonstrated an understandable reluctance to exercise this right.

The Commission does not itself gather information about action taken by member states to implement EC requirements; this role is performed by the European Environment Agency. It relies on reports which member states have to submit to it, typically in three-year cycles as required by Directive 91/692/ EEC on reports on implementation of environmental directives (OJ No. L 377/48). These reports relate only to formal implementation by the introduction of legislation and not to action on the ground (e.g. actual prosecutions of offenders). To address that issue, a network of enforcement authorities from the member states, referred to as the Chester Network after the English city where the first meeting took place in November 1992, was set up to promote an exchange of information and experience among the authorities. Since the end of 1993 it has been formalized into the European Network for Implementation and Enforcement of Environmental Law (ECONET), with the Commission participating in its meetings (Carlyle, 1994).

The third source of information on action by member states to implement directives are complaints from the public. Complaints in the environmental field have risen significantly, from ten in 1982 to 480 in 1990, which is over 40 per cent of all the complaints made to the Commission. Making complaints is a simple cost-free process involving no more than writing a letter or filling in a model form published by the Commission. The Commission's decision on the complaint is not, however, made public although the complainant is told. Additionally, the complainant cannot require the Commission to take the matter to the ECJ (Kramer, 1992).

If the Commission takes the view that a member state has failed to fulfil its obligations under the Treaty by, for example, failing to transpose a directive into national law or transposing it inadequately, the Commission issues a warning notice to the member state, requiring it to explain its position within two months. If a satisfactory explanation is not forthcoming the Commission issues a 'reasoned opinion' under Article 169 of the Treaty; this marks the start of infringement proceedings. The reasoned opinion gives a detailed account of the infringement alleged and requires compliance. Failure to comply within the period laid down results in proceedings being initiated before the ECJ. In the environmental field the ECJ has twice ruled that the UK failed to fulfil its Treaty obligations, in *Case C-337/89*, which concerned the Drinking Water Directive (80/778), and in *Case C-56/90*, which related to the Bathing Water Directive (76/160); both are discussed in Chapter 2.

Article 171 states that if the ECJ rules adversely against a member state it shall be required to take the necessary measures to comply with the judgment, but until the Maastricht Treaty it was left to the member state to decide how to respond. A member state could conceivably have ignored the judgment and risked being taken to the ECJ a second time. This is rare, however, at least in the environmental field. But where a directive has a 'direct effect' (i.e. grants individuals rights directly which they could sue upon in national courts) the ECJ ruled in *Francovich v the Italian Republic* that the individual could recover damages from the state if its failure to implement a directive caused him or her damage.

A new provision in the Maastricht Treaty may eventually result in penalties being imposed by the ECJ on recalcitrant member states. This states that if the Commission considers that a member state has not taken the measures required to comply with the ECJ's judgment it shall issue a second reasoned opinion laying down a time limit for compliance. If there is still no compliance the Commission may bring the matter before the ECJ again, this time specifying the amount of the lump sum or penalty payment to be made by the member state. The ECJ may impose that lump sum or penalty payment on the member state. There is no indication in the Treaty as to the eventual destination of the money; logically it should be deployed to remedy whatever damage the failure caused but it is far from certain that this is what would happen.

1.2.6   Environment versus the Single Market

The Treaty of Rome set out to establish a European common market. Central to achieving this objective is the need to eliminate trade barriers. Restrictions on exports and imports between member states are therefore prohibited under Articles 30 and 34 of the Treaty. Nevertheless, Article 36 allows member states to prohibit or restrict imports, exports or goods in transit if this can be justified on grounds of:

1   Public morality, public policy or public security
2   The protection of human health and the lives of humans, animals or plants
3   The protection of national treasures possessing artistic, historic or archaeological value or
4   The protection of industrial and commercial property.

At the same time, any such prohibitions or restrictions must not be a means of arbitrary discrimination or a disguised restriction of trade. The requirements of environmental protection did not feature as a possible ground of restricting free trade in the Treaty of Rome.

The question arose in the well-known 'Danish Bottles Case', i.e. *Commission v Denmark* (Case C-302/86) in which the Commission challenged provisions of Danish legislation designed to protect the environment as constituting an unjustified trade barrier. The disputed legislation required that beverages sold in Denmark be packaged in re-usable containers approved by the Danish National Environmental Protection Agency and that distributors set up and operate a system of deposit-and-return. Unapproved containers could be used to market no more than 3 000 hectolitres (hl) per year with an additional limited allowance for foreign producers testing the Danish market. The ECJ ruled that environmental protection may limit the application of the principle of the free movement of goods, but, at the same time, such measures must be necessary and proportional to the objective to be attained. As the obligation to set up a deposit-and-return system was necessary to secure the objectives of the legislation, the restriction this imposed on the free movement of goods was not disproportionate. Limiting the allowable quantity of unapproved containers to 3 000 hl per annum, on the other hand, was disproportionate and contrary to Article 30.

The *Danish Bottles Case* recognized environmental protection measures as a possible rationale for restricting the free movement of goods. This position has recently been restated by the ECJ in *Commission v The Kingdom of Belgium* (Case C-2/90), which dealt with a Belgian decree prohibiting the deposit in Belgium of waste originating in other member states. The ECJ ruled that waste has to be treated as a product the free movement of which could not, in principle, be restricted. However, the ban was justified by the mandatory requirement of the protection of the environment since there was a genuine threat given the region's limited capacity for dealing with waste. The Court also held that the ban was not discriminatory since waste should be disposed of as close as possible to the place where it is produced in order to minimize its transport.

The **Single European Act** specifically allowed member states to restrict free trade on grounds of environmental protection. First, as part of the package designed to speed up the completion of the internal market, paragraph 4 of Article 100A provides that after a measure designed to harmonize the laws of member states has been adopted by qualified majority voting, a member state may impose its own national laws on grounds of the need to protect the environment. It must, however, notify the Commission first and await the Commission's confirmation that the measures are not a means of arbitrary discrimination or a disguised restriction of trade. Germany's attempt to rely on this provision to ban pentachlorophenols (PCP) encountered difficulties when, in response to a complaint from France, the ECJ ruled that the Commission had failed to give reasons for its ruling in favour of the German ban (Case C-41/93). The Commission reinstated the decision, giving further reasons.

The second provision under which member states may restrict free trade on environmental grounds is Article 130t, which was also inserted by the Single European Act. This states expressly that environmental protection measures adopted by the Council 'shall not prevent any member state from maintaining or introducing more stringent protective measures compatible with the Treaty'. This provision has not been relied on to date by any member state.

1.3 The International Context

Although the bulk of UK environmental law originates either from the UK itself or the European Community, the wider international community is also playing an increasingly important role in shaping environmental law. This arises because of the UK's membership of several international organizations having an involvement in developing environmental standards and conventions. The European Commission also typically participates in the work of these organizations and requires member states to take action jointly to ratify the conventions. A number of these international organizations merit a mention: the United Nations Conference on Environment and Development

(UNCED), the United Nations Environment Programme (UNEP), the UN Economic Commission for Europe (UNECE), the Council of Europe, and Organization for Economic Cooperation and Development (OECD)

1.3.1   The UN Conference on Environment and Development

UNCED has already been mentioned as the organizer of the June 1992 Conference on Environment and Development in Rio de Janeiro. Four important documents arose from the conference:

1   The Framework Convention on Climate Change which is designed to control global warming; the UK ratified this Convention in December 1993 and has published a 'Climate Change Programme' setting out how it will return its emissions of greenhouse gases, of which carbon dioxide is the most significant, back to 1990 levels by the year 2000.
2   The Convention on Biodiversity which the UK ratified in June 1994—the Convention defined biodiversity as meaning 'the variability among living organisms from all sources'; the UK has published a 'Biodiversity Action Plan' setting out plans for the conservation and sustainable use of flora and fauna.
3   A Statement of Principles for the management, conservation and sustainable development of the world's forests; the UK has published its programme 'Sustainable Forestry', detailing its policy and programme.
4   Agenda 21; this is a programme of action to be followed in order to achieve sustainable development worldwide—to monitor progress on this programme a new UN body, the Commission on Sustainable Development, was set up to which annual reports would be submitted; the UK's *Strategy on Sustainable Development* has now been published.

1.3.2   The United Nations Environment Programme

UNEP was set up following the 1972 Stockholm conference on the environment and human settlements. Its headquarters are in Nairobi but with offices also in Geneva. It administers a number of significant international environmental conventions. Examples include the Vienna Convention for the protection of the ozone layer and the Basel Convention on transboundary waste movements.

The Vienna Convention for the protection of the ozone layer was agreed in 1985. The Montreal Protocol to the Convention, adopted in 1987, imposed a timetable for phasing out ozone-depleting substances. These timetables are reviewed at two-yearly intervals by state parties to this Convention; since Montreal there have been two meetings, in London in 1990 and in Copenhagen in 1992. This Convention is viewed as a success because it has achieved the elimination from production of some of these substances (e.g. halons). The Basel Convention on the Transboundary Movement of Hazardous Wastes and their Disposal was agreed in 1989. Its requirements have been transposed into EC law through Council Regulation on the Supervision and Control of Shipment of Waste within, into and out of the EC (259/93). They are implemented in the UK by the Transboundary Shipment of Waste Regulations 1994/1137.

1.3.3   The UN Economic Commission for Europe

UNECE brings together European countries as well as the United States and Canada. It is responsible for the 1979 Geneva Convention on Long-Range Transboundary Air Pollution, the 1991 Espoo (Finland) Convention on Environmental Impact Assessment in a Transboundary Context, the 1992 Helsinki Convention on the Protection and Use of Transboundary Watercourses and International Lakes and the 1992 Helsinki Convention on the transboundary effects of industrial accidents. The UK has not yet ratified the last three.

The 1979 Long-Range Transboundary Air Pollution Convention has three protocols. The 1985 Helsinki Protocol deals with the reduction of sulphur dioxide emissions, the 1988 Sofia Protocol with the control of oxides of nitrogen and the 1991 Geneva Protocol with the control of emissions of volatile organic compounds. In relation to each of these protocols the UK has published Action Programmes setting out how it intends to meet its commitments.

1.3.4   The Council of Europe

This body is often assumed to be part of the European Community which it is not, although all members of the European Community are members of the Council of Europe together with eighteen other European states. The Council of Europe was set up by the Statute of the Council of Europe signed in London in 1949 'to achieve greater unity between its members for the purpose of safeguarding and realizing the ideals and principles which are their common heritage and facilitating their economic and social progress'. It is based in Strasbourg.

The Council of Europe sees this mandate as extending to taking measures related to environmental protection and so far has initiated two environmental conventions; the 1979 Berne Convention on the Conservation of European Wildlife and Natural Habitats and the 1993 Convention on Civil Liability for Damage Resulting from Activities Dangerous to the Environment, which opened for signature in June 1993 in Lugano. The UK has not yet signed or ratified this Convention although within the EC Italy and The Netherlands have. The Convention needs only three ratifications to come into force. The European Commission has decided not to recommend that EC member states ratify it because of the current efforts within the EC to develop a proposal on civil liability.

1.3.5   The Organization for Economic Cooperation and Development

The OECD, which brings together 24 industrialized countries, was set up under a 1960 Convention signed in Paris. Under Article 5 the OECD may take binding decisions, make recommendations and enter into agreements. Its 1992 decision concerning the transfrontier movements of wastes destined for recovery operations gives effect to Article 11 of the 1989 Basel Convention on the transboundary movement of wastes under which parties may enter into agreements relating to waste movements. The decision is aimed at facilitating the movement of wastes destined for recovery within OECD countries.

References

Carlyle, S., 'From Chester Network to ECONET', *HMIP Bulletin*, Issue 27, Feb. 1991, p. 1

Comitato di Coordinamento per la Difesa della Cava v Regione Lombardia, the Lombardia case, Case C-236/92, transcript, 23 February 1994.

Commission v Council (Titanium Dioxide), Case C-300/89, *Journal of Environmental Law*, 4/1, 109.

Commission v Denmark, Case C-302/86, 1 Common Market Law Reports 408 (1989).

Commission v Council, Case C-155/91, *Journal of Environmental Law*, 5/2, 291.

Commission v The Kingdom of Belgium, Case C-2/90, *Journal of Environmental Law*, 5/1, 133.

This Common Inheritance, Cm 1200, HMSO (1990).

DoE, *Environmental Quality—The Government's Proposals for a New Independent Environment Agency* (1991).

DoE, *Strategy on Sustainable Development*, HMSO (1994).

DoE, *Water Charges: The Quality Framework* (1993).

Francovich v Italian Republic, Case C-6/90 (1993) 2 CMLR 66.

France v Commission, Case C-41/93, transcript, 17 May 1994.

House of Commons Environment Committee, *The Government's Proposals for an Environment Agency*, 1st Report, Session 1991/92, HC 55.

Kramer, L., *Focus on European Environmental Law*, Sweet & Maxwell (1992).

Marleasing, Case C-106/89 (1990) European Court Reports 4135.

OFWAT, *Paying for Quality: The Political Perspective* (1993).

Wyatt, D. and Dashwoods, A., *European Community Law*, 3rd edn, Sweet & Maxwell (1993).

2

Water Pollution Control

2.1 The Five Water Acts

The history of statutory water pollution control in England and Wales dates back to the **Rivers (Pollution) Prevention Act 1876**. In modern times, however, the **Water Act 1989** marked the most significant piece of legislation on the water industry for almost two decades. Within two years of its enactment, however, it had been replaced by five statutes made in 1991, i.e.:

The Water Resources Act 1991
The Water Industry Act 1991
The Statutory Water Companies Act 1991
The Land Drainage Act 1991
The Water Consolidation (Consequential Provisions) Act 1991

These statutes do not extend to Scotland, where the relevant legislation is in Part II of the **Control of Pollution Act 1974** as amended by Schedule 23 of the Water Act 1989.

The **Water Resources Act 1991** deals with the regulatory and operational aspects of water control. It provides for the National Rivers Authority (NRA) and gives it regulatory and operational functions. These are:

1   Water resources management, which involves essentially issuing and controlling licences for abstracting and impounding water
2   Water pollution control
3   Flood defence and land drainange
4   Fisheries management
5   The functions of a navigation authority, a harbour authority and a conservancy authority.

The NRA is thus much more than simply a water pollution control authority.

The **Water Industry Act 1991** deals with the utility functions of providing water and sewerage services. It provides for private sector companies to be appointed to supply water and sewerage services. There are ten such companies each providing services in one of ten geographical regions in England and Wales. The Act also provides for the Office of Water Services (OFWAT) headed by a Director General to regulate the activities of the water and sewerage companies, and customer service committees to protect the interests of customers. Third, the Act makes provision for the Drinking Water Inspectorate (DWI) with the responsibility of controlling the quality of drinking water supplied to the public by the companies.

The **Statutory Water Companies Act 1991** deals with the 28 statutory water companies. These are private sector companies which have been supplying water to customers since the nineteenth century under powers provided by various local statutes. Unlike the water and sewerage companies, statutory water companies are not licensed to supply sewerage services. Their share of the water services market is quite small in comparison to that of the water and sewerage companies.

The **Land Drainage Act 1991** deals specifically with the land drainage aspects of water management which is carried out by bodies known as internal drainage boards. The Act provides for the internal drainage boards, originally provided for under the **Land Drainage Act 1976** (now repealed), to be continued. It provides also for the expenses of the drainage boards which are raised through levies in their districts.

Finally, the **Water Consolidation (Consequential Provisions) Act 1991** sweeps up the bits and pieces. It repeals the previous water legislation either in full or, in a few cases, in part, depending on the extent to which the previous legislation has been incorporated into the five consolidation statutes. The repeals make it necessary to provide for actions taken under powers originally in the repealed statutes to remain valid. Thus, the Act provides that subordinate legislation and applications made, consents or approvals given, licences or certificates issued or other things done under, or for the purposes of, the repealed enactments continue to have effect as if made, given or issued or done under the provisions of the five Water Acts.

2.2 The Water Pollution Control System

The pollution of 'controlled waters' is dealt with in Part II of the **Water Resources Act 1991**. At its simplest, 'controlled waters' covers:

1 Territorial waters extending to 3 miles from the shore
2 Coastal waters
3 Inland freshwaters, which includes lakes, ponds, certain reservoirs, rivers and watercourses
4 Groundwater.

This definition is quite comprehensive and bodies of water will seldom fail to fall within the designation. Even artificial watercourses, such as canals, are covered.

Water pollution arises from two kinds of source: 'point' sources and 'non-point' or 'diffuse' sources. As the names indicate, point sources are clearly identifiable sources of discharges into watercourses, typified by a drain or a pipe deliberately constructed to conduct effluent from a particular point into a watercourse. Non-point sources are diffuse and not so easily identifiable. Often the discharge is the incidental and unintended consequence of other activity (for instance, the dressing of land with pesticides or nitrate fertilizers or leachate from a landfill). There are, however, areas of overlap; accidents, for instance, can cause both point source and diffuse pollution.

The two sources of pollution are not amenable to control by the same kinds of legal mechanisms and so different tactics are adopted. Point source pollution is controlled principally through a system whereby a regulatory authority grants in advance a consent for effluent to be discharged into a watercourse under specified conditions. Such a discharge is lawful. This system is known as 'the discharge consent system'. It has its critics among those who advocate a policy under which no discharges would be permitted, i.e. a 'zero discharges' policy. Greenpeace, for instance, argues that it is a system of legalized pollution since it enables those granted consents lawfully to discharge pollutants into controlled waters. The system's justification is that it is the only practicable way of dealing with effluents that must be discharged somewhere: at least under this system discharges are controlled.

Non-point source pollution, on the other hand, is controlled principally through legal requirements designed to prevent the pollution occurring in the first place, or, where it occurs, to minimize its consequences. Accidents and other unforeseen events such as flood storms, which can be both point source and non-point source discharges, are dealt with in both ways, through, for instance, provision for storm overflows in discharge consents.

2.2.1 Environmental Quality Objectives

Discharge consents enable polluting effluent to be lawfully discharged into watercourses and so it is necessary to have some idea of the amount of pollution that is tolerable, and beyond which no discharge will be permitted. The UK has done this by specifying the environmental quality which society wishes to achieve. This is known as the 'environmental quality objective' (EQO); it is simply a statement of the quality being aimed for in a particular environment. In relation to water, these objectives are known as water quality objectives. An objective might be to keep a particular stretch of water in a clean enough condition to provide good drinking water. Thus, watercourses across the UK can be classified on the basis of the objectives that have been set for them.

An environmental quality objective may be expressed by way of numerical standards known as 'environmental (or water) quality standards'. Such standards specify the maximum permissible level of a pollutant that may be present if that water is to meet its objective. For example, the standard might provide that if the water is to be pure enough to provide drinking water then no more than 50 mg/l of nitrates may be present in it. Where the presence of the substance in the water is desired (e.g. fluoride) then the standard would specify the minimum concentration that should be present in the water. Where watercourses have been classified, each class is given a set of such standards known as 'quality criteria'.

Discharge consents specify conditions aimed at ensuring that the concentration of pollutants discharged into the watercourse do not lead to a breach of the environmental quality standards. When dealing with point source discharges the simplest way of doing this is to specify discharge limits (more commonly referred to as 'emission limits' on account of the close connection of the term to air pollution control) which each discharge must not exceed. Such limits can be uniform for all dischargers of the particular pollutant irrespective of the class of water into which the discharge is being made so that all dischargers of, say, mercury in the UK would be required to meet exactly the same limits. Alternatively, they can vary from discharger to discharger depending on the receiving watercourse and the objective it is expected to meet.

There was a row throughout the 1970s and 1980s between the UK and the EC together with the other European member states on this very point. The EC took the view that all dischargers across the EC should meet exactly the same uniform emission limits in the interest of fair competition within the internal market. If industrialists in one country faced lower emission standards than their competitors in another country their costs of production would not, it was argued, be the same. The UK maintained that uniform emission standards was conceptually flawed: the amount of pollutant that a given stretch of water could tolerate was directly related to the class of water into which the discharge was made. In any case, conditions of competition differed between countries for all sorts of reasons; climatic, geographical and so on.

The row finally dissipated when the UK agreed to adopt a uniform emissions standard system in relation to substances deemed to be so dangerous that their discharge should not be permitted into any watercourse, irrespective of its class. Such substances are listed in a list known in the UK as the 'Red List' and in the EC as the 'Black List' (discussed under 2.2.5 'Special Category Effluent'). It is always difficult to say with confidence what the effect on watercourses of discharges will be and the UK accepted that, on precautionary grounds, a limited list of dangerous substances are most easily controlled through a uniform emissions standards approach, if not banned altogether.

The UK retains its environmental quality standards system for discharges of substances which are not on the 'Red List'. There is a good reason for doing so.

The discharge consent system does not deal with non-point sources of pollution and therefore emission standards, uniform or otherwise, do nothing to control non-point pollutants. The environmental quality standards system takes into account the effect of both point and non-point polluting sources in setting the quality standard desired for the watercourse.

History of the EQO Approach

The history of EQOs, and specifically, the water quality objectives (WQOs) in the UK dates back to 1978 when a body, the National Water Council (NWC), issued a policy statement entitled *River Water Quality: The Next Stage*, which recommended that WQOs should be set for rivers, canals and major streams. The NWC argued that, in controlling pollution, it is necessary to have regard to the uses to which water is put and the purposes for which its quality must be maintained.

Obviously, waters are managed for a variety of uses:

1   Drinking water supply
2   Safe disposal of sewage and trade effluents
3   Recreation
4   Navigation
5   Amenity
6   Fisheries
7   The support of aquatic wildlife.

Not all these uses require water of similar quality. Standards should therefore be set defining the quality needed to sustain a given use. This would clarify priorities both for pollution control and for investment of resources in clean-up.

The National Water Council suggested four classes of water as follows:

1   Class 1a was *good quality* waters suitable for drinking supply, high-class fisheries and high amenity value; Class 1b, also *good quality* waters, was nevertheless of rather less high quality than Class 1a, but still usable for similar purposes.
2   Class 2 was *fair quality* waters suitable for potable supply following treatment; of supporting reasonably good coarse fisheries; and of amenity value.
3   Class 3 was *poor quality* waters polluted to such an extent that fish were absent or only sporadically present; they are suitable for use for low-grade industrial abstraction purposes.
4   Class 4 was *bad quality* waters that were grossly polluted.

This system was adopted and implemented voluntarily by the water authorities who used it to classify watercourses across the UK. The classes were determined on the basis of data relating to the biochemical oxygen demand (BOD) and ammonia concentration. BOD is a measure of the rate at which the organic content of waters will oxidize and is thus an indication of the extent to which the water is polluted by degradable organic pollutants, like domestic sewage. The classification of estuaries, however, incorporated additional information about the biological state of the waters, that is, the quantities of living organisms in the waters.

From 1980 the water authorities used the classes to conduct the five-yearly nation-wide surveys started in 1958. These were repeated in 1985, and in 1990 when the NRA announced that future surveys would follow a different methodology by adding information drawn from the biological state of the river to the chemical data used up to then (NRA, 1991a). On the basis of the 1990 survey, the majority of rivers, canals and estuaries in England and Wales are of good or fair quality.

Statutory WQOs

In 1986 the government proposed that statutory force should be given to the concept and practice of water quality objectives and standards (DoE, 1986). In doing so account would be taken of the different uses to which bodies of water were put, the different standards such uses required and the requirements of relevant EC objectives. The system proposed would provide a framework for identifying all main waters (which would be classified as appropriate), the current quality of the water to be sustained, any improved quality to be planned and the date by which it needed to be achieved.

These proposals were implemented in the **Water Act 1989** and were later transferred to Chapter I of Part III of the **Water Resources Act 1991** dealing with 'quality objectives'. Section 82 gives the Secretary of State power to make regulations prescribing a system of classifying the quality of controlled waters according to criteria specified in the regulations. The Secretary of State has a wide discretion as regards the criteria which may relate to characteristics of the waters concerned, including its uses and chemical conentrations in them. Following the establishment of a classification system, the Secretary of State may establish statutory WQOs in respect of the various classes. Before doing so, however, the minister must publicize his or her proposals, consider any representations or objections made and then establish the statutory WQOs as proposed or amend them.

Following the establishment of the WQOs the waters concerned must at all times after that date satisfy the requirements prescribed. Section 84 imposes a duty on the Secretary of State and the NRA to exercise their water pollution control powers to ensure that the WQOs are achieved at all times so far as is practicable. The WQOs may be reviewed in two situations; if at least five years have elapsed since they were set or if the NRA, after consulting interested persons, requests a review.

Action to Establish Statutory WQOs

In 1991 the NRA put forward proposals in which it proposed introducing statutory WQOs (NRA, 1991b). The NRA proposed to build upon the NWC scheme and expand it to cover all types of waters (including coastal waters, lakes and groundwater); the NWC scheme covered only rivers and estuaries. Following a lengthy consultation period the NRA finalized its proposals and put to the Secretary of State modified recommendations on statutory water quality objectives. The Secretary of State adopted the NRA's recommendations (DoE, 1992).

The proposed statutory scheme is to be based on use classes categories and the requirements of EC Directives. Six use classes are proposed:

1 Fisheries ecosystem
2 Abstraction for drinking water supply
3 Agricultural abstractions
4 Industrial abstraction
5 Special ecosystem
6 Watersports.

It is intended that the Fisheries Ecosystem should form the cornerstone of the statutory scheme in that objectives in respect of this set of classes should be applied to all stretches of river. The Surface Waters (Fisheries Ecosystem) (Classification) Regulations 1994, SI No. 1057 implemented the proposals by prescribing the quality standards for the fisheries ecosystem use class. These standards are to be applied to individual stretches of water over the coming years. The non-statutory NWC classes will remain in place until they are overtaken by the statutory WQOs, thus providing a basis for NRA discharge consenting policy and practice.

EC Water Quality Classes

The statutory WQOs scheme is the preferred vehicle in the UK for implementating EC Directives on water quality. So far, and in advance of the introduction of a general statutory scheme, three sets of water quality classifications have been made to implement the requirements of EC Directives.

First, the classifications DW1, DW2 and DW3 are specified in the Surface Waters (Classification) Regulations 1989, SI No. 1148 to implement the requirements of EC Directive 75/440/EEC concerning the quality of surface water intended for the abstraction of drinking water. The Directive classifies waters intended for the abstraction of drinking water into three categories of A1, A2 and A3 on the basis of the three standard methods of treatment required to transform the surface water into drinking water. DW1, DW2 and DW3 mirror A1, A2 and A3.

Second, the classifications DS1 and DS2 are specified in the Surface Waters (Dangerous Substances) (Classification) Regulations 1989, SI No. 2286. This implements EC emission limits in relation to the dangerous substances on the 'Black List' as specified in the following directives:

82/176/EEC and 84/156/EEC (on mercury)
83/513/EEC (on cadmium)
84/491/EEC (on hexachlorocyclohexane)
86/280/EEC (on carbon tetrachloride, PCP, and DDT)
88/347/EEC (on aldrin, dieldrin, andrin, isodrin, hexachlorobenzene, hexa-
  chlorobutadiene, and chloroform)

A third class DS3 is added to these two classes by the Surface Waters (Dangerous Substances) (Classification) Regulations 1992, SI No. 337 which implements EC Directive 90/415/EEC on 1,2-dichloroethane, trichloethylene, perchloroethylene, and trichlorobenzene (also 'Black List' substances).

Third, the classification BW1 is specified in the Bathing Waters (Classification) Regulations 1991, SI 1991 No. 1597 which implements the quality standards in EC Directive 76/160 on the quality of bathing water.

2.2.2   Discharge Consents

A 'consent' is simply a document which defines the limits of discharges of efflu-ent into receiving waters that are deemed to be legally acceptable under given conditions. Thus consents serve a dual function, being both legal instruments and technical specifications. Accordingly, they need to define discharges in suf-ficient technical detail to protect receiving waters from damage, while, on the other hand, maintaining the clarity and precision of the legal obligations they create so that they may be readily enforced (NRA, 1990).

Basically, there are two types of consents, referred to as 'numeric' consents and 'non-numeric' consents.

Numeric Consents

Numeric consents specify quantitative limits for the discharge, usually by reference to various 'determinands' (i.e. chemical elements), of the effluent. The consent will be expressed in terms of the concentration or load of the determinands and of effluent flow where 'flow' refers to the measure of the volume of effluent passing per unit time. 'Load' refers to the quantity or mass of substances in the effluent per unit time; it is the product of the concentration of the substances and the effluent flow.

The determinants selected traditionally measure the deoxygenating capacity of the effluent in a watercourse (referred to as its BOD) and suspended solids. Therefore the tendency has been to focus on the biodegradable pollutants rather than the inorganic metals. However, the toxicity of the effluent is gaining increasing prominence and the NRA is studying the feasibility of basing consents on a toxicity standard.

The potential environmental threat posed by a discharge of effluent depends on two factors: the polluting load (the amount of material per unit time being carried by the discharge), and the scale and condition of the receiving waters relative to the discharge. A discharge of low flow into receiving waters that are large will normally have little impact in the absence of highly toxic substances in the discharge. But a discharge of moderate flow can have a serious impact on small or slow-moving receiving waters because the effluent would receive little dilution.

Numeric consents specify limits of effluent discharge which may be either absolute or percentile. An 'absolute' limit is a standard that the discharge must not exceed at any time. Compliance with the limit is tested by instantaneous spot sampling, and any exceedance detected constitutes an offence whether or not any environmental damage has been caused. A 'percentile' limit, on the other hand, is a standard that needs to be achieved only for a given percentage of the time. Compliance is measured over a time period (say, one year). The practice developed in the 1980s for consents granted to sewerage treatment works to require compliance only 95 per cent of the time; this was described as a 95 per cent limit. Percentile limits can be complemented by a limit specifying an 'upper tier' absolute limit which must not be exceeded at any time.

A corollary of percentile limits is the 'look-up table' which is essentially a system of statistical quality control. Its function is to specify the number of samples out of any particular number taken to be discounted in deciding whether or not a percentile limit has been breached. This is designed to ensure that a small number of samples give a precise picture of a continuously varying process.

Non-numeric Consents

A non-numeric consent deals with those conditions under which effluent is discharged which cannot readily be expressed in terms of quantitative limits on determinands, such as the operation and maintenance of the process from which the discharge is made. For instance, a consent may specify technical requirements with which the process must comply as a way of controlling the effluent quality, usually in addition to specifying quantitative limits on determinands. Where, however, the discharge is small and of little environmental significance, a 'descriptive consent' may cover only non-numeric parameters.

Following the recommendations set out in the Kinnersley Report (NRA, 1990) the NRA announced that it would rationalize its practice in issuing consents. First, absolute limits would be set for all new and revised consents for environmentally sensitive discharges. Second, strict limits would be set on the volume of permitted effluent where the effluent contains heavy metals, organo-chlorines or other substances which may build up in the receiving waters. Third, absolute limits tested by instantaneous spot sampling would be applied equally to all dischargers, including sewerage-treatment works. The significance of the third recommendation lies in the fact that most effluents reach watercourses through sewerage-treatment works rather than directly from industrial or other processes. Implementing these recommendations is expected to take several years.

2.2.3 Direct Discharges

Consents for direct discharges are issued by the NRA to whom an application must be made by the intending discharger. The procedure is set out in Schedule 10 of the **Water Resources Act 1991**. It would be good practice for the intending discharger to discuss the matter informally with the relevant regional office of the NRA before submitting an application just to get an indication of the kinds of conditions likely to be imposed.

The Procedure

The steps which the NRA must take following receipt of an application are specified in the Act. It must:

1 Publish notice of it, at least once in two successive weeks in a local newspaper or newspapers in the place where the discharge is to be made, and in the vicinity of controlled waters likely to be affected by the discharges proposed
2 Publish a copy of that notice in the *London Gazette*
3 Send a copy of the application to every local authority or water undertaker within whose area any of the proposed discharges is to occur
4 Where the discharges would be made into coastal waters, relevant territorial waters or waters outside the limits of relevant territorial waters, serve a copy of the application on the Minister for Agriculture, Fisheries and Food and the Secretary of State for the Environment.

Where the NRA has decided to give the consent and takes the view that the discharge will not appreciably affect the receiving waters, it may dispense with the first three steps.

Obviously, what would amount to 'appreciable effect' can be the subject of some debate. The DoE Circular 17/84 indicates that in assessing appreciable effect the discharge should not:

1 Affect an area of amenity or environmental significance;
2 Result in a major change in the flow of the receiving waters;

3   Result in such changes to water quality as to damage existing or future uses of such waters or alter by 10 per cent or more the concentration in the receiving waters of any substance important to the quality of the water and the well-being of its flora and fauna.

It is open to an applicant to apply to the Secretary of State, under para. 1(7) of Schedule 10, for a certificate exempting him or her from these publicity provisions on the ground that disclosure of information would be contrary to public interest or would prejudice, to an unreasonable degree, some private interest by disclosing information about a trade secret.

The NRA is under a duty to consider written representations made to it about the application within six weeks of the advertisements. It is also under a duty to consider whether to give the consent applied for or to refuse it. If it does not give a consent within the period of four months beginning with the day it received the application the application is deemed to have been refused, although this provision may be deleted by proposals which have been put forward by the DoE (DoE, 1993a). The NRA and the applicant can also agree in writing to a longer decision period, which may be necessary in instances where the application raises complex issues.

If the NRA proposes to give consent in a situation where representations have been made, it must serve notice on every person who made representations informing them of their right, within twenty-one days from the date of the notice, to request the Secretary of State to call in the application. No consent may be given before the 21 days have expired, and if the person makes a call-in request and serves notice on the NRA, then consent may not be given unless the Secretary refuses to call in the application. The government is currently consulting on removing this requirement, leaving only a general provision enabling the public to ask for a call-in (DoE, 1993a).

If the Secretary of State calls in an application, which he or she may, whether or not a request is made to him, he may either hold a local inquiry to consider it or give the applicant, the NRA and those who have made representations an opportunity to be heard before he decides it. A third way in which the Secretary of State may become involved is where the applicant appeals to him against an adverse decision of the NRA. The appeal must be made within three months of the adverse decision.

In deciding an application, the NRA may take into account any material factors, including the past compliance record of the discharger. The conditions subject to which a consent may be given are such conditions as the NRA may think fit and, in particular, conditions as to:

1   The place at which the discharge may be made
2   The nature, origin, composition, volume and rate of the discharge

3   Steps to be taken by way of treatment or any other process for minimizing the polluting effect of the discharge
4   The provision of facilities for taking samples
5   The keeping of records and the making of returns.

A condition may not make a consent personal to a discharger as a consent relates to premises and extends to discharges made by any person from those premises.

Reviews

The NRA is under a duty to review consents and their conditions from time to time. Following such a review it may serve a notice on the discharger revoking the consent, modifying its conditions or, if it is an unconditional consent, imposing conditions. The main restriction on the exercise of these powers is that each consent must specify a period during which no revocation or modification notice may be served. Further, each revocation or modification notice must in turn specify a period, not less than two years, during which a subsequent notice shall not be served. This is intended to create some security for the discharger, enabling him or her to take advantage of any action he has taken in reliance on the consent before it can be altered.

Revocation and modifications of consents may also be initiated by the Secretary of State by way of direction given to the NRA. There are three grounds on which the Secretary of State may make such a direction:

1   For the purpose of enabling the government to give effect to any EC obligation or to any international agreement to which the UK is a party
2   For the protection of public health or of aquatic flora and fauna
3   In consequence of any representations or objections made to him, or otherwise.

The minimum two-year period before revocation or modification can be made applies to the Secretary of State in relation to the third ground, but not to the first two grounds.

The NRA can revoke or modify a consent earlier than the stipulated two-year period but it must pay compensation to the discharger, unless the change is necessitated by EC or international obligations. However, compensation is not payable where the direction was given to the NRA in consequence of a change of circumstances which could not reasonably have been foreseen or on consideration by the Secretary of State of material information not reasonably available to the NRA at the beginning of the period of restriction. Such information could include the interaction or cumulative effect of the discharge in question with other, possibly subsequent, discharges.

2.2.4   Discharges via Sewers

For many businesses, discharge of trade effluents to sewer represents the only feasible means of disposal. For the sewerage undertakers, reception and treatment of trade effluent constitutes a commercial, profit-making undertaking. In carrying out their sewerage function, therefore, the sewerage companies walk a fine line between operating a commercial business simultaneously with a system of environmental protection. The relevant legislative scheme is set out in Chapter III of Part IV of the **Water Industry Act 1991**.

After the provision of water services, the provision of sewerage services for both industrial (described as 'trade') and domestic effluent constitutes the next main statutory function of the water and sewerage companies. Under s. 94 of the Water Industry Act 1991, sewerage undertakers have a duty to provide a sewerage system and to improve, extend and maintain it so that its area is, and continues to be, drained. On trade effluent, the sewerage undertaker must have regard to existing and likely future obligations to allow for the discharge of trade effluents into its public sewers and to the need to provide for its disposal. The intention behind this is to ensure that sewerage undertakers plan ahead for the needs of industrial dischargers.

Section 141(1) of the Water Industry Act defines trade effluent as any liquid wholly or partly produced in the course of any trade or industry carried on at trade premises. In *Thames Water Authority v Blue and White Launderettes Ltd* the court held that the difference between a trade effluent and domestic effluent lies in the purpose of the activity that generated the effluent, rather than in the nature of the discharge itself. Thus, in this instance, effluent was discharged from washing machines in a launderette which was indistinguishable in nature from effluent from domestic washing machines, but the court held that it was trade effluent since the launderette was run as a trade. Further, the effluent must have originated from premises rather than from open land (for instance, an open landfill site) because the definition of a drain or sewer in s. 219(1) appears to preclude open land.

Complementing the duty on sewerage undertakers to provide sewerage services, s. 118 gives the trader a conditional right to discharge trade effluent from a drain or sewer into public sewers, the condition being that the undertaker has granted consent. Section 118(5) makes discharging effluent into a public sewer without a consent an offence. The legislation does not specify who may prosecute for the offence and so it is open to anyone to do so: HMIP in cases of discharges of 'Red List' substances; the NRA in cases of discharges into watercourses; the sewerage undertaker itself or, indeed, any private person. The offence is committed by the occupier of the relevant trade premises and would appear to be one of strict liability in that it is not open to the discharger to argue that he or she did not intend to make the discharge unlawfully.

Thus, the mechanism for controlling discharges to sewer is one of a system of statutory discharge consents. This was preferred to a system involving simply a commercial contract between two private companies, the sewerage undertaker and the trader since the disposal of trade effluent has implications for environmental protection which make it a matter of public concern. The sewerage undertaker is able to control what is discharged into the public sewer thereby protecting the public sewer and controlled waters from being overwhelmed. At the same time, the trader has a right to discharge into the public sewer which he or she may enforce through an appeal to the Director of Water Services under s. 122. This ensures that any reasonable application must be granted by the sewerage undertaker, thus protecting the trader from arbitrary conduct on the part of the undertaker or discrimination on commercial grounds, such as imposing prohibitive charges.

Application for a Trade Effluent Consent

Section 119 of the **Water Industry Act 1991** provides that an application to a sewerage undertaker for a consent shall be by a written notice known as a 'trade effluent notice' served on the undertaker by the owner or occupier of the premises. There is no prescribed form for the notice and each undertaker will have its own standard form which applicants may use. Also, there is no requirement to publicize the application. However, each application shall state the:

1   Nature and composition of the effluent
2   Maximum quantity which it is proposed to discharge in any one day
3   Highest rate at which it is proposed to discharge.

The second means of getting permission to discharge trade effluent to a public sewer is through an agreement between the trader and the undertaker under s. 129. Although agreements are commercial arrangements, they operate within the statutory framework and the Secretary of State has supervisory functions, especially in relation to discharges of 'Red List' substances; the consenting procedure for these is set out under 2.2.5 'Special Category Effluent'.

A s. 119 consent may be made subject to conditions as to various matters including those set out in s. 121, while the s. 129 agreement may specify the terms under which the effluent is received. The sewerage undertaker is given a wide discretion as to the consent conditions which may be imposed, though appeals can be lodged with the Director General against unreasonable conditions. A traditional concern of sewerage undertakers in setting conditions has been to avoid the discharge of substances which might cause damage to the sewer system or present a risk to those operating or maintaining it. Charges for the sewerage services also may be imposed by way of a condition. This is in addition to the more general power to charge for sewerage services under s. 142.

Consent conditions are a pollution control mechanism whose contravention is an offence under s. 121(5). An agreement, however, can only be enforced by a civil suit. Again, any person is free to prosecute for breaches of consent conditions. During discussions of this Act in Parliament the government rejected the argument that it was unfair that the sewerage undertaker, a private company, should have power to prosecute its customers. Undertakers are not simply commercial undertakings but have an important role in environmental protection.

Variation of Consent Conditions

Under s. 124 a sewerage undertaker may give a direction varying, adding to or annulling conditions attached to a consent. Before doing so the undertaker must give the owner or occupier of the trade premises two months' notice of the variation. No variation may be given within two years from the date of the consent or a previous variation unless the owner or occupier of the trade premises agrees. This provision is, however, modified by s. 125 whereby in specified circumstances and on payment of compensation, a variation may be made within the two-year period. The power to vary consents does not extend to revocation of the consent, and it seems that an undertaker, unlike the NRA, cannot revoke a consent.

The circumstances in which a direction may be made varying a consent relate to the necessity to provide proper protection for persons likely to be affected by the discharges. Compensation is not payable if the variation is required because of a change of circumstances since the beginning of the two-year period which could not reasonably have been foreseen, but not arising from consents subsequently issued. Section 126 gives a right of appeal to the Director General against variations. Except in the case of a direction relating to the payment of charges, the effect of an appeal made in time is that the direction will not take effect until the appeal is withdrawn or finally disposed of.

Charging

Section 142 empowers sewerage undertakers to charge for the sewerage services they provide. There are three methods under which sewerage undertakers may fix charges:

1   In accordance with a 'charges scheme' under s. 143; this is a scheme under which an undertaker fixes the charges to be paid for the services it provides
2   In accordance with an agreement with persons to be charged made under s. 142(2)(b)
3   As a condition of the consent to discharge trade effluent into the undertaker's public sewers under s. 121(2)(e).

The distinction between these various methods is important in that the right of a consent holder to appeal against the charges to the Director General depends upon the particular method the sewerage undertaker uses to levy its charges. The right to appeal is available only where the charges are levied as a condition of the consent. This is because a charges scheme must be approved by the Director General before it goes into effect, making a right of appeal against charges under it pointless. It is self-evident that an appeal cannot be lodged against an agreement.

Under s. 121(4)(a) charges levied as a condition of the trade effluent consent shall take into account three factors:

1 The nature and composition as well as the volume and the discharge rate of the trade effluent
2 Additional expenses which the undertaker incurs or is likely to incur in connection with the reception or disposal of the trade effluent
3 Any revenue likely to be derived by the undertaker from the trade effluent (e.g. where the undertaker sells the residual sludge for, say, use as manure or in energy-generating incinerators).

These factors are derived from the so-called 'Mogden Formula' which has been used to charge for sewerage services for decades, even before privatization in 1989 (OFWAT, 1991). It is also used in Scotland where sewerage services are provided by local authorities and charging is provided for under the **Local Government Finance Act 1992**. The extent to which the polluting potential of the trade effluent discharge is reflected in the charge varies in practice, but the formula does take into account the volume discharged, any treatment provided and the costs of disposing of the sludge.

2.2.5   Special Category Effluent

EC Directive 76/464/EEC on pollution caused by certain substances discharged into the aquatic environment of the Community requires the elimination or reduction of pollution of waters by certain particularly dangerous substances. The Directive authorized the setting, through other 'daughter directives', of especially stringent limits on the discharges of these substances, with the aim of eventually achieving a zero discharge. The dangerous substances chosen for control under this regime, the 'Black' or 'Red' List, are set out above under 'EC Water Quality Objectives'.

In order to implement the requirements of Directive 76/464/EEC to reduce and eventually eliminate 'Red List' substances, s. 120 of the **Water Industry Act 1991** provides a special regime for consenting discharges of trade effluent containing 'Red List' substances or arising from 'Red List' processes. Such trade effluent is referred to as 'special category effluent'. The statutory provisions are amplified in the Trade Effluent (Prescribed Processes and Substances)

Regulations 1989, SI 1989 No. 1156 as amended by SI 1990 No. 1629, and the Trade Effluents (Prescribed Substances and Processes) Regulations 1992, SI 1992 No. 339.

The procedure requires cases relating to discharges of special category effluent to be referred to the Secretary of State who deals with them through HMIP. Such cases may arise in four instances:

1   Where an application relating to special category effluent is made to the sewerage undertaker
2   Where an appeal against a sewerage undertaker's decision is made to the Director General in a case involving special category effluent
3   Where an agreement between the undertaker and the discharger is proposed relating to special category effluent
4   Where the undertaker seeks to vary an existing consent; under ss 127 and 131 the Secretary of State may also on his or her own initiative review existing consents and agreements relating to special category effluent.

A link between the pollution control powers of HMIP under the Integrated Pollution Control (IPC) regime set up in Part I of the **Environmental Protection Act 1990** (EPA 1990) and the special category effluent regime under the Water Industry Act 1991 is made by s. 138(2) of the Water Industry Act. This provides that trade effluent shall not be special category effluent requiring referral to the Secretary of State if it is produced, or is to be produced, in any process which is prescribed for control by HMIP. This avoids duplication of the control of processes. However, the fact that a process is subject to control by HMIP does not remove the need for ordinary consent from the sewerage undertaker to discharge into the sewer; it merely means that the particular provisions relating to special category effluent do not apply.

2.3   Water Pollution Offences

The discharge consent system is underpinned by, and enforced through, provisions set out in Chapter II of Part III of the Water Resources Act 1991 which in effect prohibit discharges into controlled waters unless one has a consent from one of the regulators to make the discharge. Section 85(1), the bedrock provision, makes it an offence to cause or knowingly permit any poisonous, noxious or polluting matter or any solid waste matter to enter any controlled waters.

The rationale behind the all-enscapulating offence of polluting controlled waters is illustrated very well through the case of *NRA v Eggar (UK) Ltd*. The company had been constructing a sump which filled with run-off water from its construction site. The company staff then pumped the water into a nearby river for which the company was charged with the offence of causing polluting matter to enter controlled waters. In its defence the company argued that the run-off water had no damaging effect on the river and therefore was not 'polluting matter'; in any case the company had a consent to discharge cooling water and surface water into the river, giving it a statutory defence to the charge. The court held that the offence of polluting controlled waters is concerned with the nature of the material discharged, not with the consequences of the discharge. The proper question to ask is whether the discharge is capable of causing harm to the river, not whether harm has in fact been caused. The decision whether the material is capable of causing harm to the river is to be made before the material has actually entered the river, regardless of whether the river diluted the polluting matter and suffered no damaging effect.

This ruling reinforces the statutory scheme for protecting waters from pollution, requiring any person wishing to discharge material capable of polluting waters to seek a consent as the only way to avoid committing an offence. The question whether a person should be prosecuted for a harmless discharge relates to the discretion of the regulator to bring a charge and to the level of the penalty, rather than to the issue of whether or not an offence has been committed.

The second issue concerned the company's consent. This allowed it to discharge cooling and surface water at a temperature not exceeding 25°C and a rate not exceeding 6 litres/second. The court held that to the extent that the company discharged cooling water at the temperature and rate specified, it would have a statutory defence if charged with the offence of polluting controlled waters. But the charge in this case related to run-off water for which the consent did not provide. Therefore the company could not plead its consent in defence. The lesson to be drawn from this ruling is that in seeking a consent a discharger needs to be quite clear as to exactly what it wishes to see in the consent since it provides a defence in respect of very specific discharges only; it is not a licence to discharge whatever the company may wish to dispose of. In this respect, particular attention should be paid to the quantitative parameters which will be very precise.

2.3.1   The Offences

Section 85 creates six offences in all. One is concerned with contravention of discharge consent conditions. Of the rest, s. 85(1) makes it an offence to cause or knowingly permit any poisonous, noxious or polluting matter to enter controlled waters, while the remaining four also prohibit causing or knowingly permitting discharges or entries into controlled waters in the situations where:

1   Matter, other than trade or sewage effluent, enters controlled waters by being discharged from a drain or sewer in contravention of a 's. 86 prohibition' (see below).

2   Trade or sewage effluent is discharged either into controlled waters or from land in England and Wales into the sea outside the limits of controlled waters, by means of a pipe.

3   Trade or sewage effluent is discharged, in contravention of a 's. 86 prohibition', from a building or from any fixed plant either onto or into any land, or into any waters of a lake or pond which are not inland freshwaters.

4   Matter enters any inland freshwaters so as to tend (either directly or in combination with other matter which he or another person causes or permits to enter those waters) to impede the proper flow of the waters in a manner leading, or likely to lead, to a substantial aggravation of pollution due to other causes, or the consequences of such pollution.

Two of the above offences only arise if the NRA has exercised its powers under s. 86 to serve a notice on the discharger prohibiting the discharge. A discharger who wishes to continue making the discharge has then to apply for a consent in the normal way. This power amounts to a statutory exemption from the discharge consent requirements for the two categories of discharges on the basis that they are unlikely to have an appreciable effect on the quality of waters; they may be made without a consent until the NRA decides that particular ones need to be controlled for some reason and issues a s. 86 prohibition. If, however, the discharge is in fact poisonous, noxious or polluting, it would still be an offence under s. 85(1) notwithstanding the absence of a s. 86 prohibition.

The concepts of 'causing or knowingly permitting' are common to all six offences. Case law on the meaning of the phrase to 'cause' in this context is to the effect that the offences are 'strict liability' rather than absolute offences. The nature of a strict liability offence is that to establish guilt it is not necessary for the prosecution to prove either that the defendant intended the commission of the offence or was guilty of negligence. All that is required is proof that the defendant committed some positive act which resulted in the discharge.

The leading case is *Alphacell Ltd v Woodward*. The company's business was making manilla fibres. After washing the fibres they piped the water to settling tanks whose water level was controlled by automatic pumps. Due to a defect in one of the pumps of which the company was unaware, water overflowed into a nearby river. The company was charged with causing polluting matter to enter the river. The question for the court was whether the offence could be committed by someone who was unaware that polluting matter was entering the river and who had not been negligent. The court ruled that the offence could be committed in those circumstances. The company was guilty because, as one of the judges said,

The whole complex operation which might lead to this result was an operation deliberately conducted by [them] and I fail to see how a defect at one stage of it, even if we must assume that this happened without their negligence, can enable them to say that they did not cause the pollution.

This puts the onus on the operator to ensure that his or her system is functioning properly for any malfunction might lead to an offence being committed.

A strict liability offence is, however, distinguishable from an 'absolute' offence; there are no defences to the latter while strict liability offences have both common law and statutory defences. The common law defences fall under heads such as act of God, i.e. events beyond human control such as lightning; act of a third party, e.g. where a trespasser enters premises and opens stop valves (as in *Impress v Rees*); and absence of any positive act by the person charged.

The third defence also differentiates between the offence of causing and that of knowingly permitting. A causing offence cannot be committed by someone who has not taken any positive action. In *Price v Cromack*, under a contract, the appellant allowed a company to build lagoons on his land to contain effluent produced by the company. Two cracks in the walls of the lagoons allowed effluent to escape into a nearby river. On appeal the court dismissed the appellant's conviction for causing polluting matter to enter a river because there was no positive act on his part. As one judge said, 'I cannot myself find it possible to say that a causing of entry of polluting matter occurs merely because the landowner stands by and watches the polluting matter cross his land into the stream, even if he has committed himself by contract to allowing the adjoining owner so to act'.

Passively looking on is the kind of offence envisaged by the 'knowingly permitting' limb of these provisions. Knowingly permitting involves both a failure to prevent the pollution and a knowledge that the pollution will occur. It would be the appropriate charge where the defendant allows a potentially damaging state of affairs, either by express or implied permission, knowing that the damage will occur if no pre-emptive action is taken. A mere failure to do something which might have prevented polluting matter reaching the relevant waters unaccompanied by knowledge of the consequences is not enough to support a conviction.

Knowingly permitting is therefore a much more difficult offence to prove because of the need to prove knowledge of the consequences, as was demonstrated by *Schulmans Inc. Ltd v NRA*. Oil entered a drainage system on the company's land and found its way into a nearby brook. The NRA charged the company with knowingly permitting poisonous matter to be discharged into controlled waters, arguing that once the spillage had been brought to its attention the company did not have the drainage system cleaned out until the following day. The appeal court dismissed the charge on the ground that 'there was nothing to show recognition on [its] part that the contents of the drainage system would probably find their way into the brook before the drainage system was due to be cleaned out the following day'. To sustain a charge of knowingly permitting there had to be evidence that there was a period of time when the company both knew of the contamination of the brook and was capable of stopping it but did not. It is no surprise that this offence is rarely used in prosecutions.

2.3.2   The Defences

Twelve statutory defences to water pollution offences are set out in ss 88 and 89 of the **Water Resources Act 1991** as follows:

1   The first four relate to some or other consent system so that possessing any appropriate authorization, consent, a disposal or management licence or a licence to deposit to sea is a defence to the charge.
2   The fifth relates to discharges made for purposes of works by the NRA under s. 163 of the Water Resources Act 1991 or a water undertaker under s. 165 of the **Water Industry Act 1991**.
3   The sixth concerns discharges made under a power conferred by a local statutory provision.
4   The seventh concerns discharges permitted by some prescribed enactment.
5   The eighth relates to discharges in an emergency.
6   The last four relate to discharges from vessels, abandoned mines and by highway authorities.

The first four and the eighth defences are discussed in more depth here, as raising legal issues frequently encountered in practice.

Authorization or Consent

Section 88(1) provides a defence to an offence involving entry or discharge into any waters under s. 85 if the entry or discharge was authorized or consented. There are various consent regimes, starting with the discharge consents given by the NRA under the **Water Resources Act 1991** or by the river-purification authority under similar provisions for Scotland in Part II of the **Control of Pollution Act 1974**.

HMIP, and HMIPI in Scotland, operate a consent regime for prescribed processes designated for central control under Part I of the **EPA 1990**, issuing permits referred to as 'authorizations'. Processes prescribed for IPC control are dealt with on an integrated basis with the authorizations covering discharges to all three environmental media, including discharges to water. However, the NRA has considerable influence over conditions set for discharges to water. Specifically:

1   HMIP shall not grant an authorization if the NRA certifies that in its opinion the release will result in, or contribute to, a failure to achieve any water quality objective in force under the **Water Resources Act**.
2   Any authorization granted must include such conditions as appear to the NRA appropriate for the purposes of Part I of the 1990 Act and which are notified in writing to HMIP.
3   HMIP shall exercise its statutory powers of variation so as to vary the conditions of an authorization as required by notice in writing given by the NRA.

The third consent regime is operated by waste regulation authorities, primarily issuing 'waste management licences' under Part II of the **EPA 1990** for landfills of waste. The EPA regime replaced 'disposal licences' which were issued under the **Control of Pollution Act 1974** until 1 May 1994. Leachate percolating from a landfill site into controlled waters could constitute an offence under s. 85(1) as polluting matter which has entered controlled waters. Although a landfill site is trade premises there is at least one instance (ENDS No. 227 p. 45, 1993) where a defendant (Coal Products Ltd) argued successfully in a magistrates' court that leachate from the site could not constitute an offence under s. 85(3) which deals with discharges because percolation is not a discharge but an entry; a discharge must be from a fixed discharge point, such as a pipe.

Waste disposal or waste management licences do not normally expressly authorize discharges to water, but the defence of possessing such a licence applies also to any discharge made as a result of an act or omission under, and in accordance with, the licence. Therefore, if a discharge of leachate into waters occurred as a result of normal waste disposal operations under the terms of a licence, the landfill operator could rely on his or her disposal or waste management licence as a defence. This defence was relied on successfully by Coal Products Ltd to defeat a second charge of causing polluting matter to enter controlled waters contrary to s. 85(1). The company was thus acquitted on both charges.

The defence is, however, limited somewhat by s. 88(3) of the **Water Resources Act 1991** which excludes the following from a disposal licence defence:

1   Entries of matter, other than trade effluent or sewage effluent, discharged from a drain or sewer in contravention of a s. 86 prohibition
2   Discharges of trade or sewage effluent into controlled waters or from land (in England and Wales), through a pipe, into the sea outside the limits of controlled waters
3   Discharges of trade effluent or sewage effluent from a building or from any fixed plant onto or into any land, or into a lake or pond which are not inland freshwaters, in contravention of a s. 86 prohibition.

The fourth consent regime is operated by MAFF under the **Food and Environment Protection Act 1985**, granting licences for disposal to sea. The dumping of sewage sludge, sludge dredgings and industrial wastes at sea comes within this regime. Sea disposals of sewage sludge are scheduled to end in 1998 under an agreement between the UK and the other states bordering the North Sea (DoE, 1990). The practice is also governed by international conventions, in particular the 1992 Convention to Protect the Environment of the North East Atlantic which, once ratified, will replace both the 1972 Oslo Convention and the 1974 Paris Convention.

Emergency Actions

Under s. 89(1) the discharger has a limited defence of acting in an emergency. The defence, however, is limited. The three components which must all be satisfied are that:

1   The entry was caused or permitted, or the discharge made, in an emergency in order to avoid danger to life or health
2   All reasonably practical steps in the circumstances were taken for minimizing the extent of the entry or discharge and its polluting effects and
3   Particulars of the entry or discharge were furnished to the NRA as soon as reasonably practicable after the discharge.

The statute fails to clarify whether the defence is available where the defendant believed that an emergency existed even though it later transpired that there was no emergency. Although there is no case law directly on the point, the language appears to be objective, with no reference to the opinion or belief of the discharger. Also, it seems likely that the courts would take the view that an emergency is a situation that arises from events beyond the discharger's control, and not from his or her own fault (for instance, a failure to maintain his process).

2.3.3   The Position of the Sewerage Undertaker

Discharges of trade effluent to public sewers eventually end up in controlled waters. Consequently, the consenting system which sewerage undertakers operate has important environmental implications in terms of the quality of the treated effluent discharged from an undertaker's sewerage works. Most significantly from the undertaker's point of view, they may affect the undertaker's ability to comply with its own consent from the NRA to discharge into controlled waters.

By s. 87(3) of the **Water Resources Act 1991**, the person who discharges trade effluent into the sewer will not be guilty of an offence under s. 85(3) and (4) of the Water Resources Act in respect of a discharge, provided that the sewerage undertaker was under an obligation to receive it either uncondition ally or subject to conditions which were observed. In such circumstances s. 87(1), known as 'the deeming provision', provides that the undertaker will be deemed to have caused the discharge and may be convicted of an offence under s. 85(3) and (5). But the undertaker is not guilty where its discharge contravenes conditions of its NRA consent relating to the discharge if:

1   The contravention is attributable to a discharge which another person caused or permitted to be made into the sewer
2   The undertaker was not bound to receive the discharge into the sewer, or was bound to receive it subject to conditions which were not observed or
3   The undertaker could not reasonably have been expected to prevent the discharge into the works.

The scope of this defence came up for consideration in *NRA v Yorkshire Water Services Ltd*. The case followed a clandestine discharge of a substance at night by an unknown party into works operated by the defendant. The substance was not treatable and passed directly into controlled waters. The defendant was convicted of causing polluting matter to enter controlled waters. The Crown Court rejected the attempt to rely on s. 87, pointing out that the defence is only available where the sewerage undertaker is charged with breaching the conditions of its consent; in this instance it was charged with causing polluting matter to enter controlled waters.

In view of the fact that matter discharged from sewerage treatment works may often be polluting and that sewerage undertakers are not always aware of who might be pouring effluent down the drain, the sewerage undertakers viewed this narrow construction of the defence under s. 87 with a great deal of concern and on appeal to the House of Lords it was held that a charge of causing water pollution *was* included within the s. 87 defence.

2.4   Powers to Prevent Pollution

Non-point pollution cannot be controlled through the discharge consent system. The only effective way of tackling it is to target and control the diverse activities, such as farming and accidents, that cause it. This is the purpose of the powers given to the NRA in Chapter III of Part III of the **Water Resources Act 1991** to prevent pollution. The powers are of four different types enabling the NRA to:

1   Impose requirements to take precautions against pollution
2   Set up water protection zones
3   Set up nitrate sensitive areas
4   Draw up codes of good agricultural practice.

The first has been used to control pollution by slurry and silage from agricultural premises while the third has been used to control nitrate pollution.

These two are considered in detail but the second, which has yet to be used, and the fourth, which has been resorted to three times, are discussed only briefly.

The power under s. 97 to draw up codes of good agricultural practice has been used for three codes dealing with the protection of water (MAFF, 1991), air (MAFF, 1992) and soil (MAFF, 1993a). A Code is intended only to give practical guidance on how best to avoid pollution. Failing to follow it is not an offence, but the court may take the failure into account in legal proceedings.

2.4.1   Water Protection Zones

The power under s. 93 to establish water protection zones as a way of controlling water pollution has yet to be used, although the NRA has put forward proposals for doing so. Designating a water protection zone enables the Secretary of State to prohibit or restrict specified activities as a way of controlling water pollution. The NRA's groundwater protection zones policy, discussed below, is based on a similar concept, but it is currently non-statutory. The procedure for setting up a water protection zone requires that the NRA publicize the proposals and consider objections before submitting a draft Order to the Secretary of State, who may hold an inquiry into the proposals.

In December 1993 the Welsh Region of the NRA published proposals for setting up a protection zone around the River Dee under s. 93 (NRA, 1993). Its reason is that the river is an important source of drinking water threatened by pollution from industrial activities upstream of abstraction points. If a water protection zone is set up the NRA's consent would be needed before certain chemical substances could be stored or used. Additionally, those keeping or using such substances would be required to carry out a risk assessment to determine the degree of threat posed to the river by the chemicals and may be required to take preventive measures such as installing bunding around their chemical stores. The intention is to make an application to the Secretary of State for an Order in the course of 1994 but the zone is not likely to come into effect before 1995.

A water protection zone is thus a mechanism for introducing enhanced protection for controlled waters which are at risk from activities carried on nearby.

2.4.2   NRA Groundwater Protection Policy

In 1992 the NRA published a policy document on groundwater protection (NRA, 1992). It outlines the groundwater protection policy which the NRA applies both in relation to its own powers and in seeking to influence the policies and decisions of others whose actions can affect the protection of groundwater (for example, the planning and waste regulatory authorities).

Groundwater, which contributes up to 35 per cent of the public water supply, is particularly at risk from non-point pollution because the pollution may take many years to manifest itself, and may be impossible to clean up once it has occurred. Prevention is therefore the best option. EC Directive 80/68/EEC on groundwater protection, however, controls only a small number of dangerous substances discharged into groundwater and therefore is considered inadequate. The policy document:

1   Classifies groundwater on the basis of its vulnerability,
2   Defines source protection zones on the basis of a pollutant's travel time and source catchment areas, and
3   States the NRA's policy in relation to eight kinds of activity, including abstraction, waste disposal, contaminated land and diffuse pollution.

The NRA is currently mapping groundwater vulnerability in terms of geology and soils, a process that will go on until 1996. It is also mapping Source Protection Zones for the major public water supply sources; 750 are thought to have been completed in 1993.

The concept of groundwater vulnerability acknowledges that there are greater risks of pollution in certain hydrological, geological and soil situations than in others. Risk is assessed on the basis of the nature of the hazard, the natural vulnerability of the groundwater and the scale of proposed preventive measures. The proximity of an activity to a groundwater abstraction is a key factor in assessing the risk to an existing groundwater source, giving rise to three Source Protection Zones:

1   Zone I (Inner Source Protection)
2   Zone II (Outer Source Protection)
3   Zone III (Outer Catchment).

Zone I is located immediately around the groundwater source and is intended to protect against activities which might have an immediate effect upon the source. Zone II is larger than Zone I while Zone III covers the complete catchment area of a groundwater source.

The document states the NRA's policy objectives in relation to eight kinds of activity that pose the threat of groundwater pollution:

1   Groundwater abstractions
2   Physical disturbance of aquifers and groundwater flow
3   Waste disposal to land
4   Contaminated land
5   Disposal of liquid effluent, sludges and slurries to land
6   Discharges to underground strata
7   Diffuse pollution of groundwater, and
8   Other activities posing a threat to groundwater quality.

The threats vary depending on the vulnerability of the groundwater and the proximity of the activity to the groundwater source.

The policy statements are wide-ranging; to take two examples, the NRA will 'normally object to all activities requiring a waste management licence within Zone I'; it will 'normally refuse to consent discharges of sewage or trade effluent to be made into groundwaters'. Thus this document is invaluable to developers wishing to carry out activities that might affect groundwater quality since the NRA's likely stance on development proposals can be gleaned from it. It serves a similar function to a non-statutory water quality objective for groundwater.

2.4.3   Slurry and Silage Pollution

The regulations which the Secretary of State has power to make under s. 92 would require those intending to keep poisonous, noxious or polluting matter not to do so until they have constructed works and taken precautions to prevent or control this matter entering controlled waters. They would also require those who already possess such matter to construct works and take precautions to prevent or control their entry into controlled waters. The Control of Pollution (Silage, Slurry and Agricultural Fuel Oil) Regulations 1991, SI No. 324 have been made under these powers to deal with water pollution from silage, slurry and agricultural fuel oil. Similar regulations (the Control of Pollution (Oil) Regulations) are being considered to control pollution by oil from non-agricultural activities, such as petrol stations. The third limb of the tripod would bring in regulations to deal with industrial activities, such as the storage of industrial chemicals which frequently cause water pollution (for instance, during accidents).

The Silage, Slurry and Fuel Oil Regulations, and the promised 'Oil Regulations' impose construction standards which installations storing potentially polluting matter must meet; anyone intending to use such structures must inform the NRA 14 days before doing so to enable the NRA to inspect them. Standards relating to bunding, storage capacity, resistance to corrosion, distance from watercourses, longevity and maintenance. The requirements are reinforced by practical advice in the *Code of Good Agricultural Practice for the Protection of Water* as to how they can be achieved. The first set of Regulations exempt structures built before 1 March 1991 until 1 September 1996 unless they are substantially enlarged or reconstructed in the intervening period. Where the NRA is satisfied that the exempt structure poses a risk of polluting water it may serve a notice requiring works and precautions to be taken to minimize any risk, although the person may appeal against the notice to the Secretary of State. It is an offence to contravene the Regulations.

2.4.4   Nitrate Pollution

The concentration of nitrate in fresh water, particularly groundwater, has been rising for many years, due principally to the change in farming patterns involving greater use of inorganic nitrogen fertilizers and greater intensity of crop yield per hectare. The EC Drinking Water Directive imposes a maximum concentration for nitrate of 50 mg/l. The trend of nitrate levels in groundwater points to continued increases and the likelihood that many sources of drinking water supply in south-east England will continue to breach the 50 mg/l standard for some time to come, a situation that led to the UK being declared by the ECJ to be in breach of its obligations under the Drinking Water Directive.

The case *Commission v United Kingdom* arose when the Commission sought a declaration from the European Court that the UK had failed to implement the Directive fully in Scotland and Northern Ireland, and also failed to comply in certain water supply zones with the nitrates and lead standards. The first set of complaints related to a failure to bring in implementing regulations, a question of formal compliance which the UK rectified before the case came up for hearing. The complaint regarding lead was dismissed.

The second complaint regarding nitrates related to a failure to achieve the objectives of the directive, and went beyond formal compliance. The UK argued that the Directive did not impose an obligation to achieve a result but merely required member states to take all practicable steps to comply with the standards laid down, which it had done; and that in relation to nitrate the failure to achieve the standard was due to extraneous factors relating to particular techniques used in agriculture. The Court dismissed this argument and held that member states had to ensure that the required results were achieved, and could not rely on special circumstances in order to justify a failure to discharge that obligation. This ruling is significant insofar as it maintains that technical difficulties cannot justify a failure to comply with legal obligations assumed under EC directives. A member state would therefore need to ensure, before committing itself to a deadline for compliance, that it is achievable.

Indeed, the UK has been taking action to stop the increase in nitrate levels. The Nitrate Sensitive Areas (Designation) Order 1990, SI No. 1013 designated ten Nitrate Sensitive Areas; and a further twenty-two are in the pipeline (see S.I. 1994 No. 1729). Nitrate Sensitive Areas can be of three kinds:

1   Areas within which management agreements may be entered into voluntarily by farmers in return for compensation from the government
2   Areas in which the minister may mandatorily require, prohibit or restrict specified activities without compensation
3   Areas where the minister may require, prohibit or restrict activities but give compensation.

It is up to the NRA to apply to the Minister for Agriculture to designate Nitrate Sensitive Areas. The Minister must publicize his or her intended Order and notify local authorities and water undertakings as well as those farmers who are likely to be entitled to compensation. The proposals may be objected to, in which case a local inquiry to consider the objections may be held.

The ten areas designated to date are of the voluntary kind, primarily because they constitute a pilot scheme to provide information as to whether this method is likely to deal with the problem. The designation of the areas is for an indefinite period but farmers' obligations are to run initially for five years from May 1991. Farmers are free to join only the 'Basic Scheme' or, additionally, the 'Premium Scheme'. Under the former, farmers must limit fertilizer and manure applications to specified levels, and establish an autumn green cover to prevent leaching from bare land. The latter, on the hand, seeks a more fundamental restructuring of farming patterns, requiring conversion of arable land to grassland. The rates of compensation offered to farmers for taking action under it also differ; there is an additional payment to that given under the 'Basic Scheme'. Participation in the schemes has been high with 87 per cent of the eligible land being entered, of which 14 per cent was entered into the Premium Scheme (MAFF, 1993b).

In 1991, shortly after the introduction of the pilot Nitrate Sensitive Areas, the EC adopted Directive 91/676/EEC concerning the protection of waters against pollution caused by nitrates from agricultural sources which requires member states to take steps to protect all water sources where nitrate levels exceed 50 mg/l or are at risk of doing so. The catchment areas of these water sources are to be designated Nitrate Vulnerable Zones. States must draw up action programmes under which farmers in these zones will be required to take action to control nitrate leaching. The UK has intitated plans to designate Nitrate Vulnerable Zones; many will coincide with the Nitrate Sensitive Areas (DoE, 1994a–c).

2.5 Public Water Supplies

The term 'public water supplies' refers to water supplied by a company licensed to supply water, in contrast to 'private water supplies', which refers simply to water taken from private sources or supplied by unlicensed suppliers. Since 1989 public water supplies in England and Wales have been provided exclusively by private sector companies. Ten water and sewerage companies set up under the **Water Act 1989** provide the bulk of the service alongside twenty-eight much smaller statutory water companies which have provided a public water supply in the private sector since the nineteenth century. Collectively, these companies are known as 'water companies'.

The ten water and sewerage companies are also licensed to supply sewerage services and are referred to in the statutes as 'water and sewerage undertakers'.

The word 'undertaker' has a long history of use, but has remained unfamiliar to most people outside the industry. The licensing is through an appointment by the Secretary of State or Director General of Water Services under s. 6 of the Water Industry Act 1991 to supply water and sewerage services or, in the case of statutory water companies, water only in a specified geographical area; for example, the Thames Water Company supplies the London area. Although the law envisages companies competing in certain circumstances within each other's areas, the nature of the service provided gives them a natural monopoly in their area of appointment, and so far there have been no cases of direct competition. The companies have opted instead to compete in activities such as waste management.

Section 37 of the Water Industry Act 1991 makes it the duty of every water undertaker 'to develop and maintain an efficient and economical system of water supply within its area', the aim being to make supplies available to those within its area who need it. The Secretary of State has made regulations under s. 38 defining the standards of performance which the undertaker ought to achieve, failing which it is liable to pay a standard amount of compensation to those of its customers affected by the failure. Additionally, of course, an undertaker has to meet stringent standards of drinking water quality. These standards have significant implications for water pollution control.

2.5.1   The Quality of Water Supplies

The quality of water supplies is dealt with in Chapter III of Part III of the **Water Industry Act 1991**. Section 68 imposes two duties on the water undertaker as follows:

1   When supplying water to premises for domestic or food production purposes, to supply only water which is 'wholesome' at the time of supply
2   So far as reasonably practicable, to ensure that the sources of the undertaker's supply do not deteriorate in quality.

The juxtaposition of these two duties highlights the environmental significance of the water supply duties of the water undertakers; they have a direct interest in the ambient quality of water since it directly affects their ability to supply wholesome water.

The term 'wholesome' has a long history in water legislation but has never been given any statutory definition. In *McColl v Strathclyde Regional Council* the court held that it is water that is free from contamination and pleasant to drink. In the **Water Act 1989** the Secretary of State was given power for the first time to make regulations prescribing standards which drinking water would have to meet to be regarded as wholesome. These powers are now contained in s. 67 of the Water Industry Act 1991 and were inserted in the legislation principally to make it possible for the UK to comply with EC requirements, marking a break with the UK tradition of not prescribing quantitative standards for drinking water quality.

Standards of Wholesomeness

The EC Directive relating to the quality of water intended for human consumption (80/778/EEC), commonly referred to as the Drinking Water Directive, set standards which water intended for human consumption within the EC must meet. The Directive is implemented in England and Wales through the Water Supply (Water Quality) Regulations 1989, SI No. 1147 and through similar Regulations (SI 1990 No. 119) in Scotland.

Regulation 3 of the Water Quality Regulations provides that water supplied to premises for domestic or food production purposes 'shall be regarded as wholesome if [specified] requirements are satisfied', thus defining for the first time the concept of wholesome by reference to quantitative standards. The requirements relate to organoleptic (i.e. colour, turbidity, odour and taste), physico-chemical, toxicity and microbiological parameters, largely reflecting the EC requirements. In each case the parameters specify a maximum concentration which must not be exceeded, but in relation to a number of substances, they specify a minimum concentration.

Regulation 3 has two additional requirements which water must meet to be wholesome: it must not contain any element, organism or substance at a concentration which would be detrimental to public health; and, second, it must not contain any element, organism or substance at a concentration which in conjunction with any other element, organism or substance it contains would be detrimental to public health. The rationale for these requirements is to safeguard public health, which quantitative standards alone might not do; indeed as the second requirement recognizes, substances which are harmless on their own might, when combined, prove harmful. Public health remains the starting point in controlling drinking water quality.

The Drinking Water Directive required these standards to be achieved by 1985, but practical problems, such as the need to design and plan projects and develop and test new technology, plus the necessary investment (estimated at approximately £28 billion) required mean that, inevitably, some of the parameters have not yet been complied with. The Secretary of State has in every case sought and received from the water companies undertakings under s. 19(1)(b) (referred to as 's. 19's'—see below under 2.5.2 'Enforcement of Water Supply Duties') to carry out the works necessary to achieve the standards. Each undertaking identifies the water supply area; the particular parameter being contravened; the steps to be taken to achieve compliance; and the date by which the steps are to be completed. Additionally, in an attempt to speed things up, the government issued a circular (DoE, 1991) urging planning authorities to view sympathetically planning applications by water companies for projects such as treatment works.

Undertakings have been criticized by environmental pressure groups insofar as they extend the date by which the standards set in the Drinking Water Directive are to be achieved. In *R v Secretary of State for the Environment ex parte Friends of the Earth*, FoE sought judicial review of the Secretary of State's acceptance of undertakings from the water companies, Thames and Anglian, in relation to the pesticide standard. The court dismissed the application, holding that there were considerable complexities in bringing all water up to the required standards and the undertakings were designed to enable the companies to arrive at a situation in which all water conformed to the standards. A separate FoE complaint to the European Commission is still pending. Given the ECJ's ruling in *Commission v UK* (nitrates case) above that practical difficulties cannot be used to justify failure to meet the required standards, the UK would possibly lose the case if it ever went to the ECJ.

Relaxations

Like the Drinking Water Directive, the Water Quality Regulations do not rank the various parameters in order of priority. Legally, all the parameters must be achieved fully at the same time regardless of whether they are health-related or simply aesthetic (i.e. relating, for instance, to colour and taste). The Secretary of State is able, under Regulation 4, to relax these standards in three specified circumstances only:

1   Where it is necessary, as an emergency measure, to maintain a supply of water for human consumption
2   Where it is called for by reason of exceptional meteorological conditions, or
3   Where it is called for by reason of the nature and structure of the ground in the area from which the supply of water emanates.

Again, the bottom line is that the relaxations must not give rise to a risk to public health or to a public health hazard.

The relaxation is formalized in what is referred to as a 'Regulation 4' letter from the Secretary of State to the water company identifying:

1   The parameter for which a relaxation has been granted
2   The zones to which the water may be supplied
3   Which of the three heads the relaxation is based on
4   Conditions to which the relaxation is subject, and
5   The date when the relaxation will cease.

Thus, Thames Water Company, for instance, has repeatedly obtained relaxations in respect of the phosphorus standard under the heading allowing relaxations on the ground of exceptional meteorological conditions. An earlier attempt by the government to give relaxations in relation to the nitrate standard under the heading permitting relaxations because of the nature and structure of the ground failed when the European Commission took the view that the presence of nitrates in groundwater did not arise from the nature and structure of the ground, but rather arose primarily from farming practices and land-use patterns which could be altered.

The Extent of the Duty to Supply Wholesome Water

By virtue of s. 68(2) of the **Water Industry Act 1991** the duty of undertakers to supply wholesome water effectively ends at the point where the water leaves the undertaker's pipes and enters those of the consumer. Historically, houses had copper, lead or zinc pipes. Lead pipes dissolve when exposed to water, a phenomenon referred to as plumbosolvency. There is a risk, therefore, of water which is wholesome while in the undertaker's pipes becoming contaminated by dissolved lead in the consumer's pipes. There is little a consumer can do to counter this risk apart from replacing the piping, an expensive process.

An undertaker, however, can reduce the risk of contamination by treating the water. Special provisions exist which require the undertaker to minimize the risk of plumbosolvency by removing any lead piping belonging to it if the consumer requests it in writing, or by treating the water. However, there is no requirement to treat the water if this will not minimize the risk, or is not practicable, or the risk affects only a small part of the water supply zone.

This requirement is reinforced by the provisions of s. 68(3) which effectively extend the water undertaker's duty to supply wholesome water to cover piping contamination, by providing that water is still unwholesome if, although wholesome at the time of leaving the undertaker's pipes, it has become unwholesome:

1 While in a pipe which is subject to mains pressure or would be if some valve was not closed, and
2 Because of the undertaker's failure before supplying the water to take the specified steps to eliminate or minimize the risk that the water would become unwholesome after leaving its pipes.

Additionally, the undertaker may be liable in negligence under the common law even though the statutory duty to supply wholesome water has ended, and the contamination occurs in the consumer's pipes. *Barnes v Irwell Valley Water Board* illustrates this situation. Water supplied by the Water Board dissolved lead plumbing in the premises of the consumer who contracted lead poisoning when he drank the water. The court found the Water Board negligent in that it should have either taken steps to reduce the plumbosolvency of the water, or warned consumers that the water was liable to be dangerous to health if passed through lead pipes.

2.5.2   Enforcement of Water Supply Duties

Chapter II of Part II of the **Water Industry Act 1991** deals with the enforcement of the companies' duty to provide water and sewerage services. The task is put principally in the hands of the Secretary of State and the Director General of Water Services. The Secretary of State enforces the duties relating to water quality, special category effluent, and the general environmental and recreational duties while the Director General enforces the duties relating to the companies' conditions of appointment and, on delegation from the Secretary of State, the duty to provide a sewerage system and a public water supply system. In practice, the duty relating to special category effluent is enforced by HMIP while that relating to the quality of drinking water is enforced by the DWI, both acting on behalf of the Secretary of State.

The DWI is based within the DoE. It is appointed under s. 86 of the Water Industry Act 1991 to act on behalf of the Secretary of State as technical assessors with responsibility for determining the extent to which the water companies achieve the specified water quality standards. Principally, this consists of conducting an annual technical audit of the information supplied to it by the water companies. It does not itself conduct sampling of drinking water supplies and relies partly on the private sector consultancies in its auditing task. The results of the audit and its general assessment of the quality of drinking water supplied and the performance of the companies is published in an annual report, the DWI Drinking Water Report. In the last three years it has reported that over 98 per cent of the water supplied was of high quality and complied with the specified standards.

The enforcement procedure is outlined in s. 18 of the Water Industry Act 1991. It is a laborious process involving at least four steps. The first step is for the Secretary of State or the Director General—depending on which of them is the enforcement authority—to make a 'provisional enforcement order' if he or she is satisfied either that a company is contravening a condition of its appointment (or a statutory requirement) or that it has done so and is likely do so again. The order demands that the company comply with the condition or statutory requirement. If the company still does not comply then the Secretary of State or the Director General can ultimately confirm the order, either with or without modifications. The confirmed order or 'final enforcement order' (or simply a 's. 18 enforcement order') specifies steps which the company is required to take and a time when the order will take effect. A s. 18 enforcement order is the third rather than the second step in the enforcement process because there is an interim step which must be taken before a s. 18 order can be made.

Preceding the s. 18 order the enforcing authority has to give notice stating the intention to make or confirm the order, the reason for doing so and its effect. A notice of the proposed order must also be served on the company affected and a period of twenty-eight days allowed for objections or representations to be made and considered. As soon as possible after making the s. 18 order a copy must be served on the company affected and the Director General (where the order is made by the Secretary of State) and also publicized to those likely to be affected by it.

The final stage in the process is the enforcement of the order itself. This would require the enforcement authority to bring a civil court action to force the company to implement the order. Civil action can also be brought by any other parties affected by the failure to implement the s. 18 order. In practice, the fourth stage is unlikely ever to be reached. Any practical obstacles to implementing the requirements of a s. 18 order (such as the need to upgrade inadequate treatment works) are likely to be dealt with at the objection stage before the order is made. Thus, an order which could not be complied with in the time specified is unlikely to be made.

Section 19 sets out three circumstances in which the enforcing authority need not make a s. 18 enforcement order nor confirm a provisional enforcement order; these are where the authority is satisfied that:

1 The contraventions, or possible contraventions, are trivial; 'trivial' is not defined so the DWI uses its judgement;
2 The company is complying with an undertaking to take all such steps as appear to the enforcing authority to be appropriate to secure or facilitate compliance with the condition or requirement; or
3 The authority's duties to the company preclude it from making or confirming the order; of these the duty to ensure that the company has sufficiently secure returns on its capital to finance its water and sewerage functions is particularly important.

Where the enforcing authority decides not to proceed with making or confirming the order it must notify the company of this and publicize the notice to those likely to be affected. If the reason for not proceeding is that the company has given an undertaking, the Director General has to be notified, because undertakings by companies go into the Director's calculations in setting the 'K' factor as obligations which the company has to meet (see 2.2.5 'K Factors' below). According to the DWI, improvement programmes resulting mainly from undertakings by companies will cost £2.1 billion by 1995. Of these, work to comply with the coliform and faecal coliform standards were completed in 1991, while work to comply with the chemical and aesthetic quality standards are to be completed by the end of 1995 (DWI, 1993).

To date, no provisional or final enforcement orders have been made against any company principally because the companies have taken remedial action, given undertakings or sought and received relaxations under Regulation 4 once they were notified that enforcement action was being considered, with the result that the threatened action was dropped. The s. 18 enforcement procedure is designed as a pragmatic enforcement mechanism in the face of the reality that failures to meet specified water and sewerage standards often result from structural problems which require large-scale and long-term investments. Remedial projects take time to plan and implement and can be delayed not just by a lack of funds but also by factors such as the inability to obtain planning permission to construct the necessary works, as the *FoE case* above shows.

Incidents

Despite the DWI's repeated endorsement of the high quality of drinking water in England and Wales, the public's perception is that the quality of drinking water in the UK is deteriorating rather than improving, and increasingly large numbers of people are turning to bottled water and various water-filtering devices. This is caused partly by bad publicity resulting from a few very serious contamination incidents such as the inadvertent emptying in July 1988 of aluminium sulphate into a tank of water which went directly into public supply at Camelford in Cornwall, and is alleged to have caused widespread illness among members of the public who drank the water.

On 2 March 1990 the Secretary of State issued the Water Undertakers (Information) Direction 1990 which has since been replaced by the Water Undertakers (Information) Direction 1992 requiring companies to notify the Secretary of State as soon as possible of:

1 Any event which, because of its effect on the quality or quantity of water, gives rise to a significant risk to the health, and
2 Any matter relating to the supply of water which is of national significance, has attracted significant local or national publicity, or has caused a significant concern to consumers.

Events and matters falling within the two categories above are referred to as 'incidents'. They result from incidents such as the pollution of water sources and microbiological contamination of supplies. The Direction requires that the Secretary of State be notified both where the risk, publicity or concern is realized and where it is only likely. Fifty-six such Incidents were notified in 1992 (DWI, 1993). *Guidance on Safeguarding the Quality of Public Water Supplies* (DoE, 1989) specifies the response companies should make. One of them, issuing a public notice to boil water before drinking or cooking (a 'boil notice'), is almost guaranteed to cause public alarm and undermine public confidence although it may, of course, be necessary to protect the public from harm. Others include the notifying of the local authority, monitoring the water, rectifying the problem and, if necessary, seeking an emergency relaxation of the water quality standards.

Incidents can result in enforcement action or indeed a prosecution under s. 70 of the **Water Industry Act 1991** for supplying water unfit for human consumption. Section 70 is aimed at gross breaches of the duty to supply wholesome water; a simple breach of water quality standards would not suffice for this charge because standards are set with a wide margin of safety. The crime can only be prosecuted by either the Secretary of State or the Director of Public Prosecutions; the DoE has proposed that the power be transferred to the DWI.

Additionally, the water company has a statutory defence, that:

1 It had no reasonable grounds for suspecting that the water would be used for human consumption or
2 It took all reasonable steps and exercised all due diligence for securing that the water was fit for human consumption on leaving its pipes or was not used for human consumption.

No water company has so far been charged with this offence which has led to its criticism as an enforcement mechanism. It is notable that even cases such as the outbreak of cryptosporidiosis in a number of reservoirs in 1989/90 was not considered serious enough to justify a prosecution for this offence. Perhaps only incidents as serious as the Camelford incident would sustain such a prosecution. In the Camelford incident itself, however, the water authority was charged and convicted of causing a public nuisance, a common law offence, as the incident occurred before the offence of supplying water unfit for human consumption was enacted in the **Water Act 1989**.

The Role of Local Authorities

Local authorities have hardly any powers of enforcement in relation to the water companies' duty to supply wholesome water. It was thought that to give them enforcement powers would generate confusion; local authority areas are not coterminous with the areas of appointment of any particular undertaker and so more than one local authority would have had enforcement powers over an undertaker at the same time, with the attendant conflicting requirements. Therefore, all that s. 77 of the **Water Industry Act 1991** provides is that local authorities have a duty to take steps to inform themselves about the quality of water supplied to premises in their area. They have powers under s. 85 to obtain the necessary information for this purpose.

If a local authority believes that a water company is failing in its water supply duties it may notify the undertaker, and, where satisfactory remedial action is not taken, the Secretary of State that:

1 The supply is, has been, or is likely to become unwholesome or insufficient for domestic purposes
2 The unwholesomeness or insufficiency was or is likely to be such as to cause a danger to life or health or

3   The undertaker's duty to ensure that the quality of its source of supply
    does not deteriorate is being, has been or is likely to be contravened so as to
    affect the water supply to premises in the area.

If, however, health is threatened by the lack of supply the local authority can
require the undertaker to provide alternative supplies at the authority's
expense so long as:

1   It is not practicable at reasonable cost for the undertaker to maintain a suffi-
    cient piped supply of wholesome water to premises and
2   It is practicable at reasonable cost for the undertaker to provide such a
    supply otherwise than in pipes (e.g. by tanker or hosepipe).

2.5.3   Private Water Supplies

Under s. 93 of the **Water Industry Act 1991** private water supplies are water
supplies taken from private sources or supplied by unlicensed suppliers. It
does not matter whether the water is supplied from outside or inside the premises where it is consumed. There is no legal reason why water undertakers
who wish to supply water in their private capacity independently of their
appointment may not do so. Increasing quantities of private water supplies are
bottled for sale to the public. Such water is treated legally as having been used
on the premises where it is bottled, rather than where it is actually consumed.
Sampling for wholesomeness, therefore, must be conducted before bottling.
Private supplies are, however, only a very small proportion of the water
supplies in the UK.

A private supply of water has to meet the quality requirements set out in the
Private Water Supplies Regulations 1991, SI No. 2790, which are largely the
same as those of the Water Quality Regulations 1989 but differ in respect of
monitoring requirements. The 1991 Regulations impose a duty on local
authorities to monitor private supplies according to a classification system set
out in the Regulations. There are two classes: category 1 water is used for
domestic purposes while category 2 water is used for food production purposes
or in premises used as staff canteens; educational, hospital and other residential
institutions; or camp sites and other places providing short-term accommodation on a commercial basis.

The local authority's remedy where the private supply is not wholesome or
sufficient is to serve a notice specifying the steps to be taken and a period of at
least twenty-eight days for objecting to the notice. The notice is to be served on
either:

1   The owners or occupiers of the premises using the private supply
2   The owners or occupiers of the premises where the source of the supply is
    located or

3   Anyone else who exercises powers of management and control in relation to
that source.

The notice comes into effect once it is confirmed by the Secretary of State.
It may be enforced by the local authority themselves taking the required
steps and recovering expenses from the person who failed to act as directed.

2.5.4   Bottled Water

There is currently little specific law on which liquids qualify to be referred to
under the various labels used to describe bottled water. Waters which qualify
as 'natural mineral waters' fall under the Natural Mineral Waters Regulations
1985, SI No. 71 which implement EC Directive 80/777/EEC on the exploitation and marketing of natural mineral waters. The Regulations define the term
'natural mineral water' and other similar terms and prohibit the sale of a
natural mineral water which is not marked accordingly. This does not,
however, extend to selling water under some other name, such as 'natural
spring water' which is not covered by the Regulations.

The Regulations put in place a system under which natural mineral water
may officially be recognized as such. A person seeking recognition of a natural
mineral water applies in writing to the local authority within whose area the
source is exploited. The applicant must provide details relating to the water
including the hydrology of its source; its physical, chemical, microbiological
and toxicity standards; and evidence to the effect that the water is not polluted.
Where the natural mineral water originates outside the EC the application is to
be made to the Minister for Agriculture. In each case once the recognition is
granted it shall be published in the *London Gazette* and the *Edinburgh Gazette*
and, for it to be recognized throughout the EC, in the *Official Journal* of the
EC.

The Natural Mineral Waters Regulations are concerned only with natural
mineral waters, while the Private Water Supplies Regulations above regulate
the quality of private, but not necessarily bottled, supplies. The Drinking
Water in Containers Regulations 1994, SI No. 743 (which do not apply to
natural mineral waters) set standards which bottled water must meet. The
regulations extend to water which is bottled to the standards of EC Directive
80/778/EEC on the quality of water intended for human consumption, already
applied to public and private supplies. The Regulations make it an offence to
bottle or sell drinking water which does not comply with these standards. The
standards are enforced by local authorities in their capacity as food authorities
under the **Food Safety Act 1990**.

2.5.5 'K' Factors

As noted (see 'Trade Effluent Consents') water and sewerage undertakers may fix charges for their water and sewerage services in accordance with a Charges Scheme, by way of an agreement with persons to be charged or as a condition of the consent to discharge into the public sewers. Overall control of the level of charges lies with the Director General of Water Services. Under s. 2 the Director General must balance the interests of the companies in securing returns on their capital to finance their functions and maximize revenue with those of companies' customers who naturally desire low charges; the Director General attempts to do this through setting and reviewing what are termed 'K' factors.

The K factor is the means through which increases in the companies charges are controlled. A company is able to increase its charges annually by the sum total of the increase in the retail price index plus a variable factor, referred to as 'K' set for each company by the Director General (i.e. RPI + K). Increasing the 'K' factor means that the company is able to increase its prices and, conversely, decreasing it denies the company the level of price increase previously available to it. The way in which these changes are determined is set out in the companies' licence, specifically in Condition B, which is long and complicated, being essentially an accounting exercise. Each company must limit its price increases to the limits set by its 'K' factor, otherwise it will be in breach of its licence.

Under the terms of the licence, periodic reviews of the company's business are conducted by the Director General so that he or she can determine whether 'K' should be changed. These reviews can be initiated in one of three ways:

1   By the Director General at five-yearly intervals
2   By the company at five-yearly intervals or
3   Through regular self-initiating reviews at ten-yearly intervals.

In July 1991 the Director General gave the companies notice of his intention to carry out the first five-year review to determine whether the Ks which were set in 1989 should be changed for the ten years starting on 1 April 1995. The process is currently going ahead and the new Ks limiting increases to an average of 1% per year were set in July 1994 to come into effect in April 1995 (OFWAT, 1993a,b and OFWAT, 1994).

In addition to periodic reviews, the licence allows the company or the Director General to initiate an interim review of the 'K' factor in the intervening period between the periodic review. This enables an interim determination to be made regarding whether 'K' should be changed to allow specified costs to be passed on to the customer. The most likely reasons for this would be a 'relevant change of circumstance' and unavoidable occurrences which have an adverse effect on the company's business.

Relevant changes of circumstance refers to specified items where the actual expenditure incurred by the company is expected to diverge from levels assumed when 'K' was previously set. These items include the application of any legal requirement or change to any legal requirement; this goes beyond legislation to embrace licences, consents, authorizations, and statutory undertakings (e.g. s. 19 undertakings) given by the company. Where a company fails to take the steps required to comply with its obligations and therefore incurs fewer costs than were allowed for in its 'K' the Director General can order the excess 'K' to be 'clawed-back'. But where, on the other hand, the company complies with obligations more efficiently than was envisaged it keeps the profits, an arrangement intended to encourage efficiency.

The Director General has stressed that great emphasis is placed on the need to ensure as much stability as possible, in particular between periodic reviews, to guarantee the companies a reasonable degree of certainty about revenue and investment plans; also that a high priority is given to the need to protect customers against excessive price increases. As a general principle the Director General wants companies to restrict price increases in line with their 'K' until the next periodic review. Companies should accommodate changes in expenditure by revising priorities whenever possible rather than seeking an interim review, unless that course of action is not feasible.

Since Ks were set in 1989, major new obligations have been imposed on the water companies. These include:

1   The ban on dumping of sewage sludge at sea to come into force in 1998
2   The EC Urban Waste Water Directive which imposes stringent sewage treatment requirements
3   The accelerated programme to clean up bathing waters
4   The proposed introduction of statutory water quality objectives, and
5   The programme to remove pesticides from drinking water.

The 1994 periodic review was conducted against a background of significant increases in the companies' projected expenditure, which could lead to significant price increases. The Director General has sought to draw a distinction between the companies' 'normal' expenditure (RPI + K) and mandatory environmental improvements, termed 'Q'. The Director General will permit price rises by a factor Q over and above the RPI (RPI + Q) (OFWAT, 1993a,b).

The Director General's view is that price increases to pay for new obligations should be linked to customers' willingness to pay, and since he believes that customers do not want any price increases, he sees the only options as the postponement of implementation of new programmes or their cancellation. He goes as far as to suggest that ministers should renegotiate the UK's environmental obligations with the EC (OFWAT, 1993). This view has set the Director General on an apparent collision course with the Chairman of the NRA, who argues that increased prices reflect the lack of investment in water quality and pollution control in the 1970s and 1980s, which has to be redressed.

The government indicated its sympathy with the Director General's view that price increases should be curtailed where possible through a shift in priorities but without lowering standards (DoE, 1993b). The government has since sought a postponment of the compliance dates for the EC Urban Waste Water Treatment Directive but so far without success. This episode highlights an issue not previously appreciated; that the Director General, through control of prices, has a direct role in the extent to which the water and sewerage companies fulfil their environmental obligations.

2.6 Abstraction Licensing

Under the common law, riparian owners and other persons who have a right of access to the water (through an arrangement with a riparian owner to cross over his or her land), have a right to abstract water. This right is limited only to the extent that it is subject to an equal right of the downstream riparian owners also to abstract. The common law right to abstraction has been restricted greatly since the **Water Resources Act 1963** which, for the first time, required those wishing to abstract water in England and Wales to obtain a licence. In Scotland, it was not until 1993 that proposals were published to introduce abstraction licensing in areas identified as being at risk of water depletion. Such areas would be declared 'control areas' (Scottish Office, 1993).

The Water Resources Act 1963 was repealed but the abstraction provisions were transferred to Chapter II of Part II of the **Water Resources Act 1991**, which now constitutes the law on water abstraction licensing. In essence, s. 24 restricts the right to abstract water without a licence from the NRA with exceptions relating to small abstractions, in most cases of less than 20 m^3. Additionally, only the occupier of land contiguous to the water from which the abstraction is to be made or a person who has a right of access to such land (or will have such a right whenever the licence is intended to come into effect) is entitled to apply for a licence. In other words, an abstraction licence can be granted only to someone with a common law right to abstract water. It is an offence to abstract water without a licence, and the Water Resources (Licences) Regulations 1965, SI No. 534 set out the procedure to be followed, including publicizing the application and hearing objections.

Section 39 provides that the NRA shall not grant a licence authorizing the abstraction of water so as to derogate from any protected rights, unless the person entitled to the rights consents. A 'protected right' is:

1   A right of a person to abstract small quantities of water for domestic and agricultural purposes without a licence and

2   A right of a person who holds a water abstraction licence to the extent
    authorized by the licence.

Derogation from such rights means authorizing the abstraction of water in
such a way, or to such an extent, as to prevent persons entitled to the right
from abstracting to the extent of their entitlement. Should the NRA grant a
licence which derogates from a protected right, the person entitled to the right
may sue it for damages for a breach of statutory duty. The NRA has a statutory
defence to such an action if the derogation can be attributed mainly to an
exceptional shortage of rain, an accident, or an unforeseen act or event. Even
where the NRA is liable to pay damages, the licence itself, though granted in
derogation of a protected right, remains valid and the subsequent licensee
cannot be sued by the person suffering the derogation.

   The derogation provisions make this regime in effect a 'first come–first
served' (or 'prior use') system for apportioning water between those who wish
to abstract it, in contrast to other systems of apportionment which attempt to
balance the interests of the various competing uses. Additionally, the protected
right is based on the quantity licensed rather than the extent to which the
licence is actually exploited, raising the prospect that some people may choose
to accumulate abstraction rights. This situation is mitigated greatly by the
Secretary of State's power to call in an application for a licence, consider it by
either a hearing or a local inquiry, and if he or she so decides, direct the NRA
to grant the licence, notwithstanding that the grant would derogate from a protected right. The NRA is still liable to pay damages to the prior licensee but
the Secretary of State may choose to indemnify it, either wholly or partly.

   Following an application for a licence to abstract, the NRA is required to give
notice of its decision within three months, failing which it is deemed to have
refused it, unless in the meantime it has been called in by the Secretary of State.
The applicant and the NRA may agree in writing to extend the decision-making
period, which may be necessary where the application raises complex issues. In
reaching a decision, the NRA must have regard to the effect it will have on any
minimum acceptable flow, or where none have been set, the considerations by
which it would be set. In fact, minimum acceptable flows have never been set
for any watercourse and the NRA normally grants licences conditional on what
it refers to as 'minimum residual flows', i.e. a minimum flow below which no
abstraction is to be made. The NRA must have regard also to environmental
considerations, including whether the abstraction would reduce the capacity of
the river to dilute incoming effluent. If the licence is granted it must state the
quantity of water to be abstracted and the conditions to which it is subject, such
as whether abstraction is limited during certain periods of the year.

   By s. 43 an applicant may appeal to the Secretary of State against the
decision of the NRA by giving written notice within one month of the adverse
decision, or failure to give any decision. However, the Secretary of State may

grant an extension of the one-month appeal period. The appeal is by notice in writing served on both the Secretary of State and the NRA. The Secretary of State may hold a local inquiry or simply give the applicant and the NRA a hearing before determining the appeal. The Secretary of State's decision on appeal may not be questioned in any legal proceedings, except on procedural grounds.

An abstraction licence may be varied or revoked on the initiative of the holder, the NRA or the owner of fishing rights who sustains loss or damage because of the abstraction. Where the NRA wishes to initiate the variation or revocation of a licence, or where it has been directed to do so by the Secretary of State, it shall formulate and publicize its proposals. The NRA shall allow not less than twenty-eight days for objections and refer the proposals to the Secretary of State if the licence holder objects to them. The Secretary of State may either hold a local inquiry or hear the NRA and the licence holder before determining the proposals.

Where a licence is revoked or varied by the NRA following a direction from the Secretary of State, the NRA is liable to pay compensation if the holder can show that he or she has incurred expenditure in carrying out work which has been rendered unnecessarily abortive by the revocation or variation, or has sustained some other loss or damage through it. Failing agreement on the compensation payable, the matter would be determined by the Lands Tribunal. But no compensation is payable if the licence had not been exploited in the seven years preceding the revocation or variation. The Secretary of State may, at his or her discretion, indemnify the NRA wholly or partly for the amount it pays out in compensation.

The fact that an abstraction licence cannot be revoked or varied without compensation is seen as limiting the ability of the NRA to limit water abstraction even where over-abstraction is occurring. These concerns were highlighted in the summer of 1992, when the NRA insisted that Thames Water Company limit its abstraction from the River Darent by up to 70 per cent of its authorized abstraction. The government is currently looking into the feasibility of limiting the compensation payable where the variation or revocation is considered necessary on account of over-abstraction by licensees. Such a change would perhaps be implemented by amending legislation.

In the meantime, the NRA has published an assessment of the condition of forty low-flow rivers in England and Wales (NRA, 1993). This discusses possible technical methods of alleviating low flows, including riverbed lining; the introduction of a new source of water; recycling and relocation of the offending abstraction within the same water source. The NRA has sought, on the whole, to work with abstractors to find an appropriate technical solution where there is over-abstraction.

The water abstraction licensing regime does not expressly deal with issues of water quality, being primarily a mechanism for managing quantity. However, at times abstractions can affect water quality, for instance where over-abstraction raises the concentration of pollutants in the source of supply. It is arguable that the NRA's powers to set conditions on an abstraction licence extend to setting conditions designed to protect the quality of the water supply. The issue has not come before the courts but a series of the Secretary of State's decisions show that considerations related to the quality of water water supply may legitimately be taken into account by the NRA in determining an abstraction licence application; indeed, such considerations can be the reason for refusing an application (Mumma, 1994).

2.7   The EC Water Directives

EC action with regard to the quality of water dates back to the mid-1970s. In two decades it has imposed requirements covering various aspects of the management of water quality. In recent times, however, various member states have argued that most aspects of water management should be left to the member states in line with the principle of subsidiarity and that the EC should only concern itself with setting broad framework requirements. In response, the European Commission has outlined plans to amend several water Directives so that they would impose quality and health standards only leaving member states free to add other standards if they so choose (Commission of the European Communities, 1993).

Under the proposed regime, EC requirements for water protection will be based on two sets of directives, one dealing with water quality and the other with discharges to waters. The water quality set will have:

1   A new drinking water directive which will replace the 1980 Drinking Water Directive (80/778/EEC) and aspects of the surface water for drinking Directive (75/440/EEC)
2   A directive on the ecological quality of surface waters to replace the rest of 75/440/EEC; this was adopted by the Commission in June 1994 (COM (93) 680 final published in OJ No. C 222/6 of 10.8.94)
3   An amended directive on bathing water replacing the current one (76/160/EEC); this has been proposed (COM (94) 36 final, OJ No. C 112/3)
4   An amended groundwater directive replacing the current one (80/68/EEC).

The 'discharges set' is unchanged, containing the current directives dealing with the control of nitrates (91/676/EEC), the Urban Waste Water Treatment Directive (91/276/EEC) and the Dangerous Substances Directive (74/646/EEC). According to the Commission these already comply with the subsidiarity test since they set only framework requirements. No amendments are considered necessary. The Commission also includes in this set the proposed Integrated Pollution Prevention and Control Directive (COM (93) 423 final).

The process of introducing new or amended directives is a lengthy one and therefore all the major water directives are discussed briefly here as they currently stand. The UK's action to implement the requirements of the directives are noted where this would not otherwise be obvious from the discussion in the rest of the chapter.

2.7.1   Drinking Water

There are two EC directives dealing with the quality of drinking water: Directive 75/440/EEC (OJ No. L 194/26) concerning the quality required of surface water intended for the abstraction of drinking water in member states (the Surface Water for Drinking Directive) and Directive 80/778/EEC (OJ No. L 229/11) relating to the quality of water intended for human consumption (the Drinking Water Directive). These directives are targeted primarily at ensuring a minimum quality for drinking water; they are environmental measures only indirectly insofar as water pollution control is necessary for high-quality drinking water.

The Surface Water for Drinking Directive

The Surface Water for Drinking Directive deals with the quality requirements which surface freshwater used, or intended for use, in the abstraction of drinking water must meet. It applies only to surface freshwater, not covering ground and brackish water.

The Directive classifies surface water into three categories: A1, A2, and A3 according to forty-six specified physical, chemical and microbiological characteristics which the waters exhibit. Depending on its category, the water must have an appropriate level of treatment in order to be transformed into drinking water. A1 needs only to be filtered and disinfected; A2 needs to be filtered, chemically treated and disinfected; while A3 needs to be intensively treated physically and chemically, and disinfected. Only water of at least class A3 may be used for abstraction of drinking water, unless there are exceptional circumstances of which the Commission has been notified. The UK's action to implement this directive is set out under 'EC Water Quality Classes', p. 29.

The Drinking Water Directive

The Drinking Water Directive gave member states two years within which to bring their laws into line with it, and five years within which to ensure that the quality of their drinking water met the standards it laid down. For UK implementing action see 'Standards of Wholesomeness', p. 53.

This Directive is linked to the Surface Water for Drinking Directive because only surface water falling into one of the three classes specified there can be abstracted for use as drinking water. The Drinking Water Directive sets standards which water intended for human consumption must meet, whether it is drunk or used in food production. It does not, however, cover natural mineral waters and medicinal waters.

The Directive sets sixty-two organoleptic (colour, turbidity, odour and taste), physico-chemical, toxicity and microbiological standards which drinking water must meet. Most standards express a maximum concentration which must not be exceeded and a 'guide value' to which member states should aspire; the standard for nitrates, for instance, is a maximum concentration of 50 mg/l and a guide value of 25 mg/l. Some of the standards (e.g. boron) express a guide value only; others (e.g. those relating to toxicity) a maximum concentration only; and yet others (e.g. suspended solids) set no quantitative standards. Four standards—total hardness, pH, alkalinity and dissolved oxygen—set a minimum concentration.

The standards have come under considerable criticism in recent times because they are not related directly to health considerations. The pesticides standard, for instance, is 0.1 μg/l for each pesticide and 0.5 μg/l for the sum total of all pesticides in the drinking water. Thus a blanket standard has to be met by all pesticides, regardless of the differing toxicities, an approach which differs from that of the World Health Organization, which sets a standard for each pesticide on the basis of its toxicity. The UK, which has always opposed to the EC's approach to the pesticide standard, has set its own 'advisory values' for water suppliers based on toxicological considerations (DoE, 1989).

In *Commission v UK* (Case C-337/89) the ECJ declared that the UK had not implemented requirements of the Drinking Water Directive. The Commission complained that the UK did not implement the Directive in four areas: in respect of water used in the food industry in England and Wales; by not laying regulations for Scotland and Northern Ireland; by not achieving the nitrates standard in England; and by not achieving the lead standard in Scotland (this last complaint was rejected).

2.7.2 Bathing Water

EC Directive 76/160/EEC (OJ No. L 31/1) is the only EC directive directly on the subject of bathing water. Member states had two years within which to bring their laws into line with the Directive and ten years within which to bring the quality of their bathing water up to its standards. A member state could waive the standards in exceptional circumstances, such as bad weather for a limited period, but the Commission had to be informed. The UK has implemented the Directive administratively but the standards it sets will form part of the statutory water quality objectives.

The Commission has submitted a proposal for a new bathing water Directive to be implemented by 31 December 1995, replacing the current Directive (COM (94) 36 final, OJ No. C 112/3). There are three other major changes. A new category is introduced of 'excellent quality' for bathing waters which meet the standards of the guide values specified in the Directive. Second, member states would be required to ensure that adequate information on bathing water quality was prominently displayed at each bathing area. Third, member states would have to prohibit bathing at individual bathing areas where pollution constituted a threat to public health.

In *Commission v UK* (Case C-56/90) the Commission complained that the UK did not take measures to ensure that the quality of bathing water in Blackpool, Formby and Southport met the standards in the Directive. The Directive defines bathing water as water in which bathing is either authorized or traditionally practised by large numbers of people. The UK's view was that this definition was vague since there was no requirement to authorize bathing in the UK. Therefore in identifying bathing water it applied additional criteria based on numbers of bathers. On the basis of these criteria it designated twenty-seven resorts, excluding Blackpool, Formby and Southport. With effect from 1987, the UK designated another 389 bathing waters, which included the three resorts.

The Court held that if resorts equipped with facilities could be excluded from the scope of the Directive on the basis of the number of bathers it would defeat the objectives of the Directive, which was to protect public health. The UK argued additionally that the ten-year period for bringing bathing waters of the 389 resorts up to standard started to run from 1987 rather than 1977, but the Court held that the UK could not rely on its mistaken interpretation of the scope of the Directive by which it had excluded these resorts until 1987 to justify stopping the clock until 1987.

This constitutes only the second instance in which the UK has been held to be in breach of an environmental directive.

2.7.3 Groundwater

EC Directive 80/68/EEC (OJ No. L 20/43) on the protection of groundwater against pollution caused by certain dangerous substances is concerned with direct and indirect discharges of a small number of dangerous substances which are listed in the Annex. The substances are in two lists. List I includes organohalogens, organophosphorus, organotin, mercury, cadmium and their compounds, mineral oils and hydrocarbons, cyanides and substances with carcinogenic, mutagenic or teratogenic properties. List II has a further twenty-six groups of substances on it. These substances are the same as the 'Black List' of dangerous substances.

Discharges of List I substances into groundwater must be prohibited altogether. Discharges of List II substances, on the other hand, must be limited. Disposals which might lead to discharges of List II substances may be authorized only after a prior investigation and after technical precautions have been taken. The scope of this Directive is thought to be too limited as it deals with only a limited range of substances. The NRA's groundwater protection policy therefore seeks to go further by considering all activities which might threaten groundwater.

The directive was implemented administratively through a DoE Circular 20/90 which required waste regulatory authorities to review waste disposal licences involving the disposal of List I substances. Additionally, the Waste Management Regulations 1994, SI No. 1056 make provision for the method of dealing with applications for waste management and disposal licences in respect of waste mangement activities which could lead to the discharge into groundwater of Lists I or II substances; this requires prior investigations and conditions to protect groundwater. The Regulations also require waste regulation authorities to review current waste management licences in the light of the requirements of the EC Directive and vary them as necessary.

2.7.4 Dangerous Substances in Water

EC Directive 76/464/EEC (OJ No. L 129/23) on pollution caused by certain dangerous substances discharged into the aquatic environment sets up two lists of dangerous substances: List I, commonly referred to as the 'Black List', which contains eight groups of substances many of which are on List I of the Groundwater Directive; and List II, commonly referred to as the 'Grey List', of 29 groups of substances. The 'Black List' is known in the UK as the 'Red List' (DoE Circular 7/89)).

The Directive requires member states to take steps to eliminate pollution by List I substances; and to reduce pollution by List II substances. In relation to List I the steps include prior authorization for all discharges likely to contain the substances and the setting of emission standards which discharges must not exceed. The emission standards are to be based on either limit values or quality objectives which the Directive authorizes the Council to set. Member states may opt for either the uniform limits approach or the quality objectives approach in implementing the Directive. Only the UK opted for the quality objectives approach (see 'EC Water Quality Classes', p. 29).

The Directive itself does not lay down any of these limit values or quality objectives, but authorizes them to be laid down by subsequent, or 'daughter', directives. Seven such daughter directives have since been adopted setting the standards for seventeen substances on the Lists. The seventeen are drawn from a 'priority list' of 129 individual substances which the Commission identified in 1982 from the List I groups. The intention was to proceed down that list as quickly as possible, but in view of the slow pace at which standards were set it became clear that this was not feasible, even with the adoption of EC Directive 86/280/EEC laying down general provisions on limit values; quality objectives; time limits for compliance; and procedures for monitoring discharges to be applied to all the subsequent 'daughter directives'. Attention has turned now to the Integrated Pollution Prevention and Control proposal which will impose discharge limits for dangerous substances on the basis of the industrial sectors concerned rather than on the basis of each individual substance.

2.7.5   Fishwaters

Two directives set water standards for fishlife; EC Directive 78/659/EEC (OJ No. L 222/1) on the quality of freshwaters needing protection or improvement in order to support fish life (the Fresh Water Fish Directive) and EC Directive 79/923/EEC (OJ No. L 281/47) on the quality required of shellfish waters (the Shellfish Waters Directive).

The Fresh Water Fish Directive

This directive divides fresh water into salmonid water and cyprinid water according to the species of fish that the water either supports or would become capable of supporting if pollution was eliminated or reduced to levels set in the Directive. It is left to member states to designate such waters but they must ensure that designated waters meet the standards within five years of designation.

The UK has designated 55 000 km of river of which 88 per cent is salmonid and 12 per cent cyprinid. Standards set in this Directive and in the Shellfish Directive will form part of the statutory water quality objectives.

The Shellfish Waters Directive

This Directive applies to coastal and brackish water which a member state designates as needing protection or improvement in order to support shellfish. The Directive requires member states to ensure that, within six years of designation, designated water meet the standards imposed by the Directive for shellfish waters.

2.7.6   The Nitrates from Agricultural Sources Directive

EC Directive 91/676/EEC (OJ No. L 375/1) on the protection of waters against pollution caused by nitrates from agricultural sources requires member states to identify water affected by pollution and which could be affected by pollution on the basis that it contains or could contain more than 50 mg/l of nitrates, or is or could become eutrophic.

Having identified the waters, member states must designate areas of land which drain into those waters as 'vulnerable zones'. Within two years of the designation member states are required to establish action programmes relating to the vulnerable zones, and implement them within four years, i.e. by December 1999. The zones must be reviewed and revised as necessary every four years thereafter. The action programmes are to include rules relating to:

1 Periods when the land application of certain fertilizers is prohibited;
2 The capacity of storage vessels for livestock manure;
3 Limitation of the land application of fertilizer; and
4 Measures to ensure that the amount of livestock manure applied to the land each year does not exceed a specified amount per hectare.

The UK has proposed seventy-two Nitrate Vulnerable Zones which will complement the Nitrates Sensitive Areas scheme which is already in place (DoE, 1994a).

2.7.7 Urban Waste Water Treatment

EC Directive 91/271/EEC (OJ No. L 135/40) on urban waste water treatment requires member states to identify both 'sensitive' and 'less sensitive areas'; the latter are bodies of water not adversely affected by a waste water discharge. Water is sensitive to discharges essentially because of low dispersion characteristics. An area is sensitive if it falls into one of three categories:

1 Eutrophic (eutrophication is the enrichment of water by nitrogen compounds leading to 'algal blooms') or potentially eutrophic natural freshwater lakes, other freshwater bodies, estuaries and coastal water
2 Surface water intended for the abstraction of drinking water which has the potential to breach the 50 mg/l nitrate standard
3 Water bodies in relation to which the requirements of EC directives necessitate tertiary treatment.

Effluent (or waste water) treatment at sewerage works has three stages:

1 'Primary' treatment in which the effluent is allowed to settle in tanks and the sludge removed
2 'Secondary' treatment in which bacteria are allowed to feed on the organic content of the effluent, breaking it down into carbon dioxide, water and nitrogen compounds
3 'Tertiary' treatment in which techniques such as sand filtration, disinfection and irradiation are used.

The Directive sets waste water treatment standards which are based on both the sensitivity of the receiving waters and the size of the discharge, which ultimately depends on the size of population (or industrial effluent) from which the discharge arises. The norm for receiving waters which have not been identified as either sensitive or less sensitive is to be at least secondary treatment to be achieved between the years 2000 and 2005, depending on the size of the urban area served. Discharges into a sensitive area serving an urban area with an equivalent of more than 10 000 people must receive tertiary treatment by December 1998; while discharges to coastal waters and estuaries which are identified as less sensitive need be subjected to only primary treatment.

Apart from setting treatment standards for treatment plants the Directive imposes requirements relating to waste water generally:

1 Discharges of industrial waste water into treatment plants must be specifically authorized
2 Waste water containing biodegradable industrial waste above a defined threshold from specified food and drink processing industries which is discharged directly into receiving water—by passing treatment plants—must, by the year 2000, be expressly authorized and meet requirements imposed by member states and
3 The disposal of sludge from urban waste water treatment plants into surface waters must be phased out by December 1998.

The UK published draft Urban Waste Water Treatment (England and Wales) Regulations 1993 but these have to date not been taken forward. However, fifty-eight less sensitive areas (referred to as 'high natural dispersion areas') and thirty-three sensitive (eutrophic) areas around the English and Welsh coastlines have been identified. The areas around Scotland and Northern Ireland have been identified separately (DoE, 1994). The infrastuctural development of sewerage treatment plants necessary to achieve the standards specified in the Directive for waste waters (estimated at about £8 billion) will dominate capital expenditure by the water companies in the decade beginning in 1995.

References

Alphacell Ltd v Woodward [1972] 2 All ER 475.
Barnes v Irwell Valley Water Board [1938] 4 All ER 631.
Commission v UK, Case C-337/89 (on the Drinking Water Directive), *Journal of Environmental Law*, 5/2 273.
Commission v UK, Case C-56/90 (on the Bathing Water Directive) (1993) Part 5 Env. LR, 472.
Commission of the European Communities, *Commission Report to the European Council on the Adaptation of the Community Legislation to the Subsidiarity Principle*, COM (93) 545 final, 24 November 1993, HMSO.
DoE, *Water and the Environment*, DoE Circular 17/84, WO 35/1984.
DoE, *The Water Environment: The Next Steps*, DoE Consultation Paper (1986).
DoE, *Guidance on Safeguarding the Quality of Public Water Supplies* (1989).
DoE, *Water and the Environment*, DoE Circular 7/89.
DoE, *Third Ministerial Conference on the Protection of the North Sea: UK Guidance Note on the Ministerial Declaration* (1990).

DoE Circular 20/90, *EC Directive on Protection of Groundwater from Pollution Caused by Dangerous Substances (80/68/EEC): Classification of Listed Substances*, HMSO.

DoE, *River Quality: The Government's Proposals*, DoE Consultation Paper (1992).

DoE, *Proposed Amendments to the Water Resources Act 1991 and the Reservoirs Act 1975*, Joint Consultation Paper, DoE/WO (1993a).

DoE, *Water Charges: The Quality Framework* (1993b).

DoE, 'Minister announces treatment standards for coastal sewage discharges', Press Release No. 302, 18 May (1994a).

DoE, 'Protection for sensitive areas', Press Release No. 303, 18 May (1994b).

DoE, 'Proposed vulnerable zones designated under EC Nitrate Directive', Press Release No. 307, 18 May (1994c).

DWI, *Third Annual Report*, HMSO (1993).

ENDS Report No. 227, *Waste licence defence succeeds in river pollution case*, December 1993, p. 45.

Impress v Rees [1971] 2 All ER 357.

MAFF, *The Code of Good Agricultural Practice for the Protection of Water* (1991).

MAFF, *The Code of Good Agricultural Practice for the Protection of Air* (1992).

MAFF, *The Code of Good Agricultural Practice for the Protection of Soil* (1993a).

MAFF, *Pilot Nitrate Sensitive Areas Scheme: Report on the First Three Years* (1993b).

McColl v Strathclyde Regional Council [1984] JPEL 351.

Mumma, A., 'Water quality issues in abstraction licensing', *Environmental Liability*, 2/6 (1994).

NRA, *Discharge Consent and Compliance Policy: A Blueprint for the Future*, Water Quality Series No. 1 (1990).

NRA, *The Quality of Rivers, Canals and Estuaries in England and Wales: Report of the 1990 Survey*, Water Quality Series No. 4 (1991a).

NRA, *Proposals for Statutory Water Quality Objectives*, Water Quality Series No. 5 (1991b).

NRA, *Policy and Practice for the Protection of Groundwater* (1992).

NRA, *Low Flows and Water Resources* (1993).

NRA v Eggar (UK) Ltd (1992, unrep.), see *Water Law*, 3/6, 169 (1992).

NRA v Yorkshire Water Services Ltd, *The Independent*, 19 November 1993.

NRA Welsh Region, *River Dee Water Protection Zone* (1993).

OFWAT, *Paying for Water: A Time for Decisions* (1991).

OFWAT, *Paying for Quality: The Political Perspective* (1993a).

OFWAT, *Setting Price Limits for Water and Sewerage Services: The Framework and Approach to the 1994 Periodic Review* (1993b).

OFWAT, *Future Charges for Water and Sewerage Services: The Outcome of the Periodic Review* (1994).

Price v Cromack [1975] 2 All ER 113.

R v Secretary of State for the Environment ex parte Friends of the Earth, *The Times*, 4 April 1994.

Scottish Office, *Abstraction Controls: A System for Scotland* (1993).

Schulmans Inc. Ltd v NRA (1992) Part I Env. LR D1.

Thames Water Authority v Blue and White Launderette Ltd [1980] 1 WLR 700.

3

Waste Management

3.1   The Background

In comparison to the law on water and air, which dates back to the nineteenth century, the law on waste management is relatively recent. The first statute to deal with waste disposal in its own right, the **Deposit of Poisonous Wastes Act 1972**, was a reaction to an incident involving the dumping of cyanide in the Midlands. It was quickly superseded by provisions in Part I of the **Control of Pollution Act 1974 (COPA)**. COPA prohibited any disposal of waste unless the disposal was licensed, introducing for the first time a system of control for disposal of waste to land.

This control regime was limited to waste disposal; control began with the handling and deposit of waste and ended with the closure of a landfill, or the cancellation or return of the licence. With the exception of controls directed at the movement of 'special waste', COPA provided few controls before waste reached the disposal facility, and equally few safeguards for the environment and human health once landfilling was completed, or the licence was returned to the regulator.

The system did not take account of the three-stage process that a waste stream is, from its production through transport to actual disposal. Each stage poses dangers to the environment and human health, and must accordingly be managed in its own right. Control targeted simply at the point of waste disposal is therefore inadequate, a point that was driven home time and again throughout the 1980s by bodies such as the Royal Commission on Environmental Pollution and the House of Commons Environment Committee. The main contribution made by Part II of the **EPA 1990** is to extend control to all three stages of the waste stream.

Extending control in this way needed fundamental restructuring of the substantive law on waste management. First, Part II of the EPA 1990 imposes a 'duty of care' on every person who happens to hold waste along the chain; its producer, transporter and final disposer, but including also any person, such as

a broker, who exercises effective control over the waste without having possession of it. Second, it extends the law prohibiting disposal of waste without a
licence to cover not just disposal but also keeping and treating waste; and introduces strict requirements for the 'after-care' of the disposal site. Third, it
attempted to tackle the problem of contaminated land, a problem closely associated with waste disposal activities. This attempt subsequently foundered,
however, the government withdrawing the proposals to bring the relevant
provisions (i.e. s. 143) into force. The problem of contaminated land therefore
remains unresolved and the search for a legal mechanism for tackling the
problem continues. The EPA 1990 also continues the duties which local authorities had under COPA to collect waste and plan for its disposal and to deal
with litter in their locality.

3.2 Defining Waste

The EC Waste Framework Directive (75/442/EEC as amended by 91/156/
EEC) defines waste as any substance or object in the categories set out in [an
Annex] which the holder discards or intends or is required to discard. The
Directive then stipulates that the Commission draw up, and periodically
review, a non-exhaustive list of waste belonging to the categories listed in the
Annex. The Commission's list, known as the European Waste Catalogue
(EWC), was published on 7 January 1994 in OJ No. L 1/15 as Commission
Decision 94/3/EC. The EWC is 'a reference nomenclature providing a
common terminology throughout the Community ...'. But it adds the caveat
that the inclusion of a material does not mean that it is a waste in all circumstances, the entry being relevant only when the definition of waste has been
satisfied.

For the definition of waste to be satisfied the material must belong to the
categories listed in Annex I to the Waste Framework Directive which lists
sixteen categories of waste. Examples include products whose use-by date has
expired, contaminated materials, unusable parts, residues and so on. Categories
1 and 16, however, take much of the steam out of the remaining fourteen;
Category 1 brings in 'production or consumption residues not otherwise specified below' while category 16 sweeps up with 'any materials, substances or
products which are not contained in the above categories'. There is a second
requirement which must be met before the definition of waste can be satisfied
which is that the material must not belong to the categories of materials that
are excluded from the scope of the Directive, i.e. gaseous effluent emitted into
the atmosphere and where they are already covered by other legislation, radioactive waste, mining and quarrying waste, agricultural waste, waste waters and
decommissioned explosives.

The UK government experienced considerable difficulty in reconciling the EC definition with the UK definition of waste as set out in s. 75(2) of the EPA 1990. This defined waste as including

> any substance which constitutes a scrap material or an effluent or other unwanted surplus substance arising from the application of any process; and any substance or article which requires to be disposed of as being broken, worn out, contaminated or otherwise spoilt.

This 'technical' difficulty, as the DoE described it, led to the UK failing to meet the deadline of 1 April 1993 for implementing the EC Directive and a subsequent self-imposed deadline of 1 June 1993. The government eventually opted to drop s. 75(2) (which will be repealed in due course) and directly transpose the EC definition into UK law. The Waste Management Licensing Regulations 1994 (SI 1994 No. 1056) which came into force on 1 May 1994 now state that 'waste means directive waste'. Other provisions provide that 'any reference to "waste" in the ... [EPA] 1990 includes a reference to "directive waste" '. 'Directive waste' is defined as

> [A]ny substance or object in the categories set out in Part II of [Schedule 4 to the Regulations] (i.e. Annex I of the directive) which the producer or the person in possession of it discards, or intends or is required to discard, but with the exception of anything excluded from the scope of the [Framework] Directive ...

3.2.1   Is It Waste?

Annex 2 of the accompanying Circular (DoE 11/94) gives guidance on the definition of waste and discusses the various items which consitute waste, depending on the circumstances. Whether or not a substance or object is waste depends on the facts of each case and it is the responsibility of the holder to decide whether or not it is. The guidance is intended, however, to highlight factors to take into account in reaching that decision. Three are of crucial importance; the concepts of the commercial cycle or chain of utility, specialized recovery operations and beneficial use.

The guidance observes that waste is perceived as posing a threat to human health or the environment, which is different from the threat posed by substances or objects which are not waste. This arises because producers of the material concerned normally no longer have the self-interest necessary to ensure the provision of adequate safeguards. The aim of the law therefore is to control the management of those substances or objects which fall out of the 'commercial cycle' or 'chain of utility'. The phrases are undefined but are intended to encapsulate the concept of material losing its commercial attraction to the holder who then seeks to get rid of it.

For material to be waste it must both fall into one of the specified categories and be or be intended or required to be discarded, disposed of or got rid of by the holder. Material which been discarded so that it is no longer part of the normal commercial cycle or chain of utility is most likely waste.

Waste material may, however, remain in the commercial cycle or chain of utility precisely so that it can be collected, transported, stored, recovered or disposed of. This is because some commercial activity exists specifically to manage waste in these ways. Waste consigned to a commercial cycle of this kind is waste, notwithstanding that it is still within the commercial cycle or chain of utility. Indeed the Waste Framework Directive requires that waste consigned to recovery and disposal operations of the kind specified in Annexes to the Directive should be controlled; waste does not cease to be waste simply because it has been consigned to commercial operations which exist specifically to manage waste.

Some of the recovery operations specified, however, are not easy to distinguish from operations within the normal commercial cycle, the best example being 'use principally as a fuel'. Thus it would not be right to say that some material is waste simply because it has been consigned to a specified recovery operation. The guidance therefore suggests that in those circumstances the question to be asked is whether it can be used in its present form (albeit after repair) or in the same way as any other raw material without being subjected to a 'specialized recovery operation' and if it is likely to be used in that way. If so, then it is not waste. The term 'specialized recovery operation' describes any of the operations in Schedule 4 to the Regulations which:

1   Re-uses material which is waste because it has fallen out of the commercial cycle or chain of utility or
2   Recycles it to eliminate or diminish the threat posed by its original production as waste and produces a raw material which can be used in the same way as raw material of non-waste origin.

It is an operation, in other words, which exists to bring back waste material into the commercial cycle or chain of utility.

Waste material may not be consigned to a specialized recovery operation. Its producers or holders may retain it and put it to some use themselves or pass it on to some other person to use, free of charge or on payment. The guidance states that in such circumstances, i.e. when material is put to 'beneficial use', the question whether or not it has fallen out of the commercial cycle or chain of utility is to be determined on the basis of the answers to two questions:

1   Is the purpose of the [beneficial use] wholly or mainly to relieve the producer of the burden of otherwise disposing of the material?
2   Would the producer be likely to seek a substitute for it if it ceased to become available to him or her?

If the answers are 'yes' to the first question and 'no' to the second then the beneficial use is incidental and is not different from a specialized recovery or disposal operation. This is supported by the decision of the ECJ in *Vasseso and Zanetti* (C-206/88 and C-207/88) (1990) 2 LMELR 133, where two defendants contended in an Italian court that the objects concerned were not waste but were salvaged materials capable of economic re-use. The court ruled that 'the concept of waste ... is not to be understood as excluding substances and objects which are capable of economic re-utilization. The concept does not presume that the holder disposing of a substance or an object intends to exclude all economic re-utilization of the substance or object by others'. In summary:

1   Material which has been discarded so that it is no longer part of the normal commercial cycle or chain of utility is most likely waste.
2   Material consigned to the kind of commercial cycle whose object is the management of waste is waste notwithstanding that it is still within the commercial cycle or chain of utility.
3   Material put by its producer to a beneficial use which is simply incidental is waste.

3.2.2   Controlled Waste

The **EPA 1990** distinguishes three categories of waste; (1) household, (2) industrial and (3) commercial waste. These categories are particularly important for the purposes of allocating responsibility for the collection of waste. Section 75(4) refers to these categories as 'controlled waste'. The Waste Management Licensing Regulations 1994 SI No. 1056 provide that waste which is not directive waste shall not be treated as household, industrial or commercial waste.

Although the terms household, industrial and commercial waste are defined in the Act, the Secretary of State has the power to make regulations refining these definitions. The Collection and Disposal of Waste Regulations 1988, SI No. 819 made under **COPA 1974** and the Controlled Waste Regulations 1992, SI No. 588, as amended, made under the **EPA 1990** refine the definitions by providing categories of household, industrial and commercial waste.

Household waste is waste from domestic property; a caravan; a residential home; premises forming part of a university or school or other educational establishment or a hospital or nursing home. The 1992 Regulations add nuances to this definition. For example, contruction or demolition waste and septic tank sludge are made household waste for the purposes of the 'Duty of Care'. However, as discussed below, the Duty of Care does not apply to a householder in respect of household waste produced on his or her property, so the effect of the Regulations here is to enable the householder to treat these two types of waste like any other household waste without worrying about the Duty of Care. Conversely, mineral or synthetic oil or grease, asbestos and clinical waste are excluded from the waste which a householder can dispose of within his or her dwelling; they must be collected by a contractor.

The Regulations add a total of eleven categories of waste to those listed in the Act, such as waste from premises used by charities or for public meetings, or from prisons, royal palaces, camp sites and others.

Industrial waste is defined in the Act as waste from a factory as well as from premises used for public transport services, or for supplying the public with gas, water, electricity, sewerage, postal, or telecommunication services. The 1992 Regulations add some eighteen categories of waste to this list, such as waste from a laboratory, workshop, aircraft or dredging operations; from such businesses as sign writing, laundering, developing film, selling petrol, or breeding animals.

Commercial waste is waste from premises used for a trade or business or for sport, recreation or entertainment. Waste which might fall into these categories but is defined as household or industrial waste, or waste from a mine or quarry, or agricultural premises is excluded. The 1992 Regulations add a further nine categories of waste to these, such as waste from an office, a showroom, a hotel, a market or a fair, or waste from premises used by a court, government departments or local authorities.

3.2.3 Special Waste

Apart from the two questions: is it waste? If so, is it controlled waste? one question is still left to be considered: is it 'special waste'? Section 62 of the **EPA 1990**, which will replace s. 17 of COPA in due course, gives the Secretary of State power to make special provision for dealing with controlled waste which he or she considers to be so dangerous or difficult to treat, keep or dispose of that special provision is needed for dealing with it. Such Regulations, known as the Control of Pollution (Special Waste) Regulations 1980, SI No. 1709, were made under similar powers in COPA. They implement EC Directive 78/319/EEC which deals with toxic and dangerous waste. Directive 78/319 is due to be replaced on 27 June 1995 by EC Directive 91/689/EEC on hazardous waste, which replaces the term 'toxic' with 'hazardous'. The UK will need to bring into force new Special Waste Regulations to implement the new Directive. The DoE has already consulted on this (DoE, 1990a).

The 1980 Special Waste Regulations define special waste to cover controlled wastes which are flammable, or are likely to cause death or serious injury if ingested or inhaled, such as compounds of arsenic, mercury and lead. Medicines which can be obtained only through a prescription are included, as is radioactive waste exhibiting properties similar to the other special waste.

The special regime set up for dealing with special waste centres around the 'consignment note system'. The note is a form which all those involved in the production, movement and disposal of special waste must complete, giving details of the producer, carrier and disposer, as well as a description of the waste itself. A copy of the completed consignment note is sent to the waste regulator, and copies retained by the other players for at least two years. Unless the waste regulator has agreed in writing to be notified of special waste movements only annually, a consignment note must be forwarded for each transaction. Additionally, the waste disposer must keep a record of the location of the deposit of special waste. The consignment note regime was novel and unique to special waste before the advent of the Duty of Care regime for all controlled waste in 1992; that uniqueness is now lost with the exception of the prior notification aspect.

3.3   The Role of Local Authorities

Local authorities play a key role in waste management, arranging for the collection and disposal of waste and regulating its management by others. In all there are three waste management authorities; Waste Collection Authorities (WCAs), Waste Disposal Authorities (WDAs) and Waste Regulatory Authorities (WRAs); these are typically local authority bodies.

3.3.1   Waste Collection

Waste collection is a local authority function but under the provisions of the **Local Government Act 1988** the contract to do the job must be submitted to competitive tendering, with local authorities and private sector companies competing for the tender on equal terms. The WCA has the duty, under s. 45 of the **EPA 1990**, to arrange for household waste to be collected and for private privies and, if requested, cesspools to be emptied. This duty does not extend to isolated or inaccessible places where collection costs would be unreasonably high, and to waste which the WCA thinks the holder can dispose of adequately. The collection of waste is made without a charge to the householder but the Secretary of State has power to provide for kinds of waste to be collected only if its holder asks the WCA to do so and pays a reasonable charge.

Schedule 2 of the Controlled Waste Regulations 1992, SI No. 588 provides that a charge may be made to collect some eighteen categories of household waste. Waste of more than 25 kg or which cannot fit into collection bins, garden waste, clinical waste, waste from a residential hostel, university, school, hospital or self-catering holiday accommodation, dead pets, litter, mineral or synthetic oil or grease, asbestos, waste from a caravan or a camp site, waste from premises used for charity, and waste from a prison, a hall used for public meetings or a royal palace. The WCA may also, if asked and paid a reasonable charge, arrange for commercial waste and, with the consent of the WDA, industrial waste, to be collected.

The WCA may serve a notice requiring the householder to place the waste to be collected in receptacles or bins, and may specify their type and number. It may provide the bins free of charge or on payment of a sum agreed with the householder or it may require the householder to provide them. Failure to comply with the notice may result in a fine of up to £1 000 in a magistrates' court and so the householder has a chance to appeal against the notice to the magistrates within twenty-one days of receiving it. The WCA may also, if requested, supply bins for commercial or industrial waste which it has been asked to collect, and charge for providing them. If it appears to the WCA that the waste is of a kind which, if not stored in bins of a particular kind, is likely to cause a nuisance or a detriment to the amenities of the locality, it may serve a notice requiring those holding it to store it in specified bins. Failure to comply may result in a fine of up to £1 000 in a magistrates' court and again the person served with the notice may appeal to a magistrates' court within twenty-one days.

Waste left for collection is not abandoned for just anyone to take away. It is an offence under s. 60 to sort it over or disturb it and in a magistrates' court a fine of up to £1 000 may be imposed. Apart from the portion which the WCA decides to recycle, the waste has to delivered by the WCA to a place specified by the WDA for the area. Section 49 requires the WCA to make a waste recycling plan setting out the kinds and quantities of waste it expects to recycle and the cost and savings of doing so. If the WDA itself has arranged for the waste to be recycled it may object to the WCA recycling it, in which case the waste must be delivered to the WDA.

Section 52 deals with payments and reimbursements for the collection, recycling and disposal of waste. The general principle is that a body which has incurred expenses must be reimbursed by the body which has made a saving from the waste-handling operation. Thus if the WCA recycles some waste which would have gone to disposal, it is reimbursed by the WDA; if the WDA removes waste which it is the duty of the WCA to collect, the WCA reimburses the WDA its expenses. The extent of reimbursement to be paid is set out in the Environmental Protection (Waste Recycling Payments) (Amendment) Regulations 1994, SI No. 552.

3.3.2 Waste Disposal

Responsibility for waste disposal lies with the WDAs. Since May 1991 local authorities in England and Wales have been required under s. 32 to divest themselves of their waste disposal activities by arranging for these to be carried on in the private sector by companies which are either wholly private or in which the local authority has a financial interest. Where a local authority fails to make its own arrangements to divest itself of these activities, s. 32 gives the Secretary of State power to require it to set up a company, known as a Local

Authority Waste Disposal Company (LAWDC), to take over its waste disposal activities. The practicalities are set out in Part I of Schedule II to the **EPA 1990** (DoE, 1992a).

Once privatization is complete, waste disposal therefore will be performed by either LAWDCs, other private sector companies, or companies owned jointly by local authorities and the private sector; all are known as 'waste disposal contractors'. Waste disposal contracts, like waste collection contracts, must be awarded through competitive tendering; the procedure for this is set out in Part II of Schedule II to the EPA 1990. Additionally, under the **Local Government and Housing Act 1989**, local authorities are required to treat companies in which they have a controlling interest at 'arm's length', i.e. like any other company in which they do not have an interest. This was affirmed in *R v Avon CC ex parte Terry Adams Co. Ltd*, *The Times*, 20 January 1994, in which the Court of Appeal held that the WDA had an obligation to avoid undue discrimination in favour of one waste disposal contractor as against another when determining the terms and conditions of any contract into which it proposes to enter.

The main function of waste disposal authorities following privatization of waste disposal operations will be confined to arranging with waste disposal contractors for the disposal of controlled waste collected in their area by WCAs. They are also responsible for places known as 'civic amenity sites' under s. 1 of the **Refuse Disposal (Amenity) Act 1978** (now largely repealed in England and Wales) at which residents may deposit household waste. Residents may normally deposit waste at such sites free of charge but the authority may restrict the kind of household waste which is acceptable for deposit there and may charge for deposits on such sites of other controlled waste. In order to discharge its waste disposal functions the authority has power to provide, among other things, land, plant and equipment to enable waste disposal contractors to keep, treat or dispose of waste temporarily or, in relation to land, both temporarily and permanently. It may also contribute to the costs of commercial and industrial waste producers towards the provision of plant, equipment or other infrastructure for dealing with such waste before collection.

In Scotland where waste disposal authorities continue to carry out waste disposal activities the WDAs do not need a waste management licence under s. 33 of the EPA. Instead the local authority, acting as a WRA, authorizes by a resolution the treatment, keeping or disposal of controlled waste in or on land occupied by the WDA. The procedure prior to the passing of the resolution is comparable to that followed before issuing a waste management licence, involving consultations with bodies like the HSE and river purification authorities and a reference to the Secretary of State for Scotland in case of a dispute.

3.3.3   Waste Management Planning

WRAs are responsible for both waste management planning and for the administration of the waste management licensing regime, discussed below. Waste management planning is currently in two parts: (1) waste local planning and (2) waste disposal planning. Waste local planning is also a local authority function, carried out by the local planning authority. Waste disposal planning is undertaken by the WRA and will be taken over by the Environmental Protection Agency once it is set up.

Applications for planning permission for developments of facilities depositing, treating, storing, processing and disposing of waste are decided by local planning authorities. Town and country planning law requires these bodies to draw up 'development plans' indicating their policy on applications for planning permission for developments generally. In 1992 s. 38 of the **Town and Country Planning Act 1990** introduced a requirement for these bodies to prepare additionally a plan stating their policy on waste management facilities for their area; this is known as a 'waste local plan'. They may, alternatively, include such a plan in their minerals local plan which they are required to prepare under s. 37 of the same Act, a provision reflecting the fact that the holes remaining after mining has ceased are often used for the deposit of waste.

Separately, s. 50 of the EPA 1990 requires WRAs who are responsible for waste management in their area to form a view as to the arrangements needed to treat and dispose of waste in their area, or likely to be in their area, in order to prevent or minimize pollution of the environment or harm to human health, and to prepare a plan for dealing with it. This is the 'waste disposal plan'; most local authorities will have prepared one under COPA but they have to review and modify it as requirements change. The plan, a copy of which must be sent to the Secretary of State, must include information on:

1   The kinds and quantities of waste which the WRA expects to be present in, to be brought into or taken out of, and to be disposed of in its area during the plan period
2   Its priorities as regards the methods of treatment and disposal and the cost the methods entail; the Act requires that priority be given to recycling where practicable
3   Details of the sites and equipment available in the area for disposal and
4   Its policy on waste management licensing.

PPG No. 23 on 'Planning and Pollution Control' (DoE, 1994) explains that while a waste disposal plan is concerned primarily with the strategic issues of waste management, a waste local plan is concerned with local issues such as identifying the areas that would be suitable for the siting of waste disposal facilities. Nevertheless, there can be some overlap; planning authorities are required to have regard to the waste disposal plan in drawing up their waste local plan, but where there is a conflict PPG 12 on 'Development Plans and Regional Planning Guidance' states that the more recent of the plans prevails.

In August 1992 the government issued a consultation paper on 'Waste Disposal Planning under an Environmental Protection Agency' in which it set out the way waste disposal planning is to be conducted both before and after the Agency is set up. WRAs are expected to draw up waste disposal plans pending the setting up of the Agency to provide a policy framework for waste management in the interim period. Once the Agency is set up the Secretary of State will issue a 'Statement of Waste Policies and Priorities' on the advice of the new Agency. This will apply across the whole country and would cover the next ten to fifteen years although it would be revised every five years. The Agency would itself seek advice from local planning authorities in order to keep the link with local planning. Additionally, the Secretary of State would issue specific regional guidance on waste.

There are two main methods of waste disposal which waste local plans and waste disposal plans can make provision for: (1) landfill and (2) incineration. 'Landfill', the practice of burying waste in the ground, is the traditional means of waste disposal in the UK. It is estimated to account for up to 90 per cent of all controlled waste disposal (House of Commons Environment Committee, 1988–89).

Landfill is unlikely to continue to account for this proportion of final disposals of waste, however; it runs counter to the EC's policy which requires that landfill be treated only as the last waste management option (Commission of the European Communities, 1989). The EC has proposed a directive on landfill (93/C 212/02) introducing standards which landfill sites would be required to meet and a levy ostensibly to redress an imbalance in the low cost of landfill as against other waste management options. The UK also is considering introducing a landfill levy and commissioned two reports on its feasibility and impact (DoE, 1993b,c). Thus, the cost of landfill is set to rise appreciably in the foreseeable future. The combination of the two is likely to precipitate a decline in the use of landfill with incineration becoming the preferred disposal option.

A second factor precipitating an increase in the use of incineration is the 1998 deadline for ceasing the dumping of sewage sludge (the residue produced at a sewage treatment works) at sea as agreed between the UK and other North Sea states in 1990. Sewage sludge is now most likely to be incinerated and only the solid residue from that will be landfilled. Third, incineration of municipal waste (i.e. domestic waste together with certain commercial waste) has the added attraction that it can be linked with energy recovery, the energy being sold as electricity. This is seen as being not only environmentally beneficial but also revenue generating.

Incineration received a boost from the Royal Commission of Environmental Pollution who, in a report, argued that incineration is the best practicable environmental option for municipal waste (RCEP, 1993). The report indicates that in 1991 there were 200 licensed incineration plants in the UK handling municipal, special and clinical waste as well as sewage sludge. Another 700 or so incinerators owned by the National Health Service incinerate clinical waste. It is thought that the majority of the NHS incinerators will not be able to meet the new emission standards with which they have to comply by 1996 under the IPC regime and will therefore be closed down.

Waste incineration plants fall under either the IPC regime or, for smaller incinerators, the LAAPC regime in Part I of the EPA. HMIP regulates the IPC system while the smaller incinerators are regulated by local authorities. Additionally the EC has set standards for both existing and new municipal incineration plants in Directives 89/429/EEC and 89/369/EEC, respectively. A proposed directive dealing with the incineration of hazardous wastes (COM (92) 9, OJ C 130) has yet to be adopted although the Council has now reached a common position (No. 26/94). One of the sticking points was the exclusion from the directive of incinerators burning non-hazardous clinical wastes, including municipal waste incinerators burning such wastes.

3.4   Waste Management Licensing

Section 33 of the **EPA 1990** is the backbone of the waste management licensing system. It creates three offences:

1   Depositing, treating, keeping or disposing of controlled waste without a waste management licence
2   Knowingly causing or permitting controlled waste to be deposited, treated, kept or disposed of in or on land or by means of mobile plant without a waste management licence and
3   Treating, keeping or disposing of controlled waste in a manner likely to cause pollution of the environment or harm to human health.

The last offence was brought into force on 1 April 1992 to coincide with the introduction of the Duty of Care provisions. The first two offences came into force on 1 May 1994 when the waste management licensing regime under Part II of the EPA was implemented. On that date the waste licensing provisions under the EPA 1990 replaced those under COPA 1974. The COPA waste disposal licence automatically become an EPA waste management licence in all but a few transitory cases, such as cases of pending appeals.

A person charged with these offences has a defence if he or she:

1   Took all reasonable precautions and exercised all due diligence to avoid committing the offence
2   Acted under his or her employer's instructions, did not know and had no reason to suppose that an offence was being committed or
3   Acted in an emergency to avoid danger to the public and, as soon as practicable after that, informed the WRA in the area where the offence occurred.

An EPA 1990 site licence encompasses three types of site: a landfill where waste is deposited; a transfer station where waste is unloaded and prepared en route to some other facility for recycling, treatment or disposal; and a treatment plant where waste is altered by physical, chemical or biological treatment. Until *R v Metropolitan Stipendiary Magistrate ex parte London Waste Regulation Authority and Berkshire CC v Scott* (1993) doubt had been cast by the decision in *Leigh Land Reclamation Ltd v Walsall MBC.* (1990) on whether s. 3 of COPA, the predecessor to s. 33 of the EPA, covered transfer stations and treatment plants. Section 3 of COPA, unlike s. 33 of the EPA, did not refer to treating or keeping controlled waste; it restricted its prohibition to the deposit of and disposal of controlled waste. The question which arose therefore was whether the word 'deposit' covered permanent deposits as well as temporary deposits, such as a deposit at a transfer station.

In the *Leigh case* the company had a site licence which allowed it to deposit specified types of waste. One of its conditions required the waste to be compacted before deposit. An inspector visited the site and saw waste being deposited while some other waste had not yet been compacted. The company was prosecuted for breaching a condition of its licence, the authority arguing that waste was 'deposited' when it was set down on the site, and so had to be compacted as soon as it was set down. The magistrates convicted, but on appeal the company argued that its machine operators had instructions that before blending the waste onto the workface of the site they must remove any material with which there was a problem as well as waste in drums and seek the advice of the management. The Appeal Court quashed the conviction and held that 'waste is to be regarded as deposited when it is dumped on the site with no realistic prospect of further examination to reject goods of which deposit is not allowed under the licence'. According to the judge the requirement to compact the waste applied when the waste reached its 'final resting place', not before.

The *Leigh* decision led to the conclusion that the word 'deposit' applied only to permanent deposits and not to temporary deposits, a situation which many regulators viewed with disquiet. The issue was considered fully in *the London Waste Regulation Authority case* which overrruled *Leigh*. The case was a joined case and in the first the defendants were operating a waste transfer station without a licence, while in the second the defendants operated a skip-hire business and materials were processed and recycled on the site and then removed. In both cases the magistrates held that the waste was not deposited on the site because it was to be moved elsewhere. The High Court held that s. 3 was not concerned only with final deposits. Indeed, 'to hold otherwise would involve an unnecessary erosion of the efficacy of the Act which is as much concerned with environmental damage that may be caused by a waste transfer station as with effects created on or by a site where the waste reaches its final resting place'. The judge added that it does not matter whether the site in question has a licence or not, thus putting the law on this point beyond doubt.

This case continues to be relevant for the transitory cases in which the COPA licence did not become a waste management licence.

3.4.1   Exemptions from Licensing

Waste management licences are granted under s. 35 of the EPA 1990. The Waste Management Licensing Regulations 1994, SI No. 1056 link the pollution control regimes for the other environmental media with the waste management regime by providing that the treatment, keeping or disposal of waste which is carried out under a water pollution consent, a licence to deposit at sea or an IPC authorization does not require a waste management licence. This prevents overlap.

Not all waste management activities require a licence. The Secretary of State has power under s. 33(3) to exempt from licensing certain kinds of waste management activity including those involving small quantities of waste, waste deposited only temporarily, or waste whose treatment or disposal is innocuous. Schedule 3 to the 1994 Regulations exempts forty-three categories of waste management activities under these provisions but subject to conditions including the quantity of waste involved and the length of period over which the activity is carried on at the site. The exempted activities are wide-ranging and include waste kept at its place of production pending treatment or disposal elsewhere; treating or disposal of waste as an integral part of its production; a regulator taking samples of waste for testing; and various recycling and recovery operations.

In accordance with the requirements of the Waste Framework Directive exempt activities must be registered. The 1994 Regulations make it an offence to carry on, after 31 December 1994, an exempt activity involving the recovery or disposal of waste without a registration. The registration authority is:

1   In the case of activities which are exempt because they are linked to prescribed processes under Part I of the EPA, HMIP or the local air pollution control authority
2   In the case of animal by-products, the Minister for Agriculture, Fisheries and Food or his or her Scottish or Welsh counterparts and
3   In any other case, the WRA.

The registration is intended to be simple, containing only the name and address of the establishment or undertaking carrying on the activity, details of the activity and the place where its carried on. With the exception of the WRA, the regulators are taken to be aware of these details. The WRA shall enter the details in the register if it receives notice of them in writing or otherwise becomes aware of them.

3.4.2 The Waste Management Licence

An EPA 1990 waste management licence is granted by a WRA. It authorizes the treatment, keeping or disposal of controlled waste on or in specified land or by means of a mobile plant. A licence to treat, keep or dispose of controlled waste in or on land is known as a 'site licence' whereas a licence to treat or dispose of waste by means of a mobile plant is known as a 'mobile plant licence'. A site licence is granted to the occupier of the land while a mobile plant licence is granted to its operator.

The licensee cannot transfer the licence unless the WRA approves. A site licence continues in force until it is revoked by the WRA or is surrendered by the licensee and the surrender is accepted by the WRA. This is the key difference between the COPA and the EPA regimes; under COPA the licensee was able simply to hand back the licence. Now a licence can be surrendered only if the authority accepts its surrender under a procedure set out in s. 39. This new requirement is the main pillar of the new regime in that as a site licensee cannot simply hand it back, the licensee has the incentive to ensure that the operation meets high environmental standards.

An application for a site licence is made to the WRA in whose area the land is located while an application for a mobile site licence is made to the WRA in whose area the plant operator has his or her principal place of business. The WRA must give its decision within four months or it will be deemed to have refused the application; however, the parties may agree a longer period. Before issuing the licence the authority must consult the NRA, or in Scotland the local river purification authority; the HSE; and, where any part of the land falls within an area of special scientific interest, the Nature Conservancy Council for either England or Scotland or the Countryside Council for Wales. The consultees have twenty-one days within which to respond. If the NRA, or in Scotland the river purification authority, requests that the licence should not be issued or disagrees with conditions of the proposed licence, either party may refer the matter to the Secretary of State for a decision.

The authority can issue the licence only if it is satisfied that:

1   The land has planning permission or an 'established use certificate', i.e. a certificate which the planning authority may issue for land uses which have been carried on since 1964 without express permission; since the **Planning and Compensation Act 1991** a 'certificate of lawful use' may be obtained from the planning authority indicating that a use is lawful because, for example, the operator has an established use certificate or has acquired immunity from enforcement action—this can be shown to the WRA.

2   The applicant is a 'fit and proper person'; the DoE has issued guidance to WRAs (discussed below), on how applicants can satisfy them on this point. And

3   It is not necessary to reject the application in order to prevent pollution of the environment, harm to human health, or serious detriment to the amenities of the locality.

The requirement that the WRA take into account the potential effect of the licensed activities on the environment, human health and local amenity is a marked improvement on the considerations the WRA was required to take into account under the COPA regime. Under COPA all the WRA had to consider was the possibility of water pollution arising from the disposal activities. Even under the EPA regime the WRA is required to take into account considerations related to the possible effect on local amenity only if the land has an established use certificate but not if it has planning permission. The reason for this limitation, presumably, is that the question of amenity will have been dealt with when the planning permission was being issued, an optimistic line to adopt given the variable level of awareness of environmental issues which planning authorities at times display.

A licence may be varied on the initiative of the WRA or because the licensee has requested a variation. In the latter case, unless the two parties have agreed a longer period, the WRA must give its decision in two months or it will be deemed to have rejected the request. The WRA may, in particular, vary the licence to ensure that the activities it authorizes do not cause pollution of the environment, harm to human health or become seriously detrimental to the amenities of the locality. Unless there is an emergency or the variation will not affect a particular consultee, the WRA must consult the specified consultees in the same way as if it proposed to issue a new licence.

There are three reasons for revoking a licence entirely or partially and one further reason for revoking it only partially:

1   The holder is no longer a fit and proper person because he or she has been convicted of a relevant offence; or
2   Continuing the authorized activities would cause pollution of the environment or harm to human health or would be seriously detrimental to local amenities; and
3   The pollution, harm or detriment cannot be avoided by modifying the conditions of the licence; or
4   The licensee is no longer a fit and proper person because the authorized activities are not being managed by a technically competent person; in this case the WRA, in revoking the licence, may require that specified conditions of the licence (e.g. requiring the monitoring for gas and leachate) continue to bind the holder, the licence remaining effective to that extent.

Alternatively, the WRA may opt to suspend parts of a licence and require the licensee to take corrective action if:

1   The licensee is no longer a fit and proper person because the authorized activities are not being managed by a technically competent person; or

2   Serious pollution of the environment or harm to human health has resulted from, or is about to be caused by, activities it authorizes or an event affecting those activities; and

3   Continuing to carry on those activities or some of them in the circumstances will continue, or will cause, serious pollution of the environment or serious harm to human health.

Appeals from a WRA's decisions are to the Secretary of State who may appoint an inspector to determine it, either in private or by public hearing. A decision to modify licence conditions or revoke a licence is suspended while an appeal is pending. However, if the WRA states that the modification or revocation is necessary to prevent or minimize pollution of the environment or harm to human health then an appeal would not suspend the decision which would come into effect immediately. But the Secretary of State has the power to rule that the WRA has acted unreasonably in stating that the modification or revocation should not be suspended by an appeal (or has acted unreasonably in suspending a licence), in which case the WRA's decision will be suspended for the duration of the appeal and the licensee can recover compensation for any losses he or she has suffered as a result of the WRA's decision.

3.4.3   Fit and Proper Persons

In a report in 1985, the Royal Commission on Environmental Pollution strongly criticized the situation then prevailing under which 'any person irrespective of their competence, knowledge or training or their financial or personal profit can set themselves up as waste managers' (RCEP, 1985). The **EPA 1990** attempts to redress this situation by requiring that a licence must not be granted unless the licensee is a 'fit and proper person'. Section 74 defines a 'fit and proper person' and WRAs are required to take this into account in granting, transferring, suspending or revoking a licence.

The Act sets three criteria on the basis of which a person may be disqualified from obtaining or keeping a licence on the ground that he or she is not a 'fit and proper person':

1   He or another relevant person has been convicted of a relevant offence.

2   The management of the activities which are, or are to be, authorized are not, or will not be, in the hands of a technically competent person.

3   He has not made and either has no intention of making or is in no position to make financial provision adequate to discharge the obligations arising from the licence.

Relevant Offences

This criterion is aimed at the person both applying for a licence or holding one, as well as any other 'relevant person'. Three categories of person are 'relevant persons': an employee of the applicant or licensee; his or her business partner; and a corporation in which the applicant or licensee is a director, manager, company secretary or other similar officer. The 1994 Waste Management Licensing Regulations prescribe the main environmental and health and safety offences as 'relevant offences' for this purpose.

The WRA does have a discretion to treat a person as fit and proper despite having been convicted of these offences. In Waste Management Paper (WMP) No. 4 (DoE, 1994a) the Secretary of State issued guidance to WRAs on the three factors to take into account in exercising their discretion:

1 Whether it is the applicant or another relevant person who has been convicted
2 The nature and gravity of the offence and
3 The number of offences involved.

Where it is another relevant person who has committed the offence the WRA is advised to consider whether the circumstances merit the applicant being considered not fit and proper. On the nature, gravity and number of offences the WRA should have regard to:

1 Whether any of the offences involved controlled waste or special waste or caused serious pollution, harm to human health or detriment to local amenity
2 The severity of the penalty imposed by the courts, this being an indication of the seriousness with which the court viewed the offence, and
3 Whether the conviction is spent or would have been spent were the applicant an individual rather than a corporation.

Technical Competence

A technically competent person ('a TCP') is expected to be in a position to control the day-to-day activities carried out at the licensed site. According to WMP No. 4 a TCP does not have to be a single individual; many individuals employed by the same organization can together make up the TCP for the licensee or applicant. Consequently, the nature of adequate technically competent management will depend on the type of operation involved; for a large and complex site, several specialists can constitute the technically competent management and, in some cases, more than one site can be under the control of the same individual or group of individuals. The licensee needs therefore to give to the WRA the names and evidence of the qualifications of all the persons involved in the management of the site, with updates as necessary.

Regulation 4 of the 1994 Waste Management Licensing Regulations states that a TCP needs to hold a certificate issued by the Waste Management Industry Training and Advisory Board (WAMITAB). There are two categories of certificate, Level 3 and Level 4, and the particular certificate a TCP needs depends on the type of facility he or she seeks to manage. Level 3 certificate holders are competent to manage four types of facility:

1   Civic amenity site operations
2   Inert waste operations at landfills with a capacity below 50 000 m^3
3   Waste treatment plants not handling special waste or
4   Transfer stations not handling special waste.

Level 4 certificates are required for all other facilities; ten are listed including landfills which receive special waste or biodegradable waste; treatment plants involving incineration or chemical or physical treatment of special waste; and transfer stations dealing with biodegradable, clinical or special waste.

Two categories of people are exempted from the requirement to have a WAMITAB certificate; those who applied for one before 10 August 1994 and had been managing the particular site in the preceding twelve months, and those who were over 55 years old on that date and had, in the preceding ten years, for five years managed a facility of the type for which a certificate is required. The first category of person has a five-year exemption during which they must acquire the certificate; in the meantime WAMITAB may offer them a 'provisional certificate of technical competence'. The second category of person has a ten-year exemption which will take them to the retirement age of 65. WAMITAB may offer them a 'certificate of qualifying experience' which should suffice for the WRA.

Two further categories of person do not need a certificate of technical competence. The first is a waste manager managing a site previously licensed under the COPA regime but whose licence has been transferred into the new EPA system. There is no provision for the 'fit and proper person' test to be applied retrospectively and so this person will be able to continue until either the management changes hands or the licence is substantially modified, thus enabling the WRA to introduce the 'fit and proper person' test. Before that oppportunity arises the licence holder will be deemed 'technically competent'. The second category is a person managing an activity which is not covered by the WAMITAB certificate, such as scrap metal operations. WMP No. 4 advises that for such persons a 'Statement of Qualifying Experience' showing at least five years' relevant experience should suffice.

Financial Provision

The question of financial provision proved the most protracted of the three requirements needed to achieve 'fit and proper person' status. Financial competence is not a basis for revoking or suspending a licence, but since landfills may remain problematic long after closure, it is necessary to ensure that the applicant remains financially capable of meeting his or her commitments during the whole of the post-closure period. Therefore, authorities are advised to insert a condition in the licence requiring the licensee to maintain adequate cover during the whole period; this could then be invoked for enforcement purposes. Thus the WRA could prosecute the licensee for breaching a condition of his or her licence by not maintaining an adequate financial cover and then revoke the licence on the basis that the licensee has been convicted of a relevant offence.

WMP No. 4 offers guidance on how financial competence might be assessed. This is to the effect that authorities should seek only a general statement about financial provision with the initial application because the applicant cannot provide a detailed statement until he or she has been given a draft licence upon which to base the extent of the financial provision that would be necessary. Evidence of financial provision, including provision for environmental contingencies, can take the form of business plans, audit certificates, guarantees by the parent company or the directors, charges on company assets, insurance, self-insurance, overdraft facilities, bonds, escrow accounts, trust funds, as well as membership of the mutually funded company which the National Association of Waste Disposal Contractors has mooted. This requirement is likely to prove difficult in practice. A proper assessment of financial competence will call for considerable sophistication on the part of the regulators who may find it necessary on occasion to call in outside consultants. WRAs seem to prefer escrow accounts.

3.4.4 Surrender of Site Licences

An EPA 1990 site licence, unlike a COPA site licence, can only be surrendered if the WRA accepts the surrender. The procedure to be followed in case of a proposed surrender is set out in s. 39 which came into force on 1 May 1994. On receiving the application the WRA must inspect the land to determine whether the activities that have been carried out on it under the licence have put it in a condition which is likely to cause pollution of the environment or harm to human health. If so, the WRA must reject the proposed surrender. If, however, the WRA finds the surrender acceptable it must, before accepting it, consult the NRA, or in Scotland the river purification authority, and, in some cases, the local planning authority. Should the NRA or the river purification authorities request a rejection of the surrender the matter may be referred to the Secretary of State for a decision. The WRA has three months within which to make a decision or else it will be deemed to have rejected the surrender. However, the parties can agree a longer period. If the WRA accepts the surrender it issues to the licensee a 'certificate of completion' which signifies the end of the licensee's obligations under the licence.

This procedure is aimed at ensuring that licensees remain responsible for the landfill as long as it has the potential to cause harm or pollution, even though active landfilling has ended. At the same time, licensees cannot be expected to remain responsible for a site indefinitely; there must be a procedure under which responsibility can, at some stage, end. Section 39 provides that responsibility for the site can be transferred to the WRA if it is satisfied that the site is in a stable condition. In order to generate the information needed to make that decision, the licensee must have in place a monitoring programme addressing three questions. What is happening within the site now? What is the potential for problems in the future? What is happening outside the site?

As indicated in 3.3.3 'Waste Management Planning', landfilling is the chief method of waste disposal in the UK. The predominant form of landfilling practice in the UK is known as 'co-disposal' (DoE, 1993d). This is the joint deposition of industrial and household wastes in order to use natural microbial and chemical processes to degrade the wastes, i.e. the jointly landfilled wastes react biologically and chemically, degrade and, over time, dissipate. The two principal outputs from the microbial and chemical breakdown of co-deposited wastes are methane, a flammable gas, and leachate, a highly polluting liquid which can pose a threat of groundwater contamination. These two are the main environmental problems posed by landfilling of waste.

Older landfills were not self-contained, being simply holes in the ground. Due to this, the leachate generated has been dispersed over time into the ground, hence 'dilute and disperse' landfills. This dispersal has come to be seen as posing a threat of groundwater pollution. Modern landfills are designed through the use of clay and polythene liners to be self-contained engineered structures capable of limiting the possibility of groundwater contamination by run-off leachate. The methane gas and leachate are normally collected and disposed of under controlled conditions; the methane is vented while the leachate is discharged to a sewer under a consent from the relevant sewerage undertaker. The whole operation is backed up, typically, by a programme of monitoring which continues throughout the life of the site.

The UK insists that co-disposal of waste in modern landfills is environmentally safe, but the European Commission disagrees, preferring instead a form of landfill more commonly found in the United States known as 'mono-landfills'. This form is designed as a self-contained tomb for the safe-keeping, rather than degradation, of waste. A mono-landfill contains only one category of waste, keeping, say, domestic waste away from industrial waste. The degradation, which the UK sees as the advantage of co-disposal, is seen by proponents of mono-landfills as a problem because of the generation of leachate and methane. Mono-landfills are intended to minimize degradation, simply containing the waste material for decades on end. This debate dogged the proposed Landfill of Waste Directive (COM (93) C 212/02) which sought unsuccesfully to impose provisions requiring that co-disposal be phased out.

WMP No. 26A on 'Surrender of Licences' gives guidance on how WRAs are to determine whether the condition of the land is such that a surrender of the licence is acceptable. The licensee is expected to maintain the landfill gas and leachate control after active landfilling has ceased until the production of methane and leachate ends. When the landfill has stabilized to such a degree that it is unlikely to cause pollution or harm to human health these measures may be suspended. That stage, known as 'the point of completion', is determined on the basis of physical, chemical and biological criteria, details of which are given in the WMP. It is followed by a period of at least two years of monitoring, known as 'completion monitoring', to demonstrate that the site is stable before a surrender application can be lodged. WMP No. 26A recommends the number of leachate sampling points for different types of site, the duration and frequency for monitoring leachate and groundwater, and the chemical substances for which to monitor. All the information is then collated in a 'Completion Report' which is presented to the authority with the surrender application (DoE, 1994b).

3.4.5 Registration of Waste Brokers

The EC Waste Framework Directive (75/442/EEC) requires that establishments or undertakings which arrange for the disposal or recovery of waste on behalf of others must be registered if the laws of the member state do not require them to be authorized. The UK had no legislation requiring such people, referred to as 'brokers', to be authorized. Therefore the 1994 Waste Management Licensing Regulations introduce a registration scheme for brokers based on the waste carrier registration scheme (discussed in 3.6 'Registration of Waste Carriers'). The registration authority is the WRA in the location where the broker carries on his or her business and a broker who has been convicted of 'relevant offences' may be refused registration.

It is an offence, after 31 December 1994, for an establishment or undertaking to arrange (as a dealer or broker) for the disposal or recovery of directive waste on behalf of another person without being registered as a broker. However, the requirement to register does not apply if the directive waste is exempt from waste management licensing or has a permit under some other pollution control regime.

There is no definition of a broker in the legislation. Annex 8 of the Waste Management Licensing Regulations also refrains from attempting to define the term. However, it suggests examples of undertakings which may be brokers, such as where an environmental consultant contracts to arrange for the recovery or disposal of all the controlled waste generated by a particular producer. The consultant is acting as a broker since it is neither the producer, holder, carrier, recoverer nor disposer of the waste in question. This includes those who arrange for the transfrontier shipment of waste. The key appears to be acting as an intermediary over waste without being the waste's producer, holder, carrier, recoverer or disposer. There are exemptions from the requirement to register for:

1 Charities, voluntary organizations and local authorities
2 An undertaking whose application, lodged before 1 January 1995, is still pending and
3 Brokers who are registered as carriers—the carrier registration scheme and the broker registration scheme are to be combined; someone who is both a carrier and a broker would need to register under only one of the schemes.

3.5 The Duty of Care

The concept of the 'Duty of Care' was put forward in a 1985 report by the Royal Commission of Environmental Pollution (RCEP, 1985). This recommended that 'to prevent pollution occurring there must be a secure waste stream, achieved through the exercise of a proper duty of care by producers, handlers and transporters of waste ...' (para 1.12). The Duty of Care is now enshrined in s. 34 of the **EPA 1990**. With the exception of a householder in relation to household waste produced on his or her premises, the Duty of Care applies to every person in the waste management chain; that is, any person who imports, produces, carries, keeps, treats, or disposes of controlled waste, or, as a broker, has control of such waste.

The Duty of Care has three aspects, requiring the holder to:

1 Prevent others committing the offence of treating, keeping or disposing of controlled waste without a licence or in a manner likely to pollute the environment or harm human health
2 Prevent the waste escaping from his, or someone else's control and
3 Transfer the waste only to 'an authorized person', or only for 'authorized transport purposes' and with a written description which would enable others not to break the law on the treatment, keeping and disposal of waste and to fulfil their own duty to prevent waste escaping.

An 'authorized person' is defined in s. 34 as one of six persons: a waste collection authority; a licensed waste manager; anyone who is exempt from the waste management licensing requirements; a registered waste carrier; anyone who is exempt from the registration of carriers requirements; and a waste disposal authority in Scotland. 'Authorized transport purposes' are stated to be transport within the same premises, transport to a place within Britain of imported waste and transport by air or sea of waste being exported.

The Duty of Care does not involve an absolute responsibility. It is limited, requiring the holder of waste only to take measures which are applicable to him or her in the capacity in which he holds the waste. Thus, if he holds it as a carrier only, he may not need to write a description for it, while as its producer he would need to. Further, the measures to be taken are limited to measures that are 'reasonable in the circumstances'. Deciding that can be problematic and the Secretary of State has issued guidelines in DoE Circular 19/91 and in the Code of Practice on the Duty of Care (DoE, 1991a), both of which are useful indications on how to proceed in practice.

3.5.1   The Code of Practice

The Code recommends a series of steps to be followed which should normally be adequate to comply with the Duty of Care. But, as it points out, the Code of Practice cannot cover every contingency which will arise in practice so there will be a need at times to go back to first principles to determine what has to be done to comply, particularly in the more problematic cases. The Code divides the Duty of Care into six steps: (1) identifying and describing the waste; (2) keeping it safely; (3) transferring it to the right person; (4) receiving the waste; (5) checking up; and (6) getting expert help and advice where needed. It suggests how to proceed at each stage.

Anyone handling waste has to answer the following questions. Is it Directive waste? If so, is it controlled waste? If so, is it special waste? If the waste is controlled waste, it is necessary to identify its nature so as to be able to give subsequent holders a sufficient description to enable them to manage it properly. Attention must be paid in particular to any characteristics which may cause problems. The description of the waste will vary from very simple descriptions giving perhaps only the name of the substance to a description that incorporates a chemical and physical analysis of the waste, depending on the type of waste and whether it might cause subsequent handlers special problems. Often the transfer note (see 3.5.2 'Documentation') is able to serve also as a description of the waste.

Waste should reach not only its next holder but also the licensed facility or other final destination without escape. It therefore needs protection against spillage and loss by being put in an appropriate container and labelled. Security measures need to be taken also at sites where waste is stored to prevent theft, vandalism and scavenging. Before transferring the waste it is necessary to check that the carrier is an authorized person or, alternatively, that the carriage is for authorized transport purposes. This is done by checking the carrier's certificate or copy certificate of registration, discussed further below. Similarly, before choosing a waste manager to transfer the waste to it is necessary to check that he or she has a licence which covers the type of waste being transferred. The Code's advice is that where the transfers are repetitive—the same type of waste from the same origin to the same destination—full checks on carriers and waste managers do not need to be repeated with each transfer; once a year will suffice. The **Deregulation and Contracting Out Act 1994** amends s. 34 to give a statutory basis to the Code's advice on such annual checks.

The Duty of Care extends to the person receiving the waste and he or she must also check to avoid accepting waste from a source that seems in breach of the Duty of Care. He must also ensure that the transfer note is properly completed, that the waste is properly packaged and that its description is adequate to enable him to deal with it properly. There is no requirement that a waste producer audit his or her waste's final destination but an audit and periodic visits thereafter would be a prudent means to demonstrate the steps taken to prevent subsequent illegal treatment of the waste.

3.5.2 Documentation

No particular regulator is given the task of enforcing the Duty of Care; the government believes that the Duty of Care is self-enforcing through waste holders checking on each other primarily to avoid breaking the law. This is over-optimistic as it presumes that waste holders have adequate knowledge about the Duty of Care. In the two years following the coming into force of the Duty of Care in April 1992 there were about a dozen prosecutions for breaching various aspects of its requirements; all were mounted by WRAs.

The mainstay of the Duty of Care is a system of documentation creating an audit trail of the waste. This enables the history of the waste to be traced and assists in identifying those who breach the Duty of Care. The Environmental Protection (Duty of Care) Regulations 1991, SI No. 2839 have been made under s. 34(5) of the 1990 Act to impose requirements on waste holders to ensure that when the description of the waste is transferred it is accompanied by a transfer note completed and signed on behalf of the transferor and the transferee. In some circumstances a single note can cover multiple consignments taking place within the same year.

The transfer note must identify the waste transferred and its quantity; its packaging; the time and place of transfer; details of the parties involved; and the purpose of the transfer where it is made for authorized transport purposes. The description of the waste and the transfer note can usually be combined into one document. The note must be kept by both parties for at least two years. The waste regulatory authority may serve a written notice on anyone, whether in or outside their area, requiring its production. Failing to comply with these requirements is an absolute offence for which there are no defences.

The Code's advice is that the transfer note can also double up as the description of waste and the Code has a model transfer note which those transferring waste may use. The model transfer note must be used with caution, however, a fact highlighted by a recent magistrates' court prosecution. Leicestershire WRA prosecuted Simons Construction Ltd, a building firm, for misdescribing paint waste as 'builders' waste'. The paint, which originated from a construction site, had been placed in the bottom of a skip supplied by a waste carrier. When the skip was collected the transfer note described the waste simply as 'builders' waste'. The skip was taken to a landfill site where a further transfer note was completed, repeating the description 'builders' waste'. The paint was discovered when the skip was emptied. Since the landfill was not licensed to accept paint waste, the WRA was informed; they charged Simons Construction Ltd with a Duty of Care offence. The company's defence was that the phrase 'builders' waste' was in everyday use and that skips described as containing this kind of waste were commonly understood to contain a whole range of materials, including paint. The company argued further that, in any case, the space available on the transfer note was insufficient to accommodate a comprehensive description of waste. The magistrates rejected these arguments, convicted the company and imposed a fine of £1 500 plus costs of £400 (ENDS, 1993a).

For a waste producer, or any other person holding waste, to be able to discharge the Duty of Care, a system under which waste can lawfully be passed on to others is necessary. Not only must there be a licensed waste manager to dispose of the waste, there must be also a waste carrier to whom waste can be transferred for transport to the disposal site, or elsewhere. The waste management licensing system has already been discussed. The carrier registration system is provided for in the **Control of Pollution (Amendment) Act 1989** and the Controlled Waste (Registration of Carriers and Seizure of Vehicles) Regulations 1991, SI No. 1624.

3.6 Registration of Waste Carriers

Section 1 of the **Control of Pollution (Amendment) Act 1989** makes it an offence to transport controlled waste without registering as a waste carrier with the WRA in the area from where the business is carried on. However, only those who transport waste 'in the course of any business or with a view to profit' need to register as waste carriers. The section exempts transport within the same premises, to a place within Britain of imported waste and by air or sea of waste being exported. There are three defences which a person charged may raise:

1   The waste was transported in an emergency and the WRA in whose area the emergency occurred was informed as soon as practicable after that; an 'emergency' is limited to a situation in which it is necessary for the waste to be transported from one place to another without using a registered carrier

in order to avoid, remove or reduce any serious danger to the public or serious risk of damage to the environment

2   The person did not know or have reason to suspect that it was controlled waste being transported and took all reasonable steps to ascertain whether it was such waste or

3   That the person acted under instructions from his or her employer.

The Controlled Waste (Registration of Carriers and Seizure of Vehicles) Regulations 1991, SI No. 1624 exempt eight categories of carriers from registering: waste collection, disposal and regulatory authorities; the producer of the waste, unless it is building or demolition waste; British Rail; ferry operators carrying a vehicle which is carrying controlled waste; the operator of a vessel, aircraft, hovercraft, floating container, or vehicle disposing of waste at sea under a licence; a charity or voluntary organization; and someone whose application, made before 1 April 1992, is still pending.

3.6.1   The Registration

The application is made to the WRA in the area where the carrier's principal place of business is located. If the business is a partnership all the partners and prospective partners need to apply. If successful the carrier is issued with a certificate bearing a registration number; the certificate may not be transferred. The carrier has to inform the WRA of changes of circumstance, such as a change to the principal place of business, so that the WRA can amend the register. Where the change affects the information on the certificate it may be necessary for the WRA to issue an amended certificate; unlike the first certificate, this would be free of charge. The WRA may also, on request, issue numbered copies of the certificate which a carrier with more than one vehicle may need for the various drivers. A carrier cannot, however, apply to be registered or to renew his or her registration while a previous application is pending, or while he is registered. This is to prevent the situation arising where a carrier is registered simultaneously with more than one WRA.

The authority can refuse the application for two reasons only. The first reason is if the applicant has not complied with a requirement relating to the application. DoE Circular 11/91 advises authorities to refuse applications in cases where the application is made to the wrong WRA, a previous application is still pending or the applicant is already registered, or where not all partners and prospective partners have applied, but to exercise its discretion in relation to the other aspects of the application.

The second reason for refusing an application is where the applicant or 'another relevant person' has been convicted of a 'prescribed offence' and in the opinion of the WRA it is undesirable for the applicant to be authorized to transport controlled waste. The offences which have been prescribed for this purpose are primarily environmental and health and safety offences and they are listed in Schedule I to the Regulations. The applicant has to disclose any convictions for such offences. In one magistrates' court prosecution a waste carrier was convicted for failing to disclose in his application for registration that he had a previous conviction for a prescribed offence, in this case a water pollution offence. The waste carrier's plea in mitigation was that the form had been filled by his secretary as he has difficulty reading and writing. He was fined £500 (ENDS, 1993b).

A refusal of registration may, however, be appealed to the Secretary of State. In the first appeal under this provision, the Secretary of State's decision letter is reported to have stated that 'operators should not be forced out of business unnecessarily as a result of the registration system' (ENDS, 1993c). The WRA may also, on the same grounds, i.e. conviction for a prescribed offence, revoke an existing registration. Presumably the same sentiments expressed by the Secretary of State would apply in deciding whether to revoke the registration. The appeal must be made within twenty-eight days. In the case of an appeal from a revocation the registration remains in force until the appeal is concluded.

A person is a 'relevant person' if he or she is an employee or a partner of the applicant or if it is a corporation in which the applicant is a director, manager, company secretary or other similar officer. DoE Circular 11/91 goes into some detail regarding how this power should be exercised.

The first issue to consider is whether the conviction is spent within the terms of the **Rehabilitation of Offenders Act 1974**. This provides that the conviction of an individual who is convicted and sentenced to less than two and half years imprisonment becomes 'spent' after a rehabilitation period if he or she has not committed some other indictable offence in the meantime. Such a 'rehabilitated person' is in the same position as someone who has not been convicted of the particular offence. A spent conviction need not be disclosed and the WRA must not take it into account even if it happens to know about it. The actual rehabilitation period depends on the length of the sentence imposed; a two-and-a-half year sentence becomes spent after ten years; a fine, after five years. Corporations do not become rehabilitated in this way but WRAs may choose to take into account the fact that had it been an individual the conviction would have been spent.

The second factor is whether the WRA considers that it is undesirable for the applicant to be authorized to transport controlled waste. DoE Circular 11/91 advises that the decision is to be made on the basis of four factors: (1) the type of applicant; (2) whether it is the applicant or another relevant person who was convicted; (3) the nature and gravity of the offence; and (4) the number of offences involved. An individual, a partner or a prospective partner or a corporation constitute the possible types of applicant. Where it is not the applicant who committed the offence, the degree of his or her involvement in its commission will count, for instance, if, as a director, he or she connived at the offence or was negligent; similarly, where the offence is repeated, whether it involves controlled or special waste, causes serious pollution, or incurs a penalty.

Typically, a carrier's registration is valid for three years. Six months before the end of that period the WRA must send a notice to the carrier informing him or her of the date of expiry and the fact that, if the carrier applies for renewal before the end of the three years, registration continues in force until that application is determined. If the applicant does not apply for a renewal before the end of the three-year period he would have to apply afresh, not seek to renew his expired certificate; in this latter situation he must not transport waste while his or her fresh application is pending. A registration may expire before the end of the three years because the applicant asks the WRA to deregister him, or a partner in the business loses his registration or a person who is not registered joins the partnership unless, that is, the authority has been notified and has amended the register to reflect the change. A carrier whose registration has expired must return the certificate and any copies to the WRA.

A police officer in uniform or an officer of the WRA may stop any person who appears to be, or to have been, transporting controlled waste and ask them to show their registration certificate; the vehicle may also be searched. However, only a police officer in uniform can stop a vehicle while it is on the road. If the certificate is not produced on the spot it must be sent to the WRA's office within seven days. This is the principal way in which WRAs are able to enforce the registration requirements. It is an offence to obstruct intentionally the exercise of this power, and obstruction need not be physical.

One unresolved issue is whether the WRA officer has to have reason to believe that a vehicle is transporting waste without registration before he or she can stop it; the most practical means of enforcement is simply to stop every vehicle transporting waste whether or not there is reason to believe that the vehicle has a registration.

3.6.2   Seizure of Vehicles

Before the Controlled Waste (Registration of Carriers and Seizure of Vehicles) Regulations 1991 local authorities had to concentrate on trying to apprehend offenders in the act of tipping waste from their vehicles. Inevitably, fly-tipping was extremely difficult to monitor. The new law provides a procedure for tackling fly-tipping. Under it a warrant may be issued to a WRA to seize a vehicle if there are reasonable grounds for believing that it has been involved in the illegal disposal of controlled waste. Before applying for a warrant the authority has to check records of vehicles with the Transport Secretary for UK-registered vehicles and with the chief police officer of the area where the offence was committed if the vehicle is a foreign-registered vehicle. If that fails the authority has, second, to identify a person who can tell it who was using the vehicle when the waste was fly-tipped. Only if this also fails, and it has not yet charged anyone with the offence, can the WRA then apply for a warrant to seize the vehicle.

If the vehicle is on the road then only a police officer in uniform can actually stop it. Having been stopped it may be searched and seized, together with any property in it. The vehicle and property may be sold, destroyed or disposed of but the authority has to publicize its intention and wait for twenty-eight days to see if a claimant comes forward, unless its condition necessitates immediate destruction. These powers are not intended to enable vehicles to be confiscated as a punishment. They provide a means by which the WRAs may find out the name and address of a person who should be able to provide it with the details of the person who was using the vehicle at the time the offence was committed. Therefore, the WRA is required to return a vehicle to a claimant who satisfactorily establishes entitlement to it, since once a person has come forward to claim the vehicle the purpose of its seizure will have been served. Indeed, even after the sale, the proceeds, apart from the portion that goes to meet the WRA's expenses, may be claimed by the person entitled to them.

There have been no reports of this power being used, perhaps because the procedure for doing so is so laborious.

3.7 Litter

Part IV of the **EPA 1990** is concerned with litter, which is not defined and is not in all cases controlled waste. It makes several authorities responsible under s. 89(1) for keeping land in their control clear of litter and refuse. These are local authorities in the capacity of 'principal litter authorities'; the Crown in respect of Crown land; the Secretary of State in respect of motorways; and in respect of their land, designated statutory undertakers, educational institutions and occupiers of land.

The Litter (Statutory Undertakers) (Designation and Relevant Land) Order 1991, SI No. 1043 and the Litter (Designated Educational Institutions) Order 1991, SI No. 561 designate most educational establishments and statutory undertakers such as British Rail and airport operators. The duty is limited to the particular authority's 'relevant land', i.e. land under the direct control of the particular body. Additionally, in the case of the Crown and principal litter authorities it relates to land which is both open to the air and to which the public have access; in the case of statutory undertakers and an occupier it relates to land which is in a litter control area and to which the public have access; and in the case of an educational institution it relates to land which is open to the air.

A *Code of Practice on Litter and Refuse* (DoE, 1991b) has been issued which establishes 'cleanliness standards' at which those subject to the duty should aim.

The standards are divided into four grades ranging from A to D as follows: A—no litter; B—predominantly free of litter; C—widespread distribution of litter; and D—heavily littered. The Code also categorizes land into eleven zones recommending one of the four standards which the zone should achieve. The length of time within which the standard should be achieved depends on how far below the standard the zone had fallen; i.e. a zone A area which falls to a zone C standard should be restored back to a zone A standard much quicker than if it falls to a zone B standard. The way this works is as follows:

1   Zone 1—e.g. town centres; grade A, to which it should be restored from grade B within 6 hours and from grade C within 3 hours
2   Zone 2—e.g. high-density residential areas; grade A, to which it should be restored from grade B within 12 hours and from grade C within 6 hours
3   Zone 3—e.g. low-density residential areas; grade A, to which it should be restored from grade C within 12 hours and from grade D within 6 hours
4   Zone 4—e.g. beaches; grade A, to which it should be restored from grade C within one week and from grade D within 60 hours
5   Zones 5, 6 and 7—e.g. various categories of roads and motorways; grade A, to which it should be restored from grade C within one month and from grade D within one week depending on the category
6   Zone 8—e.g. educational institutions; grade B, to which it should be restored from grade C within 24 hours
7   Zones 9 and 10—e.g. various categories of railway embankments; grade B, to which it should be restored from grade C within two weeks depending on the category
8   Zone 11—e.g. canal towpaths; grade A, to which it should be restored from grade C within two weeks.

Various steps may be taken to deal with litter, all but the last two by principal litter authorities. The authority may declare a 'litter control area' under s. 90 because its condition is, in the authority's view, detrimental to the amenity of the locality. The Litter Control Areas Order 1991 (SI No. 1325) specifies land which may be designated as a litter control area—mostly land in private or public body ownership to which the public have access, such as public car parks, shopping centres and cinema halls.

Second, the authority may issue a 'street litter control notice' under s. 93 imposing requirements on an occupier to keep specified areas clear of litter or refuse. Under the Litter Control Notices Order 1991 (SI No. 1324) the notice may be issued in respect of commercial or retail premises that are used for the sale of food or drink for consumption off the premises such as take-away food shops. The notice may require the occupier to provide litter bins and to empty them regularly and keep the area clear of litter. Before serving the notice the authority has to inform the person concerned and give twenty-one days in which representations may be made. An appeal may also be lodged in a magistrates' court. If the person fails to comply with the notice the authority may apply to the magistrates' court for an order requiring compliance. Failure to comply with that order may result in a fine of up to £2 500.

Third, the authority may use the 'litter abatement notice' procedure under s. 92 where it considers that particular land is defaced by litter or refuse or that defacement is likely to recur. The notice imposes either a requirement to remove the litter or a prohibition on permitting the land to become defaced, or both. The person served may appeal to a magistrates' court within twenty-one days. Failure to comply with the order is an offence for which a fine of up to £2 500 may be imposed in a magistrates' court, with a further fine of £125 for each day the breach continues.

Fourth, s. 87 makes it an offence to throw down, drop or deposit and leave litter, an offence referred to as 'leaving litter', for which a penalty of up to £2 500 in a magistrates' court may be imposed. The offence applies only in public open places and the police may make an arrest for it under s. 25 of the **Police and Criminal Evidence Act 1984**. A quick method of dealing with the offence is provided in s. 88 which gives power to any litter authorities to operate fixed-penalty schemes for littering. Under this a notice to pay a fixed penalty of £10 may be given by an authorized officer of the litter authority to a person who he or she has reason to believe has committed the offence of leaving litter. No proceedings shall be instituted for the offence within fourteen days following the notice to pay the £10. If the person pays the fixed penalty in that time he or she shall not be convicted of the offence.

The final possibility is the summary proceeding under s. 91 by any person aggrieved by litter. This may be used by anyone, except the principal litter authorities, against all the litter authorities who have a duty to keep land clear of litter. The person aggrieved may bring proceedings in a magistrates' court requiring the removal of the litter or refuse. Before doing so he or she must give the authority concerned five days' notice and if the litter is removed the order shall not be made. Failure to comply with the order is an offence for which a fine of up to £2 500 may be imposed with a further fine of £125 for each day the offence continues. These provisions have hardly been relied on yet. An early attempt failed because the complainant did not specify the littered streets, complaining about the whole estate (*The Independent*, 13 March 1992). The Tidy Britain Group, which campaigns on litter issues, is keen to see the powers used.

On the question of person aggrieved the DoE's view, expressed in a 1989 consultation paper, is that a person aggrieved

> might be a local resident, someone who worked in the area, or a regular visitor to it—
> in other words anyone who had a bona fide interest in that locality and hence a
> particular right to demand proper standards of cleanliness there. The person could
> equally be an individual representing a local community organization or voluntary
> body with such an interest in the locality (DoE, 1989).

This view would appear to be borne out by the case law on the standing of environmental groups to bring proceedings, discussed in Chapter 12.

Dog fouling is included within the definition of refuse by the Litter (Animal Droppings) Order 1991, SI 1991 No. 961. This enables the application to dog fouling of those provisions which deal with both litter and refuse, that is, the duty to keep land clear of litter and refuse; the s. 91 summary procedure for a litter abatement order; the litter abatement notice procedure under s. 92; and the power under s. 93 to issue street litter control notices. The offence of leaving litter and the fixed-penalty provisions of s. 88 do not apply to dog fouling. Additional measures for dealing with dog fouling are often found in by-laws made by local authorities, and the DoE has issued model dog-fouling by-laws which local authorities may use.

3.8   EC Waste Laws

The EC's policy on waste is contained in a 1989 document which outlines a hierarchy for waste management: prevention; recycling and re-use; and safe disposal as the last resort (Commission of the European Communities, 1989). This hierarchy permeates the entire philosophy of the EC as regards waste management. The document states additionally that in relation to disposal 'provision must be made to ensure that as far as possible waste is disposed of in the nearest suitable centres ...', a principle widely known as the 'proximity principle' whose objective is to discourage the movement of waste to other member states for disposal.

The implementation of the EC's waste management strategy has had one unique feature insofar as the Commission briefly adopted a special approach involving putting forward proposals for discussion rather than introducing proposed Directives before consultation with interested parties. The new approach was adopted in 1990 when the Commission indicated that as an experiment it would draw up a list of waste streams, known as 'priority waste streams', on which representatives from governments, industry, consumer and environmental groups would work as a group. The group's task would be to quantify the scale and nature of the problem posed by each particular waste stream, put forward a waste management strategy on the basis of the EC's waste management hierachy and set targets and a timescale to be achieved. The Commission would then base its proposed directive on the agreed strategy. The idea behind this procedure was to reduce the time it takes for EC legislation to be adopted by getting interested parties behind the proposed strategy from the start.

The first four waste streams are used tyres, chlorinated solvents, redundant vehicles and healthcare waste. The reports of the project groups are expected in 1994. However, the strategy does not seem to have resulted in markedly shorter timescales and it has been reported that no further lists of priority waste streams will be drawn up (ENDS, 1993d).

EC waste directives and regulations are many and diverse. They are set out briefly here with an indication of the action taken by the UK to implement them, where this is not already obvious.

3.8.1 Waste Framework Directive

EC Directive 75/442/EEC (OJ No. L 194/39), the Waste Framework Directive, was amended by directive 91/156/EEC (OJ No. L 78//32). The directive retains the name and reference of Directive 75/442/EEC. Member states were required to implement the new provisions by 1 April 1993. The UK initially hoped to achieve that deadline but 'technical difficulties' related to aligning UK law with the EC requirements forced a postponment of the implementing Waste Management Licensing Regulations 1994 (SI No. 1056) to 1 May 1994.

The extent of alignment that was needed can be seen in the new requirement in Schedule 4 to the 1994 Regulations that all 'competent authorities' must perform their functions, insofar as they relate to the recovery or disposal of waste, in accordance with the relevant objectives. Competent authorities refers to the other pollution control authorities, i.e. planning authorities, local air pollution control authorities, HMIP, HMIPI in Scotland, the Minister for Agriculture, Fisheries and Food, the NRA and the river purification authorities. The relevant objectives to be pursued are drawn from the Waste Framework Directive and relate to ensuring that waste is recovered or disposed of without endangering human health or the environment. This obligation was reaffirmed by the ECJ in the *Lombardia case* (1994).

The directive is referred to as the 'Framework Directive' as it sets a framework for the management of waste generally and leaves it to subsequent 'daughter directives' to deal with particular categories of waste or particular instances of waste management. There are several such daughter directives.

The directive requires member states to ensure that undertakings which carry out waste disposal or waste recovery operations obtain a permit. It allows member states to exempt undertakings which carry out their own waste disposal at the place of production or which carry out waste recovery, and require them instead to be registered. Similarly, member states must ensure that undertakings which collect or transport waste on a professional basis or arrange for the disposal or recovery of waste on behalf of others, that is, dealers or brokers, are either authorized or registered. Member states must ensure, third, that holders of waste who do not lawfully dispose of it themselves or recover it, hand it over to a private or public waste collector or to undertakings which carry out waste disposal or recovery.

3.8.2   Directive on Hazardous Waste

EC Directive 91/698 (OJ No. L 337/20) on hazardous waste replaces EC Directive 78/319/EEC on toxic and dangerous waste which it repeals with effect from 27 June 1995, the date by which member states should have brought into force laws to implement the new directive (see Directive 94/31/EC, OJ No. L 168/28). The earlier directive was implemented in the UK by the Special Waste Regulations 1980, SI No. 1709 which will be replaced.

The directive is one of the daughter directives of the Waste Framework Directive, and applies specifically to hazardous wastes which is defined as waste on a list to be drawn up by the European Commission. The Hazardous Waste Directive has stipulated generic types of hazardous waste, and constituents as well as properties of waste which render them hazardous, and these are to form the basis of the list to be drawn up by the Commission. There has been considerable difficulty in compiling the list of hazardous wastes because it is argued that whether or not waste is hazardous depends on the particular circumstances; to produce a list of hazardous wastes is therefore unfeasible. These difficulties led to the postponement of the implementation of the directive from 31 December 1993 because the list was not ready. To overcome this problem the Commission intends to draw up a list of wastes considered hazardous but only beyond specified threshhold concentrations.

Arrangements for managing hazardous waste are required to be, on the whole, more stringent with records of the details of hazardous waste being kept for at least three years, except for records relating to the transport of such waste which need be kept for only 12 months. The directive excludes domestic wastes from its provisions but requires the Commission to propose specific rules for dealing with domestic waste. The Commission has yet to do so.

3.8.3   Directive on Shipments of Waste

EC Regulation No. 259/93 (OJ No. L 30/1) on the supervision and control of waste within, into and out of the European Community applied from 6 May 1994. It replaced an earlier Directive 84/631/EEC. The 1993 Regulation is implemented in the UK by the Transfrontier Shipment of Waste Regulations 1994, SI No. 1137.

Regulation 259/93 establishes a complex multi-layered control regime principally because it is the vehicle through which EC member states fulfil their international obligations with respect to transfrontier waste shipments arising from:

1   The 1989 Basel Convention on the control of transboundary movements of hazardous wastes and their disposal—this seeks to control the movement of

hazardous wastes world-wide and to prohibit illegal traffic in waste; the UK and the EC have ratified the Convention.

2   The Lomé IV Convention of 15 December 1989 which requires the EC to prohibit the export of hazardous waste to African, Caribbean and Pacific States (ACP); the ACP countries are also required to prohibit the import of such waste into their territories.

3   The OECD decision of 30 March 1992 on the control of transfrontier movements of wastes destined for recovery; this seeks to facilitate the free movement between OECD countries of categories of waste which do not present a risk to the environment as long as the waste is intended to be recovered, such waste has been listed on a 'green list' in an Annex to the Decision.

4   The European Economic Area Agreement between the EC and the European Free Trade Area (EFTA) countries which seeks to promote a free trade area in Western Europe, including the free movement of waste.

The Regulation is a 'daughter' of the Waste Framework Directive and adopts the definition of waste set out there. It does not, however, apply to categories of waste such as civil aviation waste, radioactive waste, and waste generated by the normal operation of ships and offshore platforms which are governed by other agreements. Like the OECD decision, it sets up three categories of waste in ascending order of the waste's potential to cause harm; a green list, an amber list and a red list; waste on the green list intended for recovery may be shipped with only minimal controls, particularly within the OECD, unless the importing country wishes to impose more stringent controls.

Broadly, the regulation establishes a prior notification system under which wastes may not be shipped until the country of destination has signalled its consent. In reality the system set up is extremely complex, principally because there are nuances arising from the international obligations to which EC member states are subject under the four waste movement regimes outlined above. There is an additional fifth regime for movements of waste within the EC itself. Complexity is compounded because the rules differ depending on whether the waste is intended for disposal or for recovery; waste intended for disposal is subjected to more stringent control, while the controls on waste intended for recovery are on a sliding scale, from those on the green list through amber to red.

The common rules which apply are, therefore, the most straightforward. These require that waste which cannot be dealt with as envisaged when shipped, or in an environmentally sound manner, be returned to the country which dispatched it; that a financial guarantee or insurance arrangement be provided to cover the costs of shipment and be returned only after the disposal or recovery is complete; and that documents be kept for at least three years.

Generally, a notification about a shipment is to be made by means of a consignement note which may cover several shipments of waste over a period of one year, a procedure known as a 'general notification procedure'. Each note must give such details of the waste as its source, composition and quantity; the identity of both the producer and consignee; arrangements for routing and insurance; measures to be taken to ensure safe transport; information relating to recovery and any additional information requested.

The relevant parties to a shipment are:

1   The person wishing to ship the waste—this is either the person who produced the waste or a waste collector or a broker, or the person holding the waste; he or she is the person with the legal duty to notify prior to the shipment and is the 'notifier'
2   The authorities, known as 'competent authorities', with the duty to decide whether or not the shipment is acceptable—there are three competent authorities, of dispatch, of transit and of destination, according to whether their responsibility is in the area of origin, transit or destination of the waste; in the UK competent authorities are the WRAs and, for waste in transit, the DoE
3   The person receiving the waste, referred to as the consignee.

The procedure to be followed in all cases of shipment of waste is broadly similar. First, the notifier concludes a contract with the consignee, then informs the competent authority of destination and sends a copy of the note to all the other relevant parties. The competent authority of destination must acknowledge the note within three days with copies to all the other relevant parties. There follows a period—twenty days where shipment is within the EC and sixty days where it involves non-EC countries—during which objections to the planned shipment may be lodged by the other competent authorities. The authority of destination has ten days following the period for objections to give its decision, and the waste may not be shipped before this. Approval is given by stamping the note and sending it to the notifier with copies to the other competent authorities. The notifier then completes the note and sends copies of it to the other competent authorities three days before shipment. An additional copy accompanies the shipment. On receipt of the note the consignee signs it and, within three days after receiving the waste, sends copies to the notifier and the competent authorities concerned. Finally within 180 days after receipt of the waste the consignee sends a certificate of disposal or recovery to all the other relevant parties.

The variations arising from the other international waste shipment regimes outlined above are diverse, and only the key distinguishing facets of the different regimes are highlighted here. There is a departure from the normal rules relating to the EC internal market to allow EC member states to prohibit imports of waste for disposal from other EC member states, or simply to adopt a policy of objecting systematically to all such imports. Second, written consent to shipments of waste on the amber list between EC member states for recovery is not mandatory, and the shipment may proceed after thirty days without the need to wait for a written consent. Third, imports of waste for disposal from non-EC countries are only permitted from an EFTA country which is a party to the Basel Convention or from other countries with which there are bilateral or multilateral arrangements; if such imports are for recovery, they are permitted only from OECD countries or other countries with which there are multilateral arrangements. Fourth, exports of waste for disposal are permitted only to an EFTA country which has not prohibited them and is a party to the Basel Convention; if such exports are for recovery, they are permitted only to OECD countries or to other countries with which there are bilateral or multilateral arrangements. Lastly, exports of hazardous waste to ACP states are prohibited.

3.8.4 Directive on Waste from the Titanium Dioxide Industry

EC Directive 78/176/EEC (OJ No. L 54/19) on waste from the titanium dioxide industry targets specifically waste from the titanium dioxide industry. It requires member states to draw up programmes for the progressive reduction, and eventual elimination, of pollution caused by waste from existing industrial establishments. Additionally, the Commission is to make proposals to the Council for the harmonization of these programmes across the EC.

The Commission's proposals resulted in EC Directive 89/428/EEC but this Directive was annulled by the European Court of Justice in *Commission v Council* on the ground that it had not been adopted on a valid legal basis insofar as it had been adopted pursuant to Article 130S instead of Article 100A. Directive 89/428/EEC was therefore replaced by 92/112/EEC (OJ No. L 409/11) which requires member states to put in place measures by June 1993 to prohibit or otherwise control discharges of such waste.

Directive 78/176 also required the Commission to submit proposals on procedures for the surveillance and monitoring of the environment concerned with waste from the titanium dioxide industry. The Commission's proposals resulted in Council Directive 82/883/EEC (OJ No. L 378/1).

3.8.5 Directive on PCBs and PCTs

EC Directive 76/403/EEC (OJ No. L 108/41) on the disposal of PCBs and PCTs lays down special measures for dealing with PCBs. It requires Member States to put in place measures to control the disposal of PCBs along with objects and equipment containing PCBs.

In the UK the Control of Pollution (Supply and Use of Injurious Substances) Regulations 1986 SI No. 902 banned the sale and use of PCBs in all new plant and equipment but permitted the continued use of PCBs in certain equipment already in use in 1986. Now the government is consulting on phasing them out altogether. The action required would mean the destruction of PCBs by the waste industry and the removal for incineration of PCBs from effluent discharged to watercourses (DoE, 1993e,f).

3.8.6 Directive on Batteries and Accumulators

EC Directive 91/157/EEC (OJ No. L 78/38) on batteries and accumulators containing certain dangerous substances seeks to approximate the laws of member states on the recovery and controlled disposal of spent batteries and accumulators which contain above specified concentrations of mercury, cadmium, and lead. The directive requires member states to prohibit the marketing of alkaline manganese batteries for prolonged use in extreme conditions and other alkaline manganese batteries containing more than a defined quantity of mercury, with the exception of alkaline button cells and batteries composed of button cells.

Member states are required to put in place from March 1993 programmes which would gradually reduce the pollution caused by batteries and accumulators, and to ensure that they are collected separately and recovered or disposed of. The Directive is implemented in the UK through the Batteries and Accumulators (Containing Dangerous Substances) Regulations 1994, SI No. 232 requiring the batteries to be marked with a distinguishing collection mark.

3.8.7 Directive on the Disposal of Waste Oils

EC Directive 75/439/EEC (OJ No. L 194/23) on the disposal of waste oils as amended by Directive 87/101/EEC (OJ No. L 42/43) sets up a hierarchy for dealing with waste oils; regeneration first, combustion second, and safe destruction or controlled dumping third. It requires member states to prohibit discharges of waste oils into waters, to the soil where they may be harmful, and to the air beyond prescribed limits. To ensure that these objectives are achieved, undertakings which dispose of waste oils must obtain a permit. Additionally the directive sets limit values and other standards with which the regeneration, combustion and dumping of waste oils must comply.

The directive is implemented in the UK through regulation 14 of the 1994 Waste Management Licensing Regulations 1994 (SI No. 1056) which provides that a waste management (or disposal) licence which authorizes the regeneration or keeping of waste oils must contain conditions designed to guard against toxicity and contamination with PCBs or PCTs. The remaining aspects of the directive are implemented through the general pollution control laws which impose permit requirements for polluting activities.

3.8.8   Directive on Sewage Sludge in Agriculture

EC Directive 86/278/EEC (OJ No. L 194/6) on the protection of the environment, and in particular of the soil, when sewage sludge is used in agriculture seeks to regulate the use of sewage sludge in agriculture so that harmful effects do not result from such use. Accordingly, the Directive lays down limit values for concentrations of heavy metals in soils to which sludge is applied and in the sludge itself, as well as the maximum annual quantities of such heavy metals which may be introduced into soil intended for agriculture. It requires member states to prohibit the use of sludge where the concentrations of one or more heavy metals in the soil exceeds the limits specified. Member states are required also to regulate the use of sludge so that the accumulation of sludge in the soil does not lead to these limit values being exceeded.

Additionally, the Directive requires member states to prohibit the use of sludge or the supply of sludge for use on grassland or forage crops which are to be grazed or harvested within three weeks; on soil in which fruit (but not fruit trees) or vegetables are growing; and on ground intended for the cultivation of fruit and vegetable crops, which are in direct contact with the soil and are eaten raw, for ten months preceding the harvest.

In the UK this Directive is implemented by the Sludge (Use in Agriculture) Regulations 1989, SI No. 1263.

3.8.9   Proposed Directive on Packaging and Packaging Waste

The EC proposed directive on packaging and packaging waste was first submitted to the Council by the Commission on 24 August 1992. The Council's common position is published as Common Position (EC) No. 13/94 (OJ C 137/65). The common position was achieved by a qualified majority vote, with Germany, Denmark and The Netherlands voting against. Later Belgium also raised objections and the directive failed to be formally adopted at a Council meeting on 9 June 1994.

As it stands the proposed Directive's requirements are:

1   Five-year targets for recovering and recycling packaging waste
2   A minimum of 50 per cent and a maximum of 65 per cent, by weight, of packaging waste must be recovered
3   A minimum recycling target of 25 per cent and a maximum recycling target of 45 per cent
4   At least 15 per cent of each individual packaging material must be recycled
5   Ireland, Greece and Portugal to have temporary derogations
6   Member states may exceed the maximum targets if they have already set up, or are setting up, recovery programmes but each member state would have to ensure that its recovery programme does not distort the single market

7   Member states will be allowed to favour re-use of packaged materials provided this is ecologically sound and conforms to the Treaty
8   Member states will have to put in place national programmes to encourage the prevention of the production of excess packaging.

The proposed packaging and packaging waste directive is being put forward by both the Commission and some member states to counter the problem created by unilateral measures being taken by individual member states (e.g. Germany, France and Belgium) to tackle the problem of excess packaging. These measures are seen as causing a distortion of competition and free movement of goods in the internal market. The German and the French schemes, both of which are already in operation, are the most far-reaching (London and Llamas, 1994). The two, together with the UK's efforts to introduce measures to control packaging waste, are discussed below. The details of the measures in all the other EC member states are discussed in a 1993 article (Goethem, 1993).

The German System

The German Packaging Decree of 20 June 1991 introduced strict targets for managing packaging and packaging waste as follows:

1   From 1 December 1991 packaging used to protect goods from damage as it is carried from manufacturers to the distributor has to be taken back and re-used or recycled (not incinerated or landfilled)
2   From 1 April 1992 distributors and retailers have to establish a system for taking back the excess packaging they sell and that their customers leave behind
3   From 1 January 1993 distributors are required to take back, re-use or recycle retail packaging (i.e. packaging in direct contact with the product).

Manufacturers and distributors established a used packaging-removal company called *Duales System Deutschland* (DSD) to take the actual collection off their hands. This collection system is separate from and parallel to the municipal collection system. To have packaging collected through DSD the manufacturers and distributors pay a fee to DSD and put a 'green dot' mark on it so that consumers can sort it out for separate collection. The Decree has set high collection and recycling targets to be met by DSD by 1996.

The German system has resulted in a lot of packaging waste being collected which cannot be re-used, recycled or recovered because the capacity does not exist in Germany. As the decree does not permit the collected packaging waste to be landfilled or incinerated in Germany, a great deal of it is exported to other European countries at very cheap prices, with the result that recycling industries in those countries have found themselves unable to compete, leading to an outcry across Europe against the DSD system.

The EC countries cannot ban imports from another EC state. Therefore, EC ministers met in October 1993 to work out a solution. Germany promised to stop exporting plastics to other EC countries, to look into ways of stopping exports of paper, to review its packaging legislation specifically to reduce its recycling targets and to allow incineration.

The French System

France has adopted a rather different system. A decree dated 3 April 1992 which came into effect on 1 January 1993 requires manufacturers and importers to make a contribution to, or provide for, the disposal of their packaging waste. A manufacturer may either arrange for the recovery of the packaging or make an approved organization responsible for it. The approved organizations are *Eco-Emballages*, which is approved to assume responsibility for all household packaging; *Adelphi*, which recovers only glass containers for wines and spirits; and *Cyclamed*, which recovers the packaging waste generated by medicinal products. A fee is paid to the organization and in exchange a green dot is placed on the packaging.

The French system differs from the German one in two respects; the decree strictly controls landfilling the packaging waste but permits incineration with energy recovery, and municipal authorities continue to collect the packaging but the approved organization takes it back and offers the authorities financial support for the amount collected. In this way a dual collection arrangement is avoided.

The UK System

The UK is in the process of agreeing a voluntary system with industry. On 7 February 1994 the Producer Responsibility Industry Group (PRG) published a report setting out its proposals (PRG, 1994). The PRG was set up following the challenge by John Gummer, Secretary of State for the Environment, to industry to come up with a plan for recovering between 50 per cent and 75 per cent of packaging waste by the year 2000. This report is the PRG's plan which it presented to the DoE and DTI.

The report proposes to 'recover value from' 58 per cent of packaging waste by the year 2000. An industry-wide organization called VALPAK is to be set up to administer the plan. PRG takes the view that a voluntary system would not work as some parties would attempt to opt out. Therefore, legislative backing to enforce compliance by all members of the packaging chain will be necessary and the Government has promised to introduce this soon. Revenue to fund the plan will be collected as a levy on packaging materials by VALPAK. Local authorities would retain responsibility for domestic waste collection and sorting.

3.8.10.   Proposed Directive on Landfill

The proposal for a Council Directive on the landfill of waste (91/C190/1) as amended (COM (93) 275 final, OJ No. C 212/33) is nearing adoption; the Council reached a common position on it on 9/10 June 1994. The proposal applies to landfills, transfer stations and storage facilities; all are required to obtain a permit before operating. Many of the proposal's requirements represent current trends in the UK.

Landfills are classified into three types: for hazardous waste; for municipal and non-hazardous waste; and for inert waste. A landfill may receive multiple classification provided that the disposal operations are carried out in separate areas of the site. Independently of classification wastes can be assigned to a mono-landfill, i.e. a landfill where only one type of waste is deposited.

The proposed directive provides that certain kinds of waste are not acceptable in a landfill; i.e. waste

1   In liquid state, unless compatible with the type of waste acceptable in that individual landfill
2   Which is explosive, oxidizing, highly flammable or flammable or
3   Arising from medical or veterinary establishments.

The proposed directive requires monitoring to be carried on after disposal has stopped to ensure that the landfill has stabilized. There are requirements regarding after-care for a closed landfill. The operator of the landfill shall remain in charge for at least ten years. At least thirty years after closure of the landfill or for as long as needed if the site poses an active risk, leachate from the site and the groundwater shall be monitored and analysed.

Member states are required to ensure that the operator provides a financial guarantee to cover the estimated cost of the closure procedures and after-care operations of the landfill. The guarantee shall be kept as long as the operator is in charge of the maintenance and after-care operations of the site.

Landfill after-care funds are also to be established to cover the normal after-care costs of a closed landfill and the costs of works necessary to prevent environmental damage produced by the disposal of waste where this is not covered by the financial guarantee or insurance. The fund shall not cover the costs that can be directly charged to the landfill operator as long as he or she is liable. Also the financial guarantee does not free the operator from contribution to the fund.

References

Commission of the European Communities, *A Community Strategy for Waste Management*, SEC (89) 934 final.

Commission v Council Case C-300/89, *Journal of Environmental Law*, 4/1, 109 (Titanium Dioxide Case).

DoE, *Action on Litter—A Consultation Paper*, July (1989).

DoE, *Special Waste and the Control of its Disposal*, a Consultation Paper (1990a).

DoE, *Third International Conference on the Protection of the North Sea—UK Guidance Note on the Ministerial Declaration* (1990b).

DoE, *The Control of Pollution (Amendment) Act 1989*, Circular 11/91.

DoE, *The Duty of Care: A Code of Practice*, HMSO (1991a).

DoE, *A Code of Practice on Litter and Refuse*, HMSO, (1991b).

DoE, Draft *Waste Disposal Planning under the Environmental Protection Agency* (1992).

DoE, PPG 23 on *Planning and Pollution Control* (1994).

DoE, Draft WMP No. 2/3, *The Preparation of Waste Disposal (Management) Plans* (1993a).

DoE, *Landfill Costs and Prices: Correcting Possible Market Distortions*, HMSO (1993b).

DoE, *Externalities from Landfill and Incineration*, HMSO (1993c).

DoE, *UK Landfill Practice: Co-disposal* (1993d).

DoE, Draft *UK Action Plan for Phasing Out and Destruction of PCBs* (1993c).

DoE, Draft WMP No. 6 on PCBs (1993f).

DoE, WMP No. 4, *Licensing of Waste Management Facilities*, HMSO (1994a).

DoE, WMP No. 26A, *Landfill Completion*, HMSO (1994b).

DoE, *The Environmental Protection Act 1990, Waste Management Licensing and the Framework Directive on Waste*, Circular 11/94, HMSO.

ENDS Report No. 226, 'Waste producer misses a trick in duty of care case', 45, November (1993a).

ENDS Report No. 222, 'Waste carrier convicted for failure to disclose offence', 47, July (1993b).

ENDS Report No. 217, 'Howard's permissive approach to waste carrier registration', 13, February (1993c).

ENDS Report No. 222, 'Programme on priority waste streams cut back', 42, July (1993d).

Goethem, A.V., 'Packaging and packaging waste: the regulatory framework in the twelve EU member states', *Europe Environment* (1993).

House of Commons Environment Committee, *Toxic Waste*, Session 1988-89, HMSO.

House of Commons Environment Committee, *Contaminated Land*, Session 1989-90, HMSO.

North Sea Conference, 'Ministerial declaration on the Third International Conference on the Protection of the North Sea', The Hague, 8 March 1990.

Lombardia case (Comitato di Coordinamento per la Difesa della Cava v Regione Lombardia—C-236/92) decided on 23 February 1994.

London, C. and Llamas, M., 'Packaging laws in France and Germany', *Journal of Environmental Law*, 6/1 (1994).

Producer Responsibility Industry Group, *Real Value for Packaging Waste—A Way Forward* (1994).

RCEP, *Managing Waste: The Duty of Care*, 11th Report, Cm 9675, HMSO (1985).

RCEP, *Incineration of Waste*, 17th Report, Cm 2181, HMSO (1993).

R v Avon CC ex parte Terry Adams Co. Ltd, Times Law Reports, 20 January 1994.
R v Metropolitan Stipendiary Magistrate ex parte London Waste Regulation Authority and Berkshire CC v Scott, Times Law Reports, 14 January 1993.
Vassesso and Zanetti, Case C-206 and C-207 (1990) 2 *Land Management and Environmental Law Report* 133.

4

Contaminated Land and Liabilities

According to the DoE, contaminated land is 'land which represents an actual or potential hazard to health or the environment as a result of current or previous use' (House of Commons Environment Committee, 1989–90). Exactly how much land is contaminated in the UK is uncertain, no study having been conducted to determine the point. Estimates therefore range widely and there is no way of telling how accurate any of them may be; each depends on the assumptions on which it is based.

4.1 An End-use Policy

Traditionally, government policy in relation to contaminated land has been to encourage its reclamation and development for beneficial use, contamination being seen principally as a constraint on the use to which the land may be put. To this end, grants have been made available for the redevelopment of land which is incapable of use without treatment because of damage from past use. Such land is referred to as 'derelict land', a category which more often than not overlaps with contaminated land (House of Commons Report).

No provision is made specifically for contaminated land since contamination becomes a problem only when the land is being considered for redevelopment. The House of Commons Environment Committee criticized this policy on the ground that it ignores the environmental and health and safety threats posed by contaminated land whether or not it is in active use, an example being the threat of groundwater pollution.

The Derelict Land Grant is the main source of funding targeted specifically at the treatment of derelict land and it is available to both local and other public authorities as well as the private sector. Provision for the grant is made by the **Derelict Land Act 1982** and the grant is intended to ensure that the redevelopment of derelict land costs the same amount as if the development had taken place on a site that is not derelict, i.e. a 'green field' site (DoE, 1993a). Expenditure under the scheme was forecast to reach £105.96 million in

1992/3 (DoE, 1993b). The grants were previously administered by the DoE but, in 1994, this responsibility was transferred in England and Wales to the Urban Regeneration Agency (also called English Partnerships), a new body set up in 1993 under the **Leasehold Reform, Housing and Urban Development Act 1993** with the remit of urban regeneration.

With the traditional end-use policy towards contaminated land, the level of treatment considered desirable in any particular case is dependent on the particular end-use envisaged. Use for residential purposes would require higher standards of clean-up than use for industrial purposes, for instance. Therefore, the government has never considered it necessary to specify absolute quality standards for land to be achieved in all circumstances (i.e. a multifunctionality approach). The available standards have been drawn up by the Interdepartmental Committee on the Redevelopment of Contaminated Land (ICRCL), a body set up in 1976 to consider contaminated land-related problems. The ICRCL has now been superseded and its functions taken over by a new division within the DoE, the Contaminated Land and Liabilities Division (CLL), reflecting the recent concern with the issue of potential civil and criminal liabilities associated with ownership or control over contaminated land.

In the decade and a half of its existence the ICRCL issued eight guidance notes on contaminated land as follows:

ICRCL 17/78—landfill sites
ICRCL 18/79—gasworks sites
ICRCL 23/79—sewage works and farms
ICRCL 42/80—scrapyards and similar sites
ICRCL 59/83—assessment and redevelopment of contaminated land
ICRCL 61/84—fire hazards of contaminated land
ICRCL 64/85—asbestos on contaminated sites
ICRCL 70/90—restoration and after-care of metalliferous mining sites for
    pasture and grazing.

The guidance notes set 'trigger concentrations' for a limited range of contaminants which are related to particular end-uses to assist in determining the significance of contamination found on-site. There are two kinds of trigger concentrations: 'threshold' and 'action'. If samples show values below the threshold concentration the site may be regarded as uncontaminated and development may proceed. If, however, the sample results exceed the action concentration some remedial action will be necessary before the particular development envisaged may proceed or, in the alternative, a different form of use can be considered (see ICRL 59/83). Underscoring the end-use orientation of contaminated land policy, these trigger concentrations do not apply to sites already in use. In any case, the ICRCL trigger concentrations cover only a limited number of contaminants.

4.2.   Clean-up Provisions

Thus current policy on contaminated land does not make adequate provision for the environmental and health and safety implications of leaving contaminants in place. This position is compounded by the absence of robust legal mechanisms for requiring the clean-up of pollutants, even in situations where there are potential health implications.

Land contamination is a material planning consideration which the planning authority needs to take into account before issuing planning permission (DoE, 1994). However, as the DoE PPG points out, a balance has to be struck between the risks and liabilities posed by land contamination and the need to bring the land back into beneficial use. The fact of contamination does not mean therefore that planning permission will not be granted; it may simply point to the need for remedial action before development. Second, the Building Regulations 1991, SI No. 2768 require precautions to be taken to avoid danger to health and safety caused by substances found on or in the ground to be covered by the building.

More widely cited in recent times are provisions under which various enforcement authorities could require action to be taken to clean up contaminated sites or, alternatively, do so themselves and recover their expenses from the person responsible, the land-owner or occupier, as the case may be. These provisions are available in a range of circumstances.

4.2.1   Amenity of Land

Section 215 of the **Town and Country Planning Act 1990** enables a local planning authority who believes that the amenity of a part of their area, or of an adjoining area, is adversely affected by the condition of land in their area to serve on the owner and occupier a notice requiring specified steps to be taken for remedying the condition of the land. Failure to comply with the notice is a criminal offence.

An appeal may be made against the notice to the magistrates' court on grounds including that the condition of the land is attributable to, and is such as results in the ordinary course of events from, the carrying on of operations or use of land which is not in contravention of planning requirements. If the notice is not complied with, the local planning authority may carry out the works and recover their expenses under s. 219.

4.2.2   Statutory Nuisance

Section 80 of the **EPA 1990** enables the local authority who believes that a statutory nuisance exists, or is likely to occur or recur, to serve an abatement notice requiring the execution of works to abate the nuisance. Failure to comply with the notice is a criminal offence and there are provisions for an appeal to the magistrates' court. The notice is served on:

1   The person responsible for the nuisance
2   Where the nuisance arises from a structural defect, the owner of the premises or
3   Where the person responsible cannot be found, the owner or occupier.

The local authority may abate the nuisance and recover their costs from the person responsible and, if that person is the owner of the premises, from the 'owner for the time being'.

4.2.3   Unlawfully Deposited Waste

Section 59 of the **EPA 1990** enables the waste regulatory authority in whose area controlled waste is unlawfully deposited to serve a notice on the occupier requiring him or her to remove the waste and/or take steps to reduce or eliminate the consequences of the deposit. The notice may be quashed on appeal to the magistrates' court if the person neither deposited nor knowingly caused nor knowingly permitted the deposit.

It is an offence not to comply with the requirements of the notice. The authority may remove the waste and recover their expenses from the occupier of the land or the person who knowingly deposited or knowingly caused or knowingly permitted the deposit. A similar provision under s. 61 of the EPA 1990 was not brought into force.

4.2.4   Water Pollution

Section 161 of the **Water Resources Act 1991** enables the NRA to carry out anti-pollution works to remove or dispose of polluting matter, remedy or mitigate its polluting effects or restore the waters (including any flora or fauna) to their previous state. The NRA may recover their expenses from the person who caused or knowingly permitted the polluting matter to be present in the place from where it was likely to enter controlled waters, or to be present in controlled waters.

Bruton and National Rivers Authority v Clarke represents the only case to date where the NRA has recovered its costs under these provisions. The case arose from a discharge of pig slurry into controlled waters when a lagoon burst, resulting in the death of many fish. The NRA's criminal prosecution failed on a technicality not connected with the liability of the defendant. In a subsequent civil suit the defendant admitted liability for the discharge.

The first plaintiff sued as the representative of the local anglers association and sought damage for loss of amenity (i.e. not getting the fish they had paid for) arising from the effect of the pollution incident on fisheries. The NRA sought to recover its costs for restocking fish. Its claim was based on s. 46 of the **Control of Pollution Act 1974** (which was replaced by s. 161 WRA) and on negligence. The court dismissed the negligence claim on the ground that a regulatory body cannot sue in negligence for economic loss when no property interest of its own has been damaged but upheld the s. 46 claim. The NRA won £90 000 and the first plaintiff £16 890 (ENDS, 1994a).

There are few instances of reliance on clean-up powers to require contaminants to be removed. Anectodotal evidence indicates that some polluters of groundwater have voluntarily carried out remedial measures apparently on the basis that if they did not carry out the remedial works then the NRA would rely on s. 161. Thus, for instance, it has been reported that Eastern Counties Leather plc, the defendant in *the Cambridge Water Company case* (see Chapter 12), agreed a clean-up plan with the NRA involving the removal of solvent from the aquifer (ENDS, 1994b). Details of these cases are not in the public domain, however, and therefore the considerations which led the polluters concerned to take voluntary action can only be speculated upon.

The principal difficulty facing regulators attempting to exercise clean-up powers is that the regulator concerned has to spend money first in the hope of recovering it. At a time of shrinking government grants, expenditure based on no more than the hope of recovering the money, most likely through court action, cannot be embarked upon lightly. The legal mechanism for financing clean-up must, therefore, make provision for funding to be obtained from identified sources in advance of the clean-up.

4.3 Proposals for Reform

The lack of robust legislative measures for tackling contaminated land led to a wide-ranging review of the issue by the House of Commons Environment Committee. The Committee recommended that local authorities should be required to compile registers of contaminated land which would be made publicly available. Registers would solve what the Committee saw as the 'biggest single problem with the existing system of control', the lack of identification of contaminated sites (House of Commons Environment Committee, 1990).

The government's view was that registers showing actual contamination of land were impractical since local authorities would have to spend a great deal of money conducting surveys before they could compile the registers. Further, if the registers were to be kept up to date these surveys would have to be continuous. The government therefore enacted in s. 143 of the **EPA 1990** a duty on local authorities to compile and maintain registers of land currently or previously put to a 'contaminative use', that is, any use of land which may cause it to be contaminated by noxious substances. The particular uses were to be specified in Regulations. It was argued that the information would help to identify land which may be contaminated and which therefore should be investigated

by developers and others with an interest in the land who could then take remedial action as necessary if actual contamination was identified; the registers
would thus act as a warning.

After two abortive attempts to lay Regulations identifying contaminative
uses, in May 1991 and in July 1992, the government, in March 1993, abandoned the plan to lay the Regulations mainly as a result of a sustained campaign
by diverse interest groups who feared that property listed on the registers
would be blighted (DoE, 1993c). When withdrawing the registers plan the
government cited three problems in that registers would:

1   Include uncontaminated sites simply because they had been put to a use
    appearing in the Regulations but exclude other sites actually contaminated
    by unlisted uses
2   Record the history of a site making it impossible to remove a site from the
    register even after remediation and
3   Make no provision for the action to be taken when sites were identified as
    actually contaminated and who would be liable for the cost of remediation
    or compensation.

The government instead announced a review of all the issues arising from land
contamination. As part of the review a consultation paper, *Paying for Our Past*,
was published 'to gather informed and structured views of interested parties on
the key issues identified by the review'. This paper reaffirmed the government's
commitment to the end-use approach to the clean-up of contaminated land.
The paper pointed out that this did not preclude the owner, occupier or developer from undertaking earlier or more thorough action or the regulatory authority from requiring remediation where necessary (DoE, 1994a). In November
1994 the DoE put forward formal proposals in 'Framework for Contaminated
Land'. They involve defining the circumstances under which contaminated
land constitutes a statutory nuisance to be dealt with under Part III of the EPA
1990 (DoE, 1994b).

The government's commitment to an end-use approach was incorporated
into the proposal for reform put forward by the Royal Institution of Chartered
Surveyors which was to link remediation requirements to the planning process.
Under this scheme a 'land quality statement' would have to be submitted to the
planning authority before planning permission could be granted. The proposal
was criticized because the rate at which clean-up proceeded would depend on
the rate of development and sale of land, and not on the extent and degree of
the contaminated land problem (CBI, 1993).

The third proposal, canvassed occasionally for tackling the problem of the
lack of identification of contaminated sites, is to reverse the *caveat emptor* rule.
Caveat emptor, 'let the buyer beware', is a common law rule under which the
buyer makes his or her own judgement about the condition of the item of purchase. The rule has been much attenuated by exceptions but not to the extent

that a seller would be expected to disclose to the buyer information he or she has about the condition of the property being sold.

The proposal which was put forward by the Conveyancing Standing Committee of the Law Commission in March 1989 was to place a duty on the seller to disclose all material facts of which the seller is aware. The justification for the proposal was that the seller is best placed to know the condition of his or her property (Law Commission, 1989). This proposal was not welcome, however, primarily because of the widespread fear that a seller may find itself under an obligation to survey its property for any contamination before putting it on the market. Such a solution to making information about contamination available might create more problems than it solves. The priciple is, however, being reviewed as part of the consultation exercise currently going on.

The search for funding for clean-up of contamination has gone beyond the industrial operator to include the financial sector, the business community generally and the insurance industry. The potential liability of these sectors for clean-up arises against the background of uncertain and vaguely worded legal provisions. The key question relates to the circumstances in which a person who was not primarily responsible for the polluting incident may be liable for the clean-up.

4.4 The Financial Sector and the Business Community

4.4.1 The Basis for Liability

The nature of the problem is encapsulated in a speech in 1993 by an environment minister to the British Banker's Association, in which he said

> Deciding what the liability should be and when it should fall on the polluter, the owner, or the state is not easy. For the polluter, the operator of a process, the person who left a polluting mess behind, has a responsibility. So have many landowners. So too does a prudent but constructive [sic] bank (DoE, 1993d).

The stage was set by the US Comprehensive Environmental Response Compensation and Liability Act (CERCLA), the so-called Superfund legislation. CERCLA imposed imposed strict joint and several liability on those responsible for disposing of waste substances to a facility, i.e. 'potentially responsible parties'. Liability stretches to current owners of sites, former owners and operators, those who arranged for the disposal of the substances at the facility and those who transported the substances to the facility. Also liable are all those who exercised control over the substances, whether directors, officers, shareholders or lenders but excluding those who, without participating in the management of the facility, hold a security interest (e.g. secured lenders) (Novick *et al.*, 1994).

In the *Fleet Factors case* the court held that the determining factor for liability was the nature and extent of the creditor's involvement in the facility, not whether its motive was simply to protect its security interest. Further, the touchstone for determining whether a lender had participated is financial management, as opposed to participation in waste management. The Environmental Protection Agency subsequently issued a Lender Liability Rule which sought to clarify the extent to which a lender could participate in the management of the facility without forfeiting its exemption, but this attempt failed when the court in *Kelly v EPA* held that the EPA lacked jurisdiction to adjudicate the scope of CERCLA liability (Novick *et al.*, 1994).

The UK business and financial community have come down firmly against any mechanism for funding clean-up of contaminated land which is patterned on the Superfund. According to the CBI, the existing rules on causation and the definition of potentially responsible parties must be retained or modified only if a lender exemption is provided. The CBI also argues that joint and several liability should be rejected:

> Lenders should not face liability for the remediation costs of their customers as a result of lending, providing financial advice to management, when they hold the charge of borrower's assets, when they enforce security, or in situations where they endeavour to get a firm in financial difficulties back on its feet or sold (CBI, 1993).

These arguments have been met with caution because of concern that a general lender exemption might lead to contaminated assets being transferred to 'ring-fenced' underfunded companies. *Paying for Our Past*, for instance, pointed out that 'in the complex business world of diversified control, ownership and participation in profits, regulators should not be prevented from attributing costs alongside responsibility where that is shared or the legal liability has been transferred'. Whereas fear of liability could inhibit lending towards polluting activities, the weight of opinion appears to be that regulators should be able to pursue parties other than the polluter for recovery of clean-up costs.

4.4.2 Liability under Current Provisions

Liability under the provisions currently in place might arise where the lender is considered to be either the owner or occupier of the contaminated site or to have knowingly permitted the pollution (see 4.2 'Clean-up Provisions'). The potential risks for the owner/occupier arise in various situations, including where the lender forecloses or otherwise holds title as security. A receiver appointed to realize and manage a company's property potentially risks incurring criminal responsibility as well as s. 161 liability for causing or knowingly permitting polluting activities. If the receiver obtains rents from the property he or she may be considered its 'owner'. The issue of knowingly permitting relates to the degree of involvement in the management of the activities of the polluting operator.

Tower Hamlets BC v London Docklands Development Corporation illustrates potential liability in these circumstances. The LDDC was charged with knowingly permitting works to be carried out in breach of a COPA noise consent while the contractors were charged, and convicted, of breaching the consent. LDDC had appointed consulting engineers to supervise the works and acoustic experts to monitor the noise. Evidence emerged from minutes of various meetings that LDDC was aware of the breaches. The court held that LDDC did not take reasonable steps to prevent the contractors from breaching the consent such as suspending part of the work, refusing to pay for it, forbidding the use of certain plant or, as a last resort, terminating the contract.

A lender may also risk liability through the principles governing the liability of a 'shadow director' (Pickworth, 1994). In *Re Hydrodam (Corby) Ltd (in liquidation)* the court defined a shadow director as a person who is not held out as a director, does not claim or purport to be a director and 'lurks in the shadows, sheltering behind others who, he claims, are the only directors of the company to the exclusion of himself'.

In spite of appearances a shadow director directs the ostensible directors how to act in relation to the company and they act in accordance with such directions. In *Re a Company* the court held that a company's bank, which had commissioned a financial report into the company's affairs and took steps to ensure the implementation of the report's recommendations, could be a shadow director of the company. Similarly, in *Re Tasbian Ltd (No. 3)* the court held that a management consultant appointed to advise and assist in the recovery of a company in financial difficulties could be a shadow director.

The extent to which these principles, which have been developed in the context of company law, could be transferred to environmental control are unclear since there is no case law at present. Questions therefore remain regarding the potential risk to a lender in commissioning an environmental audit and requiring the borrower to implement its recommendations or, alternatively, not insisting that the borrower act on its recommendations where it reveals pollution problems. It may be that the current government review will clarify some of these questions.

4.5   The Insurance Industry

The insurance industry has been drawn into the discussion regarding funding for clean-up of contaminated land primarily on account of its role in risk management. A contract of insurance is an agreement whereby the insurer, in return for a premium, undertakes to pay money to the insured in the event of the insured suffering economic loss. The validity of a contract of insurance is premised on the insurer having an 'insurable interest' which the law recognizes. An example of an insurable interest is a legal or contractual liability to which the insured may be exposed in either tort or contract. A contract insuring such an interest is known as 'liability insurance'. An insurance policy taken out to protect the insured against legal liability for accidental bodily injury to third parties or loss of or damage to their property is called a public liability policy (Kluwer).

The nature of an insurance contract (with the exception of life insurance) is that it is a contract of indemnity, the insurer undertaking to compensate, i.e. indemnify, the insured in the event of loss. Professional indemnity (PI) insurance, which covers professional advisors in the event that their advice causes loss to a client, takes its name from this feature of insurance contracts.

As a general rule a public liability policy covers liability arising from pollution unless specifically excluded. The terms used to refer to this kind of insurance are either Pollution Liability Insurance (PLI) or Environmental Impairment Liability Insurance (EIL) (Fields, 1993). In an attempt to limit its exposure to pollution claims, largely as a result of compensation claims in the United States, the Association of British Insurers (ABI) on 23 July 1990 recommended that insurers include wording on their policies excluding liability for gradual, as opposed to accidental, pollution which would continue to be covered. The wording was to the effect that the policy excluded liability in respect of pollution other than that 'caused by a sudden, identifiable, unintended and unexpected incident which takes place in its entirety at a specific time and place during the period of insurance'. British insurers adopted this wording with effect from April 1991 (ABI, 1990).

A claim under a public liability policy is triggered by an 'incident' occurring, hence the policy is written on an 'occurrence basis'. Typically, a claim will only be made when an injury or damage manifests itself and complex questions about the validity of the claim may arise where the injury or damage is not contemporaneous with the incident. To take the facts of the *Cambridge Water Company case*, the 'incident' was the spillage of solvent in the 1960s and 1970s and the injury or damage was the detection of the solvent in the water forcing the closure of the borehole in 1983. In the period between 1960 and 1983 a number of public liability insurance policies may have been written and the question arises whether all or any of them cover the damage. It is possible that several or all the policies would be held jointly and severally liable for the claims. This factor has led to another development in the way policies are written, i.e. so that they cover only the claims made in the year of the policy, regardless of when the incident occurred. Policies of this kind are referred to as 'claims-made' policies (Fields, 1993).

Insurance is a mechanism for managing risk. It transfers the risk of economic loss to an insurance company which spreads it among many policy holders. Premiums are calculated on the basis of the perception of the degree of risk entailed by the operation, higher risks attracting higher premiums. Risk which is so high as to amount to a near-certainty is often uninsurable, insurers fearing that the chance of loss is so high as to make the business not worth while. Ironically, those who need insurance most (because of the likelihood that they will suffer loss) are least likely to get it while those who need it least are the most likely to obtain an insurance policy. Environmental impairment liability insurance is an excellent illustration of this, insurers being prepared to offer a policy to only those operators who have in place effective environmental management systems to limit the potential for environmental damage (*Lloyd's List*, 1993)

EIL insurance is now difficult to obtain largely because of the massive claims made in the United States as a result of both asbestos injuries and contaminated land clean-up liabilities arising out of the Superfund legislation. British insurers, who often re-insure American policies, have suffered massive losses from claims made at times after a search in the archives has unearthed old policies, a practice now known as 'insurance archeology'. The potential for claims to be made under Superfund has forced an exit from the EIL market.

To obtain EIL insurance, operators must be able to demonstrate that the risk is low. This requires that they carry out an environmental audit of their activities backing it up with a programme of environmental good practice and improvement. The cover remains low, currently not exceeding several million pounds and thus inadequate to cover any major environmental incident (*Lloyd's List*, 1993). In the face of this 'captive' insurance companies are being viewed as a way to manage the risk of environmental liability.

A captive insurance company is a company owned by another to insure the risks of the parent company and its subsidiaries. Setting up a captive is considered advantageous over making provision by way of savings because a captive, like any other insurance company, can reinsure, thereby reducing its exposure. However, only large operators can afford captives since the capital outlay is large (Harvey and Simmons, 1993).

Civil liability inevitably raises the issue of insurability since insurance is a means of controlling the risk of economic loss. A number of legislative provisions have imposed a requirement that the operator carry adequate financial provision; often this will be by way of an insurance policy. Examples include the waste management provisions under Part II of the EPA 1990 which require evidence that the operator has made financial provision for contingent liabilities; the proposed EC landfill directive which requires an after-care fund to be set up; and the Council of Europe Convention on Civil Liability which also requires an after-care fund.

Since insurers link the availability of insurance cover to the quality of the insured's risk management this may promote better environmental management among operators. But if operators are required to carry insurance as a condition of their licence, there is a risk that insurers become the effective 'licensors' of operators, providing or withholding insurance cover on the basis of their assessment of the environmental management record of the operator seeking cover. This would expose operators to unjustifiably high premium demands and operators are on the whole opposed to compulsory insurance provisions. Insurers too are not in favour of finding themselves in the role of environmental regulators.

References

ABI (Association of British Insurers), Ref. G/250/065, 23 July (1990).

Bruton and National Rivers Authority v Clarke (1993, unrep.), County Court, Cambridge, Case No. 9004906, dated 23 July 1993.

CBI, *Firm Foundations: CBI proposals for environmental liability and contaminated land* (1993).

DoE, *Derelict Land Grant: Guidance Note*, Advice Note 3 (1993a).

DoE, *Derelict Land Grant: Developments and Achievement Report 1988–92* (1993b).

DoE, 'Michael Howard announces review of land pollution responsibilities', Press Release No. 209, 24 March (1993c).

DoE, *Paying for Our Past: The Arrangements for Controlling Contaminated Land and Meeting the Costs of Remedying the Damage to the Environment*, A DoE/WO Consultation Paper, March (1994a).

DoE, 'Framework for Contaminated Land' (1994b).

DoE, 'Minister challenges bankers on environmental commitments', Press Release No. 658, 13 October (1993d).

DoE, PPG 23, *Planning and Pollution Control*, HMSO (1994).

ENDS Report No. 232, 'Civil claim costs farmer £106 000', p. 45, May (1994a).

ENDS Report No. 233, 'Compromise on aquifer clean-up at Eastern Counties Leather', p. 7, June (1994b).

Fields, R., 'Impact of Cambridge water', paper presented at the 5th Annual IBC Conference on Risk Management and Insurance of Pollution, Environmental Management and Waste, 27/28 September 1993, London, IBC Financial Focus Ltd, 57/61 Mortimer Street, London, W1N 7TD, UK.

House of Commons Environment Committee, *Contaminated Land*, Session 1989–90, HMSO (1990).

Kluwer's *Handbook of Insurance*, Kluwer Publishing.

Harvey, M. and Simmons, A., 'To what extent can captives deal with pollution risk?', IBC 5th Annual Conference (1993).

Law Commission, *Caveat Emptor in Sales of Land: A Consultation Paper from the Conveyancing Standing Committee of the Law Commission* (1989).

Lloyd's List, 'Pollution insurance', pp. 8–9, 24 June (1993).

Novick, A. *et al.*, *Law of Environmental Protection*, Environmental Law Institute, Clark, Boardman, Callaghan, New York, Vol. 3, 13 May (1994).

Pickworth, J., 'Avoiding the spotlight: the role of the shadow director', *In House Lawyer* (IHL), 12 April (1994).

Re a Company (1989) BCLC 113.

Re Tasbian Ltd (No. 3) (1991) BCLC 792.

Re Hydrodam (Corby) Ltd (in liquidation), *The Times* 19 February (1994).

Tower Hamlets BC v London Docklands Development Corporation (1992, unrep.).

5

The Control of Atmospheric Pollution

5.1 Integrated Pollution Control

Like water pollution, statutory control of air pollution in the UK dates back to
Victorian times. The first **Alkali Act** was passed in 1863, targeted at the alkali
industry, the most serious cause of industrial air pollution at the time. This,
and subsequent Alkali Acts, were consolidated into the **Alkali etc. Works
Regulation Act 1906**, parts of which are still in force. Under it the Alkali
Inspectorate regulated alkali and other industrial processes, requiring them to
use the 'best practicable means' (BPM) to arrest noxious or offensive gases
within the plant and prevent their escape into the atmosphere. The concept of
BPM left discretion in the hands of the Alkali Inspectorate to balance the cost
consequences of achieving the statutory objective of controlling noxious or
offensive gases. It was described at the time as an elastic band, tightening with
developments in pollution abatement technology and changes in an industry's
financial situation.

In its 5th Report, the Royal Commission on Environmental Pollution
argued that wastes, whether solid, liquid or gaseous, should be disposed of into
the particular environmental medium where they would do the least overall
environmental damage. In the Commission's words, in disposing of wastes, the
'best practicable environmental option' (BPEO) should be adopted (RCEP,
1976). The Royal Commission on Environmental Pollution defined the
concept in a subsequent report as follows:

> A 'bpeo' is the outcome of a systematic consultative decision making procedure
> which emphasizes the protection and conservation of the environment across land,
> air and water. The 'bpeo' procedure establishes, for a given set of objectives, the
> option that provides the most benefit or least damage to the environment as a whole,
> at acceptable cost, in the long term as well as in the short term (RCEP, 1988).

ver

The government accepted this approach to pollution control on the basis
that 'the environment functions as an integrated whole' (DoE, 1988) and

133

proposed introducing into law a system of 'integrated pollution control' (IPC) to cover releases into all three environmental media from 5 000 or so major industrial processes. In charge of this system would be Her Majesty's Inspectorate of Pollution (HMIP) which had been set up in 1987 to carry the mantle of the old Alkali Inspectorate in England and Wales, and Her Majesty's Industrial Pollution Inspectorate (HMIPI) in Scotland. An IPC system therefore goes beyond merely a system for air pollution control; it is a system of controlling pollution in respect of all three environmental media.

The IPC system, subsequently implemented in Part I of the EPA 1990, marks an important stage in the evolution of the control system operated under the Alkali Acts. At the same time, it is a mechanism for implementing in the UK requirements of EC Directives relating to prior approval of industrial processes and the need to use the best available technology not entailing excessive costs to prevent or minimize noxious emissions. But the IPC system goes further; it requires the process operator to use not the best practicable means, nor the best available technology, but the best available 'techniques' not entailing excessive costs (BATNEEC). 'Techniques' is believed to incorporate not just hardware (e.g. pollution-abatement equipment) but software and manpower as well, i.e. the entire management system applied in the process.

5.1.1   Prescribed Processes and Substances

Section 2 of the EPA 1990 gives the Secretary of State power to make regulations specifying the processes which need to be authorized before they can be carried on. The Secretary of State may, additionally, specify substances whose release into the environment must be authorized in a similar fashion. Such processes and substances are referred to as 'prescribed processes and substances'. In prescribing a process or a substance the Secretary of State may designate it as one for central control, thus putting it under the control of HMIP or HMIPI, or as one for local control, thus putting it under the control of the local authority in whose area the process is carried on. The reason for this is that the IPC system is aimed at only the most polluting industrial processes. Less polluting processes are still subject to the single medium pollution control system, and in the case of emissions to air, such processes are controlled by local authorities and referred to as local authority air pollution control (LAAPC) processes.

In 1991 the Secretary of State made the Environmental Protection (Prescribed Processes and Substances) Regulations 1991, SI No. 472, which have since been amended four times, most recently by SI 1994 No. 1271 and SI 1994 No. 1329. The Regulations prescribe processes and substances for both IPC and LAAPC. They categorize the processes into Part A processes which are under HMIP's control, and Part B processes which are under LAAPC. Unlike Part B processes which have already come under local authority control, Part A processes are being brought into the IPC system in phases rather than all at once. It will be 1996 before all the Part A processes come under the IPC system. Processes which have not yet come into the IPC system remain under the **Alkali Act 1906** which will be repealed once this process is complete.

Six processes are prescribed:

1   Fuel production and combustion processes
2   Metal production and processing
3   Mineral industries
4   The chemical industry
5   Waste disposal and recycling
6   'Other industries' such as paper and pulp manufacturing and coating and printing processes.

These processes reflect those listed in the EC Directive 84/360/EEC which deals with air pollution from industrial plants and requires member states to instal a system of prior authorization for such processes and ensure that operators employ BATNEEC to minimize emissions. Fuel production and combustion processes, waste disposal and recycling processes and the minerals industry processes were brought into the IPC system in 1992 while the chemical industry was brought into the system in 1993, apart from inorganic chemical processes which were brought in 1994. Metal production and processing and the other industries category are scheduled for 1995. Combustion processes of over 50 MW, however, came under IPC on 1 April 1991 because of the need to implement EC Directive 88/609 on large combustion plants.

Unlike processes, substances are prescribed on the basis of the medium into which they are to be released: substances prescribed for release into air are drawn from Directive 84/360/EEC on air pollution from industrial plants; substances prescribed for release into water are drawn from the 'Red List'; and substances prescribed for release into land are drawn from special wastes. 'Red List' substances are listed in the Trade Effluents (Prescribed Processes and Substances) Regulations 1989, SI No. 1156 as amended (see 2.2.5 'Special Category Effluent' in Chapter 2), while special wastes are defined in the Control of Pollution (Special Wastes) Regulations 1980 SI No. 1709 (see 3.2.3 'Special Waste' in Chapter 3).

A process releasing any of the prescribed substances into any of the three media falls under the control of HMIP and not, in the case of 'Red List' substances, the sewerage undertaker, or, in the case of special waste, waste regulatory authorities. Nevertheless, these other regulatory authorities do retain control in certain crucial aspects: HMIP does not regulate the landfilling of wastes; it has to include in its authorizations conditions which the NRA considers necessary; and it cannot authorize a process if the NRA certifies that releases from the process will result in, or contribute to, a failure to achieve any statutory water quality objective (see 2.2.1 'Statutory WQOs' in Chapter 2).

5.1.2 Jurisdiction

That there are two parallel systems of control for HMIP and local authorities raises the prospect of dual control in situations where aspects of a process fall under IPC control while other aspects of the same process fall under local authority control. Dual control is undesirable, and the Prescribed Processes and Substances Regulations give rules for avoiding it. The general rule is that a 'process' includes any other process carried on at the same location by the same person. This includes operations related to the main process as long as they fall within the same generic category into which the six prescribed industrial activities are divided.

Subject to some specific exemptions relating to tyres, scrap, wastes and storage drums, the broad effect of this and the other supplementary rules is that an operator carrying on a process which includes two or more processes falling under the same generic category is controlled by HIMP only, even though some of the activities are designated for local authority control. Similarly, where because of use of different fuels or materials or disposal of different wastes, a process at some time falls under HMIP control and at other times under local authority control, the process remains under HMIP control at all times. Finally, the disposal or treatment of waste used in the course of a process is considered to be part of the description of that process.

In relation to Scotland, the IPC system is administered by both HMIPI and the river purification authorities with s. 5 giving the Secretary of State power to make regulations allocating functions between them. The Environmental Protection (Determination of Enforcing Authority etc.) (Scotland) Regulations 1992, SI No. 530 allocates functions as follows: HMIPI is responsible for processes which release prescribed substances into air only, or air and land only, or into all three media, but not those releasing into water only; river purification authorities are responsible for processes which release prescribed substances into water only, or water and land only, but not for those releasing into all three media, or into air only. Additionally, the two regulators have an obligation to consult each other on applications made to either of them for authorization.

5.1.3 The Authorization

An operator needs an authorization to carry out a prescribed process, and s. 6(2) provides that the application is made to the particular regulator responsible for the process. The procedure is set out in both Schedule 1 of the **EPA 1990** and the Environmental Protection (Applications, Appeals and Registers) Regulations 1991, SI No. 507. The application must be accompanied by supplementary information such as the details of the applicant, the process (including its location), the BATNEEC proposed, the substances which will be released and the monitoring proposed and an environmental assessment of the consequences of the proposal.

The regulator may require additional information before deciding on the application. The power to ask for further information is contained in Schedule 1 to the EPA 1990. Consequently the notice requiring further information is referred to as a 'Schedule 1 notice'. Requests for further information inevitably delay the consideration of the application and because of the poor quality of the initial batch of applications Schedule 1 notices were often served. To shorten the time taken considering applications, HMIP has adopted the approach of issuing the authorization but imposing a condition requiring further information to be submitted (ENDS, 1994).

Before deciding the application the regulator must consult a list of persons, unless it relates to waste oil burners, which have an exemption. These consultees are the HSE; MAFF (in England only); the Welsh Secretary (in Wales); the Scottish Secretary (in Scotland); the NRA (where there may be a release into controlled waters in England and Wales); the sewerage undertaker or, in Scotland, the island and regional councils where releases may be made to sewers, the three national Conservancy Councils where SSSIs may be affected; and appropriate harbour authorities.

The application must also be advertised. The applicant may apply to the Secretary of State to be exempted from these requirements on the ground that the information touches on national security or is commercially confidential. A survey of 666 applicants revealed that of 97 claims for commercial confidentiality, 63 had been granted by HMIP (ENDS, 1994).

The application must be decided within four months otherwise it is considered refused unless the applicant and the regulator have agreed a longer time period. This may be necessary in cases of applications which raise complex issues where the necessary information may only become available in stages, as the project progresses towards commissioning. As a large number of waste oil burners have been affected, local authorities (as pollution control authorities for these processes) were granted a blanket extension for authorizing the processes.

If the question whether the information affects national security or is commercially confidential has arisen, the four-month period starts to run from the day a decision is reached on it, and if the decision is appealed, time does not run until the appeal is concluded. Powergen and National Power's applications for combustion plant authorizations (which are under HMIP's control) were not decided for over one year while HMIP waited for the Secretary of State to determine the companies' appeals seeking to keep some information commercially confidential. In the event National Power's appeal succeeded but Powergen's failed (DoE, 1992).

5.1.4   BATNEEC

In operating these processes, the key objective is to use BATNEEC to prevent the release of the prescribed substances, or where that is not practicable, to minimize any releases and render them harmless. Where the process might release the substances into more than one environmental medium, BATNEEC must be used also to minimize the pollution which the releases might cause to the environment taken as a whole. Any releases must be made on the basis of what is best for the environment as a whole, that is, the BPEO.

The twin objectives of BPEO and BATNEEC are unique to the IPC system as against the single-media pollution control systems; BATNEEC alone applies to the LAAPC system. The permit takes into account discharges to all three media on an integrated basis, hence the phrase 'integrated permitting' sometimes heard. The European Commission has put forward an Integrated Pollution Prevention and Control (IPPC) proposal (COM (93) 423, OJ No. C 311, 17/11/93) which would require member states to introduce a system which is quite similar to the UK's IPC system.

HMIP has produced a 'practical guide' which fleshes out the concept of BATNEEC, breaking it down into its constituent parts (HMIP, 1993a). 'Best' means the most effective in preventing, minimizing or rendering harmless polluting releases. 'Available' means procurable. 'Techniques', the only component of the term defined in the **EPA 1990**, embraces both the plant in which the process is carried on and how the process is operated. It includes matters such as numbers and qualification of staff, working methods, training and supervision and the design, construction, layout and maintenance of buildings; in other words, it goes beyond the hardware to incorporate the software, unlike the EC Directive 84/360 on emissions from industrial plants, which it implements.

The 'not entailing excessive costs' limb has two meanings depending on whether it is applied to new or existing processes. In either case, however, should it be that the cost of applying the best available techniques would be excessive in relation to the nature of the industry and the environmental protection to be achieved, the particular 'best available techniques' may be modified on the basis of these economic considerations.

For a new process, the decision over whether the costs entailed are excessive is made on the basis of the following principles:

1   The greater the environmental damage posed by the process, the greater the costs of the 'best available techniques' that can be required before the costs are considered excessive
2   If after applying BATNEEC serious harm would still result the application can be refused
3   Concern is directed at whether costs in general are excessive, with the

unprofitability of the particular business seeking authorization not affecting the determination.

For existing processes there is an additional concern, to establish timescales over which old processes need to be upgraded to the standards applied to new processes or ultimately closed down. This decision is to be made on the basis of factors outlined in the Air Framework Directive (84/360/EEC), which are:

1 The plant's technical characteristics
2 Its rate of utilization and the length of its remaining life
3 The nature and volume of polluting emissions from it and
4 The desirability of not entailing excessive costs for the plant concerned, having regard in particular to the economic situation of undertakings belonging to the category in question.

BATNEEC is expressed as a performance standard, specifying the technique which produces particular release levels, or better. It does not constrain the development of cleaner techniques nor restrict unduly an operator's choice of means to achieve the specified standard. Strictly speaking, BATNEEC is specific to a process but in reality, the BATNEEC for one process is likely to be the BATNEEC for a comparable process, and guidance has therefore been issued on what constitutes BATNEEC for each description of process, specifying, among other things, emission limits which the processes must achieve and the standards expected of operators.

Guidance is in two forms. For the LAAPC system, the Secretary of State has issued seventy-eight UK-wide statutory process guidance notes, running from PG1 to PG5, covering each process, and another five General Guidance Notes (GG1-5) covering general matters such as interpretation of common terms, authorization, applications and appeals. The process of revising guidance has started with the cement industry guidance note being the first to be reissued. One general Upgrading Guidance Note (UG1) has been published to upgrade aspects of previous guidance. Additionally, the DoE has issued a series of non-statutory guidance to local authorities under an Air Quality (AQ) series on concepts such as 'triviality', i.e. emissions which may be disregarded.

The Secretary of State has not issued any guidance for IPC processes. Instead the Chief Inspector of HMIP has adopted the practice of issuing non-statutory guidance to his inspectors, under the reference IPR. The first five guidance documents are industry sector guidance notes for the first five sectors under IPC (IPR 1-5). The second set describe a generic BATNEEC for the inspectors to take into account when dealing with a specific application. HMIP consults publicly on the guidance notes before issuing them, and they are published just before the particular sector comes under IPC control. Guidance for the metal production and processing and the 'other industries' sectors will therefore be issued in time for 1995 when these processes come under IPC.

Additionally, HMIP has started issuing 'Technical Guidance Notes' (TGNs) on various technical issues. Those published so far deal with stack heights for polluting emissions, monitoring emissions, pollution abatement technology for reducing solvent vapour emissions and pollution abatement technology for particulate and trace gas removal (HMIP, 1993b,c, 1994a,b).

There is no statutory duty on the regulators to issue guidance; HMIPI has not issued guidance of this kind, and considers HMIP's guidance as no more than 'persuasive' in Scotland. However, it has issued some brief notes to guide those applying for authorization (Scottish Office, 1992a and 1992b).

5.1.5 Assessing BPEO and BATNEEC

The fundamental change in pollution control which the IPC system introduced were the twin concepts of BPEO and BATNEEC. Yet the key problem identified by the ENDS survey of the way IPC is working in practice is that most applicants do not make an assessment of the potential environmental impact of their process. The reason according to the report of the survey is because 'HMIP has failed to produce clear guidelines on how to assess environmental effects . . .' (ENDS, 1994). In an effort to close this loophole HMIP released for consultation proposals for formalizing the methodology for assessing BPEO and BATNEEC for processes to determine their environmental impact (HMIP, 1994c).

Under this model the applicant is expected to predict the environmental concentration (PEC) of the pollutants that would be released if any of the range of available process options or abatement techniques were used. The PEC will either:

1 Exceed a chosen benchmark (i.e. a statutory limit such as an EQS where one exists, but if one does not, then a non-statutory limit referred to as a 'Regulatory Assessment Level' (RAL) set by HMIP in the interim)
2 Fall below a benchmark, dubbed the 'Action Level', which HMIP has decided is not sufficiently significant to require abatement action (set at 10 per cent of the RAL) or
3 Fall somewhere between the Action Level and the RAL.

In 1 above, an authorization cannot be issued and the applicant has to put forward proposals (i.e. an alternative process or abatement technique) which would reduce the PEC to an accceptable level below the RAL. Number 2 above is the opposite of 1; the PEC is negligible and no additional expenditure for pollution abatement purposes is to be necessary; the process is authorized as BATNEEC. It is 3 above which calls for an assessment of which of the range of process options or abatement techniques represents BATNEEC: BATNEEC is the option which would reduce the PEC as far towards the Action Level as possible without becoming excessively costly. If the option which the applicant chooses is not the process capable of achieving the lowest PEC in the circumstances, the applicant must justify it on the basis of excessive cost, giving details.

To assess BPEO the applicant should express the PEC as a proportion of the EQS or the RAL to create a tolerability quotient (TQ) for each medium (i.e. air, water and land). The various tolerability quotients can then be summed up, giving a BPEO index. Indices can be created in this way for a range of processes and abatement techniques. The option with the minimum index would constitute the BPEO. If it is not the option chosen by the applicant, the chosen option must be justified on the basis of cost, the applicant giving details of the annual costs of the various process options.

These proposals are at an early stage but, if successfully implemented, would introduce objectivity into the assessment of BATNEEC and BPEO.

5.1.6 Variations

An authorization may be subject to a variation which can be initiated by both the regulator, at times at the instigation of the Secretary of State, or the operator. Variations are necessary because of the need to keep BATNEEC up to date; as pollution control techniques improve, or as the perception of environmental risk changes, the standards can be expected to change. In fact, conditions in any authorization are required to be reviewed at least every four years. The procedure is to serve a 'variation notice' on the operator specifying the variations and the date on which they are to take effect. The operator must then inform the regulator of the action he or she proposes to take to implement the variation. The action may involve making a 'substantial change' to the process. If it does, the proposed change must be publicized and consulted on as if it were a fresh application. Each of the process guidance notes indicate what change to that process would be considered substantial. A change is either 'substantial' or 'relevant'; the latter describes all but inconsequential adjustments.

An operator initiates a variation by asking the regulator whether a change he or she proposes to make would breach conditions of his authorization; if not, whether the regulator would vary the authorization because of the change and whether the variation would involve a substantial change. The operator can then apply formally for a variation allowing him to make the change; this will be advertised if it is a substantial change.

Processes in the organic chemical industry sector in particular change their input, throughput and output constantly. To apply for a variation each time this happened would be crippling given the four or so months it takes to process an application and the application costs. HMIP has developed 'envelope authorizations' as the way to allow operators room to make changes without needing a variation. The word 'envelope' is intended to convey the idea of a box defined by chemical compounds, release limits and pollution-abatement techniques within which the operator may lawfully make changes; at one time using specific compounds, emitting certain substances, and employing a particular abatement technique while, at another, resorting to a different combination, without requiring a variation. Envelope authorizations are a new idea and the concept is mentioned only briefly in the Guidance Note, *Batch Manufacture of Organic Chemicals in Multipurpose Plant*, IPR 4/5. It is therefore still too early to say how it will work in practice.

5.1.7 Enforcement

An authorization is enforced administratively by giving either an 'enforcement' or a 'prohibition' notice. The operator may appeal against either type of notice but the appeal does not suspend the notice. An enforcement notice is served when the operator is believed to be breaching any of the conditions of his authorization. It must specify the nature of the breach and require that particular steps be taken within a given period to remedy the situation. A prohibition notice is served when there is an imminent risk of serious pollution, irrespective of whether there has been a breach of the authorization. It too specifies the risk, the steps which must be taken to remove it and the time by which they must be taken. Its effect is to suspend the authorization wholly or partially; it may also impose further conditions on those parts of the process not suspended.

The regulator may prosecute the operator for not complying with these notices, and the court may order that specified remedial steps be taken within a given period. In March 1993 HMIP announced its first successful prosecution under the IPC system; the company, Brookridge Ltd, treated timber with tributyltin naphthanate without being authorized to do so. The company had simply not applied for an authorization; it pleaded guilty and was fined £1 650 with costs of £3 000 (HMIP, 1993d). Overall, prosecutions under Part I of the **EPA 1990** are still rare. At present most of HMIP's prosecutions are under other legislation which it also enforces, such as the **Radioactive Substances Act 1993**, the **Alkali Act 1906** and aspects of the **Health and Safety at Work etc. Act 1974**.

Apart from mounting a prosecution, HMIP, with the approval of the Secretary of State, may itself take remedial steps and recover its expenses from the operator; it has not yet exercised this power. Ultimately, an authorization may be revoked, particularly where the process has not been carried on for twelve months. The operator may appeal and this suspends revocation.

The Act is silent on whether an appeal against authorization conditions has the effect of suspending the authorization conditions. The issue was the subject of a dispute between Leigh Environmental and HMIP (ENDS, 1993a). Leigh challenged authorization conditions imposed by HMIP requiring it to upgrade its process within a period of six months, arguing that this was the time allowed for appeals to the Secretary of State against the condition. In case its appeal were to succeed it would have spent money upgrading its process unnecessarily. Leigh's judicial review application was, however, put on hold by the court when HMIP gave an undertaking that no enforcement action would be taken against Leigh until the appeal had been determined. The issue whether or not an appeal suspends authorization conditions therefore remains undetermined.

Appeals against the regulator's decisions are made to the Secretary of State, and there are different time limits depending on the matter at issue: six months for a refusal to grant an authorization or a condition attached to an authorization; two months for a variation or a prohibition notice; twenty-one days where a request to keep information confidential is turned down and before the date on which a revocation comes into effect. The Secretary of State may extend these time limits, except in the case of an appeal against a revocation.

A government review of the LAAPC system indicated that there had been three appeals from local authorities' decisions; one concerning the refusal of an authorization, another the conditions in the authorization and the third against an enforcement notice (ENDS, 1993b). On the other hand, there had been sixty seven appeals over HMIP authorizations by October 1993, most of them over confidentiality claims (ENDS, 1994). Appeals need to be lodged within the stipulated time limits but may take well over a year to determine.

5.2 The Control of Dark Smoke

The control of dark smoke is now carried out under powers in the **Clean Air Act 1993** which consolidated and repealed previous legislation, i.e. the **Clean Air Acts 1956 and 1968** and the **Control of Smoke Pollution Act 1989**. The 1956 Act was introduced after a severe smog in London in 1952 which killed several thousand people. The smog was precipitated by unusual weather conditions which combined with generally poor-quality air around London, the result of the practice at the time of burning dark smoke-emitting fuels. The 1968 Act simply extended the remit of the 1956 Act. The Acts, now consolidated in the 1993 Act, define 'dark smoke' as smoke which, if compared with the Ringelmann Chart, would appear to be as dark as, or darker than, shade 2 on the chart. The chart, which runs from 0 to 5, is the standard means local authority environmental health officers use to monitor dark smoke emissions.

Section 1 prohibits the emission of dark smoke from a chimney of any building or any other chimney which serves the furnace of any boiler or industrial plant. The Dark Smoke (Permitted Periods) Regulations 1958 (SI No. 498 in England and Wales and SI No. 1399 in Scotland) have been made specifying periods during which, in certain cases, emissions are exempt. Contravening the prohibition is an offence for which the maximum fine is £1 000 where the chimney is part of a private dwelling and £5 000 in all other cases. No offence is committed, however, where the emission occurred because of:

1   The lighting up of a furnace which was cold and all practicable steps were taken to prevent or minimize the emission of dark smoke
2   Some failure of a furnace or a connected apparatus which could not reasonably have been foreseen or provided against and the emission could not have been prevented after the failure or
3   The use of unsuitable fuel when suitable fuel was unobtainable and all practicable steps were taken to prevent or minimize the emission.

Additionally, in relation to industrial premises the Clean Air (Emission of Dark Smoke) (Exemption) Regulations 1969 SI No. 1263 have been made exempting categories of fuel from this prohibition. No offence is committed also where the emission was inadvertent and all practicable steps were taken to prevent or minimize it.

The Act imposes several requirements designed to minimize the emission of dark smoke of which the first two do not apply to domestic furnaces. First, it requires that new furnaces shall be, as far as practicable, smokeless. To this end, before a furnace is installed the plans and specifications shall be submitted to the local authority enabling it to ensure that the furnace is, so far as practicable, capable of operating continuously without emitting smoke when burning fuel of the type for which the furnace was designed. Second, chimneys serving furnaces must not emit grit or dust at a rate exceeding limits prescribed in the Clean Air (Emission of Grit and Dust from Furnaces) Regulations 1971 (SI No. 162 in England and Wales and SI No. 625 in Scotland). If no limit has been prescribed for a chimney practicable means must be used for minimizing the emission of grit or dust from it.

The third requirement applies to all furnaces, domestic and non-domestic alike, but there are differences of detail. Non-domestic furnaces burning pulverized fuel or other solid matter at a rate of 45.4 kg or more an hour or liquid or gaseous matter at a rate equivalent to 366.4 kW or more must be provided with grit or dust arrestment plant installed according to plans and specifications approved by the local authority and maintained and used properly. However, the Clean Air (Arrestment Plant) (Exemptions) Regulations 1969 (SI No. 1262 in England and Wales and SI No. 1388 in Scotland) have been made exempting classes of furnaces from this requirement. Further, an application may be made to the local authority to exempt a furnace being used for a particular purpose without installing arrestment plant if emissions will not be prejudicial to health or a nuisance. The local authority has eight weeks in which to give a decision (unless the parties have agreed a longer period) otherwise it will be deemed to have granted the application. There are provisions for an appeal to the Secretary of State.

Domestic furnaces must install arrestment plant for grit and dust in accordance with plans and specifications approved by the local authority if they are to burn pulverized fuel or solid fuel at a rate of 1.02 tonnes an hour.

A fourth requirement deals with the height of chimneys for both domestic and non-domestic furnaces. The heights of chimneys burning pulverized fuel, solid matter at the rate of 45.4 kg or more an hour or liquid or gaseous matter at a rate of 366.4 kW or more must be approved by the local authority. The Clean Air (Heights of Chimneys) (Exemption) Regulations 1969 (SI No. 411 in England and Wales and SI No. 465 in Scotland) have been made exempting certain boilers from this requirement. The local authority shall not grant approval unless the height of the chimney will be sufficient to prevent, so far as practicable, the emissions from becoming prejudicial to health or a nuisance having regard to consideration such as its purpose, position, the buildings nearby and the levels of the neighbouring ground. The local authority's decision must be given within four weeks or a longer agreed period otherwise the application shall be deemed to have been granted. An appeal against the local authority's decision may be made to the Secretary of State.

The Act also makes provision for a local authority to declare the whole or parts of its area a 'smoke control area'. It is an offence to emit smoke in such an area unless fuel authorized under the Smoke Control Areas (Authorized Fuels) Regulations 1991 SI No. 1282 are used. Regulations have been made exempting various classes of fireplaces from the prohibition of the emission of dark smoke in smoke control areas on the ground that they can be used for burning unauthorized fuel without producing any or a substantial quantity of smoke. It is an offence to acquire or sell unauthorized fuel in a smoke control area.

As part of the deregulation initiative announced in early 1993 the government consulted on repealing parts of the Clean Air Act 1993 arguing that local authorities had sufficient powers under the LAAPC system and the statutory nuisance provisions (see Chapter 6) to control dark smoke and did not need all its powers under the Clean Air Act 1993 (DoE, 1993a). The powers affected relate to:

1   The approval of new furnaces
2   The requirement to fit approved arrestment equipment for new furnaces
3   Limits on the rate of emissions of grit and dust from furnace and
4   The approval of chimney heights.

The proposals were not welcomed by local authorities who view these powers as useful pre-emptive powers, unlike statutory nuisance control powers. The proposals may be effected through the powers given to the Secretary of State to repeal or amend legislation in the **Deregulation and Contracting Out Act 1994.**

5.3   Controls on Energy Use

Energy use, unlike other areas of environmental control, has typically been the subject of voluntary measures. However, since the Climate Change Convention, agreed in Rio de Janeiro in June 1992, requiring countries to reduce their carbon dioxide emissions by the year 2000 to 1990 levels, considerable momentum has been generated for putting binding legal measures in place. Carbon dioxide, emitted in burning fossil fuels to generate energy, is considered the main greenhouse gas (methane is also thought significant) responsible for raising atmospheric temperature, thus causing climate changes.

The European Commission put forward four proposals for reducing energy use and carbon dioxide emissions.

5.3.1   A Carbon/Energy Tax

This proposal (COM (92) 226 final, OJ No. C 196/1) aims to introduce a tax equivalent to $3 a barrel on fuels, rising, by the year 2000, to $10 a barrel. It made little headway due to disagreements within the Council: the UK objected to the principle of a Community-wide tax; France insisted on a tax limited to carbon fuels, thus excluding its nuclear energy generating industry; and the four Cohesion countries (Spain, Portugal, Greece and Ireland) sought exemptions on the ground that their national carbon dioxide emissions are below the Community average.

Initially the remaining six countries (particularly Germany and The Netherlands) threatened to veto Council decision 94/69/EC (OJ No. L 33/11) approving the Climate Change Convention for ratification by the Community. They argued that the Council could not approve ratification of the Convention without agreeing a mechanism (and the carbon/energy tax was their preferred mechanism) for fulfilling the commitments made under it. The argument was rejected, the UK taking the position that member states did not need the approval of the Council to ratify the Convention since states had individual, not joint, commitments under the Convention. The UK proceeded to ratify the Convention before the Council decision of 15 December 1993 which approved the Convention for ratification.

The carbon/energy tax proposal has not yet been formally abandoned but it is unlikely to be adopted in the near future since its adoption has to be unanimous, being a tax measure.

5.3.2   A Monitoring Mechanism of Community Greenhouse Gas Emissions

This Directive (93/389/EEC, OJ No. L 167/31) established a monitoring programme for carbon dioxide and other greenhouse gas emissions. It requires member states to devise, publish and implement national programmes for limiting emissions of these gases in order to achieve the Climate Change Convention commitment of returning emissions back to 1990 levels by the year 2000. Reports are to be submitted to the Commission by 31 July each year.

5.3.3   A Programme on Energy Efficiency (SAVE)

EC Directive 93/76/EEC (OJ No. L 237/28) to limit carbon dioxide emissions by improving energy efficiency (SAVE) must be implemented by 31 December 1994. It requires member states to draw up and implement programmes in the following fields:

1   Energy certification of buildings
2   The billing of heating, air conditioning and hot water costs on the basis of actual consumption
3   Third-party financing for energy efficiency investments in the public sector
4   Thermal insulation of new buildings
5   Regular inspection of boilers and
6   Energy audits of undertakings with high energy consumption.

The UK has already commenced action which would go towards fulfilling some of these requirements; details were given in the UK's Action Plan on CO_2 emissions, discussed below.

5.3.4   An Alternative Energy Programme (ALTENER)

Council decision 93/500/EEC (OJ No. L 235/41) set up an alternative energy programme (ALTENER) lasting five years between 1993 to 1997 and supported by Community funds amounting to ECU 40 million. ALTENER consists of 'specific actions for greater penetration of renewable energy sources', as follows:

1   Studies and technical evaluations for defining technical standards or specifications, the Community meeting all the costs
2   Measures to support member state initiatives for extending or creating infrastructures concerned with renewable energy sources, the Community meeting between 30 per cent and 50 per cent of the costs
3   Measures to foster the creation of an information network, the Community meeting between 30 per cent and 50 per cent of the costs and
4   Measures aimed at assessing the feasibility and advantages of the industrial exploitation of biomass for energy purposes, the Community meeting up to 30 per cent of the costs.

5.3.5 The UK's Energy Programme

This programme was outlined in *Climate Change—The UK's Programme*, published as the UK's report under the Climate Change Convention (DoE, 1994a). The programme aims to reduce carbon dioxide emissions by 10 million tonnes of carbon (MtC) by the year 2000 as follows:

1   *Energy consumption in the home (4 MtC)*: There are six elements to this:
   (i) A VAT of 8 per cent on domestic energy use was introduced in April 1994 to rise to 17.5 per cent in April 1995 but Parliament voted against the rise.
   (ii) An Energy Saving Trust was set up in November 1992 by the government and the companies supplying energy to promote its efficient use, initially in the domestic sector. It provides financial assistance towards gas condensing boilers, combined heat and power systems (these maximize the energy extracted from the primary energy source by utilizing waste heat from electricity generation), Local Energy Advice Centres and incentives to purchasers of low-energy light bulbs.
   (iii) Energy efficiency advice and information including 'Helping the Earth Begins at Home' publicity.
   (iv) Eco-labelling: this is an EC programme which assesses the environmental impact (including energy use) of products and awards labels which may influence the purchasing decisions of consumers. The first products assessed were washing machines and dishwashers (see 9.2 'Eco-labelling').
   (v) EC Save Programme: Energy consumption standards for household appliances are to be set under this programme. Also, labels giving information about this are being developed (see 9.2 'Eco-labelling').
   (vi) Building Regulations are to be revised to strengthen energy efficiency requirements.
2   *Energy consumption by business (2.5 MtC)*: There are five elements to this:
   (i) Energy efficiency advice and information; this consists of
   • Making a Corporate Commitment Programme: this was launched in October 1993 and seeks the commitment of top management in private and public sector organizations to energy efficiency within their organizations. The programme asks organizations to give a board-level director responsibility for developing and reassessing their energy efficiency strategy, to set improvement targets and publicize them and to ensure that plans are considered regularly at board level.
   • Best Practice Programme: this campaign advocates a management approach to energy. It is run by the DoE's Energy Efficiency Office, which has eleven regional offices.
   • The Energy Management Assistance Scheme: this was set up in April 1992 to help small companies obtain advice on the design and implementation of energy-efficiency projects.

(ii) Energy Saving Trust Schemes programme (applied currently to the domestic sector) will be applied to small businesses.

(iii) Energy Design Advice Scheme: this was launched in 1992 to ensure that the design of business projects incorporates the latest energy-saving techniques available.

(iv) The EC SAVE Programme (above) will cover office machinery.

(v) The promised Buildings Regulations amendments will cover the business sector as well.

3   *Energy consumption in the public sector (1 MtC)*: Public sector bodies are expected to set targets for a reduction in their energy consumption.

4   *Transport (2.5 MtC)*: The government sees the key to its transport strategy as the provision of price incentives. In 1993 fuel duty increased by 3 pence per litre representing an increase of 8–10 per cent. Further increases will be made of 5 per cent a year above the rate of inflation. Other possible initiatives include charging for the use of roads, e.g. tolling and increased parking fees.

5   *The Non-fossil Fuel Obligation*: The government also has a policy of subsidising the development of new and renewable energy sources so that they can compete in the market against fossil fuels. Currently coal contributes 68 per cent of the total electricity generated in the UK and oil 6 per cent while imported fuel accounts for about 25 per cent. Renewables make up only about 2 per cent. The policy is to increase this proportion to about 3 per cent by the year 2000 by promoting wind power, nuclear energy, the generation of energy from waste (i.e. incineration with energy recovery), biomass, and other such schemes.

The policy is implemented through 'The Non-fossil Fuel Obligation' (NFFO) for renewables which requires electricity companies to buy a proportion of their electricity from renewable and nuclear sources, thus guaranteeing renewables a market for a set period and enables investors to recoup their investment in renewables. Electricity generated from renewables costs more but the electricity companies pass on the higher price to consumers (McCue, 1994).

Companies generating energy from renewable sources apply to the DTI for aid under an 'Order' which specifies the sources from which the renewable energy is to be purchased and the amount of such electricity. Nuclear energy currently gets the bulk of the Order. The first 'Renewables Order' in England and Wales was announced in 1990, the second in 1991, the third is planned for 1994, the fourth for 1996 and the fifth for 1998. The first Scottish Renewables Order is planned for 1994 and further Orders are likely in 1996 and 1998.

In view of the increase in planning applications for wind energy projects which the NFFO engendered the DoE published PPG 22 on 'Renewable Energy' in February 1993 (DoE, 1993b). This guides local planning authorities on the implications of these projects for land-use planning and on how to deal with applications for planning permission. Ironically, the increase in wind energy projects has created a concern about their environmental effects, chiefly noise and visual impact on areas which, typically, are rural and considered very attractive (Wilkinson, 1994).

5.4   The EC Atmospheric Pollution Directives

The EC has been particularly active on atmospheric pollution and a wide range of directives have been adopted. These directives have driven many legislative measures in the UK as indicated below.

5.4.1   Air Quality Standards

EC air quality standards have been set in relation to sulphur dioxide and suspended particulates, nitrogen dioxide, lead and ozone; the first three are implemented in the UK by the Air Quality Standards Regulations, SI 1989 No. 317 while the ozone standard one is implemented separately (see below). However, proposals for a new framework directive on ambient air quality assessment and management have been published (COM (94) 109 final, OJ No. C 216/4 of 6.8.94). This will be followed by daughter directives on individual pollutants, the first group of which will revise the present four directives which set air quality standards while the second will set standards for an agreed list of pollutants, e.g. cadmium, carbon monoxide and benzene, currently not covered (ENDS, 1993c).

The UK has also issued a consultation paper on the need to set standards for specific air pollutants on the basis of their effect on health and the environment (DoE, 1994b). In line with this policy the government's independent expert panel on air quality standards has commenced studies with a view to recommending standards for air pollutants such as ozone, carbon monoxide, 1,3-butadiene, nitrogen dioxide, sulphur dioxide and particulates (DoE, 1994c).

Monitoring for compliance with the standards set in directives is carried out both by the DoE and local authorities using both automatic and sampler techniques from various monitoring sites established according to requirements specified in the directives. In addition, the DoE established in 1993 an Enhanced Urban Monitoring Network consisting of nine sites which provide public information on general air quality. The information is available on Ceefax, Teletext, Freephone 0800 556677, and the news media and states on any day whether the air quality is 'very good', 'good', 'poor' or 'very poor'. In order to improve the quality of monitoring the government is currently consulting on extending cooperation on automatic air quality monitoring at the national and local levels (DoE, 1993c).

Directive on Sulphur Dioxide

EC Directive 80/779/EEC (OJ No. L 229/30) on air quality limit values and guide values for sulphur dioxide and suspended particulates has the aim of fixing limit values and guide values for sulphur dioxide and suspended particulates in the atmosphere in order to protect human health and the environment, and these are set out in annexes. 'Limit values' are concentrations which member states are required to have achieved by 1 April 1993 at the latest. 'Guide values', on the other hand, serve three purposes, being concentrations:

1   To be aimed for
2   Which serve as long-term precautions for health and the environment and
3   Which are to be achieved in zones in which member states consider it necessary to limit or prevent a foreseeable increase in pollution following development, or consider should be afforded special environmental protection.

Directive on Nitrogen Dioxide

EC Directive 85/203/EEC (OJ No. L 87/1) on air quality standards for nitrogen dioxide requires member states to ensure that the limit values laid down are achieved all over their territories by 1 January 1994 at the latest. Additionally, the Directive sets guide values which member states are to use for setting standards to be achieved in zones which they consider should be afforded special environmental protection. They may also serve as guides for setting standards in zones where member states consider it necessary to limit or prevent a foreseeable increase in pollution in the wake of development.

Directive on Lead in the Air

EC Directive 82/884/EEC (OJ No. L 378/15) on a limit value for lead in the air fixes a limit value for lead which member states had to achieve by December 1987, and in relation to areas where this limit could not be achieved by that date, plans had to be drawn up to achieve the limit by December 1989.

Directive on Air Pollution by Ozone

EC Directive 92/72/EEC (OJ No. L 297/1) on air pollution by ozone has the purpose of establishing a harmonized procedure across the EC for monitoring, exchanging information and informing and warning the public about air pollution by ozone, which, at ground level, is highly toxic to human health and to vegetation.

The Directive establishes standards (referred to as 'thresholds' because they are intended as action-triggering mechanisms) of ozone concentration on the basis of four parameters: (1) health; (2) vegetation; (3) population information; and (4) population warning. Should the concentration of ozone in the air exceed the population information and population warning thresholds, the member state shall inform or warn the public, giving details of the protective action the public should take.

The Directive is implemented through the Ozone Monitoring and Information Regulations 1994 (SI No. 440) which enable the Secretary of State to establish measuring stations as required by the Directive and to take steps to inform the public if the specified ozone concentration values are exceeded.

5.4.2   Industrial Emissions

Five EC directives impose air quality controls on industrial emissions; they relate to emissions from industrial plants, large combustion plants, municipal waste incinerators, hazardous waste incinerators and asbestos.

Directive on Air Pollution from Industrial Plants

EC Directive 84/360/EEC (OJ No. L 188/20) on the combating of air pollution from large industrial plants requires member states to introduce a system of prior authorization for new, or substantially altered, plants in six categories of industries; energy, metal production and processing, the manufacture of non-metallic mineral products, chemicals, waste disposal, and others. The authorization must ensure that:

1   The best available technology not entailing excessive cost is used to prevent air pollution
2   The plant does not cause significant pollution by emitting sulphur or nitrogen compounds, carbon monoxide, organic compounds except methane, chlorine and fluorine and their compounds, and dust, asbestos and glass and mineral fibres.

The Directive also requires member states gradually to adapt existing plants belonging to the six categories so that they too employ the best available technology. In doing so, however, account must be taken of:

1   The plant's technical characteristics
2   Its rate of utilization and the length of its remaining life
3   The nature and volume of its polluting emissions
4   The desirability of 'not entailing excessive costs' for the plant in question, having regard to the economic situation of undertakings of that category.

Finally, the directive provides that the Council may, in subsequent (or 'daughter') directives, fix emission limit values for pollutants; in that sense it is a framework directive, hence the name 'the Air Framework Directive'. So far, limits have been fixed for asbestos, large combustion plants, municipal waste incinerators and hazardous waste incinerators.

The directive and its daughters (below) are implemented in the UK through the Prescribed Processes and Substances Regulations 1991 SI No. 472, as amended, under the IPC system. The requirements and timetables for their achievement which these directives set have dictated the timetables within which the prescribed processes are brought under IPC control and the period allowed for existing processes to meet the standards set for new processes. The standards imposed by IPC authorizations are themselves drawn from the standards imposed by these directives. Details of the standards to be met by the various processes are set out in the HMIP Process Guidance Notes.

Directive on Large Combustion Plants

EC Directive 88/609/EEC (OJ No. L 336/1) on the limitation of emissions of certain pollutants into the air from large combustion plants applies to combustion plants of at least 50 MW net rated thermal input, although certain plants are exempted, including those powered by diesel, petrol and gas engines.

The Directive aims to reduce sulphur dioxide and oxides of nitrogen in emissions from large combustion plants. It sets national emission ceilings and reduction targets which each member state has to achieve in three phases from 1990 to 2003 for SO_2 emissions and in two phases to 1998 for NO_x emissions. The national emission ceilings are in effect national quotas of SO_2 and NO_x which a member state is permitted to emit. Each member state is required to draw up a programme for reducing emissions to comply with the quotas.

The UK's programme was published in 1990 (DoE, 1990). The plan is made under powers provided to the Secretary of State in s. 3 of the **EPA 1990**. It allocates the UK's quota between England and Wales, Scotland and Northern Ireland. In England and Wales it shares out the electricity industry quotas between National Power and Powergen, the two major power generators. The Commission has room to make proposals to the Council in 1994 to revise the third phase for SO_2 emissions and the second phase for NO_x emissions of the reduction targets.

Second, the Directive sets emission values which plants licensed after 1 July 1987 ('new plants'), must meet, although there are derogations for certain larger plants as well as plants burning categories of indigenous solid fuels. The limit values are based on the best available technology not entailing excessive cost and the Commission is under a duty to submit to the Council before 1 July 1995 proposals for revising them.

Directives on Municipal Waste Incinerators

Two directives set emission limits to be met by municipal waste incineration plants, one for new plants and the other for existing plants. EC Directive 89/369/EEC (OJ No. L 163/32) on the prevention of air pollution from new municipal waste incineration plants sets emission limit values and other operating conditions with which new plants (plants authorized from 1 December 1990) must comply. EC Directive 89/429/EEC (OJ No. L 203/50) on the reduction of air pollution from existing municipal waste incineration plants lays down the timetable by which plants authorized before 1 December 1990 are to achieve the standards set for new municipal waste incineration plants. With one exception, plants with a capacity of 6 t/h must achieve the standards by 1 December 1996. Plants below that capacity must achieve these standards by 1 December 2000, but the Directive imposes interim standards to be achieved by 1 December 1995. It is thought that many National Health Service incinerators will have to close in 1996 because they will be unable to meet the standards set in this Directive, which will be implemented through the IPC system.

Proposed Directive on Hazardous Waste Incineration

The proposal for a directive on the incineration of hazardous waste (COM (92) 9 final—SYN 406, OJ No. C 130/1, 21.5.92) was submitted by the Commission on 23 March 1992. It was subsequently amended (OJ No. C 190/5, 14.7.93) and has yet to be adopted by the Council although a common position has been agreed. The proposed directive requires incineration plants to be authorized. It sets emission limit values which plants should not exceed and also imposes other requirements relating to their operation. The requirements and standards are to be met within three years of the directive's coming into force.

Directive on Pollution by Asbestos

EC Directive 87/217/EEC (OJ No. L 85/40) on the prevention and reduction of environmental pollution by asbestos requires member states to ensure that asbestos releases into air, water and land are reduced at source and prevented, using, where the activity is a production, manufacturing or industrial finishing process involving at least 100 kg per year of raw asbestos, the best available technology not entailing excessive cost. Additionally, it sets emission limit values for emissions to both air and water, and requires that measures be taken to ensure that asbestos is not released in the course of work such as demolishing buildings or transporting waste containing asbestos. The Directive is implemented in the UK through the Trade Effluents (Prescribed Processes and Substances) Regulations 1989 SI No. 1156 (see 2.2.5 'Special Category Effluent' in Chapter 2).

5.4.3   Regulation on Substances that Deplete the Ozone Layer

EC Regulation 91/594/EEC (OJ No. L 67/1) on substances that deplete the ozone layer was adopted on 4 March 1991. It implements the Montreal Protocol of 1987 on substances that deplete the ozone layer within the EC and controls the import, export, production and consumption of CFCs, halons, carbon tetrachloride, and 1,1,1-trichloroethane, referred to as 'controlled substances'. The Regulation imposes a schedule for phasing out the production and consumption of ozone-depleting substances. At the 4th Meeting of the Parties to the Montreal Protocol which was held in Copenhagen from 23 to 25 November 1992 the parties agreed to phase out the production of CFCs and carbon tetrachloride by 1 January 1996; halons by 1 January 1994; and 1,1,1-trichloroethane by 1 January 1996. The EC Council of Ministers subsequently agreed to adopt a faster phase-out schedule in the EC. Consequently Council Regulation 3952/92 which was adopted on 30 December 1992 amended EC Regulation No. 594/91 to introduce the new phase-out schedule under which CFCs and carbon tetrachloride must be phased out within the Community by 1 January 1995, one year ahead of the Copenhagen schedule. The regulation applies in the member states directly.

In the UK the Environmental Protection (Non-Refillable Refrigerant Containers) Regulations 1994 SI No. 199 impose restrictions on the importation, supply and storage of non-refillable containers containing CFCs and HCFCs for use as refrigerants in air conditioning and refrigeration machinery. A 'Refrigerant Users Group' has been set up to put those who need to continue using recycled CFCs in touch with those who have spare CFCs for sale (DoE, 1994d).

There is a procedure for a limited amount of production to be allowed for 'essential uses' which meet the following criteria:

1   It is necessary for the health or safety or is critical for the functioning of society.
2   There are no technically and economically feasible alternatives or alternatives that are acceptable from the point of view of environment and health.
3   The substance is not available in sufficient quantity and quality from existing stocks of banked and recycled substances.

The procedure is for each state party to nominate uses it considers essential either six months for halons or nine months for the other substances prior to each annual meeting of the state parties. The nominations may or may not be accepted by UNEP which administers the Montreal Protocol. The practice of the DoE is to ask producers to put forward nominations to the DoE; the DoE then forwards some of these to the Commission. The DoE has indicated, however, that it will not put forward requests for essential uses for halons as there is sufficient supply in established 'halon banks'.

The Commission has put forward a proposal (COM (93) 202 final, OJ No. C 232/6, 28.8.93) to consolidate the 1991 and 1992 Regulations and additionally introduce controls on methyl bromide and HCFCs. Under this proposal, using a 1991 baseline, 25 per cent of methyl bromide marketed should be phased out by the end of 1996 while HCFCs are supposed to be phased out altogether by 2015.

5.4.4   Content of Fuels

A number of directives set standards which fuels must meet, and thus limit the pollution thereby caused. EC Directive 75/716/EEC (OJ No. L 307/22) relating to the sulphur content of certain liquid fuels as amended by EC Directive 87/219/EEC (OJ No. L 91/19) sets a limit of 0.3 per cent, which member states may, in certain situations, reduce to 0.2 per cent, for the sulphur compound content of the gas oil used as domestic fuel.

EC Directive 85/210/EEC (OJ No. L 96/25) concerning the lead content of petrol as amended by Directive 87/416/EEC (OJ No. L 225/33) sets a limit on the lead content of leaded petrol and a benzene content of both leaded and unleaded petrol. It also requires member states to ensure that unleaded petrol is available within their territories.

These directives are implemented in the UK through the Motor Fuel (Sulphur Content of Gas Oil) Regulations 1990, SI No. 1097 and the Motor Fuel (Lead Content of Petrol) Regulations 1981, SI No. 1523, as amended, made under the **European Communities Act 1972** and ss 30 and 31 of the Clean Air Act 1993 under which the Secretary of State may make regulations about motor fuel and impose limits on the sulphur content of oil fuel for furnaces or engines.

5.4.5   Engine Construction

A second way in which polluting vehicle emissions are controlled is to set emission standards which newly designed types of vehicles must be capable of meeting in order to gain approval ('EC type approval'). Typically, there is one year between the period when new 'type approvals' must comply with the standards and when new 'registrations' must comply. This is intended to enable manufacturers to dispose of old stock. The UK type approval authority is the Vehicle Certification Agency of the Department of Transport, based in Bristol.

The history of EC type approval goes back to 1970 with the adoption of Directive 70/220/EEC on the approximation of the laws of member states relating to measures to be taken against air pollution by emissions from motor vehicles. EC requirements are implemented in the UK through Construction and Use Regulations, as amended, made under the **Road Traffic Act 1988**. Vehicles are categorized into three for purposes of requirements related to vehicle emissions standards; passenger cars, light commercial vehicles and heavy goods vehicles.

Passenger Cars

Emission standards for passenger cars (i.e. cars with not more than six seating positions) are set out in Council Directive 91/441/EEC (OJ No. L 242) which amended Directive 70/220/EEC, establishing the following emission standards as from 1992:

Carbon monoxide	Hydrocarbons and oxides of nitrogen	Particulates
2.72 g/km	0.97 g/km	0.14 g/km

These standards are met by fitting three-way catalytic converters. Directive 91/441/EEC has been amended by the introduction of new emission standards (see COM (92) 572 final, OJ No. C 56/34) to come into effect from January 1996 as follows:

Carbon monoxide	Hydrocarbons and oxides of nitrogen	Particulates
petrol 2.2 g/km	0.5 g/km	
diesel 1.0 g/km	0.7 g/km	0.08 g/km

Light Commercial Vehicles

This category of vehicles is heterogeneous and is composed of vehicles whose engines are derived from both passenger cars and heavy commercial vehicles. Therefore this category of vehicles is classified as follows:

Class I   reference mass of up to 1 250 kg
Class II   reference mass of between 1 250 and 1 700 kg
Class III   reference mass of between 1 700 kg and 3 500 kg

Emission standards for this category of vehicles are set out in Council Directive 93/59/EEC (L 186/21) which amended Directive 70/220/EEC in relation to this category of vehicles. New vehicles in this category have had to meet the following new emission standards from 1 October 1993 in order to get EC type approvals:

	Carbon monoxide	Hydrocarbons and oxides of nitrogen	Particulates
Class I	2.72 g/kg	0.97 g/km	0.14 g/km
Class II	5.17 g/km	1.4 g/km	0.19 g/km
Class III	6.9 g/km	1.7 g/km	0.25 g/km

The emission standards for passenger cars and light commercial vehicles are comparable to those in other countries, such as the USA and the EFTA states. As is the case with passenger cars for which new emission standards have been agreed to take effect in 1996, new standards are to be proposed for light commercial vehicles to come into force as from 1 January 1996 for Class I approvals and 1 January 1997 for Class II and III approvals.

Heavy Goods Vehicles

Emission standards for vehicles in this category (i.e. over 3 500 kg) were set in Directive 87/77/EEC. This has been amended by Directive 91/542/EEC (OJ No. L 295/1) which sets the following standards:

Date	Carbon monoxide	Hydrocarbons	Nitrogen oxides	Particulates
New types (figures are in g/kWh)				
1/7/92	4.5	1.1	8.0	0.36
1/10/95	4.0	1.1	7.0	0.15
New registrations (figures are in g/kWh)				
1/10/93	4.9	1.23	9.0	0.4
1/10/96	4.0	1.1	7.0	0.15

5.4.6 Proposed Directive on VOCs

Volatile organic compounds (VOCs) are carbon-containing gaseous pollutants which are emitted from a wide variety of sources such as motor vehicles, solvent usage, industrial processes, oil refining, petrol storage and distribution, food manufacture and even natural sources. VOCs react with oxides of nitrogen to form ground-level ozone, an aggressive pollutant with adverse effects on human health, plant growth and building materials. The 1991 Geneva Protocol to the 1979 UN Economic Commission for Europe (UNECE) Convention on Long-range Transboundary Air Pollution requires member states to take action to control VOC emissions. In December 1993 the UK published a document setting out its strategy for meeting its commitments under the UNECE Convention (DoE, 1993d). The strategy is premised on the controls imposed under Part I of the **EPA 1990** which requires processes emitting organic solvents to be dealt with as LAAPC processes and on action to be taken under forthcoming EC directives.

The European Commission is tackling VOCs in two parts. The first part is a forthcoming directive on solvents which will require controls similar to those currently under the LAAPC system to be imposed on solvent-emitting processes. This proposal has yet to be published; the drafts are still being discussed with a view to the Commission putting forward a formal proposal. The second part covers fuel VOCs in two stages. Stage I (COM (92) 277 final, OJ No. C

227/3, 3.9.92) concerns losses due to the storage of petrol and its loading, transport and unloading at or between refineries, distribution terminals and petrol stations. The Commission's proposal requires equipment to be fitted to minimize vapour losses and to ensure the recovery of vapours displaced during storage and unloading. Stage II covers losses during vehicle refuelling; a proposal is expected from the Commission which will require alterations to the design of vehicle filler necks and the installation of vapour recovery equipment at petrol stations.

5.4.7 Proposed IPPC Directive

The proposal for a directive on integrated pollution prevention and control (COM (93) 423 final, OJ No. C 311/6, 17.11.93) was submitted by the Commission on 30 September 1993. The proposal introduces a system of pollution control that is similar to the UK's IPC system of pollution control.

It requires member states to ensure that new installations do not operate without a permit and that any existing installations obtain a permit by 30 June 2005. The permit shall be based on a system of integrated environmental protection taking into account air, water and land. Permitted emission limits must not breach environmental quality standards or, where these have not been set, World Health Organization standards. The technology to be used shall be the best available and permits shall be reviewed at least every ten years; however, the costs of the technology shall be considered.

References

DoE, *Programme and National Plan for Reducing SO$_2$ and NO$_x$ Emissions from Large Combustion Plants* (1990).

DoE, 'Michael Howard announces decisions on first commercial confidentiality appeals under IPC', News Release 760, 19 November (1992).

DoE, *A Proposal to Repeal Provisions of the Clean Air Act 1993* (1993a).

DoE, *PPG 22 on Renewable Energy* (1993b).

DoE, *The Future of Air Quality Monitoring Networks in the UK—A Consultation Paper* (1993c).

DoE, *Reducing Emissions of VOCs and Ground Level Ozone: A UK Strategy* (1993d).

DoE, *Climate Change—The UK's Programme*, HMSO (1994a).

DoE, *Improving Air Quality—a discussion paper on air quality standards and management* (1994b).

DoE, 'Air quality standards for ozone recommended', News Release No. 310, 18 May (1994c).

DoE, 'Refrigerant users group launched', News Release No. 200, 24 March (1994d).

ENDS Report No. 225, 'Leigh goes to court over IPC authorization', p. 12, October (1993a).

ENDS Report No. 222, 'Official review of local authority air pollution controls', p. 4, July (1993b).

ENDS Report No. 225, 'Framework rules on air quality promised by end of year', pp. 39–40, October (1993c).

ENDS, *Integrated Pollution Control—the First Three Years*, 1994.

HMIP, *Integrated Pollution Control: A Practical Guide*, HMSO (1993a).

HMIP, *Dispersion: Guidelines on Discharge Stack Heights for Polluting Emissions*, HMSO (1993b).

HMIP, *Monitoring Emissions of Pollutants at Source*, HMSO (1993c).

HMIP, 'First prosecution for HMIP under EPA 1990', News Release No. 170, 16 March (1993d).

HMIP, *Pollution Abatement Technology for the Reduction of Solvent Vapour Emissions*, HMSO (1994a).

HMIP, *Pollution Abatement Technology for Particulate and Trace Gas Removal*, HMSO (1994b).

HMIP, *Environmental, Economic and BPEO Assessment Principles for Integrated Pollution Control* (1994c).

McCue, S., 'Northern Ireland non-fossil fuel obligation', *Utilities Law Review*, 7, Spring (1994).

RCEP, *Air Pollution Control: An Integrated Approach*, 5th Report, Cmnd 6371, HMSO (1976).

RCEP, *Best Practicable Environmental Option*, 12th Report, Cmnd 310, HMSO (1988).

Scottish Office, *Environmental Protection Act 1990 Part 1: A Practical Guide—Central Control* (1992a).

Scottish Office, *Notes for the guidance of applicants for authorization for processes prescribed for regulation by HMIPI for Scotland or a river purification authority* (1992b).

Wilkinson, H.W., 'Windfarms', *NLJ*, 314/315, 4 March (1994).

6

Statutory Nuisance and Noise Control

6.1 Statutory Nuisance

The history of statutory nuisance goes back to the 1840s when the Victorians faced a major public health crisis caused by the lack of a comprehensive sewerage system at a time of rapid urbanization. Sewage was discharged straight into watercourses without treatment, causing not just a nuisance but also a threat to public health. The poor condition of housing, the streets and the air made living in the rapidly growing cornubations extremely unpleasant and public health reform and street cleansing became the main issues of the day (Wohl, 1983).

The common law remedy of an action for nuisance proved woefully inadequate; typically, action had to be taken by private individuals at great expense and, in any case, the court procedure was slow and cumbersome. The solution was to single out the most common nuisances and prescribe a speedier procedure for tackling them. Nuisances which could be dealt with under this procedure became known as 'statutory nuisances'. The procedure, adopted nearly 150 years ago, is currently to be found in Part III of the EPA 1990.

Section 79 of the EPA 1990 sets out nine statutory nuisances:

1 Premises in such a state as to be prejudicial to health or a nuisance
2 Smoke emitted from premises so as to be prejudicial to health or a nuisance
3 Fumes or gases emitted from premises (which are private dwellings) so as to be prejudicial to health or a nuisance
4 Dust, steam, smell or other effluvia arising on industrial, trade or business premises and being prejudicial to health or a nuisance
5 Any accumulation or deposit which is prejudicial to health or a nuisance
6 Any animal kept in such a place or manner as to be prejudicial to health or a nuisance
7 Noise emitted from premises so as to be prejudicial to health or a nuisance
8 Any other matter declared by any enactment to be a statutory nuisance

9   Noise that is prejudicial to health or a nuisance and is emitted from or
    caused by a vehicle, machinery or equipment in a street (this was added by
    the **Noise and Statutory Nuisance Act 1993**).

6.1.1   Prejudice to Health

The procedure applies where the thing complained of is 'prejudicial to health
or a nuisance'. The courts have construed this phrase to mean that in order to
constitute a statutory nuisance the thing complained of must relate to health.
Thus, not all common law nuisances are statutory nuisances. The court in
Bishop Auckland Local Board v Bishop Auckland Iron and Steel Co. Ltd took
the view that

> the natural sense of the word seems ... to [be] ... a nuisance either interfering with
> personal comfort or injurious to health ... the legislature intended to strike at
> anything which would diminish the comfort of life though not injurious to health,
> and at anything which would in fact injure health (pp. 140–1).

But a transient interference with personal comfort would not be a statutory
nuisance as it is not related to health. This principle is illustrated by *Great
Western Railway Company v Bishop* which concerned rain water dripping from
a railway bridge onto persons beneath.

The facts in *Coventry CC v Cartwright* illustrate the public health nature of
this remedy. The local authority owned a vacant plot of land on which indiscriminate tipping of building materials, scrap iron, broken glass and tin cans took
place. The authority took no action to remove the refuse. A complaint was
made on the ground that the accumulation of materials constituted a statutory
nuisance. The magistrates held that the accumulation was prejudicial to health
because people who went onto the land might hurt themselves on things tipped
there and that it constituted a nuisance because of its visual impact on people
living in neighbourhood houses. On appeal the court held that the statutory
nuisance provisions were aimed at an accumulation of something which produced a threat to health in the sense of a threat of disease, vermin or the like.
An accumulation could not constitute a 'nuisance' merely because of its visual
impact nor could an accumulation of inert matter be 'prejudicial to health'
merely because the inert matter might cause injury to persons who came onto
the land.

6.1.2   Statutory Nuisance Abatement

Abatement Notice

Section 79 of the **EPA 1990** makes it the duty of every local authority to inspect
its area to detect statutory nuisances and also to investigate complaints made by

local residents about statutory nuisances. The procedure for dealing with a statutory nuisance is set out in s. 80.

The local authority must serve an 'abatement notice' on the person responsible for the nuisance. The notice is served on the owner of the premises in two situations: where the nuisance arises from any defect of a structural character or where the person responsible for the nuisance cannot be found. The notice must require the abatement of the nuisance or prohibit or restrict its occurrence or recurrence. It may also require works to be carried out and steps to be taken to abate the nuisance. An appeal against the notice may be made to the magistrates' court within 21 days. Failure to comply with the requirements of the notice without reasonable excuse is an offence for which the maximum fine is £5 000 or, where the offence is committed on industrial, business or trade premises, £20 000.

It is a defence, under s. 80(7), to prove that best practicable means were used to prevent, or to counteract, the effects of the nuisance. This defence is carefully restricted and is not available in cases of a nuisance arising from:

1   Any premises
2   Dust, steam, smell or effluvia arising on industrial or business premises
3   Accumulations or deposits
4   Animals
5   Noise emitted from premises unless the nuisance arises on industrial, trade or business premises
6   Noise emitted from or caused by a vehicle, machinery or equipment in a street unless these are being used for industrial, trade or business purposes
7   Smoke emitted from premises unless it is emitted from a chimney or
8   Fumes or gases emitted from premises or any other statutory nuisances declared by statute.

There is an additional defence relating to noise-related statutory nuisances which covers noise emitted under the provisions of **COPA 1974**. These enable a local authority to serve a notice controlling the noise emitted from construction sites; issue a noise-related consent for work on construction sites; in a noise-abatement zone, serve a noise-reduction notice; and to determine the noise level for a new building. It is a defence to prove that the noise was covered by such notice or consent, or that the level of noise emitted did not contravene a noise-reduction notice or exceed the level stipulated for a new building.

The local authority may itself abate the nuisance where the abatement notice is not complied with and recover its reasonable expenses from the person who caused the nuisance, including the current owner. This provision has raised considerable concern in recent years given its potential for use in the clean-up of contaminated land. It is under review as part of the government's review of local authorities' powers in respect of contaminated land (see Chapter 4).

Abatement Order

Section 82 enables a 'person aggrieved' by a statutory nuisance to take abatement proceedings. The person makes a complaint to a magistrates' court which, if satisfied that a nuisance exists or is likely to recur on the same premises, makes a statutory nuisance abatement order and may at the same time impose a fine of up to £5 000. Before making the complaint twenty-one days' or, for noise-related statutory nuisances, three days' notice of it must be given. The penalty for failing to comply with an abatement order is a fine of up to £5 000 plus £200 for each day on which the offence continues. If a nuisance which existed at the time of the complaint is abated before the trial the court shall order the defendant to pay the complainant's reasonable expenses. If the court is satisfied that the nuisance renders premises unfit for human habitation it may prohibit their use until they are fit for that purpose. The available defences are the same whether proceedings are instituted by a person aggrieved or by a local authority. The court may, after giving the relevant local authority a hearing, direct it to do what the abatement order required.

The statutory nuisance abatement procedure is additional to the specific pollution control provisions available to regulators. It is intended to be a quick remedy for nuisances. It is well suited to cases of gross pollution which are demonstrably prejudicial to health.

6.2 Noise

Provisions for the control of noise are found in Part III of the **COPA 1974**, except for the statutory nuisance provisions which are in Part III of the EPA. The COPA provisions relate primarily to construction sites, noise-abatement zones, new buildings and plant and machinery.

6.2.1 Construction Sites

Local authorities have power under s. 60 of COPA to serve a notice imposing requirements as to how work is to be carried out on construction sites. The notice may specify the appropriate plant or machinery, the hours during which the work may be carried out and the level of noise which may be emitted from the premises. It may also provide for any change of circumstances.

The notice is to be served on the person carrying out or about to carry out the works or on such other persons appearing to the local authority to be responsible for, or to have control over, the works. It may specify the time within which compliance is required, and may require the execution of works and the taking of other necessary steps. In *Walter Lilley & Co. Ltd v Westminster CC* the court held that the notice is limited to works being undertaken or contemplated at the time such notice was issued and that its application does not extend to uncontemplated works at the same premises for which a fresh notice should be issued.

The local authority is required to have regard to approved codes of practice. The Control of Noise (Code of Practice for Construction and Open Sites) Order 1984, SI No. 1992 has approved British Standards Institution (BSI) codes of practice for this purpose. The local authority must also take into account the need to:

1 Ensure that best practicable means are employed to minimize noise
2 Specify equally effective means of minimizing noise more acceptable to the recipient of the notice before specifying any particular methods or plant or machinery
3 Protect any persons in the locality of the construction from the effects of the noise.

The recipient may appeal against the notice to a magistrates' court within twenty-one days of service. It is an offence to contravene the requirements of the notice.

Section 61 of COPA enables a person who intends to carry out work on a construction site to apply to the local authority for a consent. The application must contain particulars of the works and the method by which they are to be carried out and of the steps proposed to be taken to minimize noise resulting from the works. If the local authority considers that the application contains sufficient information and that, if the works are carried out in accordance with the application it would not need to serve a notice to control the noise, it shall give its consent to the application. The local authority is required to have regard to the same factors as in serving a notice and the decision in the *Walter Lilley case* would apply to the works covered by the consent. It may attach conditions to the consent, including limiting its duration.

It is an offence to breach the conditions of the consent. *Tower Hamlets LBC v London Docklands Development Corp.* provides an instance of a developer being convicted of breaching noise consent conditions through a failure to supervise adequately an independent contractor who was carrying out the works.

The local authority must inform the applicant of its decision on the application within twenty-eight days. It may publish notice of the consent, and of the works to which it relates. There is provision for the applicant to appeal to a magistrates' court against a failure to give a consent in twenty-eight days or against its conditions.

A consent does not provide a defence to a charge of causing a statutory nuisance or to an action for common law nuisance. In *Lloyds Bank v Guardian Assurance and Trollope & Colls* the first defendant engaged the second defendant to carry out demolition and reconstruction work at a site adjacent to the bank's premises. Because of the noise the bank sought an injunction limiting the hours of working. Contemporaneously, the local authority issued a notice under s. 60 of COPA restricting the hours of work but to a lesser extent than specified in the injunction. The court dismissed the defendant's argument that the court had no jurisdiction to grant an injunction in the circumstances where a s. 60 notice had been, or was to be, issued.

However, in *Gillingham BC v Medway (Chatham) Dock Co. Ltd* the court held that planning permission so altered the character of the locality that the local planning authority which had granted the planning permission could not succeed in an action for a common law nuisance arising from the noise and dust consequent upon the development. This underscores the fact that the existence of a permit is a relevant factor in determining whether a nuisance exists but having decided that, on the facts, a nuisance exists, the court may award an injunction or damages in spite of the permit.

6.2.2 Noise-abatement Zones

Section 63 enables a local authority to designate all or any part of its area a noise-abatement zone. The order designating the zone shall specify the classes of premises to which it applies. Having so designated its area the local authority must measure the level of noise emanating from premises within the zone which are of any class to which the order applies and record them in a 'noise level register' which it must keep and make available for public inspection. The Control of Noise (Measurement and Registers) Regulations 1976, SI No. 37 specifies the particulars to be included in the register. A copy of the record shall be served on the owner or occupier of the premises in respect of which the measurement was taken. There is provision for an appeal against the record to the Secretary of State within twenty-eight days.

It is an offence under s. 65 to contravene the level of noise recorded in the register in respect of any premises except with the local authority's written consent, which may be subject to specified conditions. If the authority does not give its consent within two months it shall be deemed to have refused the application, although this period may be extended by agreement. The applicant may appeal within three months to the Secretary of State against the authority's decision or deemed refusal. If a person is convicted of exceeding the level of noise recorded in the register the court may, if satisfied that the offence is likely to continue or recur, order the execution of any works necessary to prevent it. The court may also direct the local authority to carry out the works.

Where the local authority believes that the level of noise from any premises exceeds the level specified in a noise-abatement order and that a reduction is practicable at reasonable cost and would afford a public benefit, the local authority may serve a notice on the person responsible under s. 66. This 'noise-reduction notice' requires the person to reduce the level of noise to a specified level and to prevent a subsequent increase without consent.

The notice shall specify a time, not being less than six months, within which the noise level is to be reduced to a specified level. Such a notice overrides any consent which the local authority has issued allowing the level of noise to exceed that recorded in the register and there is provision for an appeal to the magistrates' court within three months. It is an offence to contravene the requirements of a noise-reduction notice but if the noise was caused in the course of a trade or business it shall be a defence to prove that best practicable means were used to prevent or counteract its effects.

6.2.3 New Buildings and Intruder Alarms

Where the local authority believes that a building is to be constructed to which a noise-abatement order will apply or that any premises will, as a result of any works, become premises to which a noise-abatement order applies it may, under s. 67, determine the level of noise which will be acceptable. It may do this either on the application of the owner, the occupier or the person negotiating to acquire an interest in the premises or, in the alternative, on its own initiative. It shall then record that level of noise in the register. Before determining the noise level the authority shall give notice of its intentions to the person responsible who may appeal to the Secretary of State within three months.

Section 9 of the **Noise and Statutory Nuisance Act 1993** gives local authorities powers to resolve that provisions dealing with the installation and operation of intruder alarms shall apply in their area. These provisions enable the entry into premises to turn off alarms after one hour of continuous audible operation. These provisions have not yet been brought into force because of unresolved issues relating to possible liability should a burglary occur after an alarm has been turned off under these powers.

6.2.4 Aircraft Noise

Provisions for the control of aircraft noise are contained in Part III of the **Civil Aviation Act 1982**. These provide for the designation of aerodromes, grants towards the cost of soundproofing buildings, consideration of environmental factors in licensing and consultation procedures. The designation provisions, set out in s. 78, are the basis of aircraft noise control.

Under s. 78 the Secretary of State may, by notice, make it the duty of the operator of an aircraft at a designated aerodrome to secure that, after the aircraft takes off or before it lands, requirements in the notice for limiting or mitigating the effects of noise and vibration are complied with. The Secretary of State may also, by notice, prohibit aircraft from taking off or landing during specified periods, specify the number of occasions on which aircraft may be permitted to take off or land during specified periods and determine the operators who shall be entitled to arrange for aircraft to take off or land during specified periods.

The notices (known as NOTAMs) are issued by the Civil Aviation Authority on behalf of the Department of Transport (DOT) in respect of the three designated airports Heathrow, Gatwick and Stansted. The restrictions on night movements of aircraft which were introduced in 1988 lasted until 1993. The DOT's proposals for replacing them failed following a successful judicial review application in *R v Secretary of State for Transport ex parte Richmond upon Thames LBC and Others.*

The proposal was to introduce in October 1993 a quota system of night-flying restrictions to replace the system of restrictions on the number of aircraft movements then in operation. The new proposals assigned to each airport a maximum number of quota points. Within the ceiling defined by the quotas operators would be free to choose how to distribute the quota points between noisier and quieter aircraft, operating a greater number of quieter aircraft or a lesser number of the noisier types. The intention was to give aircraft operators an incentive to replace their older, noisier aircraft by modern, quieter ones.

The applicants' complaint was that the quota system was contrary to the provisions of s. 78 since it did not specify the 'maximum number of occasions on which aircraft may be permitted to take off and land' and ignored the effect of frequent aircraft movements on the health of inhabitants. They argued that ground noise arising from aircraft movements is not diminished by using quiet aircraft. The court rejected the Secretary of State's argument that the scheme dictated a maximum number of movements for each aircraft type, and involved a specification of maximum numbers, ruling that whatever maxima the quota system generated were purely notional and were not the real basis on which the Secretary of State proposed to regulate noise at the airports. The court held that under s. 78 a maximum number of movements 'must be the linchpin of any order made' and struck down the Secretary of State's proposal.

The Secretary of State therefore issued a replacement notice which combined the quota system plus a specified maximum number of movements to come into force on 27 March for the 1994 summer season (NOTAM, 1993; DOT, 1994a). Subsequently, arrangements to apply from the winter of 1994/5 until the end of the 1998 summer season were announced (NOTAM, 1994; DOT, 1994b).

The DOT has announced proposals to repeal s. 78 and replace it with a new power of designation. In the government's view the drawback with s. 78 at present is that it places responsibility for operating noise-amelioration measures in the hands of the Civil Aviation Authority (on behalf of the Secretary of State) rather than on the aerodrome operator. The new power would give designated aerodromes explicit power to prepare noise-amelioration schemes and to penalize operators who do not comply with them. The aerodrome would be required to consult locally about the scheme and seek agreement to it from a 'lead' local authority although there would be provision for disputes to be referred to the Secretary of State (DOT, 1991; DOT, 1993).

References

Bishop Auckland Local Board v Bishop Auckland Iron & Steel Co. Ltd (1882) 10 QBD 138.

Coventry v Cartwright (1975) 2 All ER 99.

DOT, 'Revised summer season night flying restrictions at Heathrow, Gatwick and Stansted', Press Notice No. 40, 1 February (1994a).

DOT, 'Night flying restrictions at Heathrow, Gatwick and Stansted', Press Notice No. 162, 6 May (1994b).

DOT, *Control of Aircraft Noise—A Consultation Paper* (1991).

DOT, *Review of Aircraft Noise Legislation: Announcement of Conclusions*, March (1993).

Gillingham BC v Medway (Chatham) Dock Co. Ltd (1992) 4/2 JEL 251.

Great Western Railway Co. v Bishop (1872) 7 LR QB 550.

Lloyds Bank v Guardian Assurance and Trollope & Colls (1987) 35 Build. LR 34.

NOTAM, *Heathrow, Gatwick and Stansted Airports Noise Restrictions (No. 2) Notice*, S45/1993, 15 October (1993).

NOTAM, *Heathrow, Gatwick and Stansted Airports Noise Restrictions (No. 1) Notice*, S5/1994, 18 February (1994).

R v Secretary of State for Transport ex parte Richmond upon Thames LBC and Others, [1994] 1 WLR 74.

Tower Hamlets LBC v London Docklands Development Corporation (1992).

Walter Lilley & Co. Ltd v Westminster CC, *The Times*, 1 March (1994).

Wohl, A.S., *Endangered Lives: Public Health in Victorian Britain*, J. M. Dent (1983).

7

Hazardous Substances and Genetically Modified Organisms

7.1 The Background

The control of hazardous substances is carried out primarily under the **Health and Safety at Work etc. Act 1974**. Genetically modified organisms are controlled under further, more specific, legislation.

The aims of the Health and Safety at Work etc. Act 1974 are stated to be

1 To protect the health, safety and welfare of persons at work:
2 To protect the public against risks to their health and safety arising from the activities of persons at work and
3 To control dangerous substances and emissions into the atmosphere.

These aims are clearly closely related to those of environmental protection, particularly in relation to the protection of the public and the control of atmospheric emissions.

In order to achieve its aims, ss 2 to 9 of the Act impose a series of 'general duties' on employers, manufacturers, importers and suppliers of articles as well as on employees. Employees have a duty to take reasonable care for the health and safety of themselves and other persons at work. An employer's duties under the Act are to:

1 Ensure the health, safety and welfare at work of all employees so far as is reasonably practicable
2 Prepare and revise a written statement of general policy with respect to the health and safety of employees and the organization and arrangements in force to carry out that policy and bring it to the notice of all employees
3 Conduct activities so as to ensure that, so far as is reasonably practicable, persons not in employment who may be affected by a company's activities are not exposed to risks to their health or safety.

Similarly, manufacturers, importers and suppliers of articles or substances have a duty to ensure, so far as is practicable, that they are safe and free of risk to health and that the necessary information about possible risks is available. These duties have been developed by a series of 'health and safety' regulations and codes of practice made under ss 15 and 16 of the Act.

To administer and enforce the Act, s. 10 established the Health and Safety Commission (HSC) and the Health and Safety Executive (HSE) as the Commission's executive arm. Coordination between the HSE and the environmental protection authorities is ensured through Memoranda of Understanding which the HSE entered into on 17 October 1990 with both the NRA and HMIP, similar to an earlier one of 7 December 1990 between the NRA and HMIP. The HSC and HSE also have to liaise closely with both the DoE and local authorities over planning permissions, authorizations and enforcement. The HSC is advised on matters relating to toxic substances by the Advisory Committee on Toxic Substances (ACTS). In June 1993 ACTS' remit was extended to take account of environmental and consumer interests in addition to toxic substances in the workplace, reflecting the close link between health and safety and environmental concerns.

The HSC and HSE regulate all issues of health and safety in the workplace. This extends to the regulation of offshore installations; hazardous substances, including radioactive susbstances; pesticides regulation; and the transport of dangerous goods on either rail or road. However, where there are issues which have a health and safety–environment interface then the jurisdiction is shared between the HSE and departments of the central government; the principle is that the HSE controls the health and safety aspects while the government departments control the environmental aspects. Pesticides regulation, for instance, is shared with MAFF, while hazardous substances control is shared with the DoE. The regulation of genetically modified organisms is also shared; their deliberate release into the environment is under the DoE while the HSE is in charge of controlling their contained use.

The HSE operates through Inspectorates who conduct 'field inspections' of relevant installations for which it is responsible. The various Inspectorates are the Factory Inspectorate, the Agriculture Inspectorate, the Mines and Quarries Inspectorate, the Nuclear Installations Inspectorate, the Railways Inspectorate and the Offshore Safety Division. The names indicate quite clearly the remit of each Inspectorate.

7.2 Hazardous Substances Control

Hazardous substances are regulated through a wide range of measures. These relate to the need for planning permission from a local authority; prior notification of the HSE about a proposed installation involving the use or storage of hazardous substances; risk assessment of the hazards presented by exposure to the substances; the classification, packaging and labelling of the hazardous substances; special transport arrangements to counter risks that their transport might pose; and restrictions and controls on supply, storage and use. These measures are discussed below.

7.2.1 Planning Permission

Activities which involve the handling of hazardous substances come up for consideration in the normal way under the development control system (see Chapter 8). This stipulates that planning permission is required for most development activities. However, additional specific provision has been made for dealing with hazardous substances at the planning permission stage under the **Planning (Hazardous Substances) Act 1990**. In Scotland the provisions are contained in Part II to Schedule 7 of the **Housing and Planning Act 1986** which amended the **Town and Country Planning (Scotland) Act 1972** to introduce specific planning controls on hazardous substances. These provisions came into force on 1 June 1992 in England and Wales and 1 May 1993 in Scotland (DoE, undated, and DoE/SO, 1993).

Control under the Planning (Hazardous Substances) Act 1990 is exercised by the local authority in its capacity as the 'hazardous substances authority'. Section 4 provides that the presence of a hazardous substance on, over or under land requires the consent (the 'hazardous substances consent') of the hazardous substances authority unless the quantity present is less than the 'controlled quantity' for that substance. The Planning (Hazardous Substances) Regulations 1992, SI No. 656 prescribes seventy-one toxic, highly reactive, explosive and flammable substances as hazardous substances for the purposes of the Planning (Hazardous Substances) Act 1990. It also prescribes the controlled quantities for the particular substances; with the exception of methyl bromide, phosphine and TCDD which are in kilograms, the quantities are specified in tonnes. The Town and Country Planning (Hazardous Substances) (Scotland) Regulations 1993, SI No. 323 (S.31) prescribes the same substances and quantities in relation to Scotland.

A consent is not required where the substance is:

1   Present in less than the 'controlled quantity'—this is the aggregate quantity of the substance within 500 metres of the site in or on land or a structure which is, in either case, under the control of the same person
2   Present on the land only temporarily while it is being transported between places
3   Is a controlled or a radioactive waste
4   Is contained in an aerosol dispenser with a capacity of less than 1000 ml, or does not contain flammable substances or any of a number of several listed hazardous substances in excess of 1000 ml

5   Is an 'exempt pipe' or a 'service pipe'; the former is a pipeline used to convey a hazardous substance to or from a site while the latter is a pipeline used by a public gas supplier to supply gas to an individual consumer from a mains of that supplier

6   Is unloaded from a ship in an emergency and no more than 14 days have passed since the unloading.

A hazardous substances consent may be either an 'express consent' or a 'deemed consent'; the former is applied for while the latter is 'claimed' under s. 11. Section 12 makes provision for another variant of a hazardous substances consent; this is a consent granted as part of a government authorization for a development by a local authority or a statutory undertaker which involves the presence of a hazardous substance in circumstances in which a consent would otherwise be required.

The application for an express consent is made on Form 1, supplied by the hazardous substances authority and includes a map and a substance location plan indicating where the substance is to be stored, manufactured, treated or otherwise processed. The applicant must also certify that either he or she was the owner of the land in the twenty-one days preceding the application or, where he was not, that he has endeavoured to notify the owners of the application. The application shall be publicized and consulted on before it is determined. The authority is required to determine the application within eight weeks but the applicant and the authority may agree a longer period.

The consent may be granted subject to a number of conditions relating to:

1   The commencement or execution of development on the land which is authorized by a planning permission

2   How and where the substance is to be kept or used

3   The times when the substance may be present and

4   The permanent removal of the substance.

Unless the consent is granted by the minister, conditions relating to how the substance is to be kept or used may only be imposed on the advice of the HSE.

Section 11 states that where a hazardous substance was present on, over or under land at any time in the year before the Act came into force, referred to as the 'establishment period', a hazardous substances consent may be claimed in respect of its presence. The claim had to be made in the six months following the coming into force of the Act, i.e. by December 1992 in England and Wales and by October 1993 in Scotland, a period referred to as 'the transitional period'. The deemed consent, which is automatically granted once claimed, is subject to the conditions that:

1   The consented quantity does not exceed the 'established quantity', a quantity calculated in one of two ways: (i) where before the Act came into force on 1 June 1992 (in Scotland, 1 May 1993), the presence of the substance

was notified to the HSE under the Notication of Installations Handling Hazardous Substances Regulations 1982, SI No. 1357, (see below), it is the quantity last notified or twice the quantity notified or last notified before the establishment period whichever is the greater; (ii) where notification was not required the amount is one and a half times the maximum quantity which was present on, over or under the land within the establishment period.

2 It is kept and used in the place and manner in which it was kept and used before the Act came into force.
3 None of the substance is kept or used in a container greater in capacity than the largest of the containers in which the substance was kept or used before the Act came into force.

The conditions subject to which a consent, whether express or deemed, has been given may be varied on application to the authority. A variation application of this sort does not throw open other aspects of the consent not related to the conditions (e.g. other substances consented) for review. The authority also has power to modify or revoke the consent, in which case compensation shall be payable by the authority for damage suffered by the consent holder for the loss of the consent. A revocation of the consent may result from:

1 A material change of use of the land
2 The commencement of development which would involve a material change of use of the land
3 The absence for five years from the land of the substance consented; in this case the revocation must relate to the entire consent.

A revocation does not take effect, however, until it is confirmed by the Secretary of State either wholly or in part.

Although a hazardous substances consent enures to the benefit of the land, when there is a change in the person in control of the land a 'continuation application' must be lodged with the authority otherwise the consent could be revoked. The authority may take advantage of a continuation application to revoke or modify the consent but if it does it must pay compensation to the previous consent holder. If the continuation application is granted the authority shall state that the land, the hazardous substances, the quantity involved and the conditions to which it is subject are unchanged, or if any of them have changed, the nature of the change. The Secretary of State may direct that applications be referred to him or her to determine. Appeals may be made within six months to the Secretary of State whose decision is final.

The authority may enforce the consent by issuing a 'hazardous substances contravention notice'. This specifies the contravention and requires specified steps to remedy it within a stated period. The notice takes effect on a specified date which must be at least twenty-eight days from its service. It may require the hazardous substance to be removed from the land, in which case it may direct that the consent ceases to have effect either wholly or partially from a given date. The notice may, however, be withdrawn before it comes into effect and shall be suspended if an appeal is lodged against it to the Secretary of State.

It is an offence to have in, on or over land hazardous substances above the controlled quantity without a consent. A fine of £5 000 may be imposed in the magistrates' court with a further £200 on each day on which the offence continues.

7.2.2   Prior Notification of the HSE

Three sets of Regulations require prior notifications of dangerous activities before they commence, giving the HSE an opportunity to impose safety requirements to pre-empt possible dangers. The Regulations, which pre-date the **Planning (Hazardous Substances) Act 1990** and its Scottish equivalent, complement their provisions.

Notification of Installations

The Notification of Installations Handling Hazardous Substances Regulations 1982, SI No. 1357 made under the **Health and Safety at Work etc. Act 1974** make provision for installations handling hazardous substances (but not licensed waste disposal sites) to be notified to the HSE. The HSE has power, however, to exempt any person or activity from this requirement if it is satisfied that the health and safety of persons who are likely to be affected by the exemption will not be prejudiced because of it. The regulations specify the substances and their threshhold quantities, referred to as the 'notifiable quantity', which bring the specified substance within its parameters.

A 'notifiable quantity' is a similar concept to 'controlled quantity' under the Planning (Hazardous Substances) Act 1990. It is also determined by taking into account all the hazardous substances under the control of the same person within 500 metres of the site whether in a pipeline or in a vehicle, vessel, aircraft or hovercraft used for storage. Substances in the course of transport are, however, excluded from the calculation.

The regulations require that the HSE must be notified three months before any activity is embarked upon in which there is, or is liable to be, a notifiable quantity of a hazardous substance. Further, the HSE must be updated of changes in the quantity of the hazardous substance or the cessation of the activity. Where the quantity of the substance on the site increases to three times that originally notified the HSE must be notified afresh as if it were a new activity.

Industrial Accident Hazards

The second set of regulations requiring prior notification is the Control of Industrial Major Accident Hazards Regulations 1984, SI 1902, as amended, which implements in the UK EC Directive 82/501/EEC on major accident hazards of certain industrial activities, the 'Seveso Directive'.

The Regulations apply to specified categories of industrial installations if they conduct an industrial activity which is liable to involve a dangerous substance. The dangerous substances to which the Regulations apply are either those listed in the Regulations in the specified quantities or substances which are toxic, flammable, explosive or liable to oxidize. The Regulations also apply to the storage of specified quantities of a number of specified dangerous substances or preparations. In calculating the quantities involved account is taken of all the substances within a distance of 500 metres under the control of the same person. The Regulations do not apply, however, to nuclear intallations, installations under the control of the Secretary of State or an international organization, explosives factories, and mines and quarries. A previous exemption for industrial activities carried on under a waste disposal licence was removed by amending Regulations 1994, SI No. 118.

The industrial installations involved are categorized into 'top tier' and 'lower tier' on the basis of the quantity of hazardous substances handled: installations handling greater quantities of hazardous substances are seen as posing a greater hazard. In relation to smaller intallations, the operator must identify the major accident hazards posed, take adequate steps to prevent their occurrence and limit their consequences. They must also provide their workers with information, training and equipment necessary to ensure their safety. Should an accident occur the HSE must be notified with details, including the steps taken to prevent a recurrence. The HSE shall then inform the European Commission of the occurrence.

Three months before an activity involving a 'top tier' installation is begun, a written report must be sent to the HSE detailing the dangerous substances involved, the nature of the installation, the management system for controlling the industrial activity and the potential major accidents. Changes which could materially affect the particulars in the report may not be made to the activity subsequent to the report unless, three months before the changes, a further report taking account of the changes is sent to the HSE. Three years after the report a further report shall be prepared taking account of new technical knowledge which materially affects the particulars of the previous report relating to safety and developments in the knowledge of hazard assessment. A copy of the new report must be sent to the HSE within one month.

The Regulations give the HSE power to serve a notice on the manufacturer seeking additional information for evaluating the major accident hazards created by the activity. They also require that the person in charge of the 'top tier' activity prepare and regularly update an 'on-site' emergency plan showing how major accidents will be dealt with and giving the names of those responsible for safety on the site and for acting in accordance with the plan. For its part, the local authority also has to prepare and update, in consultation with the manufacturer, the HSE and other relevant people, an 'off-site' emergency plan showing how such an accident would be dealt with; it may recover its costs from the manufacturer.

The responsibility for giving the public information, such as how they will be alerted and how they should behave in the event of an accident, falls on the operator but he or she is required to arrange with the local authority to disseminate it. Empirical evidence suggests that the public often show apathy towards information given to them, throwing leaflets in the bin, for instance (ENDS, 1994a). This suggests that more imaginative ways of informing the public must be constantly sought. This has been underscored by recent high-profile industrial accidents with significant off-site effects. In one incident at the Allied Colloids factory in Bradford, the fire created a plume of black toxic smoke which drifted many miles from the site and caused injuries to several fire and police officers involved in dealing with the emergency (ENDS, 1994b).

Marking of Sites

In relation to storage, the Dangerous Substances (Notification and Marking of Sites) Regulations 1990, SI No. 304 make provision for the HSE and the fire authority to be notified of the presence at a site of more than 25 tonnes of dangerous substances. There are a number of exemptions including those situations where the HSE has been notified under other Regulations. Where there are changes involving a reduction of the quantity of dangerous susbstance present on the site or the classification of the dangerous substance present, the changes must be notified as well.

While the dangerous substances are present in those quantities safety signs bearing hazard-warning symbols specified in the Regulations must be displayed to warn fire officers of their presence in case of an emergency. The Regulations also contain provisions for directions to be given to the person in control of a site to display safety signs bearing the hazard-warning symbols, the details of which are set out in the Regulations, if the warning is necessary to warn fire officers in an emergency of the presence of the substances.

7.2.3   Risk Assessment of Hazards Posed by Exposure

The third step in the sequence of planning permission and prior notification is the assessment of risk before actual work commences. Historically, this has been in the context of health and safety rather than environmental control, although there is an environment–health and safety interface at this stage.

Two sets of Regulations are relevant: the Control of Substances Hazardous to Health Regulations (COSHH) 1988, SI No. 1657, as amended, and the Management of Health and Safety at Work Regulations 1992, SI No. 2051 which came into force on 1 January 1993. The two sets of Regulations flesh out the duties set out in ss 2 to 9 of the **Health and Safety at Work etc. Act 1974** requiring employers and those who supply articles for use at work to take reasonably practicable measures to secure the health, safety and welfare of their workers and others who may be affected by their activities.

The Control of Substances Hazardous to Health Regulations 1988 apply to a range of 'substances hazardous to health' which they list. The Regulations seek to prevent the exposure of employees and others to such substances. They require the employer before starting work to assess and review the risks created by the work to the health of employees and the steps needed to prevent or, where this is not reasonably practicable, adequately control the risks. The employer must monitor the exposure of the employees to the substances and keep a record for forty years where it represents the personal exposure of identifiable employees, but where it does not, for five years. In certain circumstances, a health, or medical, surveillance of employees may be appropriate in which case the employer shall ensure that it is undertaken. Additionally, the employer must provide the employees with the information, instruction and training relating to the risks created by the exposure and the precautions which should be taken including the results of any monitoring and health surveillance undertaken.

The Management of Health and Safety Regulations 1992 are part of the 'six-pack' Regulations which implement the EC Framework Directive 89/391/EEC on measures to encourage improvements in the safety and health of workers at work. The other five deal with display-screen equipment, manual handling operations, the provision and use of work equipment, personal protective equipment and the workplace itself, i.e. ventilation, temperature, and so on.

Like COSHH, these Regulations require the employer to assess and review the risks to the health and safety of employees and others in order to identify and put in place measures needed to counter these risks. Where more than five people are employed these Regulations, unlike COSHH, require that the employer record the significant findings of the assessment, groups of employees identified as being especially at risk and details of the arrangements to counter the risks. As under COSHH, the employer has to provide employees with health surveillance, information and training. The 1992 Regulations introduced a new requirement for employers to appoint competent persons to assist them in undertaking the necessary health and safety measures. This requirement does not, however, apply to an employer who is in partnership with someone who has the competence to carry out the necessary measures.

7.2.4   Classification, Packaging and Labelling

Two regulations deal with classification, packaging and labelling (CPL) of dangerous substances. The first, The Chemicals (Hazard Information and Packaging) Regulations 1993, SI No. 1746 (CHIP), make provision for the classification, packaging and labelling of dangerous substances for supply purposes only. The second, the Carriage of Dangerous Goods by Road and Rail (Classification, Packaging and Labelling) Regulations 1994, SI No. 669 (CPL 1994), make provision for the classification, packaging and labelling of dangerous goods intended to be consigned for carriage purposes. The requirements in both cases are similar. The HSE has proposed introducing new regulations, CHIP 2, to replace CHIP 1 in order to implement requirements of EC directives relating to child-resistant fastenings and tactile danger warnings for the blind (HSE, 1994).

CPL for Supply

CHIP came into force on 1 September 1993, replacing the Classification, Packaging and Labelling of Dangerous Substances Regulations 1984, SI No. 1244 (as amended). A one-year transition period was given for persons already complying with the requirements of the 1984 Regulations so that until 1 September 1994 they did not need to implement the requirements of the 1993 Regulations. In relation to certain small packages the transition period runs up to 1 March 1995.

The regulations implement four EC directives which provide for classification, packaging and labelling: 92/32/EEC amending for the seventh time Directive 67/457/EEC (dangerous substances); 88/379/EEC (as amended) (dangerous preparations); 78/631/EEC (pesticides); and a fourth directive, 91/155/EEC, which provides for an information system, i.e. 'data sheets', on dangerous preparations.

The regulations apply to substances or preparations which are 'dangerous for supply', although there are a number of exceptions. The substances and preparations are listed in a Schedule to the Regulations and in an HSE document known as the 'Approved Supply List' (HSC, 1993). This gives, in respect of these substances:

1   The names
2   Index and CAS, or reference, numbers
3   Risk or 'R-phrases'
4   Safety or 'S-phrases'
5   Classification and labelling data and concentration limits approved by the HSC for the classification of preparations containing that substance and
6   Oral toxicity values for classifying pesticides.

The Regulations provide that a substance or a preparation must not be supplied unless the supplier has classified it on the basis of:

1   Its entry in the Supply List
2   Its notification under the Notification of New Substances Regulations 1993, SI No. 3050 which implement the requirements of the 7th amendment to EC Directive 67/548/EEC on classification, packaging and labelling
3   The categories of danger set out in a Schedule to the Regulations (e.g. flammable, toxic, corrosive and so on)
4   Criteria in a Schedule (Schedule 4) to the Regulations dealing with the classification of preparations or
5   Criteria set out in a Schedule (Schedule 5) to the Regulations for the classification of pesticides.

The supplier must also provide the recipient with a 'safety data sheet' containing specified information to enable the recipient to take the necessary health and safety and environmental protection measures.

The second requirement of the Regulations relates to packaging. A substance or a preparation shall not be supplied unless it has been suitably packaged. The packaging of the substance or preparation must be labelled with:

1   Details of the substance or preparation and its supplier or consigner
2   A danger symbol drawn from the Schedule to the Regulations giving indications of danger
3   'R-' and 'S-phrases' giving indications of risk and safety measures and
4   The EEC number, if any, and, in relation to carriage, a hazard warning sign.

Finally, the Regulations make provision for labelling. They specify the methods of marking and the dimensions of the label, basing these on the capacity of the package. There are limited exemptions for transfers between workplaces, small quantities of substances or preparations and small packages. Additionally, special provision is made for the labelling of specified preparations, for example very toxic, toxic or corrosive preparations sold to the general public.

CPL for Carriage

The Classification, Packaging and Labelling of Dangerous Goods for Carriage by Road and Rail 1994, SI No. 669 came into force on 1 April 1994. The Regulations revoke the carriage requirements previously in CHIP which now deals solely with CPL for supply.

The Regulations require all consignors of dangerous goods for transport by road or rail to ensure that they are classified correctly according to the nature of the hazard and then packaged and labelled accordingly. The classification shall be in accordance with the 'Approved Carriage List' published by the HSC (1994a). This gives, in respect of the dangerous goods:

1 The name
2 The UN number
3 The codes for the classification for carriage
4 The code for any subsidiary hazard
5 The emergency action code
6 The hazard identification number
6 Whether the goods may be carried in tanks
8 Whether the goods may be carried in bulk
9 The packing group, if any and
10 The code for any special provision.

The Regulations provide that dangerous goods must not be consigned for carriage in packages unless these are suitable for the purpose. The packages must, among other requirements, be designed, constructed, maintained, filled and closed so as to prevent their contents from escaping.

Finally, dangerous goods must not be consigned for carriage in packages unless these have been labelled with the following particulars:

1 The designation of the goods
2 The UN number
3 The danger sign and
4 If one is given, the subsidiary hazard sign.

The HSC has published approved methods for the classification and packaging of dangerous goods (HSC, 1994b). This gives the appropriate methods for ascertaining in relation to the dangerous goods:

1 Their hazardous properties in order of degree of hazard
2 Their flash points
3 Their relevant properties and
4 The suitability of packaging.

7.2.5 Transport

There are a number of international instruments dealing with the carriage of dangerous goods and the UK has, on the whole, based its rules and regulations on them. Although requirements under the UK Regulations are not in all cases the same as those under the international rules, compliance with the international rules will in the majority of cases be sufficient to exempt the carrier from the comparable UK rules. Globally, there are:

1 The United Nations Recommendations for the Transport of Dangerous Goods
2 The Regulations on the International Carriage of Dangerous Goods by Rail
3 The International Maritime Dangerous Goods Code issued by the International Maritime Organization
4 The European Agreement on the International Carriage of Dangerous Goods by Road, or simply, the ADR, which is not yet harmonized with the UN Recommendations (DTp, 1993).

Five sets of regulations make provision in the UK for the transport of dangerous substances and preparations: the Road Traffic (Carriage of Dangerous Substances in Packages etc.) Regulations 1992, SI No. 742 as amended; the Road Traffic (Carriage of Dangerous Substances in Road Tankers and Tank Containers) Regulations 1992, SI No. 743 as amended; the Road Traffic (Training of Drivers of Vehicles Carrying Dangerous Goods) 1992, SI No. 744 as amended; the Dangerous Substances in Harbour Areas Regulations 1987, SI No. 37 as amended; and the Carriage of Dangerous Goods by Rail 1994, SI No. 670

Carriage in Packages

The Carriage of Dangerous Substances in Packages Regulations 1992, SI No. 742, as amended, impose a number of duties on the operator of a vehicle carrying dangerous substances. These are to ensure that:

1 The vehicle and, where the substance is placed in a freight container, the container is properly designed, is of adequate strength and good construction, is maintained properly and is suitable for the purpose
2 Where the substance is carried in bulk, the parts of the vehicle and freight container which are likely to come into contact with it are made of material which would not be affected by the substance or react with it to form a substance which creates a health and safety hazard
3 The operator obtains from the consigner of the substance the information needed to be able to comply with the operator's duties and to be aware of the hazards created by the substance
4 The driver of the vehicle carries on the vehicle information about the identity and quantity of the substance, the nature of the hazards created by it and actions to be taken in an emergency concerning it. The information is often supplied by way of a document known as a Transport Emergency Card (Tremcard) which the driver carries in the vehicle; the driver must ensure that information about a dangerous susbstance which is not being carried on the vehicle is not left in it
4 Where the vehicle carries at least 500 kg of a dangerous substance, it must

display two rectangular orange-coloured plates conforming to specifications set out in the Regulations; these must be removed or covered when the vehicle is empty.

Carriage in Tankers and Tank Containers

The Carriage of Dangerous Substances in Road Tankers and Tank Containers Regulations 1992, SI No. 743 as amended apply, with certain exceptions, to carriage in a road tanker or a tank container carried on a vehicle. The obligations imposed by these regulations on operators of the vehicles are similar to those dealing with the carriage in packages Regulations. They relate primarily to the road tanker and tank container's design, strength, construction and suitability for the purpose; information about the health and safety hazards created by the substance; information to be carried on the vehicle about the identity and quantity of the substance; and the actions to be taken in an emergency.

A number of other requirements are different, as follows:

1 The road tanker and tank container must be tested, examined and certified both initially and periodically under a written scheme prepared for the purpose
2 The road tanker must display three, and the tank container four, hazard-warning panels conforming to specifications set out in the Regulations
3 Additional labelling requirements where a load consists of two or more substances, i.e. a multi-load, requiring labels to be carried in seperate uncompartmented tanks or in separate compartments of a compartmented tank
4 Requirements relating to unloading of petrol at premises where it is kept.

Driver Training

The Road Traffic (Training of Drivers of Vehicles Carrying Dangerous Goods) 1992, SI No. 744, as amended, makes provision for the training of drivers of vehicles carrying dangerous goods. However, there are cases of carriage which are exempt from its provisions.

The operators must ensure that the drivers have been instructed and trained to enable them to understand the dangers to which the particular goods being carried may give rise and the action to be taken in an emergency as well as the drivers' health and safety duties. The drivers must hold a vocational training certificate showing that they have been trained and have passed the relevant examinations. The Regulations provide for the validity of provisional vocational training certificates, which expire on 1 January 1995, and for existing training certificates which were issued under earlier provisions. The certificate must be available during the whole of the carriage and shall be produced on request to any police officer or vehicle goods examiner.

Harbour Areas

The Dangerous Substances in Harbour Areas Regulations 1987, SI No. 37, as amended, make provision for the carriage, loading, unloading and storage of dangerous substances in harbour areas. The regulations require in most, but not all, cases that notice of at least twenty-four hours be given to the harbour master or, where the substance is to be brought to a berth, the berth operator; they may, however, require up to fourteen days' notice. The notice must provide adequate information for evaluating the health and safety risks created by the substance and, where appropriate, an indication as to whether the vessel has fitness and safety certificates. The harbour master may give directions regulating or prohibiting its entry into the harbour area; its handling, movement or position within it; or requiring its removal from the harbour area. The vessel shall be anchored or moored only at such places and at such times as the harbour master may direct. The harbour authority in its turn must prepare and update an effective emergency plan for dealing with emergencies which involve, affect or could affect the dangerous substances in the harbour area. The authority may, additionally, make by-laws prohibiting the entry, or regulating the entry, carriage, handling and storage of dangerous substances in the harbour area.

Vessels carrying specified quantities of certain dangerous substances must display flags and lights conforming to requirements set out in a Schedule to the Regulations. Other vessels are required to keep a safe distance from moored or anchored vessels displaying such lights and flags unless they have permission to move close. Similarly, a barge carrying 3 000 kg or more of a dangerous substance, or in the case of a tank barge, any quantity of a dangerous substance, must display hazard-warning panels which conform to requirements set out in a Schedule to the Regulations dealing with form, colour, information and specification. These labels must be either removed or covered once the tank and compartments have been emptied.

Finally, the Regulations require that a freight container containing dangerous substances shall be accompanied by a certificate given by the person who loaded it certifying that the dangerous substance has been safely packed inside the container. A dangerous substance brought in a freight container, portable tank, or receptacle shall be labelled as required and the labels shall be removed once their purpose has been served.

Carriage on Rail

The statutory rules for the carriage of dangerous goods by road and in harbour areas were not matched by similar statutory rules in relation to rail transport until the Carriage of Dangerous Goods by Rail Regulations 1994, SI No. 670 were made. These have applied to carriage on rail as from 1 April 1994. Prior to this British Rail relied on its own conditions of carriage, i.e. the 'List of Dangerous Goods and Conditions of Acceptance by Rail on Freight Services and Parcels Services, BR 22426'. But with impending privatization of rail services the prospect of several rail operators transporting dangerous substances meant that reliance could no longer be placed on non-statutory arrangements; these Regulations therefore replace the BR conditions of carriage.

The Regulations impose requirements relating to the construction of containers and wagons and their packaging and labelling which are similar to the requirements for carriage on roads. The classifcation, packaging and labelling provisions contained in the Carriage of Dangerous Goods by Road and Rail (Classification, Packaging and Labelling) Regulations 1994, SI No. 669 (above) apply equally to carriage on rail.

7.2.6 Supply, Storage and Use

Section 140 of the **EPA 1990** gives the Secretary of State power to make regulations prohibiting or restricting the import, use, supply and storage of any specified substances or articles if he or she considers it appropriate to do so to prevent the substance or article from causing pollution of the environment or harm to human health or to the health of animals or plants. Power is also given to the Secretary of State to establish a committee which he or she is required to consult before putting forward proposals for regulations. The proposals are then to be publicized and fourteen days allowed for representations to be made before the regulations are laid. These requirements may be by-passed where it appears to the Secretary of State that there is an imminent risk of serious pollution of the environment. The Advisory Committee on Hazardous Substances Order 1991, SI No. 1487 set up the committee with effect from July 1991.

Several regulations have been made under these powers implementing requirements of EC directives:

1   The Environmental Protection (Controls on Injurious Substances) Regulations 1992, SI No. 31 deal with the supply of lead paint, mercury, arsenic and organostannic compounds and another substance, DBB. The regulations also amend the Control of Pollution (Supply and Use of Injurious Substances) Regulations 1986, SI No. 902 by lowering the quantity of PCBs and PCTs permitted for supply or use.
2   The Environmental Protection (Controls on Injurious Substances) (No. 2) Regulations 1992, SI No. 1583 prohibit, with a number of exceptions, the marketing of Ugilec 141 from June 1994, the marketing of Ugilec 121 and of another substance, DBBT.
3   The Environmental Protection (Controls on Injurious Substances) Regulations 1993, SI No. 1 controls the marketing and use in certain applications of PCPs.

4   The Environmental Protection (Controls on Injurious Substances) (No. 2) Regulations 1993, SI No. 1643 made under the **European Communities Act 1972** but also dealing with hazardous substances restrict the use and marketing of cadmium for various applications.

7.3   The Control of Pesticides

Part III of the **Food and Environment Protection Act 1985** (FEPA) makes provision for the control of pesticides, rendering obsolete the non-statutory Pesticides Safety Precautions Scheme and the Agricultural Chemicals Approvals Scheme under which pesticides were controlled between 1957 and 1986. The core of the provisions is the power given to ministers under s. 16 jointly to make regulations on a range of issues relating to pesticides.

The power to make regulations controlling pesticides is exercised by the Minister for Agriculture, Fisheries and Food and the Secretary of State for the Environment in consultation with the Pesticides Advisory Committee established, also under s. 16, to advise the ministers. The Committee works through a scientific sub-committee and follows a set procedure in advising the approval or otherwise of pesticides; it also publishes an Annual Report, the first of which came out in 1987. FEPA gives enforcement powers to persons authorized by the minister, i.e. officials of MAFF and the HSE, and officers of a local authority who are authorized to exercise enforcement powers. Enforcement is thus carried out by the HSE in the context of the use of pesticides as part of work activities, and by local authorities in the context of local authority duties in relation to environmental health.

The Control of Pesticides Regulations 1986, SI No. 1510 have been made under s. 16 and constitute the primary legal control on pesticides. The Regulations prohibit the advertisement, sale, supply, storage or use of pesticides unless the person has a provisional or full approval and a consent from the ministers and he or she complies with the conditions subject to which it was given. Approval may take one of three forms:

1   An 'experimental permit' to enable testing and development to be carried out to obtain safety and other data for ministers. It is granted automatically for one year or one season to any substance or organism which is the subject of research or development for possible use as a pesticide.
2   A 'provisional approval' given for a limited renewable period, normally one year, to enable data to be gathered to satisfy the ministers' requirements. Unlike the experimental permit it allows use of the pesticide in the environment outside experimental premises.
3   A 'full approval' granted when all necessary data requirements have been met.

A full approval for a pesticide is subject to three kinds of review: every ten years from the date of provisional approval; randomly in response to new evidence; and routinely under a routine review programme introduced for all pesticides on the market in order of date of first registration, starting with pre-1965 registrations, 1965 to 1975, 1975 to 1985 and so on. These routine reviews were introduced in 1989 because of concerns that early registrations were based on inadequate data.

The ministers also have power jointly to give their consent to the advertisement, sale, supply, storage and use of pesticides subject to various 'basic conditions' set out in Schedules to the Regulations. These consents were given and published in the *London Gazette* on 21 November 1986 for advertisements and 6 October 1986 for sale, supply, storage and use. The basic conditions subject to which the advertisement consent is given is that the advertisement shall:

1   Relate only to such uses of a pesticide as are permitted by the approval in relation to that pesticide
2   Include the name of the active ingredient of each pesticide mentioned in the advertisement, a warning to read the label and use the pesticide safely and, where required by the approval, a statement of any special degree of risk and
3   Include no claim for safety which is not permitted on the approval label for that pesticide.

Basic conditions subject to which the consent for the sale, supply and storage is granted oblige the employer to:

1   Ensure that employees have the necessary instruction and guidance
2   Obtain a certificate of competence issued by the British Agrochemical Standards Inspection Scheme (BASIS) or be supervised by a person holding one where he or she is storing to sell or supply a pesticide approved for agricultural use in quantities over, at any one time, 200 kg or 200 litres
3   Obtain a BASIS certificate where the employer sells, supplies or markets to the end user a pesticide approved for agricultural use.

To give practical guidance on these requirements the HSE has issued two codes of practice, for suppliers of pesticides to agriculture, horticulture and forestry (MAFF, 1990) and on the storage of pesticides (HSE, 1988).

The basic conditions subject to which the consent for use of a pesticide is granted also require:

1   Instruction and training and
2   A certificate of competence or supervision where a pesticide approved for agricultural use is used in the course of a commercial service or by a person born after 31 December 1964.

Aerial applications of pesticides can only be undertaken by a person who, or whose employer or main contractor, holds an aerial application certificate granted under the Air Navigation Order 1985, SI No. 1643. Additionally, the pesticide must have been approved for the intended aerial application and various authorities such as the NRA, the district Chief Environmental Health Officer and occupants of nearby property must have been notified of the intended application. Records of each aerial application must be kept for three years and yearly summaries made available to the minister. The MAFF and the HSE have jointly issued a code of practice for the safe use of pesticides on farms to give practical guidance to farmers on the application of pesticides (HSE/MAFF, 1990).

7.4   Genetically Modified Organisms (GMOs)

The genetic modification of an organism is defined by the Genetically Modified Organisms (Contained Use) Regulations 1992, SI No. 3217 as 'the altering of the genetic material of that organism by a way that does not occur naturally by mating or natural recombination or both'. These Regulations and the Genetically Modified Organisms (Deliberate Release) Regulations 1992, SI No. 3280, as amended, specify various techniques of genetic modification. The resulting organisms may be put to a contained use or released into the environment. The Contained Use Regulations define contained use of GMOs as

> any operation in which organisms are genetically modified or in which such genetically modified organisms are cultured, stored, used, transported, destroyed or disposed of and for which physical barriers or a combination of physical with chemical or biological barriers or both, are used to limit their contact with the general population and the environment.

Section 107(10) of the **EPA 1990** states that a GMO is 'released' if it is deliberately caused or permitted to cease to be under control and to enter the environment.

Legal control of GMOs is based on whether the GMO is intended for contained use or deliberate release. There is a distinction between organisms and micro-organisms (GMMOs); the term 'organism' covers all micro-organisms and multi-cellular organisms, including plants and animals but excluding human and human embryos. The Contained Use Regulations cover the human health and environmental risks associated with GMMOs but only the human health risks associated with GMOs. The environmental risks arising from both the contained use and the deliberate release of genetically modified plants and animals are covered under s. 108(1)(a) of the EPA 1990 but the substantive legal requirements are the same.

7.4.1 Contained Use

The Genetic Manipulation Regulations 1989, SI No. 1810 made under the **Health and Safety at Work etc. Act 1974** first provided for control of genetic manipulation in the UK. Subsequently, EC Directive 90/219/EEC on the contained use of genetically modified micro-organisms required member states to bring into force implementing laws by 23 October 1991 although it was not until 1 February 1993 that the Genetically Modified Organisms (Contained Use) Regulations 1992, SI No. 3217 came into force, implementing the Directive and revoking the 1989 Genetic Manipulation Regulations. They were supplemented shortly afterwards by SI 1993 No. 15 in regard to risk assessment provisions.

The Contained Use Regulations categorize GMMOs into Group I or Group II, and contained uses into Type A operations (teaching, research, development, or non-industrial or non-commercial purposes) and Type B operations (i.e. the non-Type A operations). The Regulations provide that premises shall not be used for activities involving genetic modification unless an assessment has been conducted of the risks posed to human health and the environment. Additionally, a genetic modification safety committee must be established at each centre where activities involving genetic modification are undertaken. The risk assessment must classify the GMMOs involved according to criteria set out in a Schedule to the Regulations and decide the level of containment required taking account of specified parameters. A record of the risk assessment must be kept for at least ten years.

Although the HSE, which administers these Regulations, may subsequently approve a method for risk assessment it has not yet done so; the guidance prepared by the Advisory Committee on Genetic Modification is relied on (DoE, 1993a). The guidance indicates that there are four main elements to risk assessment: (1) hazard identification; (2) assessment of exposure to the hazard and the consequences of that exposure; (3) assessment of the level of risk (by consideration of the magnitude of harmful consequences and the likelihood of their being realized); and (4) selection and assignment of appropriate control measures (i.e. risk management).

Where the risk assessment shows that as a result of any reasonably foreseeable accident the health or safety of persons outside the premises is liable to be affected or there is a risk of damage to the environment, an emergency plan must be prepared in consultation with the appropriate bodies. Both the persons liable to be affected by an accident and the emergency services must be informed of the emergency plan. Should an accident occur the HSE must be notified with details of the accident and the HSE shall in its turn inform the European Commission. The HSE's guide to the Contained Use Regulations states that spillages of Group I GMMOs are unlikely to count as significant releases which present a hazard and will not routinely require notification (HSE, 1992).

The HSE has to be notified of the intention to use premises for activities involving modification for the first time at least ninety days in advance. The notification must give information about the activity proposed together with a summary of an assessment of the risks posed by the proposal. Where the activity involves Group II GMMOs the HSE's consent, which has to be given within ninety days, must be awaited but otherwise the activity may proceed after the ninety-day period unless the HSE has objected. The risk assessment under these Regulations will not cover the environmental risks arising from the contained use of GMOs. Individual activities involving genetic manipulation must also be notified to the HSE sixty days before the activity commences giving specified information. Type B operations involving Group II GMMOs must await the consent of the HSE before proceeding. The HSE must forward a copy of each notification to the Secretary of State and, insofar as it relates to a release into the environment, the HSE cannot grant, vary or revoke a consent without the Secretary of State's agreement.

7.4.2   Deliberate Release

The Royal Commission on Environmental Pollution recommended, in a report on the release of GMOs into the environment, that statutory control on releases of GMOs must be provided to complement the controls on contained use that were already in place (RCEP, 1989). This recommendation was accepted and Part VI of the **EPA 1990** was enacted in 1990 giving power to the Secretary of State to control GMOs. In the same year EC Directive 90/220/EEC on the deliberate release into the environment of genetically modified organisms was adopted requiring member states to bring into force implementing laws by 23 October 1991.

The Gentically Modified Organisms (Deliberate Release) Regulations 1993, SI No. 3280 made under the EPA 1990 came into force on 1 February 1993 to implement the EC directive. The Regulations were amended shortly afterwards by SI 1993 No. 152. The Secretary of State was also given power to appoint a committee, known as the Advisory Committee on Releases to the Environment (ACRE), to advise on whether a consent to release or market a GMO should be granted and the conditions to be attached to the consent; the Committee has been appointed.

Consent

Section 111 makes provision for obtaining the consent of the Secretary of State to import or acquire, release or market any GMOs either in cases prescribed in Regulations or where the Secretary of State has given directions that a consent is required. The Genetically Modified Organisms (Deliberate Release) Regulations 1992 make provision for applications for consent. Applications are made to the DoE which acts for the Scottish Office as well. The application for a consent to release a GMO may be of two kinds; it may relate (1) to the same site or (2) to more than one site. In the first case the application may include more than one release of more than one type of GMO while in the second it can only relate to one type of GMO albeit for many releases.

An application for a consent to market a GMO must be made to a competent authority in EC member states both where it is intended to market the GMO for the first time and where it is intended to market it for a use for which it has not previously been marketed. The application must be accompanied by details specified in Schedules to the Regulations together with an evaluation of the impact and risk posed to human health and the environment from the release. In relation to the application to release a GMO there are provisions requiring publicity for the application.

The Secretary of State must, within thirty days of receiving the application for a consent:

1 Forward to the European Commission a summary in a format specified by the Commission (see Commission Decision 94/211/EEC, OJ No. L 105/26)
2 Examine it and evaluate the risks posed
3 If necessary, carry out tests or inspections
4 Take account of comments received and
5 Record his or her conclusions in writing.

The Commission shall inform the competent authorities of the other member states who have sixty days in which to object. If there is no objection the Secretary of State may grant the consent and inform the Commission and the other competent authorities that he has done so. Consent cannot be granted, revoked or varied, insofar as it relates to the protection of human health, without the consent of the HSE. Where a member state objects, a decision on the application is taken by the Commission. The involvement of the European Commission and the other member states is necessary because a GMO cleared for release in one member state may be released in any of the other member states without restriction. This application procedure is outlined in a DoE guidance document (DoE, 1993b).

The Regulations require the decision on the application to be communicated to the applicant within ninety days from the date of the application. This period and the procedures involved in obtaining consent have been criticized by the biotechnology industry as unnecessarily bureacratic (House of Lords Select Committee on Science and Technology, 1992/3). It argues that product legislation based on the use to which the GMO is put (e.g. pesticides legislation) is adequate and that there is no need for additional 'GMO-specific' legislation which adds to the delay in obtaining consent.

In a bid to reduce the time taken to process applications the DoE has introduced a 'fast-track' procedure for obtaining consent to release low-hazard, low-risk GMOs or for repeat releases with which the DoE has experience. Under this procedure, which does not involve a full risk assessment, the application is handled within thirty days. The DoE has released guidance on the criteria to be used to determine which applications qualify for this procedure (DoE, 1994). Separately, the European Commission has established the criteria for simplified procedures for the deliberate release of genetically modified plants which also relate to previous experience with the plant species involved (93/584/EEC, OJ No. L 279/42). Member states may apply to the Commission to be able to apply the simplified procedures. It is also proposed that where product legislation requires risk-assessment procedures which are similar to those applied to GMOs, 'GMO-specific' procedures will be dispensed with (DoE, 1993c).

Risk Assessment

The assessment of the risks posed by GMOs has been the subject of considerable public debate. The Royal Commission of Environmental Pollution recommended, in a report, that the risk appraisal methodology it referred to as GENHAZ be adopted for every proposal (RCEP, 1991). GENHAZ, which is developed in detail in the Royal Commission's Report, is a highly structured methodology for the assessment of risk arising from the release of GMOs. It follows from a procedure known as HAZOP (Hazard Operability Study), which is a technique for evaluating hazards in chemical manufacturing plants.

The government did not accept this proposal, taking the view that GENHAZ does not provide the flexibility required to assess releases of low, medium or high risk. In the government's view GENHAZ is likely to be the preferred methodology for risk assessment primarily for releases involving high risk only. Additionally, the government argued, to prescribe a particular method of risk assessment to be applied in every case would result in over-regulation; far better to issue guidelines requiring no more than hazard identification, risk estimation and risk evaluation to be implemented as circumstances dictate, which has been done (DoE/ACRE, 1993).

The guidelines stipulate seven steps to be followed in assessing the risks posed and require that the information obtained be submitted as part of the application. The steps are:

1   Identify the hazards associated with the GMO
2   Identify how each hazard could be realized in the particular receiving medium
3   Estimate the magnitude of the harm likely to be caused by each hazard, if realized
4   Estimate how likely or how often each hazard will be realized as harm

5   Estimate the risks of harm being caused by the release or marketing proposal
6   Modify the proposal if necessary until the lowest possible level of risk in relation to each hazard is reached
6   Evaluate the combined effects of the steps followed in terms of risk to the environment (including human health).

7.5   EC Health and Safety Law

The EC's requirements in relation to health and safety have tended to drive requirements in the UK, especially in relation to the setting of technical standards. This is particularly the case in respect of the classification, packaging, and labelling of dangerous substances.

7.5.1   Directive on Classification, Packaging and Labelling of Dangerous Substances

Directive 67/548/EEC on the classification, packaging and labelling of dangerous substances required the Commission to draw up an inventory of substances which were available on the EC market by 18 September 1981. The inventory, known as the European Inventory of Existing Chemical Substances (EINECS) (OJ No. C 146/4), was finally published in 1990.

The term 'existing chemical substances' refers to chemical susbtances that were on the EC market in 1981 as listed in EINECS. Substances *not* on EINECS are referred to as 'new chemical substances'. EINECS has great practical significance for importers, manufacturers and distributors of chemicals; substances listed in EINECS can continue to be marketed while those not listed on it must, before being put on the market, be notified and subjected to a risk assessment procedure set out in Directive 67/548/EEC before being put on the market. The Commission is required to keep a list, the European List of Notified Chemical Substances (ELINCS), of the new substances notified to it. The first list of ELINCS, which has to be updated annually, appeared on 11 April 1992 in OJ No. C91/1.

Directive 67/548/EEC has been amended repeatedly; Directive 92/32/EEC (OJ No. L 154/1) which was adopted on 30 April 1992 is the seventh and latest amendment.

The purpose of the Directive is to approximate the laws, regulations and administrative provisions of the member states in four areas: (1) the notification of substances; (2) the exchange of information on notified substances; (3) the assessment of the potential risk to humans and the environment of notified substances; and (4) the classification, packaging and labelling of substances dangerous to humans or the environment. The Directive does not apply to medicinal or cosmetic products, wastes, foodstuffs, animal feeding stuffs, pesticides, radioactive substances, and other substances or preparations for which EC notification or approval procedures exist.

Notification

The Directive requires member states to ensure that new substances cannot be placed on the market unless they have been notified to competent authorities appointed for this purpose. In the UK where the notification requirements are implemented by the Notification of New Substances Regulations 1993, SI No. 3050 the competent authority is the HSE and the DoE acting jointly. Notification is made by the manufacturer of the substance to the competent authority of the member state in which the substance is manufactured. If the substance is manufactured outside the EC the notification is made by the person responsible for placing it on the EC market to the competent authority of the member state in which the person is based.

The notification has to include:

1 A technical dossier of information needed to evaluate any foreseeable risks to humans or the environment; the kind of information required is set out in the Directive and includes its proposed uses, physico-chemical properties, results of toxicological and eco-toxicological studies, and the possibility of rendering it harmless; reduced information may be submitted where the amount of substance involved is less than one tonne per annum

2 A declaration concerning the unfavourable effects of the substance in terms of its foreseeable uses

3 The proposed classification and labelling of the substance (discussed below)

4 In the case of dangerous substances, a proposal for a safety data sheet; the Directive requires the notifier to include with the substance a safety data sheet to enable users to take the measures necessary to protect the environment and health and safety.

The substance may be placed on the market sixty days—thirty days for quantities less than one tonne—after the notification unless the competent authority has indicated that the dossier is not in conformity with the Directive.

On receiving the notification the competent authority shall carry out an assessment of the risks entailed on the basis of principles and methods laid down in EC Directive 92/37/EEC (OJ No. L 154/30). Within sixty days, or thirty days as the case may be, it shall inform the notifier whether or not the notification has been accepted and, if not, what further information is required. It shall also inform the Commission of the dossier submitted and any additional information it requests. The Commission shall inform the competent authorities of the other member states who may suggest that further tests and information be requested from the notifier. The notifier may request that commercially sensitive information be kept confidential from everyone except the other competent authorities and the Commission.

Risk Assessment

The principles for the assessment of risk to humans and the environment of notified substances were laid down in EC Directive 93/67/EEC (OJ No. L 227/9). This Directive provides that risk assessment shall entail:

1 Hazard identification
2 As appropriate, dose or concentration–response or effect assessment, i.e. an assessment of the response of the target to a given dosage of the substance
3 Exposure assessment
4 Risk characterization.

These risk-assessment requirements have been adopted by the HSE.

Classification

The Directive requires that substances be classified on the basis of their intrinsic properties according to the categories laid down in the Directive. Fifteen categories of danger are laid down: explosive; oxidizing; extremely flammable; highly flammable; flammable; very toxic; toxic; harmful; corrosive; irritant; sensitizing; carcinogenic; mutagenic; toxic for reproduction; and dangerous to the environment.

Labelling

The Directive requires member states to ensure that dangerous substances are not marketed unless their packaging has been labelled with details of:

1 The name of the substance using one of the designations given in the Directive
2 Details of the notifier
3 The symbols indicating the danger involved in the use of the substance
4 Standard or 'R-phrases' indicating the special risks arising from the dangers involved in using the substance
5 Standard or 'S-phrases' relating to the safe use of the substance and
6 The EEC number of the substance obtained from either EINECS or ELINCS.

The danger symbols, R-phrases or S-phrases are either laid down in the Directive already or can be assigned on the basis of a procedure laid down in the Directive. The labelling requirements do not apply to munitions and explosives and shall not apply to butane, propane and liquefied petroleum gas until 30 April 1997.

The Directive is implemented in the UK by the Chemicals (Hazard Information and Packaging) Regulations 1993, SI No. 1746 which came into force on 1 September 1993. The 1993 Regulations, referred to as CHIP, replace the Classification, Packaging and Labelling Regulations 1984, SI No. 1244 which implemented requirements of Directive 79/831/EEC, the sixth amendment to Directive 67/548/EEC. CHIP implements most of the requirements of the seventh amendment although provisions relating to notification of new substances are implemented through the Notification of New Substances Regulations 1993, SI No. 3050.

7.5.2 Regulation on the Evaluation of Risks of Existing Substances

EC Regulation 793/93 (OJ No. L 84/1) on the evaluation and control of the risks of existing substances extends the risk-assessment requirements that already apply to new chemical substances to existing chemical substances on EINECS not previously subjected to prior risk assessment. From June 1993, any manufacturer or importer of an existing substance must submit to the Commission information about the substance, including:

1   Its name and EINECS number
2   The quantity produced or imported
3   Classification
4   Foreseeable uses
5   Physical-chemical data
6   Environmental fate and pathways
7   Eco-toxicity and toxicity
8   Data on carcinogenity, mutagenicity and toxicity for reproduction.

This requirement applies to those who have maunfactured or imported these substances in quantities of over 1 000 tonnes per year at least once in the three years preceding March 1993 and/or in the year to March 1994. The information has to be submitted by June 1994 for the EINECS substances listed in the Regulation as produced or imported in quantities exceeding 1 000 tonnes and by June 1995 for those EINECS substances not listed in the Regulation. There are reduced data requirements for substances in quantities of between 10 and 1 000 tonnes per year which has to be submitted from June 1998. Further, the Regulation exempts some substances altogether.

The Regulation allows a member state to require that information submitted to the Commission be submitted simultaneously to other competent authorities as well but the Commission shall in any case send copies of the information to member states. Those submitting the information must update it as necessary and, in relation to the production and import volumes, must do so every three years. It also allows the manufacturer or importer to request that commercially sensitive information to remain confidential.

The Regulation requires the Commission to draw up, by June 1994, a 'priority list' of substances requiring immediate attention because of their potential effects on humans or the environment. Manufacturers and importers of substances on the priority list who have already submitted information shall, within six months of the publication of the list, submit to the 'designated rapporteur' all relevant available information and study reports on the risk assessment of the substance concerned. A designated rapporteur is a competent authority designated by the member state to evaluate the information submitted and identify whether further information and testing is needed. If so, it shall inform the Commission who will make a decision according to laid-down procedures. The rapporteur shall recommend measures for limiting the risk.

On the basis of the rapporteur's risk evaluation recommendations the Commission shall submit to a Committee set up under the Directive a proposal which shall be adopted at Community level. The Commission shall also decide whether it is necessary to propose measures for restricting the marketing and use of the substance.

This Regulation applies in the UK directly and no implementing regulations were made. However, the DoE and HSE jointly published a guide on how to report data on existing substances (DoE/HSE, 1994).

7.5.3   Directive on Dangerous Preparations

EC Directive 88/379/EEC (OJ No. L 187/14) on the classification, packaging and labelling of dangerous preparations aims to approximate the laws of member states on the classification, packaging and labelling of preparations dangerous to humans and the environment when they are placed on the market. It complements Directive 67/548/EEC on dangerous substances, preparations being mixtures or solutions of substances at least one of which is classified as dangerous within the meaning of 67/548/EEC. They must also be labelled and packaged accordingly. The Directive is implemented in the UK through the Chemicals (Hazard Information and Packaging) Regulations 1993, SI No. 1746.

7.5.4   Directive on the Marketing and Use of Dangerous Substances and Preparations

EC Directive 76/769/EEC (OJ No. L 262/201) relating to restrictions on the marketing and use of certain dangerous substances and preparations requires member states to ensure that certain dangerous substances and preparations are marketed only if specified conditions are met. The Directive list PCBs and PCTs as subject to its provisions and stated the relevant conditions to be met.

Subsequent amendments have added ornamental objects, benzene in toys, fire retardants and novelties, asbestos, lead paints, anti-fouling applications, alkaline manganese batteries, PCPs, cadmium, Ugilec 21 and 141 and DBBT to the list.

The implementation of this Directive in the UK is discussed in 7.2.6 'Supply, Storage and Use'. A separate Directive (78/631/EEC) (OJ No. L 206/13) applies to pesticides. This is discussed below.

7.5.5   Directive on the Marketing and Use of Plant Protection Products

EC Directive 79/117/EEC (OJ No. L 33/36) prohibiting the marketing and use of plant protection products containing certain active substances (pesticides) prohibits the marketing and use of pesticides which contain one or more specified active substances, with limited exceptions. The Directive provides that every two years the Commission shall examine whether the exceptions should be modified in the light of scientific and technical knowledge; accordingly, pesticides whose use is allowed and the circumstances in which they may be used constantly change. The Directive does not apply to pesticides intended for export. It is implemented in the UK through the Control of Pesticides Regulations 1986, SI No. 1510 which gives powers to approve and control pesticides in the UK.

7.5.6   Directive on the Classification, Packaging and Labelling of Pesticides

EC Directive 78/631/EEC (OJ No. L 206/13) relating to the classification, packaging and labelling of pesticides seeks to approximate the laws of member states on the classification, packaging and labelling of pesticides, complementing the Dangerous Substances Directive 67/548/EEC. It is implemented through the Chemicals (Hazard Information and Packaging) Regulations 1993, SI No. 1746.

7.5.7   Directive on Placing Plant Protection Products on the Market

EC Directive 91/414/EEC (OJ No. L 230/1) concerning the placing of plant protection products on the market, as amended by Directive 93/71/EEC, establishes a 'list of active substances' which are authorized for incorporation into plant-protection products. Active substances may be included on the list for an initial period of ten years if their residues are not harmful to the environment and to human and animal health.

For an active substance which was not on the market in July 1993 to be included on the list an applicant must submit a dossier of information for evaluating the foreseeable risks and the proposed classification and labelling of the substance to member states and the Commission, who shall refer it to the EC's Standing Committee on Plant Health for an opinion. The applicant must submit also a second dossier of information on at least one preparation containing that active substance to enable evaluation of efficacy and foreseeable risks. An application may be made to renew the listing of an active substance for a further ten years; inclusions may, however, be reviewed at any time.

The Directive requires member states to ensure that pesticides are not authorized for marketing and use unless their active ingredients are included on the EC list of active substances. An authorization shall be granted for a fixed period of up to ten years but may be renewed, reviewed, modified or cancelled if necessary. To assist member states in evaluating pesticides for authorization 'uniform principles' have to be agreed at EC level and published. The Commission's proposals on this, to be known as the 'Uniform Principles Directive' (COM (93) 117), were published in September 1993.

The Directive also provides that previous and subsequent applicants for authorization may agree to share data to avoid duplication of tests. Authorizations are to be mutually recognized in member states to the extent that agricultural, plant health and environmental conditions in the member states are comparable. Each member state has to draw up a list of authorized pesticides in its territory annually.

The Directive provides that an authorization may be granted for a provisional period of up to three years to enable a gradual assessment of new active substances. If, after three years, a decision has not been made to include it in the list of active substances a further provisional authorization may be granted. Second, a twelve-year derogation from the authorization requirements is granted for active substances that were already on the market in July 1993. During the twelve-year period the Commission will be evaluating these active substances for possible inclusion in the list and may request data to be submitted to it. To facilitate this programme separate EC Regulations will be published; the first, Commission Regulation 3600/92 (OJ No. L 366/10), listed ninety active ingredients to be reviewed.

7.5.8   Regulation on the Export and Import of Dangerous Chemicals

EC Regulation 2455/92 (OJ No. L 251/13) concerning the export and import of certain dangerous chemicals applies to the European Community the 'prior informed consent' (PIC) procedure established by the United Nations Environment Programme (UNEP) and the Food and Agriculture Organization (FAO) (UNEP, 1987; FAO, 1986). Briefly, PIC is a system which seeks to ensure that countries importing pesticides, banned or severely restricted in the exporting country, are informed of this fact before the shipment so that they have an opportunity either to refuse or give 'informed consent' to the import. Additionally, Regulation 2455/92 extends the provisions of the Dangerous

Substances Directive (67/548/EEC) to substances intended for export, requiring them also to be classified, labelled and packaged accordingly.

The Regulation establishes two lists:

1 Of 'chemicals subject to notification', i.e. banned or severely restricted chemicals in the EC
2 Of 'chemicals subject to PIC', i.e. banned or severely restricted chemicals established by UNEP and FAO and of the countries in the scheme; this was published as Regulation 41/94 (OJ No. L 8/1).

The Regulation also requires each member state to designate an authority to be in charge of administering PIC. When a chemical subject to notification is about to be exported from the EC for the first time the exporter shall provide the designated authority of that member state with details of the export including information relating to the substance or preparation, the category of danger or risk and precautions to be taken, thirty days before export. The designated authority shall notify the importing country of the intended export at least fifteen days before export. If the importing country is participating in PIC a chemical which is banned or restricted in the EC is not to be exported to it without the importing country's consent.

A copy of the notification shall be sent by the designated authority to the Commission which shall inform other member states and the International Register of Potentially Toxic Chemicals (IRPTC). Where there is a 'significant reaction' to the notification from the importing country the Commission must be informed. Notifications are to be assigned a reference number and periodically published in the OJ where prospective exporters can check whether an export of a chemical has occurred before. The Commission shall also inform member states about notifications it receives regarding imports of chemicals which are banned or severely restricted in non-EC countries into the EC.

In the UK, the Export of Dangerous Chemicals Regulations 1992, SI No. 2415 designated the Health and Safety Commission as the administering authority.

7.5.9   Directive on Major Accident Hazards

EC Directive 82/501/EEC (OJ No. L 230/1) on the major accident hazards of certain industrial activities aims to prevent major accidents which might result from certain industrial activities and to limit their consequences to humans and the environment. Its adoption was prompted by an industrial accident in Seveso in Italy on 10 July 1976 which caused widespread environmental damage and personal injury and it is therefore often referred to as the 'Seveso Directive'. The Directive has been amended twice, by Directive 87/216/EEC and Directive 88/610/EEC. A third amendment has recently been proposed

(COM (94) 4). It is implemented in the UK through the Control of Industrial Major Accident Hazards Regulations 1984, SI No. 1902, as amended.

The directive applies to a wide range of industrial processes and to the storage of specified dangerous substances beyond specified threshold quantities. It requires member states to introduce measures under which manufacturers have to notify competent authorities of a proposed industrial activity or storage involving dangerous substances beyond the specified quantities. The notification shall include information showing that the manufacturer has identified possible major accident hazards entailed by the activity or storage, drawn up appropriate safety measures including emergency plans and safety equipment and provided persons working on the site with information, training and equipment in order to ensure their safety. It shall also include information necessary to enable the competent authorities to prepare emergency plans, known as 'off-site emergency plans', for use outside the establishment. Additionally, where a major accident does occur the manufacturer is required to inform the competent authorities giving details of the substances involved, the emergency measures taken and the steps envisaged to alleviate their effects and prevent a recurrence.

7.5.10   Directive on the Contained Use of Genetically Modified Micro-organisms

EC Directive 90/219/EEC (OJ No. L 117/1) on the contained use of genetically modified micro-organisms (GMMOs) categorizes the contained use of GMMOs into Type A operations which are teaching, research and development, or small-scale non-industrial use or non-commercial purposes use, and Type B operations which are all the remaining operations. It also classifies GMMOs into Group I and Group II according to criteria listed in the Directive.

The Directive requires that when an installation is to be used for the first time for operations involving the contained use of GMMOs the user must carry out a prior assessment of the risks entailed and notify the competent authority giving a summary of the assessment. Users of Group I Type A GMMOs are required to keep records of work carried out to be made available to the competent authority on request while users of Group I Type B, Group II Type A and Group II Type B operations must submit to the competent authority specified information before commencing the contained use.

Users of Group I GMMOs may, in the absence of indications to the contrary by the competent authority, proceed ninety days after submission of the notification, or earlier with the agreement of the authority but users of Group II GMMOs must await the decision of the competent authority which shall be given within ninety days. Further, Group I Type B operations and Group II Type A operations may proceed after sixty days in the absence of any indications to the contrary from the competent authority while Group II Type B operations have to await the decision of the competent authorities which shall be given within ninety days. The competent authority may require that before an operation commences an 'off-site' emergency plan is drawn up and the public informed of the emergency measures in the event of an accident. Should an accident occur, the user must inform the competent authority.

The Directive is implemented in the UK through the Genetically Modified Organisms (Contained Use) Regulations 1992, SI No. 3217, as amended.

7.5.11   Directive on the Deliberate Release of Genetically Modified Organisms

EC Directive 90/220/EEC (OJ No. L 117/15) on the deliberate release into the environment of genetically modified organisms (GMOs) imposes different requirements where the deliberate release is for research and development purposes or any other purpose other than the placing on the market of products containing GMOs. Where the release is for research and development, a notification must be submitted to the competent authority including a technical dossier for evaluating the foreseeable risks to human health and the environment. The notifier must await the decision of the competent authority which shall be given within ninety days. After completion of the release the notifier must send to the competent authority the result of the release in respect of any risk to human health or the environment. The competent authority shall send to the Commission within thirty days a summary of each notification received and Council Decision 91/596/EEC (OJ No. L 322/1) sets out the format to be used for this summary.

Where a product containing a GMO is to be placed on the market its manufacturer or importer must submit a notification to the competent authority in the member state of release giving specified detailed information. Within ninety days of the notification the competent authority shall either reject the application or forward to the Commission the dossier with a favourable opinion. Commission Decision 92/146/EEC (OJ No. L 60/19) sets out the format for sending this information to the Commission. The Commission must forward the dossier to the other member states and if none of them objects the competent authority shall give its consent within sixty days of the distribution. If a member state objects and an agreement proves impossible the Commission shall take a decision. The Commission is required to publish a list of all the products which receive consent in the OJ.

The Directive enables a competent authority which considers that sufficient experience has been obtained of releases of certain GMOs to request the Commission to apply simplified procedures for releases of such GMOs. Commission Decision 93/584/EEC (OJ No. L 279/42, 12.11.93) sets out the criteria by reference to which the Commission shall take the decision.

The Directive is implemented in the UK through the Genetically Modified Organisms (Deliberate Release) Regulations 1992, SI No. 3280, as amended.

References

DoE, *Hazardous Substances Consent: A Guide for Industry* (undated).

DoE, *Planning Controls for Hazardous Substances*, Scottish Office Circular 5/1993, DoE/ WO Circular 11/92.

DoE/ACRE, *The Regulation and Control of the Deliberate Release of Genetically Modified Organisms*, DoE/ACRE Guidance Note 1 (1993).

DoE, *Guidelines for Risk Assessment of Operations involving the Contained Use of Genetically Modified Micro-Organisms*, ACGM/HSE/DoE Note 7 (1993a).

DoE, *Format for Application for Consent to Release or Market Genetically Modified Organisms* (1993b).

DoE, *Government's Response to the Thirteenth Report of the Royal Commission on Environmental Pollution: the Release of Genetically Engineered Organisms to the Environment* (1993c).

DoE, *Fast Track Procedures for Certain Genetically Modified Organisms Releases*, DoE/ACRE Guidance Note 2 (1994).

DoE/HSE, *How to Report Data on Existing Chemical Substances* (1994).

DTp, *European Agreement Concerning the International Carriage of Dangerous Goods by Road (ADR)*, HMSO (1993).

ENDS Report No. 229, 'Octel accident revives worries about pollution from chemical fires', p. 3, February (1994a).

ENDS Report No. 228, 'Allied Colloids: shooting the chemical industry in the foot', pp. 25–28, January (1994b).

FAO *International Code of Conduct on the Distribution and Use of Pesticides*, Rome (1986, as amended in November 1989).

HSC, *Information Approved for the Classification and Labelling of Substances and Preparations Dangerous for Supply*, HSE Books (1993).

HSC, *Information Approved for the Classification and Labelling of Substances and Preparations Dangerous for Carriage*, HSE Books (1994a).

HSC, *Approved Methods for the Classification and Packaging of Dangerous Goods for Carriage by Road and Rail*, HSE Books (1994b).

HSE, *The Storage of Pesticides: Guidance for Farmers and Other Professional Users*, CS 19 (1988).

HSE, *Guide to the [GMOs] Contained Use Regulations* (1992).

HSE, *CHIP 2—New Chemicals (Hazard Information and Packaging for Supply) Regulations Proposed*, C18:94.

House of Lords Select Committee on Science and Technology, Session 1992/93, *Regulation of the UK Biotechnology Industry and Global Competitiveness*, 7th Report, HMSO.

MAFF, *Code of Practice for the Suppliers of Pesticide to Agriculture, Horticulture and Forestry* (1990).

MAFF/HSE, *Code of Practice for the Safe Use of Pesticides on Farms and Holdings* (1990).

RCEP, 13th Report, *The Release of Genetically Engineered Organisms into the Environment*, Cm 720, HMSO (1989).

RCEP, *GENHAZ: A System for the Appraisal of Proposals to Release GMOs into the Environment*, Cm 1557, HMSO (1991).

UNEP, *The London Guidelines for the Exchange of Information on Chemicals in International Trade*, Decision 14/27 of UNEP dated 17 June 1987, as amended in May 1989.

8

Environmental Assessment and Environmental Auditing

8.1 Town and Country Planning

Before the introduction of town and country planning any land-owner could develop their land as they liked so long as they kept within common law rules. With the adverse impact that such unplanned development threatened, town and country planning legislation was introduced to control development; it made the local planning authority the custodian of the public interest in development proposals (The Nuffield Foundation, 1986).

Until the late 1980s town and country planning law was the only comprehensive body of law which was concerned with the natural environment. Indeed, it can be said to have laid the foundations of environmental law in the UK. It remains a robust and largely self-contained body of law which is very closely linked to environmental law in the UK. It sets the context within which certain environmental laws and, in particular, environmental assessment rules, operate.

8.1.1 Development Plans

In England and Wales the word 'planning' is used to refer to the control of development. The control is in two parts: preparing development plans and determining applications for development projects. If an application for a development project succeeds the applicant is granted 'planning permission'. Both the preparation of development plans and the determination of planning applications are the responsibility of the local authority in its role as the local planning authority. The development plan sets out the local planning authority's policy on land use in its area and provides the basis on which applications for planning permission are determined. Town and country planning, currently in the **Town and Country Planning Act 1990 (TCPA)**, as amended by the **Planning and Compensation Act 1991**, has, on the whole, remained unchanged since the **Town and Country Planning Act 1947**.

Except in London and the other metropolitan areas the development plan is in two parts; a 'structure plan' drawn up by the county council and a 'local plan' produced by the district council. The structure plan:

1   States the policies and general proposals for the development and other use of land in its area
2   Takes account of the policies at national and regional level insofar as they affect the physical and environmental planning of its area and
3   Provides the framework for local plans.

A local plan:

1   Develops the policies and general proposals of the structure plan and relates them to a precise area of land
2   Provides a detailed basis for development control and
3   Brings local planning issues before the public.

A local plan may cover the whole of a district, a substantial area of it or an 'action plan area' which has been singled out for comprehensive treatment. Draft plans must be publicized to enable residents to make comments before they are approved (in the case of structure plans, by the Secretary of State).

The distinction between structure and local plans does not exist in London and the metropolitan areas which, since 1986, have not had county councils. The London boroughs and the metropolitan district councils, therefore, draw up 'unitary plans'; these are divided into Parts I and II which resemble the structure and local plans respectively.

Development plans serve the function of translating national policy to the circumstances of the locality to which the plan applies thus providing the local policies on which case-by-case development control is based. Policy is inherently ever changing according to changing circumstances and needs. In relation to land use, national policy is spelt out in ministerial 'Planning Policy Guidance Notes' (PPGs) and government circulars. On the basis of national policy, structure plans give a general indication of the location of development projects and their scale while local plans spell out the detailed locations of land for such developments as housing, industry, waste disposal, quarrying and so on. Development planning therefore constitutes a strategic stage in environmental protection and makes development control possible.

Development control is effected by requiring that all developments seek planning permission from the planning authority (i.e. the district or the metropolitan borough council) under s. 57. This gives the planning authority an opportunity to bring its policies and plans to bear in relation to proposed development projects. It is unlawful to proceed with the proposal without planning permission or in contravention of the conditions subject to which the permission is given.

8.1.2   Development Control

Section 55(1) of the TCPA 1990 defines 'development' as 'the carrying out of any building, engineering, mining or other operations in, on and over or under land or the making of any material change in the use of any buildings or other land'. Development, therefore, may arise either through the carrying out of building, engineering or other operations or, alternatively, through a material change of use of land.

Three categories of development do not require planning permission:

1   Certain building, engineering or other similar operations which are specifically excluded from the definition of development by s. 55(2); an example is the use of land and buildings for agriculture or forestry.
2   Types of development which are permitted either under the TCPA 1990 itself or by a general or specific consent laid down in the General Development Order 1988, SI No. 1813, as amended; examples include developments by the Crown (the DoE has proposed the removal of this exemption—DoE, 1992a), most mining operations and developments in simplified planning zones and enterprise zones (i.e. zones set up under ss 82 to 89 of the TCPA 1990 with only limited planning requirements to promote the regeneration of depressed areas).
3   In relation to changes of use, certain changes of use which are exempted by the Use Classes Order 1987, SI No. 764, as amended; this specifies eighteen classes of use (e.g. use as an 'industrial building') within which changes of use may be made without planning permission—a change of use from, say, a hair salon to a grocery shop may not need planning permission.

Planning authorities have a wide discretion in considering a planning application. However, s. 70(2) requires that the authority have regard to the development plan, so far as material to the application, and to any other material considerations. Previously, the development plan was no more than one of the material factors to be taken into account but the **Planning and Compensation Act 1991** inserted a new s. 54A in the TCPA 1990 which requires an application to be determined in accordance with the development plan unless material conditions indicate otherwise. As PPG1 on 'General Policy and Principles' (DoE, 1992b) points out, 'in effect, this introduces a presumption in favour of development proposals which are in accordance with the development plan' (para. 25). The corollary to this is that a development proposal which is in conflict with the development plan must be accompanied by a convincing demonstration of why it should not be rejected. Apart from the development plan there are ministerial policies as set out in circulars and guidance notes, and ministerial decisions given on appeal which must also be taken into account so far as they are relevant.

Environmental considerations are material considerations in determining planning applications. The Town and Country Planning (Assessment of Environmental Effects) Regulations 1988, SI No. 1199 and other environmental assessmnent regulations require that, where appropriate, an environmental statement be taken into account in the development control process. However, because there is a pollution control system in place the local planning system should not duplicate that system. The general principle is that the local planning authority must not substitute its own judgment for that of the pollution control authority on pollution control issues. This was underscored in *Gateshead MBC v Secretary of State for the Environment and Northumbrian Water plc*.

The facts were that the planning authority challenged the Secretary of State's decision to allow the appeal of the second defendant from the authority's refusal of permission for a clinical waste incinerator on the basis that there was insufficient data on the possible impact of the proposed development on the air quality of the locality. The court held that although the environmental impact of emissions to the atmosphere is a material planning consideration at the planning stage so too is the pollution control system under the EPA. Therefore in appropriate cases the planning authority or the Secretary of State may decide that they are satisfied that any remaining pollution concerns are capable of being dealt with under the EPA. The Secretary of State's decision that this was such a case could not be challenged. This judgment was upheld by the Court of Appeal (transcript, 1994).

The planning authority is also required to take into account the representations made by statutory consultees; these include the HSE and the NRA (see Article 18 of the GDO 1988). The views of the statutory consultees notwithstanding, the final decision remains with the planning authority, and must be based on planning considerations. In *Ynys Mon MBC v Secretary of State for the Environment* the planning authority rejected an application for the development of residential housing because the NRA had vetoed further residential development as the sewerage in the area was inadequate. The court held that the policy objectives of the NRA were important policy considerations but they must be weighed together with all other relevant matters and a planning decision properly arrived at which breached the NRA's veto was not unlawful simply because it did so.

However, serious consideration must be attached to the representations of statutory consultees; this was underscored by a call-in decision where the Secretary of State overturned a planning authority's decision to grant permission for the development of a restaurant near a hazardous installation against the HSE's advice (Secretary of State, July 1993).

Finally, the authority is required to take into account any objections made by members of the public but only if they are material planning considerations. To alert the public to development proposals in their area, applications must be publicized in accordance with a set procedure. But as PPG1 points out, 'local opposition to a proposal is not in itself a ground for refusing planning permission, unless that opposition is founded upon valid planning reasons which can be substantiated' (para. 42). In other words, the fact that the proposal is unpopular, as are many proposals for waste disposal facilities, is no reason for rejecting it; opponents must have valid arguments against it which raise land-use planning issues (for instance, the likelihood of intolerable noise pollution or dust nuisance).

Under s. 320 of the TCPA, rejecting an application without valid planning reasons may expose the planning authority to costs being awarded against it if the matter goes to a local inquiry following an appeal to the Secretary of State. A recent example of an award of costs against a planning authority involved a successful appeal by Browning Ferris Environmental Services Ltd whose application for a chemical treatment facility had been rejected by Newport Borough Council (Welsh Office, 1993).

The local planning authority may grant or refuse planning permission or grant it subject to conditions. Although the discretion to impose conditions is wide *Pyx Granite Co. Ltd v Ministry of Housing and Local Government* and *Newbury DC v Secretary of State for the Environment* indicated that, to be valid, conditions must be for a planning purpose, fairly and reasonably relate to the proposed development and not be arbitrary or manifestly unreasonable. Where permission is refused, Article 25 of the General Development Order 1988 requires the authority to give its reasons which must be precise, specific and relevant to the development.

The applicant may appeal to the Secretary of State under s. 78 against a refusal or adverse conditions. Although a member of the general public may not appeal, he or she may request the Secretary of State to 'call in' an application for consideration and determination. The Secretary of State's power to call in an application, which he may exercise on his own initiative or following a request, is granted by s. 77. The Secretary of State may choose to hold a public inquiry before determining the appeal or a called-in application, although they are more often determined on the basis of either written representations or an informal hearing. The Secretary of State's decision can be challenged in court only on points of law by way of an application for judicial review.

8.1.3   The Local Inquiry

Local inquiries are a familiar feature of British public administration. When triggered by planning applications they are known as 'local public inquiries'.

Bushell v Secretary of State for the Environment defined a local inquiry as an inquiry held in public:

1 In the locality in which the works that are the subject of the proposal are situated
2 By a person appointed by a minister charged with the duty of determining the question at issue
3 To inquire into the objections to the proposal by persons in the vicinity of the proposed works whose interests may be adversely affected
4 To provide the minister with as much information about those objections as will ensure that in reaching a decision the minister will have weighed the harm to local interests and private persons against the likely public benefit from the proposal and will not have failed to take into consideration any matters which he ought to have taken into consideration.

In reality, the duties of the Secretary of State over routine planning matters have largely been delegated to the Planning Inspectorate based in Bristol. The Secretary of State deals only with a few major or controversial matters. The procedure for holding planning inquiries is set out in the Town and Country Planning (Inquiries Procedure) Rules 1992, SI No. 2038 and the Town and Country Planning Appeals (Determination by Inspectors) (Inquiries Procedure) Rules 1992 SI No. 2039 made under the **Tribunals and Inquiries Act 1971**. The rules make provision for the procedure to be followed before the inquiry (including a pre-inquiry meeting), during the inquiry (including the rights of the public at the inquiry) and after the inquiry (including communicating the decision to interested parties).

Most inquiries are routine, lasting only a few days but occasionally there is a 'major public inquiry'. As the House of Commons Environment Committee noted, the distinguishing feature of major public inquiries is that they deal with national or, at least, regional policy issues rather than local ones and, in this sense, are qualitatively different from the local planning inquiry (House of Commons Environment Committee, 1986). The controversial question at such inquiries is whether there is a *need* for the project. The inquiry into the Sizewell B nuclear plant in a good example of an extremely controversial inquiry which lasted many months (O'Riordan *et al.*, 1988). Most controversial inquiries normally concern proposals for road and highway developments, some of which are fought over for years.

By its very nature, the local inquiry is not suited to considering national or regional policy issues, not least because it relies on the adversarial process. Therefore s. 101 of the TCPA provides for a Planning Inquiry Commission which the Secretary of State may constitute as necessary to consider such controversial questions of policy; no such Commission has been set up although this power has been on the statute book for several years.

8.1.4   Planning and Environmental Protection

One of the key factors in environmental protection is the geographical location of the activities which, because of their potential environmental impact, need to be controlled. For this reason, planning authorities in charge of development planning and control are key to environmental protection. Provision has been made therefore in the **TCPA 1990**, as amended, for them to take account of environmental considerations in development planning, both in plan making and in development control. The process for taking into account environmental considerations in development control is considered in detail in 8.2 'Environmental Assessment'.

In making both structure and local plans ss 31(3) and 36(3) respectively require planning authorities to include policies in respect of the conservation of the natural beauty and amenity of the land, the improvement of the environment and the management of traffic. Further, the Town and Country Planning (Development Plan) Regulations 1991, SI No. 2794 which provide for the form, content and approval of plans require that the plans take environmental considerations into account. PPG 12 on 'Development Plans and Regional Planning Guidance' fleshes out these requirements at some length (DoE, 1988a).

PPG 12 notes that most policies and proposals in all types of plan will have environmental implications. It advises that these should be systematically appraised using, where appropriate, the DoE's guidance on policy appraisal and the environment (DoE, 1991a). There is no requirement to conduct a full environmental assessment of the plan (para. 5.52). Chapter 6 of the PPG, 'Plans and the Environment', outlines the environmental considerations that plans need to take into account. These include:

1   Energy conservation and global warming
2   Reclamation of contaminated and derelict land
3   Reduction of nuisance such as noise, smell and dirt
4   The need to protect water quality
5   The location of hazardous installation
6   Mineral extraction, processing and tipping operations and
7   The conservation of natural beauty and amenity of the land.

The DoE has given specific guidance on the relevance of pollution control to the exercise of planning functions in PPG 23 on planning and pollution control (DoE, 1994a). PPG 23 advises planning authorities not to duplicate the functions of pollution control authorities, even where, in another capacity (e.g. as litter control authorities), they are the pollution control authority. Nevertheless, pollution remains a material planning consideration and the PPG indicates, in relation to each sector—IPC, air quality, water quality, waste management, contaminated land and environmental assessment—how the planning authority can take pollution considerations into account.

8.2   Environmental Assessment

Environmental assessment is essentially a technique for ensuring that environmental considerations are taken into account in any decision on development activities. In principle, it should apply to all actions likely to have an environmental impact, i.e. policies, plans, programmes and projects of all kinds. Indeed, it is the nature of decision making that the form of action at one level is conditioned by prior action, thus limiting feasible alternatives available to subsequent decision makers. The implementation of a project, for instance, is conditioned by the policy decisions already taken at higher levels which may have pre-empted some alternative strategies.

Although the benefits of undertaking an environmental assessment is widely acknowledged, for policies, plans and programmes it remains a complex undertaking whose methodology is very much in its infancy. Environmental assessment has been undertaken, therefore, mainly at the project level where the methodology is further advanced. In recognition of this more limited focus of current environmental assessments, the official definition of environmental assessment describes it as

> a technique and a process by which information about the environmental effects of *a project* is collected, both by the developer and from other sources, and taken into account by the planning authority in forming their judgment on whether the development should go ahead (DoE, 1989, p. 3).

The DoE has published a guide for government departments on policy appraisal and the environment which attempts to show how environmental effects can be taken into account both in environmental policies and in policies in other areas which have significant environmental impacts (DoE, 1991a). Its checklist for policy appraisal advises the following steps:

1   List the policy's aims and the constraints on the choices
2   Consider the environment from the outset
3   Consider the key issues
4   Identify a wide range of policy options
5   Seek expert advice
6   Identify impacts to be analysed and ameliorated at the policy stage
7   Choose the method of analysis carefully, preferably a cost-benefit approach
8   Analyse the environmental effects as much as is possible
9   Keep the appraisal under review
10 Monitor and evaluate the policy.

8.2.1   Directive on Environmental Assessment

EC Directive 85/337/EEC (OJ No. L 175/40) on the assessment of the effects of certain public and private projects on the environment requires member states to ensure that before projects receive consent their environmental effects are assessed. The Directive applies only to projects which are likely to have significant effects on the environment by virtue of their of their nature, size or location.

Two categories of project are specified as meeting the criteria for an environmental assessment. The first category, specified in Annex I, is subject to a mandatory assessment. Projects in this category are major developments, such as integrated chemical installations and construction of motorways. The second category, specified in Annex II, is subject to an assessment where the member state considers that the project's characteristics require it. Member states may specify certain types of project in this category as subject to an assessment or they may establish criteria and/or thresholds for determining which of the projects in the list are to be subject to an assessment.

The Directive provides that the information necessary for the assessment shall be collected and supplied to the relevant authorities by the developer. It shall consist of a description of the project, mitigating measures envisaged, the data needed to identify and assess the main environmental effects of the project and a 'non-technical' summary. It provides also that arrangements must be in place for consulting the public and authorities with environmental responsibilities with concerns about the project. The information may also be forwarded to another member state on whose environment the project is likely to have significant effects. A decision on the project, with reasons, must be made available to the public.

Amendments

The Commission has submitted a proposal (COM (93) 575 final, OJ No. C 130/8) to amend Directive 85/337 with the aim of correcting deficiencies relating to the scope of the Directive as well as the content of the impact study. The scope of the Directive depends on the thresholds defined for Annex II projects and member states' requirements have varied widely; those who set high thresholds require assessment in only a few cases while those who set low ones require assessments of projects with limited impact. The content of the information submitted by the developer has also varied greatly in the absence of minimum standards, most developers submitting only the bare minimum of information.

The first set of amendments are intended to clarify the circumstances in which Annex II projects will be required to undergo an environmental assessment, i.e. in every case where the project is liable to have a significant effect on 'special protection areas' designated by member states. The amendments also clarify the selection procedure for Annex II projects which member states must apply in all other cases in order to ascertain whether an assessment is necessary, using criteria defined and agreed at Community level and accompanied, where appropriate, by thresholds laid down by member states.

The second set of amendments are intended to improve the quality of the information by introducing the concept of scoping. This will enable an indication to be given of the nature of information which should be gathered. Additionally, there must be an indication of the alternatives considered by the developer. This amendment is important since the quality of the decision depends crucially on the quality of information considered in the process.

Implementation of the Directive in the UK

The Directive required member states to bring into force implementing measures within three years. The UK implemented it principally through the Town and Country Planning (Assessment of Environmental Effects) Regulations 1988, SI No. 1199, as amended, which came into force on 15 July 1988. The argument that the Regulations should be read as applying from 3 July 1988 was rejected in *Wychavon DC v Secretary of State for the Environment*. The Regulations apply widely to a range of projects. There are, however, other regulations which apply to specific types of project:

1 Trunk roads and motorways
2 Power stations, overhead power lines and long-distance oil and gas pipelines
3 Afforestation
4 Land drainage
5 Ports and harbours
6 Marine salmon farms
7 Marine dredging for minerals and
8 Projects in Simplified Planning Zones.

Parallel regulations apply in Scotland, the general one being the Environmental Assessment (Scotland) Regulations 1988, SI No. 1221. Additionally, the Houses of Parliament amended their standing orders to require an environmental assessment to be deposited with any Bill to approve a project which would require assessment under the Directive if it were not approved under the parliamentary procedure.

An attempt was made in *Twyford Parish Council v Secretary of State for the Environment* to argue that the implementing Regulations should be read as applying to projects 'in the pipeline' at the time the Regulations came into force (i.e. projects for which an application had been submitted but not yet determined). The argument was rejected, the court holding that the Directive required member states to ensure that the environmental effects of projects in relation to which decision-making processes or the development consent procedures had not yet started by 3 July 1988 would be assessed; it did not extend to projects in relation to which those processes or procedures were already on course.

The Regulations were made under the **European Communities** Act **1972**; at the time there was no specific statutory provision enabling the Secretary of State to make regulations requiring an environmental assessment of projects. Since then, the **Planning and Compensation Act 1991** has introduced powers enabling the Secretary of State to make regulations requiring environmental assessments. SI 1994 No. 677 (in Scotland, SI 1994 No. 2012) has therefore added wind generators, motorway service areas and coast protection works to the classes of development to which the Regulations apply. Salmonid farming, water treatment plants, golf courses, and privately financed toll roads may also be added to the list (DoE, 1992c).

The DoE has promised to close a loophole which enabled projects not requiring planning permission to escape environmental assessment even where their environmental effect was significant. Regulations will be laid requiring all such projects to be subjected to the normal planning permission procedure. Regulations will also be laid to require environmental assessment of projects which may significantly affect 'special protection areas' designated under the EC Directive 79/409 on Birds Conservation or 'special areas of conservation' under EC Directive 92/43 on Habitats (DoE, 1993), in line with the proposed amendment to Directive 85/337.

8.2.2   The Environmental Assessment Procedure

The Town and Country Planning (Assessment of Environmental Effects) Regulations 1988, SI No. 1199, as amended, require that an environmental assessment must be carried out before the relevant project proceeds. 'Environmental assessment' refers to the assessment made by the planning authority of the likely environmental impact of the proposed project. The factual basis for the assessment is the consideration of the 'environmental information' before the authority; this comprises the developer's 'environmental statement' (i.e. the developer's account of his or her proposal's likely environmental impact) together with any representations made as a result of consultations. The planning authority is not obliged to publish the environmental assessment and, where it does not, the general public has access only to the developer's environmental statement.

The Regulations apply to two categories of project referred to as Schedule 1 and Schedule 2 projects; the schedules originate from Annexes I and II of EC Directive 85/337. Schedule 1 projects, all of which are listed in the Regulations, require an environmental assessment in every case, while Schedule 2 projects require an environmental assessment only if they are likely to have a significant effect on the environment by virtue of their nature, size or location. DoE Circular 15/88 sets out criteria for deciding whether a project is a Schedule 1 or Schedule 2 project and thresholds for determining whether a Schedule 2 project would require an environmental assessment (DoE, 1988b). The thresholds are quantified while the criteria are general, indicating that a project will require an environmental assessment if it is:

1   Of more than local significance
2   Intended for a particularly sensitive location, e.g. a national park or a site of special scientific significance or
3   Likely to give rise to particularly complex or adverse effects, e.g. through the pollutants discharged.

A person seeking planning permission may ask the local planning authority to give its opinion on the category in which the proposed development falls and to state also, if in its opinion it falls in Schedule 2, whether its likely effects require an environmental assessment. The planning authority must respond within three weeks although a longer period may be agreed. If the authority believes that an environmental assessment would be required it must give its reasons in writing. The planning authority's opinion that an environmental assessment would be required (or failure to give an opinion) may be challenged by an application to the Secretary of State for a direction who also has to give a decision within three weeks. The planning authority is free to make representations to the Secretary of State but there is no statutory requirement to do so since the Secretary of State will have its reasoned opinion before him. The Secretary of State also has the power to direct that an environmental statement be submitted even if no application is made to him for a direction.

A developer may, alternatively, submit an environmental statement with an application for planning permission. DoE Circular 15/88 indicates that a planning authority should take it into account whether or not the project is one to which the regulations apply as long as the statement is relevant.

If, on the other hand, an application for planning permission for a project which requires an environmental assessment is submitted without an environmental statement the planning authority must, within three weeks or a longer agreed period, notify the applicant that an environmental statement is required, giving reasons. The applicant has three weeks in which to indicate that he or she will submit an environmental statement or that he or she is applying to the Secretary of State for a direction on the matter. If the applicant fails to state his intentions within that three-week period the application is deemed refused, from which there is no appeal. Also, if having stated that he will submit an environmental statement the applicant fails to do so, the planning authority must refuse the application. The same procedure applies also in those cases where an application for planning permission is either referred to, or called in by, the Secretary of State for a decision and to the case in which an appeal from the planning authority's decision is made to the Secretary of State. If no environmental statement is submitted where the Secretary of State believes one is needed, he shall notify the developer within three weeks and if the developer fails to respond, or states that he will submit one but does not, the application shall be refused.

An applicant who intends to apply for planning permission without an environmental statement must first publicize the statement by publishing a notice in the local newspaper and posting a copy on the site for the proposed development. The application for planning permission shall not be considered until the planning authority or the Secretary of State receives the environmental statement together with a copy of the notice advertising it and a certificate to the effect that a copy was posted on the site, or an explanation of the failure to post it. The applicant must provide enough copies of the environmental statement to enable the planning authority to submit copies to the Secretary of State as well as those statutory consultees who wish to receive one; these include the NRA and HMIP. Before the application is determined, fourteen days after the service of the environmental statement on these consultees must pass to enable them to comment on it.

Once all the documents have been submitted the planning authority has to give its decision on the application within sixteen weeks. It may not refuse it on the ground that the environmental statement is inadequate; the remedy is to ask the applicant to submit further information. This has denied planning authorities the single most effective means of controlling the quality of environmental statements submitted to them. In practice, local authorities do not always have the expertise for evaluating environmental statements and have had, at times, to retain external consultants for the purpose. The planning authority's decision on the application can be appealed to the Secretary of State and since the environmental effects of the project are only one of the factors to be considered in the planning process, the fact that a project is likely to have an adverse environmental effect does not mean that the application must be refused; permission may still be granted and made subject to specified conditions.

There is no central registry of planning applications involving environmental assessments since the task is undertaken by planning authorities across the country. However, evidence indicates that between July 1988 and March 1993 1142 environmental statements were submitted in support of planning applications. The quality of a significant proportion of these statements was reported to be unsatisfactory (ENDS, 1993a). This highlights the need for some benchmark quality for environmental statements; this could take the form of a guide of good practice, on which the DoE is currently working (DoE, 1994b).

8.3 Environmental Auditing

A widely used definition of environmental auditing states that it is a management tool comprising a systematic, documented, periodic and objective evaluation of how well the environmental organization, management and equipment are performing. Its aim is to help safeguard the environment by:

1 Facilitating management control of environmental protection and
2 Assessing compliance with company policies which would include meeting regulatory requirements (ICC, 1988).

Thus, environmental auditing (or eco-auditing) is an audit of the management systems of an organization with a view to determining how well the organization manages the effects of its activities on the environment. Its premise is that regular audits lead to a continuous improvement in the organization's management of these effects and their reduction over time.

The basic distinction between an environmental assessment and environmental auditing is that while the former is an assessment of the likely effects of *proposed* activities, the latter assesses *existing* ones. The purpose of the assessment in auditing is to ensure that the project is being conducted according to accepted standards and that the standards are maintained and improved upon; it links an environmental assessment to the manner in which the activity is eventually operated once it gets under way.

8.3.1 Standard Setting

Preceding an environmental audit there must be a standard against which the audit is conducted. This enables performance to be assessed objectively and improvements to be assessed. It also enables the audit to be verified by third parties, including the general public. Therefore, the rapid acceptance of environmental auditing necessitated the development of an environmental management system as the standard against which an environmental audit would be conducted.

In the UK the body responsible for setting standards is the British Standards Institution (BSI), a private organization based in Milton Keynes. BSI standards are given a BS number by which they may be referred to (e.g. BS 7570). At the European level standards are set by the European Committee for Standardization (CEN), based in Brussels; qualifying products carry an 'EN' (euronorm) mark. Internationally, the body in charge of standard setting is the Geneva-based International Standards Organization (ISO); standards set by the ISO take precedence over both national and European standards, thus avoiding duplication and the multiplication of contradictory standards.

Traditionally, standards have been 'product standards' specifying product quality. This trend culminated in BS 5750, the management standard for products and services. BS 5750 was quickly adopted by both the CEN and the ISO, thus establishing the international reputation of the BSI. With the advent of environmental management, BSI has developed an environmental management standard, BS 7750, to parallel BS 5750 with the hope that CEN and ISO would adopt BS 7750 also as a model environmental management system (BSI, 1994). The ISO is currently working on an environmental management standard but it is not clear that it will adopt BS 7750; the North Americans are not of the view that BS 7750 should be adopted, preferring a less prescriptive system along the lines of Responsible Care (see below). The European Community has adopted a Regulation on eco-management and audit (EMA) (No. 1836/93) whose requirements are similar to those of BS 7750.

A second type of standard is industry specific standards such as 'Responsible Care', the chemical industry's performance standard. This originated in Canada in 1984 and has been applied by the UK's chemical industry since 1989. Its requirements have similar aims to BS 7750 and the EC's EMA, having been designed essentially to enable a company's management system to be certified to the standards. The UK's Chemical Industry Association has made signing up to its Guiding Principles a condition of membership since July 1992 (Chemical Industries Association, 1992).

8.3.2   Regulation on Eco-management and Audit Scheme

EC Regulation No. 1836/93 (OJ No. L 168/1) on eco-management and audit, from May 1995, set up a voluntary scheme for companies performing industrial activities through which their environmental performance would be evaluated and information about it provided to the public. The Regulation defines a company as 'the organization which has overall management control over activities at a given site', thereby covering large and small organizations alike. It also provides that member states may apply principles similar to those set out in the scheme to sectors outside industry, such as the distributive trade and public service. The UK has indicated its intention to apply it to local authorities.

The scheme's objective is to promote continuous improvements in the environmental performance of industrial activities through a process under which organizations:

1   Establish and implement in relation to their sites environmental policies, programmes and management systems
2   Evaluate their performance systematically, objectively and periodically and
3   Inform the public about the environmental performance of the sites.

To register a site in the scheme the organization must:

1   Adopt an appropriate environmental policy
2   Conduct an environmental review

3   Introduce an environmental programme and management system
4   Carry out an environmental audit
5   Set objectives for the continuous improvement of environmental performance
6   Prepare an environmental statement
7   Have the environmental policy, programme, management system, review or audit procedure verified and the environmental statement validated
8   Submit the validated statement to the authorities and
9   Publicize the statement.

The environmental audit may be conducted either by auditors belonging to the organization or by external auditors. They are required to follow procedures set out in the Regulation which identify the issues to be covered but also set requirements in relation to the objectives, scope, organization and resources, planning and preparation, audit activities, reporting findings and conclusions, follow-up and frequency of the audit.

The statement reporting the audit findings must be validated by a verifier who is both independent of the organization and accredited by an accreditation body. The accreditation must meet requirements set out in the Regulation relating to personnel, independence and objectivity, procedures and organization. Further, the Regulation provides for items which the accreditation process is to include, the supervision of accredited environmental verifiers and extension of the scope of accreditation of a verifier. The verifier's function is essentially to confirm that the organization has complied with the requirements of the scheme in relation to the registered site and to validate the organization's statement.

The environmental statement is to be prepared following an initial environmental review and the completion of each audit cycle for every site participating in the scheme. Audit cycle refers to the period of time, whose length is not specified in the Regulation, in which all the activities in a given site are audited. In principle, a simplified unvalidated version of the statement must be prepared annually where the audit cycle exceeds one year. However, no further environmental statement is required until completion of the next audit where the accredited environmental verifier considers, for small and medium-sized enterprises, that the nature and scale of operations makes this unneccessary or, alternatively, where there have been few significant changes since the last statement.

The Regulation requires member states to establish an independent system for the accreditation of environmental verifiers and for the supervision of their activities. However, accreditations are mutually recognizable in member states and a Community list of accredited verifiers shall be published in the *Official Journal*. Member states are required also to establish competent bodies to register sites. A site may be deregistered if it fails to submit a validated environmental statement within three months of being required to do so or if the site ceases to comply with the requirements of the Regulation. Registered sites will be published in the *Official Journal* and organizations may publicize the site's participation, using the appropriate EC logo as specified in an Annex to the Regulation. The site's participation may not be used to advertise products, on the products themselves or on their packaging.

Recognizing that there are already some environmental management standards, like BS 7750, the Regulation provides that organizations implementing such certified systems and audits shall be considered as meeting the corresponding requirements of the EC scheme on two conditions:

1 The standards and procedures have to be recognized by the Commission and
2 The certification must be undertaken by a body whose accreditation is recognized by the member state where the site is located.

This enables BS 7750 to be used as one way of complying with the EC scheme: an organization registered under BS 7750 would be able to register a site under the EC scheme. But the organization would also have to make the public statement as required under EMA; a key difference between the two schemes is that a verified public statement is not a requirement under BS 7750.

8.3.3   BS 7750

BS 7750 is the standard specifying the elements of an environmental management system which an organization could use to establish environmental policies and objectives, achieve compliance with them and demonstrate such compliance to third parties. Additionally, it gives guidance on how the management system could be implemented and assessed. BS 7750 came into effect for the first time on 16 March 1992 for pilot trials and a revised version was published in March 1994. It shares common management principles with EN 29000 and ISO 9000, the European and international quality systems standards. Organizations may therefore use an existing management system developed in conformity with BS 5750 as a basis for environmental management.

The following ten elements are specified as necessary to an environmental management system:

1 A documented environmental policy with set objectives and targets
2 Key personnel with the responsibility and authority to manage, perform and verify work affecting the environment
3 A procedure for assessing the direct and indirect environmental effects caused by the organization
4 A programme for achieving the objectives and targets

5   A manual describing all the elements of the management system and a procedure for controlling the documentation

6   Procedures for verifying compliance with requirements and for documenting the results

7   Procedures for investigating non-compliance and taking corrective action

8   A system of records for demonstrating compliance with requirements and the extent of achievement of objectives and targets

9   An audit plan for the environmental management system and a system for acting on any deficiencies the audit identifies

10 A procedure for periodically reviewing the environmental management system to determine its continued suitability.

An organization wishing to implement an environmental management system therefore has to first review its operations with a view to setting its policy, objectives and targets. Then it has to establish an internal management programme with the necessary personnel and procedures aimed at delivering the objectives and targets. The third step is to document the requirements of the management system and train its personnel on its requirements. It is then necessary, after a suitable period, to audit the functioning of the structures and correct any deficiencies identified. The final step is to review its operations once again, marking the completion of the cycle and the start of another one.

For the organization to be registered under BS 7750, however, the management system would have to be 'certified'. There is a similar requirement under EMA for a site seeking EMA registration to have its management system 'verified'. Certification and verification are different terminologies for the same process of checking that the management system complies with the standards and, in the case of verification, confirming that the public statement is accurate. In both cases it would be conducted ideally by accredited environmental auditors. In the UK the auditors are drawn primarily from a range of environmental consultancies.

8.3.4   Environmental Consultancies

The statutory requirement for environmental assessments and the introduction of environmental management systems brought a dramatic increase in the number of 'environmental consultancies' offering services in drawing up the environmental statements and related environmental services (ENDS, 1993b). There are no mandatory qualification requirements to be met by environmental consultants. The variable quality of the environmental statements submitted to planning authorities in the initial stages caused concern and, in a bid to raise standards, the Institute of Environmental Assessment (IEA) and the Association of Environmental Consultancies (AEC) were formed in 1990 and 1991 respectively.

Environmental consultancies provide services in relation to both environmental assessments and environmental auditing and the two bodies have set up mechanisms for registering environmental consultants to provide both kinds of service. The mechanisms differ in their requirements. In relation to environmental assessments, the IEA's approach is to evaluate environmental statements submitted to it by a consultancy before registering those who qualify as 'registered assesssors'; the key criterion is the quality of the statement the consultancy is capable of producing. The AEC, on the other hand, registers consultancies as 'qualified environmental assessors' on the basis of the qualifications and experience of their staff who need to satisfy minimum requirements in terms of academic qualifications and years of experience, while the consultancy itself needs to demonstrate that it has undertaken work for a minimum number of clients and has procedures for ensuring the quality of its work. The environmental statement itself is not, however, evaluated (AEC, 1991; EARA, undated, a).

In relation to environmental auditing work, the IEA at first made no provision for registering environmental auditors. It now provides the secretariat for a second body, the Environmental Auditors Registration Association (EARA), set up in 1992 to register individuals as environmental consultants on the basis of their qualifications and training. EARA has three categories of auditor depending on the qualification and experience of the individual: Associate Environmental Auditor, Environmental Auditor and Principal Environmental Auditor. The individual, rather than the consultancy, is the holder of the registration. It believes that it has 'captured 80 per cent of the current UK consultancy resources active in this field' (EARA, undated, b). Unlike the IEA, the AEC has from inception made a distinction in the qualification of the individuals working in the consultancies it registers so that a consultancy registered as a 'qualified environmental auditor' is registered as qualified to conduct 'technical audits' or alternatively 'management and compliance audits' or both. Both bodies have drafted codes of conduct with which registered auditors must undertake to comply (AEC, 1991; EARA, undated, a).

The relationship between the registration systems for environmental auditors run by these bodies and the accreditation scheme to be run by the National Accreditation Council for Certification Bodies (NACCB) (see below) is under consideration. EARA and the AEC have approached the NACCB for recognition so that a registration certificate from the schemes they run would count as one way of demonstrating competence to act as a verifier or a certifier, as the case may be, under EMA or BS 7750. If matters develop in this way, a body like EARA would act as a standard setter for auditors wishing to achieve accredited status. Other professional associations, such as the Institute of Chemical Engineering, are likely to set up similar registration schemes and seek recognition from the NACCB. Whereas EARA covers the whole range of environmental consultancy services, not all the schemes may do so; some may confine themselves to offering more specialized certificates.

8.3.5 Accreditation and Registration Bodies

EMA requires member states to set up a system to accredit environmental verifiers and to supervise their activities, conferring a stamp of offical recognition on certifiers and the verifiers. BS 7750 is not an official scheme and the government has no obligation to introduce an accreditation system for it. But EMA requires that participants who use recognized national standards to meet requirements must have their compliance with those standards verified by a body whose accreditation is recognized in the member state where the site is located. The government chose therefore to extend the accreditation system for EMA to those certificating compliance with BS 7750 (DTI, 1993). This enhances the chances of BS 7750 being recognized by the Commission as adequate to satisfy the requirements for registration under EMA.

The National Accreditation Council for Certification Bodies (NACCB), originally formed as a Council of the British Standards Institution to run the accreditation system for BS 5750, has been designated by the government to accredit certifiers for BS 7750 and verifiers for EMA. The NACCB's role is to review a verifier's application and, if satisfied, make a formal recommendation to the President of the Board of Trade (i.e. the DTI) with whom the power lies to grant accreditation. The scope of an organization's accreditation can be extended if it acquires expertise in a new area and the NACCB will be defining in due course the competence levels required for the various elements of the certification process (ENDS, 1993c).

EMA also requires that member states designate an independent and neutral body to run the scheme. This would involve receiving and processing applications to register sites and considering whether to suspend or strike out sites which no longer meet the requirements of the scheme. The government initially suggested widening the remit of the UK Eco-labelling Board (see Chapter 9) to make it a competent body for EMA but subsequently opted to retain the role within the DoE (DoE, 1994c). It is thought that the task will go to the Environmental Protection Agency once it is set up.

8.3.6 The Audits

Conducting environmental audits has become fairly common practice within organizations in recent years, particularly as environmental liabilities in the form of prosecutions, fines, insurance premiums and so on have become a reality for many companies. In practice an audit is triggered by a diverse range of factors. It is these factors which dictate the scope of the any particular audit undertaken. Audits can be classified loosely into several groups (Salter, 1992) with the caveat that they may fall into more than one group and need not be either one or the other.

Types of Audit

There are four types of audit:

1 A 'compliance audit'; this is an audit undertaken by the company itself primarily to test compliance with company environmental policy and standards and with regulatory requirements.
2 An 'environmental due diligence check'; this is an audit undertaken by a purchaser or a seller to check the environmental status of a company as a prelude to a commercial merger or an acquisition of that company or its assets and liabilities with, or by, another.
3 A 'property audit'; this is an audit undertaken by a purchaser, a lender or a seller to check the environmental status of particular land to facilitate a property transaction such as a purchase, a loan or sale—the dominant issue being whether the land is contaminated and, if so, the extent of the contamination.
4 An 'environmental risk assessment'; this is an audit undertaken to assess the prospective environmental liabilities of a company for the purpose of assessing the level of insurance premium that the company needs to pay.

Depending on its scope, an environmental audit can be a 'corporate audit' covering the entire company, an 'activity audit' covering only some activities in which the company is engaged or a 'site audit' covering a particular site. Typically, compliance audits start off with one sector and spread out to cover the entire company's operations simply because this is more practicable. An audit can be conducted by either the employees of the company or by an outside consultancy or a combination of the two. Due diligence audits and property audits are, however, far more likely to be undertaken by external environmental consultants because the results of the audit are intended primarily for external consumption; the involvement of ostensibly impartial third parties lends objectivity and authority to the results.

The environmental audit provides the necessary information to assist the company's management in deciding on the appropriate course of action. This may range from the abandonment of the merger or acquisition should it be decided that the environmental status of the company would not warrant proceeding to continuing but subject to appropriate warranties and indemnities agreed between the parties. An audit thus provides the information necessary for informed decisions to be taken.

A 'warranty' is a term inserted in a contract by which one party makes promises to the other regarding the subject of the contract, for example that there are no outstanding environmental liabilities in relation to the property of which the vendor is aware; breach of the warranty enables the party suffering loss to claim compensation for any loss. A standard form of warranties relating to environmental matters which might be included in a contract is available (*Encyclopedia*, 1992).

An 'indemnity' covers similar issues to a warranty. It is a term in the contract to the effect that one party will compensate the other should it incur specified costs, for instance as a result of a suit arising from the contaminated state of the property. Warranties and indemnities are standard mechanisms in contract law for dealing with potential loss in the event of a contract failing to live up to expectations. They are now being adapted to serve the same function in respect of potential environmental liabilities in commercial transactions.

The information provided by an environmental audit may affect the contract price depending on the parties' evaluation of the real or potential environmental liabilities. For a loan agreement it may affect the assessment of the property as security for the loan and a seriously contaminated piece of property may be rejected as security. Indeed, a secured creditor might choose not to foreclose on a piece of property if an audit reveals that it is contaminated where the potential liabilities created by taking possession exceed the residual value of the property.

A compliance audit may indicate that a remediation programme is necessary to put right the problems identified by the audit (for example, cleaning up contaminants found on the site). Under BS 7750 a commitment to act on the results of the audit is a requirement for registration. This is good practice since the rationale for environmental audits is that they lead to continuous improvements in environmental performance; that would not be possible without the commitment to deal with the problems identified. Often the environmental consultancies who conduct the audits also implement remediation programmes. However, not all environmental problems are amenable to correction by external organizations; a number, such as sloppy work practices, must be tackled internally.

The Auditing Process

An environmental audit has three distinct components (Hillary, undated):

1 A desk-based review of the relevant issues and documents; this may include contacting the relevant regulators for information about the company's environmental record
2 A site visit which, depending on the scope of the audit, can extend to physical sampling and on- or off-site testing and
3 An analysis of the results of the site visit and the drawing up of recommendations for action.

The stages are dependent on each other; the desk-based study sets the stage for the site visit and the site visit also sets the stage for the subsequent analysis. Thus, for instance, the desk study should draw up a checklist of issues to look out for during the site visit. The cost of the audit increases appreciably from a purely desk-based study through a site visit and possible testing and sampling to analysis and follow-up action.

An environmental audit which is limited to a desk-based study and a perfunctory site visit runs the risk of leaving potential environmental problems undetected. There are a number of reasons for not conducting a full audit. First, the cost of conducting an audit increases the more comprehensive the audit becomes. Second, many environmental audits are sought when the associated commercial transaction has progressed to a stage that insufficient time is left to conduct a full audit. Third, there is concern that adverse results of an audit may be used as evidence against a company or become public, to the detriment of the company's image. Organizations are therefore wary of putting on record all the information that might emerge (see Chapter 4).

A desk-based study is only as good as the information on which it is based and where this is flawed or incomplete its conclusions may be unreliable. Accordingly, if the benefits of conducting an audit are to be achieved the necessary time and resources need to be set aside. An audit conducted without a full investigation or under time pressure may lead to conclusions which turn out to be unfounded, as the *Foliejohn case* below illustrates. The concern relating to an adverse use of the information that emerges from the audit can be met to some extent by a proper policy of document management (see 'Privilege' below).

Foliejohn Establishment v Gain SA, the first case in which a property environmental audit was litigated in UK courts, illustrates graphically the pitfalls of conducting an audit against tight deadlines. Gain owned some land, Foliejohn Estate, on which there was laboratory researching into the development of very high purity metal alloys. It decided to sell the land, having moved the laboratory elsewhere. Agreement was reached with the buyer on 14 July 1992 under which the sale was to take place no later than 28 September 1992, just over two months later. On the date of the agreement for sale the buyer introduced a provision in the contract under which the seller, Gain, gave warranties to the effect that the land was not contaminated.

The buyer then engaged a firm of environmental consultants to conduct an environmental audit of the land who, after a desktop study, reported towards the end of August (with a more detailed report on 25 September) that the laboratory, the drainage system and its surroundings and a stream running through the land was seriously contaminated and put the cost of remediation at nearly £250 000; the conclusion was that the seller had breached the warranties given. The seller, who saw the report for the first time on 25 September, retained another firm of environmental consultants who disagreed with the conclusions of the buyer's consultants. In the meantime, 28 September having passed, the buyer commenced proceedings against the seller in relation to what they claimed was a breach of warranty.

In court the judge rejected the buyer's claim for a breach of warranty on the basis that the buyer's consultants' report was flawed on three grounds. First, to identify contamination, they had resorted to 'spot sampling' rather than 'area sampling', looking in the drainage system and such places; the former technique takes samples from selected spots rather than covering a representative area. Second, the extrapolation of the results of the sample made no allowance for this factor, giving the impression that the whole laboratory was equally seriously contaminated. Indeed no record of the precise places from which samples had been taken was kept. Finally, the standards used to interpret the sample results were misleading; the report indicated that the levels of contamination present constituted a threat to human health when in reality there could be no human uptake from these sources, i.e. drains and filter beds.

Making Audit Results Public

The question of making the report of the results of environmental audits public is a sensitive one. It is the one area of significant difference between the EMA and BS 7750; the former requires a statement of the results to be made public whereas the latter does not. The concern is that an adverse audit may affect the company's public standing. There is also concern over the question of whether environmental audit information could be obtained by the regulators for use in a prosecution or be the subject of an order for 'discovery' in civil litigation, a point discussed in 11.1 'Self-incrimination'.

Environmental reporting generally has grown in recent years in the form of audit results in annual reports published by major companies. A frequent criticism of these annual reports is that they are subjective and qualitative, tending to report the good news only without giving a balanced report of the impact of the company's activities on the environment. It is for this reason that the EMA scheme requires verifiers to validate the accuracy of the environmental statement following an audit. Such validation would enhance the standing accorded to environmental reports. However, this requirement is seen as an obstacle to companies joining the EMA scheme as they argue that auditing is an internal management tool, not a mechanism for public information.

The Institute of Chartered Accountants in England and Wales (ICAEW) has recommended that an environmental report should cover a number of areas:

1   The company's environmental policy and objectives
2   Its director for environmental affairs
3   Action taken and expenditure on environmental objectives

4 The main environmental impacts of its activities
5 The extent of its compliance with regulations and industry guidelines
6 Significant environmental risks caused by its activities (ICAEW, 1992).

In a bid to stimulate and reward companies which provide factual information in their reports, the Chartered Association of Certified Accountants set up the Environmental Reporting Award in 1992. Separately, the Chemical Industries Association compiles data on the performance of the chemical industry in the UK in order to assess the effectiveness of its Responsible Care programme. These data are aggregated and published annually, beginning in 1993, without identifying individual companies. The data cover six issues: environmental project spending, safety and health, waste emissions, incidents during distribution, energy consumption and complaints. The regulatory authorities also maintain registers of information supplied to them by companies (see Chapter 9).

References

AEC, *The Association of Environmental Consultancies: Code of Practice and Registration Procedures* (1991).
BSI, BS 7750: Specification for environmental management systems (1994).
Bushell v Secretary of State for the Environment [1980] 2 All ER 608.
Chemical Industries Association, *Responsible Care* (1992).
DoE, PPG 12, *Development Plans and Regional Planning Guidance* (1988a).
DoE, *Town and Country Planning (Assessment of Environmental Effects) Regulations*, Circular 15/88 (1988b).
DoE, *Policy Appraisal and the Environment*, HMSO (1991a).
DoE, *Planning, Policy and the Environment* (1991b).
DoE, *Removal of Crown Exemption from Planning Law*, a Consultation Paper (1992a).
DoE, PPG 1, *General Policy and Principles*, HMSO (1992b).
DoE, *Environmental Assessment and Planning: Extension of Application*, a Consultation Paper (1992c).
DoE, *General Development Order: Permitted Development, Environmental Assessment and the Implementation of the Habitats Directive*, a Consultation Paper (1993).
DoE, PPG 23, *Planning and Pollution Control* (1994a).
DoE, *Guide on Preparing Environmental Statements for Planning Projects: Consultation Draft* (1994b).
DoE, 'Lord Arran announces competent body for the EC EMA scheme', News Release No. 648, 10 May (1994c).
DoE/WO, *Environmental Assessment: A Guide to Procedures* (1989).
DTI, *Implementation of the EC Eco-Management and Audit Regulation and Accreditation Arrangements for Certification to BS 7750*, a Consultation Paper (1993).
EARA, *Environmental Auditors Registration Scheme: Guidelines* (undated, a).
EARA, *Details of the EARA Scheme* (undated, b).
Encyclopedia of Forms and Precedents: Vol 11 (Companies), Butterworths (1992).

ENDS Report No. 221, 'Taking stock of environmental assessment', June, 20–24 (1993a).

ENDS, *Directory of Environmental Consultants*, 3rd edn (1993b).

ENDS Report No. 226, 'NACCB to be accreditation body for BS7750 and EC eco-audits', November, 36 (1993c).

Foliejohn Establishment v Gain SA (1993, unrep.).

Gateshead MBC v Secretary of State for the Environment and Northumbrian Water plc (1994) Env LR 11. Court of Appeal's judgment [1994] *Estates Gazette* 92.

Hillary, R., *The Eco-management and Audit Scheme: A Practical Guide*, Technical Communications Ltd (undated).

House of Commons Environment Committee, 5th Report, *Planning: Appeals, Call-ins and Major Public Inquiries*, Session 1985-86, HMSO.

ICC, *Environmental Auditing*, ICC Position Paper on Environmental Auditing, ICC Publication 468 (1988).

Institute of Chartered Accountants in England and Wales, *Business, Acountancy and the Environment: A Policy and Research Agenda* (1992).

Newbury DC v Secretary of State for the Environment [1981] AC 578.

Nuffield Foundation, *Town and Country Planning: Report of a Committe of Inquiry appointed by the Nuffield Foundation* (1986).

O'Riordan, T. *et al.*, *Sizewell B: An Anatomy of the Inquiry*, Macmillan (1988).

Pyx Granite Co. Ltd v Ministry of Housing and Local Government [1958] 1 QB 554.

Salter, J., *Corporate Environmental Responsibility: Law and Practice*, Butterworths (1992).

Secretary of State's decision PNW/5291/219/7 of 15 July 1993 (application by D. Henderson).

Twyford Parish Council v Secretary of State for the Environment (1992) *JEL*, vol. 4/2 272.

Welsh Office, Secretary of State's decision P34/919 P34/971 of 23 August 1993, Welsh Office (application by Browning Ferris International).

Wychavon DC v Secretary of State for the Environment, *The Times*, 7 January (1994).

Ynys Mon MBC v Secretary of State for the Environment [1993] JPL 225.

9

Environmental Information and Environmental Communications

In an era of greatly hightened public awareness and concern in relation to environmental protection the extent and nature of the information that is available to the public has become one of the key issues in regard to environmental management. The question arises in two contexts both of which are looked at in some detail below.

First, the demand by the general public for increased involvement in the process of environmental control has brought enhanced rights of public access to wider categories of environmental information. Second, the attempt to market various products as 'environmentally friendly' raises the need to control and channel positively the advertisement of products and services as well as the labelling of products to make the labels reliable. The public's preference for 'environmentally friendlier' products is likely to act as an incentive for manufacturers to produce less environmentally damaging products, a factor that can be harnessed by ensuring that the public are able to rely on advertisements and labels.

9.1 Public Access to Environmental Information

Public access to environmental information is seen as vital in enabling the general public to be involved in the process of environmental protection. Public involvement can take various forms such as:

1   Making representations to the regulators when an application for a permit is being considered
2   Taking legal action; the first case of this kind was brought by the Anglers Cooperative Association who successfully prosecuted a water authority for water pollution on the basis of data in the public register (*D.A Wales v Thames Water Authority* (1987)) or

3 Putting pressure on regulators and industry alike to pay greater attention to their environmental responsibilities.

These considerations led the Royal Commission on Environmental Pollution to recommend 'a presumption in favour of unrestricted access for the public to information which pollution control authorities obtain or receive by virtue of their statutory powers ...' (RCEP, 1984).

A much less publicized role for environmental information is its use by industry and other commercial entities to aid their strategic planning and investment decisions. The word 'public' in this context, though typically thought to refer to the disinterested public (i.e. 'the man on the Clapham bus') and environmental pressure groups, is equally applicable to industry and other commercial entities who, perhaps ironically, may themselves find the availability of environmental information of great benefit. Information about current holders of water abstraction licences with details such as quantities licensed, to take one example, is of crucial importance to anyone planning a development that requires the abstraction of water from a particular water source. This is because prior licensees are likely objectors to any application for an abstraction licence which may derogate from their licence. Accordingly, an agreement with prior licensees may need to be part of the strategic plan before embarking on the development. Such an agreement is only possible if one can find out details of the interest the prior licensees hold.

Public access to information can be provided in two ways: first, by giving the public a general right of access to information on the environment which is held by public bodies and, second, by giving the public a right to a limited amount of carefully defined categories of information only provided by means of a register. The register model, to which the UK traditionally adhered, has the advantage that it is administratively practical and is transparent insofar as it is clear exactly what information the public are entitled to and where they can get it; its disadvantage is that the quantity of information is limited. The 'general access' model, championed by the European Commission, has the advantage of giving a right to far greater categories of information than the register model could ever hope to provide, but it suffers the serious disadvantage that the public has the difficult task of first identifying what information is available, and its location, before requesting it. Those seeking information will therefore often have to go on a 'fishing expedition', making ill-defined and vague requests which are quite difficult to satisfy. This makes it possible for a public body which is reluctant to supply the information to avoid having to do so by giving the excuse that it does not hold the information. In practice, most benefit will be gained by using these two sources of information in tandem; examining the register first to see what information is available and then requesting additional information under the general access rights.

There is a third source of environmental information, the Chemical Release Inventory (CRI) operated by HMIP. The three sources of environmental information—the European Community general access rights, the registers and the CRI—are considered in turn.

9.1.1   EC Directive on Access to Environmental Information

The EC Directive 90/313/EEC (OJ No. L 158/56) on freedom of access to information on the environment required member states to have their public authorities 'make available information relating to the environment to any natural or legal person at his request and without his having to prove an interest'. This requirement is implemented in Britain by the Environmental Information Regulations 1992, SI No. 3240 which came into force on 31 December 1992.

The Regulations impose an obligation on bodies, referred to as 'relevant persons', holding information relating to the environment to make it available to any person who requests it within two months of the request or else give a written reasoned refusal. The phrase 'relevant persons' refers to two categories of body: first, public authorities such as ministries, government departments, local authorities and other national, regional or local public administrators with environmental responsibilities; and, second, bodies with environmental responsibilities which do not fall into the first category but which are under the control of a body falling into that category.

A public body could refuse a request for environmental information for one of six reasons:

1   It does not consider itself subject to the Regulations in that it is not a 'relevant person'; speculation has centred on whether bodies such as privatized utilities are relevant persons but so far the question has not been tested although on the face of it, the water companies, for instance, meet the criteria—they have public responsibilities for the environment (e.g. consenting trade effluent discharges) and are under the control of a public body with environmental responsibilities (the OFWAT) in at least some aspects of their operations.

2   It does not consider that the information requested is 'environmental'; environmental information is defined widely to cover the state of air, water, land, flora, fauna and activities or measures adversely affecting them or designed to protect them.

3   It does not hold the information requested; the DoE has advised relevant persons to publicize the categories of information they hold in publications such as their annual reports thus minimizing the frequency of misdirected requests (DoE, 1992a). HMIP, the NRA and the Drinking Water Inspectorate all have a duty to publish annual reports.

4 It uses the information in a judicial or legislative capacity; there is a long-standing tradition of protecting information being used in a judicial or legislative capacity from public disclosure and this is recognized by the EC Directive.
5 The request is manifestly unreasonable or formulated in too general a manner; this is likely to be a significant problem because people will often not have a clear idea what precise information to request.
6 One or more of a number of exemptions apply; more than any of the above reasons the exemptions, which are set out below, are likely to give rise to the greatest difficulty in interpretation.

Two categories of information are exempt from disclosure under the Regulations; information which is 'capable of being treated as confidential' and information which 'must be treated as confidential'. Five kinds of information fall under the first category:

1 Matters affecting international relations, national defence or public security
2 The subject matter of legal or other proceedings
3 Confidential deliberations or the contents of internal communications
4 A document still in the course of completion or
5 Matters to which commercial or industrial confidentiality attaches or affecting intellectual property.

Another four kinds of information fall under the second category of exemption as follows:

1 Information capable of being treated as confidential and whose disclosure would contravene a statutory provision or rule of law or would breach an agreement
2 Personal information contained in records relating to an individual who has not given his or her consent to disclosure
3 Information supplied by a person under no legal obligation to supply it, who did not supply it in circumstances entitling its disclosure and who has not consented to its disclosure or
4 Information likely to increase the likelihood of environmental damage if disclosed.

There will probably be controversy regarding the interpretation that relevant persons put on these exemptions. Relevant persons are likely to interpret them widely, enabling them to restrict the information disclosed because, among other reasons, wrongful disclosure might leave them vulnerable to legal action by those whose interests are prejudiced by the disclosure. On the other hand, those seeking disclosure may argue for narrower interpretation. Anecdotal evidence indicates, for instance, that public bodies often decline to supply information on the basis that it might be used in legal proceedings even when there are no legal proceedings in prospect. This would appear to be against the provisions and spirit of the Regulations.

In relation to commercially confidential information the DoE advised that, to avoid wrongful disclosure, relevant persons should classify the information either when it is received or when access to it is first requested after first giving its supplier the opportunity to indicate whether he or she considers it confidential, and if so, for what reason. Where only part of the information is deemed restricted relevant persons could prepare an edited version containing any non-sensitive information and mark it 'Public Access Copy' (DoE, 1992b). Classifying information in this way is particularly important for information pre-dating the Regulations since suppliers will not have had an opportunity at the time of supply to indicate whether they consider it confidential.

Compounding the difficulties to be encountered through relevant parties interpreting exemptions widely, the Regulations have not provided for appeals against the decisions of relevant persons. The DoE guidance was no more helpful, indicating only that, in appropriate cases, an aggrieved party could approach the local government ombudsman or his or her member of Parliament or resort to court action (DoE, 1992a). These remedies are limited and, in any case, whether they are feasible and effective in practice is speculative; court action, for instance, is protracted and costly. The government appears to have recognized this and has stated that for a right of access to information to be meaningful there must be a clear and effective means of challenging a relevant person's decision; the government therefore is examining the possibility of setting up a tribunal to determine such disputes (*Open Government*, 1993). Such a move would also assist in meeting anticipated objections from the European Commission to whom FoE has formally complained about the failure by the UK to provide a forum for appeals.

The general right of access to environmental information in the Environmental Information Regulations 1992 does not replace the right already in existence to defined categories of information provided through various registers. The Regulations specifically provide that they do not apply to information which is required, in accordance with any statute, to be provided to any person who requests it or to information contained in records which statute requires to be made available for inspection by any person. The two sources of information are complementary.

9.1.2 Registers of Information

All the main environmental statutes have set up public registers of information. The registers are maintained by the regulatory authorities in charge of the particular environmental medium; i.e. the NRA is in charge of the water pollution control registers, HMIP is in charge of the IPC registers and so on. The registers can be inspected free of charge, normally at the regional or area office of the authority in which the process or activity is located. Not all authorities allow photocopies to be taken but where they do a 'reasonable' charge may be made. In practice the amount varies significantly between the authorities. Information can also be obtained over the telephone and, at times, by fax.

Information may be excluded from the register on grounds either of national security or commercial confidentiality (i.e. information which is likely to prejudice to an unreasonable degree a person's commercial interest). In the case of commercial confidentiality the application for exclusion is usually made to the enforcing authority although there are a few variations in the statutory provisions; an application to exclude information from the pollution control register maintained by the NRA, for instance, is made to the Secretary of State. An appeal may be made to the Secretary of State from the decision of the enforcing authority. Where national security is the reason for seeking exclusion then the application has to be made to the Secretary of State who directs the enforcing authority to exclude the information.

There are more applications for exclusion of information on the basis of commercial confidentiality from IPC registers than from water pollution control registers. This is because IPC applications involve details of the processes, with implications for commercial confidentiality. Decisions on appeal by the Secretary of State for claims by the power generators, National Power and Powergen, gave an indication of the considerations which are taken into account in determining such claims. Powergen's claim about information regarding the forecast schedules of emissions for the coming year failed while National Power's claim about information regarding the future fuel consumption at its power station succeeded on the basis that the information could benefit its competitors and fuel suppliers (DoE, 1992c). Table 9.1 gives details of the public registers and the authorities that maintain them.

9.1.3   The Chemical Release Inventory

In 1992 the DoE published proposals to establish an annual inventory of releases of substances from industrial processes (DoE, 1992b). The inventory, the *Chemical Release Inventory* (CRI), was to have been published for the first time in 1993 with 1992 data. On the conclusion of the consultation exercise it was decided to proceed with the idea but its implementation was postponed to 1994 (DoE, 1993). Thus, the CRI constitutes the third mechanism in Britain for obtaining environmental information. However, the CRI covers only chemical releases from industrial processes under the control of HMIP and radioactive waste discharges.

The key feature distinguishing the CRI from the Environmental Information Regulations 1992 and the public registers is that the CRI is an annual aggregation of data on chemical releases making an 'annual inventory'; the data

Table 9.1   Registers and reports maintained by public bodies

Statutory provision	*Name of register/report*
The National Rivers Authority under the Water Resources Act 1991	
1 S.189 and SI 1965 No. 574	Register of Abstraction and Impounding Licences.
2 S.190 and SI 1989 No. 1160	Pollution Control Register (i.e. register of discharge consents).
3 S.191	Register of discharges made by the NRA for purposes of carrying out works.
4 S.192	Maps of freshwater limits.
5 S.195	Maps of waterworks.
6 S.187	Annual Report of the NRA.
The Office of Water Services under the Water Industry Act 1991	
1 S.195	The Director's Register (i.e. register of appointments and regulation of water companies).
2 S.193	Annual Reports by the Director General of Water Services.
3 S.194	Reports by Customer Service Committees.
4 S.201	Information published by the Secretary of State or the Director about the water industry (e.g. the Drinking Water Inspectorate Annual Report).
The water and/or sewerage companies under the Water Industry Act 1991	
1 S.196	Trade Effluent Registers (i.e. registers of trade effluent discharges into public sewers).
2 S.197	Register of discharges by the companies for purposes of works.
3 S.198	Maps of waterworks.
4 S.199	Sewer maps (i.e. records of the location of sewers etc.).
HMIP Under Part I of the EPA 1990 and other statutes	
1 S.20 and SI 1991 No. 507	Register of IPC Processes regulated by HMIP.
2 No specific statutory provision	HMIP's Annual Report (published by HMSO).
3 S.122 and SI 1992 No. 3280	Register of consents for the deliberate release into the environment of GMOs (maintained on behalf of DoE).
4 SI 1988 No. 1652	Information relating to Transfrontier Shipment of Hazardous Wastes (not a Register).
5 S.39 of the Radioactive Substances Act 1993	Records relating to radioactive substances. (Copies are kept also by local authorities.)
Local authorities under the EPA 1990 and other statutes	
1 S.64 and SI 1994 No. 1056	Public registers of waste management licences.
2 S.67 (EPA)	Annual Report of the Waste Regulatory Authority.
3 S.95 (EPA)	Public register of litter abatement orders and control notices.
4 S.1 of the Environment and Safety Information Act 1988	Register of notices relating to safety of sports grounds.
5 S.28 of the Planning (Hazardous) Substances Act 1990 and SI 1992 No. 656 and SI 1993 No. 323 (Scotland)	Register of hazardous substances consent.

(continued)

Table 9.1   Registers and reports maintained by public bodies (*concluded*)

Statutory provision	*Name of register/report*
6 S.69 of the Town and Country Planning Act 1990	Register of planning applications etc.
7 S.3 of the Control of Pollution (Amendment) Act 1989 and SI 1991 No. 1624	Register of carriers of controlled waste.
8 SI 1994 No. 1056	Register of waste brokers.
9 SI 1982 No. 600 and S.64 of COPA 1974	Noise level registers.

MAFF under the Food and Environment Protection Act 1985

1 SI 1986 No. 1510	Information relating to approved pesticides (available from the Pesticides Safety Directorate of MAFF based in Harpenden).
2 S.14	Register of disposals of sewage sludge at sea and of dredgings and industrial wastes disposed of at sea (available from Marine Environment Protection Division of MAFF).

The Health and Safety Executive under the Health and Safety at Work etc. Act 1974 and Environment and Safety Information Act 1988

1 SI 1992 No. 3217	Register of notifications relating to contained use of GMOs.
2 SI 1982 No. 1357	Register of notifications of Installations Handling Hazardous Substances.
3 S.1 of the Environment and Safety Information Act 1988	Register of enforcement notices (maintained at Area Offices). The HSE has proposed extending registers to cover information on all enforcement notices it issues (HSE, 1994).
4 SI 1993 No. 3050	List of new substances notified under SI 1993 No. 3050 (EC; HMSO).

are already available in the public registers maintained by HMIP and, in appropriate cases, local authorities thus avoiding duplication since operators do not have to submit information twice. The idea of an annual inventory was first implemented in the United States which, in 1987, set up a *Toxics Release Inventory*. Its advantages are said to lie in assisting regulators in identifying and targeting problem areas; providing operators with an idea of the environmental impact of their operations; and giving the public additional information (Sarokin and Underwood, 1990).

The CRI is compiled annually by aggregating data submitted to HMIP by operators as a condition of their authorization. Releases from processes are included from the date on which they are authorized by HMIP and so the CRI will expand as more processes are authorized under the IPC system. It covers primarily those substances on which a prescribed limit on release is imposed in the authorization but, additionally, includes any non-prescribed substances which are subject to authorized limits, covering a total of about 300 substances. The government indicated that the data available would be:

1 The prescribed substance group or groups to which an authorized substance belongs
2 The medium (i.e. air, water or land) into which the substance is authorized for release
3 The process and industry type involved
4 The county, country (England or Wales, the Scottish HMIP1 not having indicated its own intentions yet) and the HMIP Region and Division in which the process is located

In terms of compiling the CRI the government indicated that 150 or so substances are to be included at the start as reference data but that additional substances will then be entered as required by specific authorizations. As each authorization is issued, substance release limit data will be recorded in the inventory and authorizations will require that at intervals, at least annually, operators provide HMIP with monitoring data giving actual quantities of each authorized substance released. Where direct measurement is not practicable, HMIP will calculate quantities from an inferential measurement agreed in advance with the operator or estimate them in accordance with an agreed procedure. Conditions in authorizations require that operators report the release of any substance in excess of authorized limits and of any substance not included in the authorization at the time of the unauthorized release. The total of the unauthorized releases reported by the operator and identified by HMIP through its own monitoring will be recorded in the inventory.

The government also indicated that the data will be available in the public register maintained by HMIP and local information in the relevant local authority register. Additionally, a series of comparative tables will be published annually including total or substance specific releases by industry sector or sub-sector, geographic spread of releases of a given substance; actual releases as a percentage of authorized release limits; and quantities and sources of unauthorized releases. Third, HMIP will provide an inquiry service at its regional offices in Bristol, Leeds and Bedford to enable the public to obtain information not covered in the tables.

9.2 Eco-labelling

Eco-labelling is a mechanism for displaying information about the different impacts on the environment of products which provide similar uses and compete with one another in the market. It has recently attracted EC legislation due to the growing practice by member states to devise their own eco-labelling schemes. The main provision is to be found in EC Regulation 880/92 (OJ No. L 99/1) on a Community Eco-label award scheme.

An official scheme for awarding labels was seen as vital to counter the growing rise in unverified and confusing claims of 'environmental friendliness' which producers began making in an attempt to capture the growing market in environmentally sound products. The scheme seeks to ensure that all such claims are verified and officially endorsed. Initially, it is to operate alongside the current national schemes such as the German Blue Angel which is one of the oldest of such schemes in Europe; the hope, however, is that in time the EC scheme will supersede the national ones.

For an eco-labelling scheme to function, 'product groups' have to be selected; these are products which are equivalent in purpose and also compete in the market so that they can be compared (e.g. two modes of transport which compete in the market, one kind of car as against another). Second, criteria for awarding the label must be set on the basis of the environmental impact of the product over its entire life cycle, from production to final disposal (i.e. from 'cradle to grave') (House of Commons Environment Committee, 1990; DoE, 1991). This has led to the science of 'life-cycle analysis' which is still at a very early stage and remains controversial given the paucity of information about the environmental impact of the vast majority of products. Sceptics argue that the results of quantifying the ecological damage caused by the manufacture, use and disposal of products are too unreliable to give consumers proper guidance and that it is far better to 'attack pollution the old-fashioned way' (Arnold, 1993).

The debate about whether the testing of products on animals should be one of the criteria illustrates the inherent difficulties; is the impact on the animals on which the product is tested an 'environmental impact'? Additionally, it is impossible to take into account *all* environmental impacts of a product; boundaries have to be drawn but agreement on where those boundaries should lie and their validity is not easy to attain. These difficulties have not daunted proponents of life-cycle analysis who have gone ahead to develop models for analysing the various environmental impacts of products, sometimes with surprising results. An example is the recent life-cycle analysis which came to the conclusion that replacing phosphates in detergents offers no environmental advantages, a conclusion that flies in the face of conventional wisdom which has held for a long time that phosphates cause eutrophication in rivers and lakes. This led to questions being raised about the soundness of the methodology used to conduct the study (ENDS, 1994a).

Assuming that these hurdles are overcome, the third stage is to make a decision on the products which qualify for the award; if the award is to encourage products which have a low impact on the environment then only those with the lowest impact should receive an award. At the same time, if the number of products qualifying is too small consumers will not have a range of choice. Thus pitching the criteria to be met by a product to receive an award involves a delicate balancing act; the criteria to be met must not be so high as to put off most competitors but, at the same time, they must not be so low as to enable most competitors to qualify. It is argued that only between 10 per cent and 20 per cent of the products on the market should qualify.

9.2.1   The EC Eco-label Award Scheme

EC Regulation 880/92 (OJ No. L 99/1) establishes an eco-label award scheme in order to promote the design, production, marketing and use of products which have a reduced environmental impact during their entire life cycle and provide consumers with better information on the environmental impact of products. It provides for a community eco-label to be awarded to products which meet the two objectives and which, at the same time, conform with Community health, safety and environmental requirements.

The Regulation provides that the conditions for awarding the label are to be defined by product groups together with the ecological criteria for each group. This is for a three-year period after which the groups and criteria may be revised; anyone is free to put forward proposals for the establishment of criteria and product groups and a committee chaired by the Commission has been set up to evaluate them. Each product group shall be defined so that all competing products which serve similar purposes and which have equivalence of use are included in the same group. The ecological criteria are to be established on the basis of a 'cradle to grave' approach. The Regulation defines this to mean the life cycle of a product from manufacturing, including the choice of raw materials, distribution, consumption and use to disposal after use.

The procedure for the award of the label is set out in Article 10. The application is made to the competent body of the country in which the product is manufactured or first marketed or into which it is imported; in the UK this is the Eco-labelling Board which was set up by the UK Eco-labelling Board Regulations 1992, SI No. 2383. The competent body assesses the environmental performance of the product and, if it decides that the label should be awarded, notifies the Commission of its decision, enclosing the full results and a summary of the assessment. These documents have to be forwarded by the Commission to the competent authorities of the other member states within five days of notification. The competent body may implement the decision to award the eco-label thirty days after the notification to the Commission unless the Commission has informed it of an objection to the award. Any objections are to be resolved by informal means, failing which the Commission shall take a decision.

Where a competent body decides to award a label to a product already rejected by a competent body in another member state it shall inform the Commission, who shall make a decision on it. Both in this case and where the Commission has to take a decision on account of a failure by the competent bodies to resolve an objection by one to another awarding a label, the Commission shall, within forty-five days of being notified of the decision by a competent authority to award a label, submit a draft of the measures to be taken to a committee of representatives of member states set up under the Regulation to assist the Commission.

Where a label is awarded, a contract in standard terms shall be concluded between the competent body and the applicant. A model contract was published as Commission Decision 93/517/EEC (OJ No. L 243/13). It deals with advertisements, compliance monitoring, confidentiality of information, suspension and withdrawal of the label, limitation of liability and indemnity, fees, complaints from the public concerning the label, contract duration and the applicable law.

Following the adoption of this Regulation, work commenced under the leadership of various member states to develop criteria for a selected range of products as follows:

1 Denmark—paper products, textiles and insulation materials
2 France—batteries, paints and varnishes and shampoos
3 Germany—laundry detergents, dishwasher detergents, and household cleaning products
4 Italy—floor and wall tiles, packaging materials and refrigerators
5 The Netherlands—cat litter and shoes
6 The UK—anti-perspirants/deodorants, dishwashers, washing machines, soil improvers or growing media, hairsprays, hairstyling aids and light bulbs.

In June 1993 when the scheme was launched, criteria were ready for only two of these products: dishwashers and washing machines. The criteria, published as No. 93/430/EEC (washing machines) and No. 93/431/EEC (dishwashers) are of three kinds: the key criteria relate to energy consumption, water consumption, and in the case of washing machines, detergent consumption; the second category of criteria relate to best practice, concentrating on user instruction and the encouragement of recycling; and the third category of criteria are performance criteria dealing, for washing machines, with wash performance and rinse efficiency and, for dishwashers, with wash performance and drying efficiency.

The scheme has taken off slowly and, by mid-1994, only one company had applied for and been awarded an eco-label for washing machines (ENDS, 1994b). Other problems have also dogged the scheme; several member states have not yet set up competent bodies and the criteria put forward by some lead countries for awarding the label have been questioned, further delaying the scheme. This has led the Commission to launch a review of the guidelines for drawing up criteria and to promote a study on ways of standardizing life-cycle assessment methodology and of compiling a list of priority groups of products for assessment (ENDS, 1993).

9.2.2   Energy Consumption Labelling for Household Appliances

EC Directive 92/75/EEC (OJ No. L 297/16) on the indication by labelling and standard product information of the consumption of energy and other resources by household appliances aims to enable customers to choose more energy-efficient appliances of the following types: refrigerators, freezers and their combinations; washing machines, driers and their combinations; dish-washers; ovens; water heaters and hot water storage appliances; lighting sources; and air-conditioned appliances. The Directive envisages the addition of further household appliances to the list 'where significant energy savings are likely to be achieved'. Member states had until 1 January 1994 to bring into force provisions necessary to comply with the Directive.

The Directive provides that information relating to energy consumption be brought to the consumer's attention by means of a fiche and a label on house-hold appliances offered for sale, hire, hire-purchase or displayed to end users. Details relating to the information and the fiche are to be defined by subsequent directives relating to each type of appliance. The first daughter Directive 94/2/EC (OJ No. L 45/1) covered household electric refrigerators, freezers and their combinations. All suppliers of household appliances specified in the 'daughter' Directives must provide a label and a product fiche while dealers displaying the product must attach an appropriate label in a clearly visible position. Where the appliance is offered for sale, hire or hire-purchase by mail order, by catalogue or by other means where potential customers cannot be expected to see the displayed label the daughter Directive will seek to ensure that potential customers obtain the information before buying the appliance.

9.3   Advertisements

In the UK five bodies have responsibility for controlling claims, including environmental claims, in advertisements: the Trading Standards Departments of local authorities; the Director General of Fair Trading; the Independent Television Commission; the Radio Authority and the Advertising Standards Authority.

9.3.1   Trading Standards Departments

Local authorities through their Trading Standards Departments enforce provisions of the **Trade Descriptions Act 1968**. Section 1 makes it an offence for anyone, in the course of a trade or business, to apply a false trade description to any goods or to supply or offer to supply any goods to which a false trade description is applied. The Act defines a 'trade description' as a direct or indirect indication about the characteristics of the goods. The trade description is false if either it is false to a material degree or, simply, is misleading. Section

14, dealing with services as opposed to goods, makes it an offence for any person in the course of any trade or business to make a statement which he or she knows to be false or recklessly to make a statement which is false about those services.

The provisions of the Trade Descriptions Act 1968 do not specifically refer to environmental claims relating to goods and services and therefore some doubt has been expressed on whether the provisions apply to environmental claims. The House of Commons Environment Committee, for instance, recommended that the Trade Descriptions Act 1968 be amended to put beyond doubt that it covers environmental claims (House of Commons Environment Committee, 1990). The government accepted this recommendation but no amendment has yet been made to the Act.

But even if the Trade Descriptions Act were to be amended, there is the problem that it will usually be difficult to prove beyond reasonable doubt, as is required in a criminal prosecution, that an environmental claim relating to goods and services is false. This is because there will often not be sufficient evidence to demonstrate falsity. Nevertheless, there have been successful prosecutions under this piece of legislation demonstrating that, in those cases where the prosecution is able to marshall the evidence to prove a claim to be false, the Act can be a potent mechanism for controlling environmental claims.

Leigh Environmental Ltd v Walsall MBC is one example of a successful prosecution for making a false environmental claim; the case went to the Crown Court on appeal. Leigh, through one of its subsidiaries, operated a waste treatment and disposal plant on the site of a former brickworks on which there was a pit from which clay had been extracted. They received hazardous liquid industrial waste, chemically treated it to neutralize its toxicity and then mixed it with cement or fly-ash to form a slurry, which in turn was pumped into the pits where it formed in thin layers over previously deposited material. This was supposed to harden after a few weeks into a solid mass by forming cross-linked polymerics. The idea was that the waste would be trapped and sealed in the solid polymers in safety, a principle which is reflected in the trade name given to the product, 'Sealosafe'. In 1988 Leigh made a promotional film showing a person walking with the sound of boots on a hard surface and saying 'this polymer is the end result'.

One of those receiving the film thought the depiction of the site as having a firm, solid surface was false. He sent it to the Walsall Metropolitan Borough Council who charged Leigh under s. 14 of the Trade Descriptions Act 1968. The magistrates convicted, fining Leigh £7000 with £72 500 costs. Leigh appealed to the Crown Court. Walsall's case was that the polymer was stated falsely to be a hard, solid material, an impression given by the sound of boots on the surface and the sight of the person walking on apparently solid ground. They argued that the polymer was not insoluble, nor non-toxic, nor impermeable, nor non-leaching. Leigh maintained, however, that the claims of hardness, solidity and being safe to stand on were true and that there was insufficient evidence to prove solubility or toxicity. They admitted that the polymer was permeable and that it leached but argued that the claims were so nearly true that any falsity was immaterial.

The Crown Court held that the phrase 'false to a material degree' in s. 14 of the Trade Descriptions Act meant false to a degree which mattered in the context of the subject of the statement and bearing in mind the people to whom it was directed. After reviewing the evidence the court accepted that a great deal of the polymer was to a material degree neither hard nor solid and was not entirely safe to walk on. It thus failed to a material degree to correspond to the statement in the film and Leigh knew that it was not a correct statement to make. The court held further that any customer would think that it made a great difference whether the material really was hard or not. Consequently, even if the film were true as regards all the other claims made in it the falsity of the hardness and solidity claim would in itself render the whole statement false to a material degree. The appeal therefore failed.

9.3.2   The Director General of Fair Trading

The Fair Trading Act 1973 established the Office of Fair Trading with a Director General to monitor the supply to consumers of goods and services in order to ascertain circumstances and practices which may adversely affect their interests. In relation to advertisements, the Director General additionally enforces the Control of Misleading Advertisements Regulations 1988, SI No. 915 which are aimed at protecting the public from misleading advertisements. The Director's powers do not apply to advertisements carried on commercial TV, cable and satellite services or on commercial radio, which fall under the control of the Independent Television Commission and the Radio Authority respectively and, second, to advertisements relating to investment business and to most financial services advertisements.

The Regulations define a misleading advertisement as one which 'in any way deceives or is likely to deceive ... and which by its deceptive nature is likely to affect the economic behaviour or injure a competitor ...' The Office of Fair Trading fact sheet, *Misleading Advertisements* (Office of Fair Trading, undated), indicates that an advertisement can be misleading because it: contains a false statement of fact; conceals or leaves out important facts; promises to do something which there is no intention to carry out; or creates a false impression even though everything it says may be literally true. It also indicates that an advertisement will be likely to affect economic behaviour if it induces those reading it to part with money for what is being advertised; an advertisement which is neither likely to have this effect nor injure a competitor would not give rise to a complaint even though what it says is untrue.

The regulations require the Director General to consider any complaint made to him or her that an advertisement is misleading, unless the complaint appears to be frivolous or vexatious. The Director General may, however, ask the complainant to show that he or she has exhausted the normal channels for dealing with such advertisements, and may decide to pass the complaint to an appropriate body. The Director General will usually act where the complaint raises issues serious enough to justify an immediate court injunction even though existing channels have not been used, where there are no existing channels or where the existing channels have not dealt with the complaint adequately, but not where the complainant is simply not satisfied with the outcome.

Where the Director General thinks that an advertisement is misleading the remedy is to seek an injunction in court. The Regulations require that he or she give reasons for deciding either to apply or not to apply for an injunction to prevent the publication of the advertisement. He or she cannot seek an award of compensation or other punishment. The fact sheet, *Misleading Advertisements*, indicates that the Director General will consider such matters as health and safety, the nature of the goods or services advertised, loss suffered by the complainant, the nature and size of the target audience, the cost of the products or services, the need for speed in seeking a ban and the likelihood of continued publication if court proceedings are not started in deciding whether to seek an injunction.

The court may require the person responsible for the advertisement to furnish evidence of the accuracy of any factual claim it makes. Evidence that the advertisement was intended to be misleading or was made negligently is not necessary for the granting of the injunction. If an injunction is granted continued publication of the advertisement would amount to contempt of court which can be punished by imprisonment. By 1994 the Director General had sought an injunction in only two cases, neither of which related to an environmental claim.

9.3.3 Advertisements on Television and Radio

Advertisements on television and radio are under the control of the Independent Television Commission (ITC) and the Radio Authority respectively. Both the ITC and the Radio Authority are established by the **Broadcasting Act 1990**, the ITC to license and regulate commercial television and the Radio Authority to license and regulate independent radio services. The Act requires the ITC as well as the Radio Authority, in consultation with interested parties, to draw up and from time to time review a code of governing standards and practice in advertising and in the sponsoring of programmes. The two regulators may also impose requirements going beyond those of any code of practice which they have drawn up.

The ITC's code of advertising standards and practice (ITC, 1991) and the Radio Authority's advertising code are similar in substance. They also have many similarities with the code for governing advertising in non-broadcast media issued by the Committee of Advertising Practice (CAP, 1988); this is discussed below. In relation to the environment the codes state that advertisements should not encourage behaviour prejudicial to the environment and should comply with approved guidelines. The guidelines currently in use for television advertising were published in June 1990 by the Independent Television Association, an association of the commercial television services. The guidelines for use in radio advertising are also based on the Independent Television Association's guidelines and so the two are largely the same. The guidelines (DTI, 1991) state that:

1   Generalized claims for environmental benefit will be assessed on a 'cradle-to-grave basis'; categorical statements such as 'environment friendly' are inappropriate and should be eschewed in favour of more limited claims which can be backed by factual evidence.
2   Where a qualified claim such as 'friendlier' is made, its basis should be clearly explained.
3   Claims based on the absence of a harmful chemical or damaging effect are unacceptable when products in that category do not generally include that chemical or cause that effect; equally, if the product contains other, equally harmful elements a claim that it does not contain a particular element, even if true, may be disallowed.

Both the ITC and the Radio Authority enforce compliance with the codes and guidelines through a requirement that they vet advertisements before transmission; licensees are required to employ trained staff to check the accuracy of advertisement claims and, if necessary, to require supporting evidence. In practice advertisers use the 'Copy Clearance Secretariat' maintained by the Independent Television Association to clear advertisements before national broadcasting. Local and regional radio advertisements are checked by the station staff only. Where, following a complaint and an investigation, the ITC or the Radio Authority concludes that an advertisement breaches the code they may require it to be discontinued or suspended. Compliance is a condition of the licence which ultimately may be prejudiced if there are repeated breaches.

9.3.4   The Advertising Standards Authority

Advertising in print, posters, cinema, leaflets, direct mail and Teletext services, together known as the 'non-broadcast media', is not regulated by statute. Rather, control emanates from an industry-based self-regulating regime set up by the advertising industry which has agreed a code of advertising practice known as the 'British Code of Advertising Practice' (CAP, 1988) to govern advertisements. The first version of the BCAP was agreed in 1961, based largely on the International Code of Advertising Practice which was first published in 1937 by the International Chamber of Commerce. The current BCAP is the 8th edition, published in 1988 by the Committee on Advertising Practice which is charged with the daily responsibility of ensuring that members of the advertising industry comply with the code and with offering pre-publication advice on the acceptability of advertisements (CAP, 1988).

To give this self-regulating system credibility, the Advertising Standards Authority (ASA), a non-statutory body independent of the advertising industry, was set up in 1962 to participate in the work of the Committee on Advertising Practice but additionally to monitor advertisements and investigate complaints from the public about advertisements. Each complaint is investigated by the ASA and recorded in a monthly 'Case Report' which is publicly available on request. Complaints from commercially interested parties are handled by the Committee on Advertising Practice, not the ASA. Where the conclusion is that a complaint breaches the standards of the code the advertiser is asked to withdraw or amend it. Typically a failure to comply will result in a withdrawal of advertising space by the industry. The Code states that the advertiser should have ready the evidence to back up any claim made and the general rule is that all advertisements should be legal, decent, honest and truthful.

In relation to environmental claims the Committee on Advertising Practice's guidelines require that the basis of claims should be explained and that claims should not be absolute, cloaked in extravagant language, or spurious (CAP, 1990). In December 1991 the International Chamber of Commerce also released a substantively similar code on environmental advertising (ICC, 1991).

An example of the application of the guidance in these codes in practice is useful in understanding how life-cycle assessments are applied in assessing advertisements. Friends of the Earth complained against the following advertisement:

> We make newsprint from recycled fibre and home grown sitka spruce . . . sitka trees help to counter the greenhouse effect by absorbing carbon dioxide and producing oxygen as they grow . . .

The complaint was that the advertisement was likely to mislead since the paper would degrade and release carbon dioxide, thus negating any beneficial effect of the original planting. The complaint was upheld by the ASA on the ground that the advertisers had drawn attention to the stage in the trees' life cycle that fixed carbon, hence providing an environmental benefit, without making clear that at another stage the carbon was released in one form or another, thus negating the benefit (CAP, 1990).

Overall such complaints are being made with increasing frequency and advertisers are finding that misleading claims quickly come under the scrutiny of one or another environmental pressure group. In 1992, for instance, 107 complaints were received resulting in eleven advertisements being withdrawn or amended (ASA, 1993). Decisions by the Advertising Standards Authority, the Committee on Advertising Practice and the Independent Braodcasting Authority have related to advertisements about a wide range of products and services including cars, electricity, nappies, toilet tissue, insulation products, catalytic converters, shampoo, gas, peat-based soil conditioners and photo-copiers (ENDS, 1990)

References

Arnold, F., 'Life cycle doesn't work', *The Environment Forum*, September/October (1993).

ASA, *Environmental Claims: Briefing Background*, June (1993).

CAP, *The British Code of Advertising Practice*, 8th edn (1988).

CAP, *Ad Alert: Guidance No 1/90, Environmental Claims* (1990).

D A Wales v Thames Water Authority (1987, unrep.).

DoE, *Giving Guidance to the Green Consumer —Progress on an Eco-labelling Scheme for the UK: A Report by the National Advisory Group on Eco-Labelling* (1991).

DoE, *Freedom of Access to Information on the Environment: Guidance on the Implementation of the Environmental Information Regulations 1992 in Great Britain* (1992a).

DoE, *Proposed Chemical Release Inventory*, a Consultation Paper (1992b).

DoE, 'Michael Howard announces decisions on first commercial confidentiality appeals under IPC', News Release No. 760, 19 November (1992c).

DoE, 'Chemical release inventory launched today', News Release No. 244, 2 April (1993).

DTI, *Environmental Claims in Advertising: A Single Guide to all the Applicable Advertising Codes* (1991).

ENDS Report No. 191, 'Advertising and the environment: uneasy bedfellows', December, 16–23 (1990).

ENDS Report No. 227, 'Review aims at speeding up eco-labelling process', December, 26 (1993).

ENDS Report No. 228, 'Controversial LCA study backs phosphate-based detergents', January, 29–31 (1994a).

ENDS Report No. 229, 'Disappointing start to eco-labelling scheme', February, 24 (1994b).

House of Commons Environment Committee, 8th Report, *Eco-Labelling*, Session 1990, HMSO.

HSE, *Open Government Proposals for an Extension of the Public Registers of Enforcement Notices*, Press Release C4;94, 31 January (1994).

ICC, *ICC Code on Environmental Advertising* (1991).

Independent Television Commission, *The ITC Code of Advertising Standards and Practice* (1991).

Leigh Environmental Ltd v Walsall MBC (1992, unrep.).

Office of Fair Trading, *Misleading Advertisements* (undated).

Open Government, Cm 2290, HMSO (1993).

RCEP, *Tackling Pollution*, 10th Report, HMSO (1984).

Sarokin, D. and Underwood, J., 'The Toxics Release Inventory: the new era of the 'Right-to-Know' in the United States', *UNEP Industry and the Environment*, July/December, 38 (1990).

10

Paying for Pollution Control

10.1 Charging Schemes

Schemes drawn up by regulatory authorities under which they impose charges for pollution control are referred to as 'charging schemes'. In environmental protection, charging schemes are of predominantly two kinds: 'cost recovery' and 'incentive'. Cost-recovery charging schemes are aimed at recovering from dischargers the costs to the public purse of administering a prior consent or authorization system of pollution control. Incentive charging schemes are directed at giving the discharger an incentive to reduce or even eliminate discharges into the environment from his or her operations. Charges under the latter scheme would include a charge towards the cost of administering a prior consent or authorization scheme; it therefore subsumes a scheme of the first kind.

The UK introduced cost-recovery charging schemes for consents to discharge into controlled waters and for IPC and LAAPC authorizations in 1991. A cost-recovery charging scheme for waste management licensing under Part II of the **EPA 1990** was introduced in May 1994 when the waste management licensing provisions came into force. Under **COPA 1974** the costs for waste disposal licensing were met out of the Council Tax (or its predecessors, the Community Charge and the rates). This was also the case with regard to water and air pollution control costs in the UK before 1991. The current policy is to require prior consenting systems to be self-financing by recovering their costs from consent holders. The corollary to this is that charges for administering the pollution control systems are not imposed on those who do not hold a consent or an authorization or other permit; indeed there would be no justification for doing so.

With the exception of the tax differential in favour of diesel fuel which was introduced in 1987, the UK has yet to introduce incentive charging schemes although several studies have been conducted into the feasibility of introducing a landfill levy, a packaging levy, a carbon/energy tax and tradeable permits.

Whether any of these will be introduced is speculative at the moment despite the government's commitment to market instruments (*This Common Inheritance*, 1990).

10.1.1   The NRA's Cost-recovery Charging Schemes

Chapter II of Part VI of the **Water Resources Act 1991** gives the NRA power to impose charges for its various activities among which are administering discharges into controlled waters and water abstractions. The former type of charge is a charge for direct discharges into controlled waters and is distinct from trade effluent charges which sewerage companies make for the provision to industry of sewerage services. Provision for charging consent holders in Scotland are contained in the **Local Government Finance Act 1992** which has applied since April 1993.

Charging for Discharging

The NRA's power to charge for discharging into controlled waters is aimed at enabling it to recover its costs for administering the discharge consent system; it is a cost-recovery scheme. But the NRA's water pollution control responsibilities go beyond merely administering the discharge consent system. They include, in addition, the control of diffuse pollution and unauthorized discharges, general catchment management, implementing the statutory WQOs system, and general monitoring of water quality for compliance with EC directives and other international requirements. These costs are not intended to be recovered from consent holders and therefore do not form part of the charges scheme. They are met out of a grant from central government.

The provisions enabling the NRA to charge consent holders for discharging into controlled waters or, in the case of an application for a consent, to charge for the application, are set out in ss 131 and 132. Charges are to be imposed in accordance with the terms of a scheme, known as a 'scheme of charges', made by the NRA under s. 131. The procedure for making the scheme is set out in s. 132 which requires the NRA to publish proposals for the scheme, specifying a period during which objections may be made to the Secretary of State and to submit it to the Secretary of State for his and the Treasury's approval. In giving approval the Secretary of State has to ensure that the scheme enables the NRA to do no more than recover its costs. The scheme, not being an incentive charging scheme, does not allow the NRA to make a profit in its water pollution control work but it should not make a loss.

The first charging scheme was introduced in 1991 and expired in March 1994. It has been replaced by a similar scheme from April 1994 (NRA, 1994). The costs to be recovered under the scheme from year to year are the costs for:

1   Processing the application
2   Sampling, inspecting and monitoring the impact of the discharge
3   Laboratory services
4   Reviewing the consent and
5   Direct administrative costs.

The costs are calculated on the basis of four factors: the volume of the discharge, its content, the receiving waters into which it is discharged and the 'financial factor' (discussed below). No attempt is made to calculate exactly the individual costs incurred in administering a particular discharge consent since this would be cumbersome and, in the NRA's view, increase the overall cost to be recovered from dischargers by adding to the administrative costs. Rather, consents are banded on the basis of the three factors on which the costs are based (volume, content and receiving waters) and multiplied by a weighting factor which is intended to represent the NRA's efforts and costs. Similarly, costs are calculated on what is consented rather than what is actually discharged. There is thus a disincentive for a discharger to hold a consent which he or she does not fully utilize.

Volume

Most significant discharges have a condition limiting the volume which may be discharged. The Scheme of Charges has banded these volumes into seven bands and assigned each a weighting factor; they range from less than 5 m^3/day (with a weighting factor of 0.3) to greater than 150 000 m^3/day (with a weighting factor of 14). The weighting factor increases with the volume of the consented discharge because higher discharges are more costly to monitor. For particularly high discharges such as those relating to discharges from sewerage treatment plants, the NRA normally requires the discharger to install automatic monitoring devices. Such a requirement can result in a lowering of the NRA's monitoring costs and so the current scheme of charges envisages granting an appropriate reduction to the charge per year (NRA, 1993a).

Content

A second important factor in the impact that a discharge is likely to have is its content. Most consents impose numerical limits on the substances (known as determinands) in a discharge. The scheme of charges places these determinands into seven bands and assigns each a weighting factor. The bands range from A (with a weighting factor of 14) to G (with a weighting factor of 0.3). Band A relates to effluents with the most polluting substances such as pesticides and phenolic compounds while Band G relates to minimally polluting effluents such as cooling water. A discharge is placed in a particular band on the basis of the highest weighted consented determinand so that a discharge containing, among other substances, pesticides, will fall into band A.

Receiving Waters

There are four bands of controlled waters into which a discharge may be made and each has been assigned a weighting factor; ground waters (0.5), coastal waters (0.8), surface waters (1.0) and estuarial waters (1.5).

Financial Factor

In 1991 the NRA indicated how the charge is calculated (NRA, 1991). When the factors have been determined for each discharge, they are multiplied to give the number of chargeable units. The latter is then multiplied by a unit rate to give the charge for the year, the 'annual charge'. The relevant unit rate is determined by dividing the total costs by the total number of chargeable units, giving the figure known as the financial factor. Thus the charge is derived as follows: volume factor × content factor × receiving water = chargeable units. Chargeable units × unit rate (financial factor) = annual charge. The financial factor itself is to be set by the NRA annually thus enabling it to recover its costs that year; for 1994/5 it has been set at £389.

Apart from the annual charge the NRA imposes an application fee whether or not the consent is granted, since even a failed application has to be processed. The NRA opted to impose a standard application fee for all applications. The first scheme of charges set this at £350 with a reduced application fee of £50 for minor discharges while the second scheme of charges set £504 with a reduced application fee of £72. A standard application fee provides administrative simplicity although it does mean that those whose applications are straightforward subsidize those whose applications raise complex issues.

Abstraction Charges

The procedure for making a Scheme of Charges for water abstraction, set out in sections 123 and 124 of the Water Resources Act 1991, is similar to the discharging scheme of charges. There is provision in s. 126 for the NRA to enter into an agreement with persons liable to pay charges for abstraction either exempting them from payment or reducing the rates to be paid.

The current NRA Scheme of Charges for water abstraction came into effect on 1 April 1993. Although it is a national scheme unlike its predecessors which were regional, its rates are related to the costs incurred in the region where the abstraction occurs. Therefore there are regional variations which have to be checked with the particular region of the NRA in which the abstraction point is located (NRA, 1993b).

Abstraction fees, like discharge licensing fees, have an application fee and annual charge components. The application fee is a flat fee reviewed annually to reflect the NRA's charges for processing applications. The annual charge is based on the volume licensed to be abstracted rather than the volume actually abstracted. It is weighted on the basis of three factors: the source of the abstraction, the season it is made, and the quantity of abstracted water lost.

Source of Abstraction

There are three types of sources of water for abstraction: (1) unsupported sources, i.e. reservoirs, surface river sources and underground strata; (2) supported sources, i.e. sources, set out in a Schedule to the Scheme of charges, which are augmented by schemes owned, operated or financed by the NRA including inter-basin transfers and river regulation; and (3) tidal sources. Supported sources have the highest weighting factors (3.0) while tidal sources have the lowest (0.2).

Season of Abstraction

Abstractions are categorized into three seasons as follows: (1) all year round; (2) winter abstractions from November to March; and (3) summer abstractions from April to October. Abstractions for spray irrigation are typically summer abstractions. Summer abstractions have the highest weighting factor (1.6) reflecting the scarcity of water in the summer, and winter abstractions the lowest (0.16).

Quantity of Abstracted Water Lost

The loss factor is intended to account for the return of water to the source after use; the actual quantity returned varies with the purpose for which the abstraction was made. The scheme has categorized various uses into high, medium, low and very low loss categories; spray irrigation, for instance, is a high loss use while power generation is a very low loss use. The weighting factors applicable to these loss categories range from 1.0 in the high category to 0.003 in the very low loss category.

Charge Factor

In order to determine the annual charge the three factors (source, season and loss) are multiplied; the resulting figure is known as the 'charge factor'. The charge factor is multiplied with the volume licensed for abstraction and with a figure known as the 'standard unit charge' which is set annually by the NRA for each of its regions to reflect that region's costs—[Annual charge = volume

× charge factor (source factor × season factor × loss factor) × standard unit charge].

10.1.2 Fees and Charges for Waste Management Licensing

Section 41 of the **EPA 1990** provides for fees and charges for waste management licences to be paid to WRAs. Details of the fees and charges are set out in a Scheme made by the Secretary of State with the Treasury's approval (DoE, 1994). The fees are to be paid whenever an application is made:

1 For a waste management licence
2 To modify the conditions of a licence
3 To surrender a licence or
4 For the transfer of a licence (for which a standard fee applies).

There is also an annual charge (called a 'subsistence' charge) to be paid for a subsisting licence.

Unique to the waste management licensing scheme is a provision under which the NRA and the river purification authorities (RPA) in Scotland, are to be paid a portion of the fees and charges for their work as statutory consultees in the waste management licensing system. The fees and charges scheme is therefore in two parts. Part I prescribes the fees and charges to be paid to the WRA while Part II prescribes an additional 'consultation component' to be levied and passed on to the NRA or RPAs when they are consulted by the WRA. Consultation is to be undertaken where a person applies for a licence, to modify licence conditions, to surrender the licence or where it appears that water pollution is likely to be caused by the licensed activities. In the last-mentioned situation consultation will not occur every year and so the 'consultation component' (paid at the start of the financial year following consultation) will be paid only where a consultation actually took place. Similarly, in the other three situations where the application is refused without consulting the NRA or RPAs the appropriate amount shall be refunded to the applicant.

The scheme makes provision for the range of waste management activities which can be licensed under Part II of the EPA 1990, i.e. the treatment, keeping, and disposal of controlled waste in or on land. In respect of treatment a distinction is made between treatment for the purpose of recycling and treatment for other purposes, which attract higher fees. For keeping, a distinction (attracting higher fees) is made between keeping waste:

1 For any purpose at the site where it was produced
2 For the purpose of recycling at a civic amenity site
3 For the purpose of recycling at a site not falling within the first two sites
4 At a civic amenity site for any purpose other than recycling
5 At a transfer station for any purpose other than recycling.

Finally, for disposal, a distinction is made between continuing disposal operations and operations that have ceased although the licence has not yet been surrendered; the fees are much lower in the latter case because the monitoring
undertaken by the WRA is lower. Fees are prescribed also for a mobile plant
licence.

The fees and charges to be paid in any particular case are determined on the
basis of the description of the licensed activity (i.e. keeping, treatment or disposal), the description of the controlled waste and the amount of controlled
waste involved as stated in the application, or, in the case of a subsistence
charge, as stated on the licence. The descriptions of controlled waste set out in
the scheme include special waste, household or commercial waste not including
special waste; other building, demolition or inert waste and industrial waste not
including special waste. The amount of controlled waste is defined as 'the
maximum annual amount which the licence authorizes to be received at the site
or treated, kept or disposed of on the site on which it was produced'. The
amounts are placed into three bands, and a charge calculated on the basis of the
relevant band.

Special provision has been made for the transition from waste disposal
licences under COPA 1974 (for which no annual subsistence charge was
payable) to the licensing regime under the EPA. This requires the WRA to
serve a notice in writing on the holder of the old licence stating the date on
which the subsistence charge will be due; the amount; the descriptions of activities, controlled wastes and amounts of controlled waste by reference to which
the charge has been calculated and the method of payment. The WRA will not
be able to exercise its power to revoke the licence for non-payment of charges
until this period is over. This same information is to be served on all other
licensees a month before the subsistence charge is due each year since failure to
pay the charge is a ground for revoking the licence.

10.1.3   Fees and Charges for IPC and LAAPC

Section 8 of the EPA 1990 provides for charges to be paid to HMIP for IPC
authorizations and to local authorities for LAAPC authorizations under a
scheme of charges drawn up by the Secretary of State with the Treasury's
approval. The charges paid should cover the expenses incurred by the regulators in implementing these two systems together with the NRA's expenses (the
river-purification authorities in Scotland) in exercising its functions in relation
to those IPC processes which may involve releases of substances to water.
Costs arising from issuing authorizations include compliance monitoring by
sampling and analysis, running the public register of information and over-
heads. Expenses which are not related directly to the regulatory function, such
as advising ministers or gathering data for submission to the European Commission, are not recovered from operators.

The particular scheme which the Secretary of State chose was outlined in a 1990 document (DoE, 1990a). Like other cost-recovery charging schemes, the scheme has an application fee and an annual fee. IPC processes vary greatly in size and complexity and therefore some processes consume more of HMIP's time and resources than others. The mechanism which the Secretary of State introduced for relating charges to workload involves dividing a process up into a number of 'components', each component being a proxy for the time and resources spent on the process. For the sake of administrative simplicity each component attracts a flat rate fee. Since, however, the more complex a process, the more the components it will be divided into, complex processes attract higher fees. Thus, for example, the process of storing chemicals in bulk is one component if one or two named chemicals are stored, two components if three or four named chemicals are stored and three components if five or six named chemicals are stored. LAAPC processes, which are not considered as complex, have not been divided into components and are charged on the basis of standard charges, as if they all represented one component; the one exception is waste oil burners which attract lower fees.

Provision has also been made for incidental matters. Processes transferring from a previous registration system into an IPC registration pay only two-thirds of the application fee; a substantial variation attracts a fee of one-third the application fee; and where the process involves releases to water the annual charge will include an additional amount representing the charge the NRA would have imposed had it issued a consent for the discharge. LAAPC processes generally attract lower fees than IPC processes and a flat rate annual charge. However, the fee for a substantial variation of an LAAPC process represents two-thirds of the application fee.

The charge per component is set each year in a Fees and Charges Scheme; the components also are reproduced in the Scheme. In the first year of IPC, 1991/2, HMIP did not recover its costs fully because it had underestimated the fees it needed to charge per component. It has therefore levied an additional charge on operators who had submitted applications in that year; the levy is being recovered over a period of four years which began in 1992/3.

Following sustained complaints about the high charges imposed on operators, HMIP consulted in 1993 on proposals to revise the definition of components with a view to reducing the number of components per process and therefore the fees charged. Certain minor modifications were put forward to be implemented in the 1994/5 charging year. Additionally, in October 1993, HMIP put forward for consultation a wide-ranging review of the 'components' method of charging. This latter review considered alternatives, including charging operators for the time actually spent on regulating the process and relating charges to the level of pollution.

The consensus was to retain the component-based charging system. As a way of reducing costs HMIP has indicated that it will consider the extent to which corporate participation in schemes such as BS 7750 and EMA might lead to a reduction in HMIP inspection with a corresponding reduction in charges. This would be complemented by a proposal HMIP is studying on the possibility of moving to direct recovery of costs for monitoring of operators' compliance with authorizations. Finally, it will also consider charging for any pre-application guidance it gives operators since this occupies much time (HMIP, 1994a,b).

10.2 Market Mechanisms

Various market mechanisms for making polluters pay for the costs of pollution are under active consideration in the UK. One of them, the carbon/energy tax (discussed in Chapter 5), has met stiff resistance. The others, including tradeable permits and a landfill levy, may be introduced at some future unspecified date, with the landfill levy being the more likely to be introduced soon. Currently the debate relates to whether funds generated from these measures should be retained for environmental purposes or handed over to the Treasury in the normal way, with the weight of opinion being in favour of their being used for environmental objectives.

10.2.1 Tradeable Permits

A 'tradeable permit' is a permit or authorization which the operator may sell or, conversely, buy (*This Common Inheritance*, 1990, Annex A). Like other market instruments it is based on the theory that market instruments may achieve the objective of reducing environmental emissions at a cheaper cost than regulatory measures. Under such a system the regulator allocates permits signifying a quantity of emissions or discharges into environmental media which the operator may make. The operator is free either to use up its quota of allocations or use only a portion of them (on the basis that the operator can achieve a lower level of emissions without using the entire quota) and sell the rest to another operator who finds it cheaper to buy additional quotas than to abate emissions. This would enable operators to adopt a cheaper combination of measures rather than being required by the regulator to abate emissions to a specified level. The regulator retains control of the total quantity of allocations and can reduce this over a period of time in order gradually to achieve a cleaner environment.

The concept of tradeable permits has been implemented in the United States of America. The first sale occurred in March 1993 when the Chicago Board of Trade auctioned, on behalf of the US Environmental Protection Agency (EPA), permits (or 'rights') to emit sulphur dioxide mainly to power-generating companies. Each permit represented one tonne of sulphur dioxide emissions and cost less than the cost of installing pollution-abatement equipment. It is expected that some companies will be able to reduce their emissions by installing abatement equipment and they can then sell off the unused portion of their permits. Other companies might consider it cheaper to delay installing abatement equipment now and buy additional permits to tide them over until they are able to instal the abatement equipment at a later stage. It was reported that a few permits were purchased by environmental pressure groups presumably in a bid to take them out of circulation, thus reducing emissions to the atmosphere (*Financial Times*, 1993a,b).

For a system of tradeable permits to work, a market in emission rights must exist; that requires that an overall quota of emissions which may be made into environmental media has been set, e.g. that emissions of sulphur dioxide will not exceed x tonnes per annum. This quota can then be bought and sold. In the UK, emission rights in respect of sulphur dioxide emissions represent the only rights in which such a market could conceivably be developed at present. Section 3(5) of the EPA 1990 empowers the Secretary of State to make plans for establishing limits for the total amount of any substance which may be emitted and for allocating quotas to persons carrying on processes in respect of which any such limits are established.

The power has been used to give effect to EC Directive 88/609/EEC on the limitation of emissions of certain pollutants into the air from large combustion plants. This requires member states to draw up programmes for the progressive reduction of total annual emissions of sulphur dioxide and oxides of nitrogen from existing large combustion plants. The UK's Programme and National Plan, published on 20 December 1990, allocates SO_2 and NO_x emission quotas within an overall national limit to the main power generators, National Power and PowerGen, with smaller allocations going to Scottish and Northern Ireland power generators. The emission quotas are progressively reduced towards the years 2003 and 1998 respectively (DoE, 1990b). Although the emission quotas could in theory be traded between the two power generators it is unlikely that a market with only two players would be a genuine market.

Other legislative frameworks upon which a tradeable permit market could be built include the EC Urban Waste Water Treatment Directive (91/271/EEC) and the UK's statutory WQOs system. The former sets dates by which waste water discharged by treatment plants must meet minimum standards. Treatment plant operators in turn are expected to require industrial dischargers (who discharge into the treatment plants) to treat their discharges to a specified standard before discharge into sewers. The latter sets quality objectives to be achieved by controlled waters. Discharge consents are then set with an eye to meeting these quality objectives by specified dates. A tradeable permit system could conceivably be built around these systems, consent holders either installing abatement equipment or buying additional quotas from other dischargers. Realistically, however, this is unlikely to happen in the near future.

10.2.2 A Landfill Levy

Since 1992, the DoE has been examining prospects for introducing a levy on landfill, commissioning two reports on the subject (DoE, 1993a,b). The two studies indicate that a levy could serve any of a number of functions. It could:

1 Change people's waste management behaviour and encourage waste reduction
2 Tackle externalities arising from waste disposal, i.e. methane gas generation and other environmental problems from landfills
3 Redress the perceived imbalance in prices for waste disposal between land-filling and other means of disposal such as incineration
4 Generate funds for environmental projects, e.g. clean-up of contaminated land.

Should a landfill levy be introduced its long-term effect would most probably be to encourage increased incineration of waste.

The EC proposal for a directive on landfill of waste (COM (93) 275 final — SYN 335) (discussed in Chapter 3) requires the establishment of a 'landfill after-care fund' to cover the normal after-care costs of closed landfills and the expenses necessary to prevent or remedy the damage to the environment produced by the disposal of waste in case it is not covered by the insurance or financial guarantee. The proposal envisages that each landfill operator would contribute to the fund in the light of the class of landfill and the type and tonnages of waste landfilled. The landfill levy currently under consideration by the DoE would be one way of fulfilling this requirement once the directive is adopted.

Introducing a landfill levy will involve defining the level of the levy, the point at which it is collected, whether it needs to be backed by a statutory requirement in order to avoid a circumstance where some sectors of the industry do not pay the levy and how to prevent the funds from going to the Treasury (in case the objective is to fund environmental projects). These difficulties have contributed to delaying the introduction of a levy although recent indications suggest that a levy will be in place in 1996.

10.3 Financial Assistance for Environmental Projects

Council Regulation No. 1973/92 (OJ No. L 206/1) establishing a financial instrument for the environment (LIFE) repealed and replaced previous financial instruments on its entry into force on 23 July 1992. It states that the general objective of LIFE is to contribute to the development and implementation of EC environmental policy and legislation by providing funding for action in three areas:

1   Priority environmental actions in the EC
2   Technical assistance actions with non-EC countries from the Mediterranean region or bordering on the Baltic Sea
3   In exceptional circumstances, actions concerning regional or global environmental problems provided for in international agreements.

LIFE is implemented in phases; the first phase for which ECU 400 million has been allocated ends on 31 December 1995.

Five fields of action are identified as eligible for funding:

1   The promotion of sustainable development and the quality of the environment (40 per cent of the funding)
2   Protection of habitats and of nature (45 per cent of the funding)
3   Administrative structures and environment services (5 per cent of the funding)
4   Education and training (5 per cent of the funding)
5   Action outside the EC (5 per cent of the funding).

LIFE provides only a portion of the funding, with the exception of 'measures designed to provide the information necessary for the execution of an action and technical assistance measures implemented on the Commission's initiative' for which 10 per cent funding is available. Otherwise ceilings apply as follows: 30 per cent of the cost for actions involving income-generating investments; 50 per cent of the cost of other actions; and 75 per cent of the cost of actions to conserve biotopes or habitats facing extinction. Funding is available to private and public sector applicants alike.

The procedure for allocating the grants requires that by 30 September each year, the Commission must establish priority actions for funding that year within the five fields of action. The Commission is required also to specify additional criteria to be used for selecting the actions to be financed. Proposals for funding are to be submitted to the Commission by Member States, normally by 31 March each year. The DoE, Scottish Office, Welsh Office and Northern Ireland Office normally request proposals to be forwarded to them by 15 February for initial screening before onward transmission to the Commission. The request is announced through a News Release.

The evaluation process at the Commission normally takes about six months and so allocations are made in the last quarter of the year. The Commission then enters into contracts with successful applicants under which funding is released. In 1993 the first year of allocations, 121 out of 1 500 applications received funding; fourteen were from the UK out of a total of 167 applications (Commission of the European Communities, 1994; DoE, 1993c).

References

Commission of the European Communities, *LIFE: 1994 Information Package* (1994).

DoE, *Pollution Regulation: Cost Recovery Charges* (1990a).

DoE, *The UK's Programme and National Plan for Reducing Emissions of SO$_2$ and NO$_x$ from Existing Large Combustion Plants*, DoE/WO/SO (1990b).

DoE, *Landfill Costs and Prices: Correcting Possible Market Distortions*, HMSO (1993a).

DoE, *Externalities from Landfill and Incineration*, HMSO (1993b).

DoE, 'EC financial instrument for the environment (LIFE)', News Release, 4 November (1993c).

DoE/WO/SO, *Waste Management Licensing (Fees and Charges) Scheme* (1994).

Financial Times, 'Pollution rights go to auction', 29 March (1993a).

Financial Times, 'Mixed start to pollution permit sale', 31 March (1993b).

HMIP, *Fees and Charges for IPC and Radioactive Substances Act Regulation: Proposed 1994/95 Charges* (1994a).

HMIP, *Fees and Charges for Integrated Pollution Control, 1994/95* (1994b).

NRA, *Proposed Scheme of Charges* (1991).

NRA, *Charging for Discharging*, a Consultation Paper (1993a).

NRA, *Proposed Scheme of Abstraction Charges 1993–94* (1993b).

NRA, *1994/95 Annual Charges: Discharges to Controlled Waters* (1994).

This Common Inheritance, Cm 1200, HMSO (1990).

11

Criminal Law and the Environment

The term 'enforcement' refers to the process of compelling compliance with legal requirements. It covers all the activities and mechanisms available to enforcement agencies to achieve compliance, from inspection (or monitoring) at one end of the continuum to prosecution at the other. 'Monitoring' means no more than checking and, in the context of environmental protection, it refers to the activity of checking the quality and quantity of the physical, chemical and biological characteristics of environmental media. Where the aim is to ensure compliance with regulatory requirements then the phrase commonly used is 'compliance monitoring'. Ultimately the aim of compliance monitoring where breaches of the law are detected is to assemble the information necessary to sustain a prosecution in court. Consequently, the procedure for gathering information is central in compliance monitoring; both legal requirements and non-statutory guidance set out the rules to be followed with the overriding aim of ensuring that the process is fair and is seen to be so.

Monitoring is normally carried out by both the process operator and the enforcement agency. Third parties, who are free to bring prosecutions for most environmental offences, may carry out monitoring where they suspect a breach of the law. However, their ability to do so is seriously restricted by a lack of resources and the fact that third parties, unlike enforcement agencies, do not have a right of entry and would be trespassing if they entered premises without permission. Only rarely, therefore, do third parties prosecute. There are, however, exceptional circumstances when they will be able to carry out monitoring successfully. In 1991 Greenpeace collected samples of the effluent discharge from the chemical company, Albright & Wilson, into the Irish Sea. They were able to do so because the point of discharge was tidal waters over which the public have a right of access. The data were later used to prosecute the company successfully (LMELR, 1991, 1992).

Operators monitor their processes both as an aid to process efficiency and because it is a often a condition of their consent or authorization from the enforcement agency. All the environmental protection statutes—the **Water**

Resources Act 1991, the **EPA 1990** and the **Control of Pollution Act 1974**—make provision for the enforcement authority to impose conditions on the consent, licence or authorization requiring the operator to carry out monitoring of the activity which is authorized, keep the information and submit reports to the enforcement agency, or alternatively, keep the information and make it available when requested.

Despite the increasing importance of self-monitoring for enforcement purposes, compliance monitoring is carried out predominantly by the enforcement agencies who have wide enforcement powers. These are as follows:

1   HMIP's powers in relation to processes prescribed under the IPC system and a local authority's powers in relation to processes prescribed under the LAAPC system are set out in s. 17 of the EPA 1990.
2   A WRA's powers in relation to waste management are contained in s. 69 of the EPA 1990.
3   The HSE's powers in relation to workplaces are found in s. 20 of the Health and Safety at Work etc. Act 1974.
4   The NRA's powers in relation to controlled waters are set out in s. 169 of the Water Resources Act 1991.
5   The water companies' powers in relation to public sewers are set out in ss 170 and 171 of the Water Industry Act 1991.

These provisions give inspectors wide powers of entry, examination, investigation, sampling, detention of substances and articles and requisition of information and other evidence. It is an offence to obstruct the exercise of these powers.

Whether information obtained under these powers can be used in court to sustain a charge, and the extent to which that can be done, is tied up with the common law rule against 'self-incrimination'.

11.1   Self-incrimination

11.1.1   The Rule Against Self-incrimination

The rule, stated in *Blunt v Park Lane Hotel Ltd and Briscoe* is that 'no one is bound to answer any question if the answer thereto would expose him to any criminal charge . . .', i.e. incriminate him. This rule, commonly known as the privilege against self-incrimination, covers both verbal and written answers and the requirement to produce documents. It gives the suspect the right to choose not to answer questions posed by investigating officials or produce documents demanded. If in court, the accused has the right to choose not to give evidence but the court has a duty to make sure that the privilege is properly claimed. Accordingly, the mere fact that a person claims that his answer would incriminate him is not conclusive; the court must examine the facts in order to satisfy itself that the claim is soundly based.

This rule is curtailed by the Criminal Justice and Public Order Bill 1994 which allows the court to 'draw inferences' from the suspect's silence in two respects:

1 Where the suspect relies in his defence on a fact which he failed to mention when questioned or charged, which he could reasonably have been expected to mention or
2 Where he fails to give evidence at his trial.

This curtailment allows the court, once these provisions enter into force, to infer guilt from the suspect's silence. But the Bill also states that a person shall not be charged or convicted solely on the grounds of failure or refusal to answer questions.

The privilege against self-incrimination extends also to civil litigation where it protects a litigant from being forced to disclose incriminating evidence through an order for discovery of documents. The term 'discovery' describes the process under which litigants are able to obtain, within limits, information of the existence and contents of documents which are relevant to the litigation. It involves the disclosure in writing of all the relevant documents in the possession, custody or power of the litigant and the production of the documents disclosed, except for those subject to privilege, either for inspection by the opposing party or to the court (*Halsbury's*). Concern has been expressed that the records of an environmental audit would have to be disclosed as part of an order for discovery and this has raised interest in the extent to which they can be protected by privilege.

The rule applies to both natural and legal persons. As was held in *Triplex Safety Glass Co. Ltd v Lancegaye Safety Glass*, privilege can be claimed by a corporation in the UK. In the United States and Australia, the courts have held that the privilege does not extend to corporations. The leading Australian case on the point is *Environment Protection Authority v Caltex Refining Co. Pty Ltd* which concerned an order to disclose water pollution records kept by a discharger. The reasoning of these courts is that the privilege was designed, among other reasons, to protect suspects from being forced to make confessions under threat or torture, pains which cannot be inflicted on a corporation. But the English court in the *Triplex case* took the view that a corporation, like a natural person, can be convicted and punished and so deserves the same protection.

11.1.2 Legal Professional Privilege

A separate but allied rule to the privilege against self-incrimination is the doctrine of *legal professional privilege*. Under the common law, confidential communication between a person, his or her legal adviser and third parties is privileged from disclosure; this privilege is known as 'legal professional privilege'. The privilege is strictly circumscribed, however, and is available only if the communication was made to enable the client to obtain legal advice, or with reference to a litigation that was either actually taking place or was contemplated at the time of the communication.

If the communication is not between client and the legal adviser but, rather, is between either of them and third parties, then it is privileged only if it was made in reference to a litigation that was actually taking place or was contemplated and with the objective of being submitted to the legal advisers for the purpose of obtaining advice upon the litigation. Communication between a client and his or her legal adviser is privileged even where it was not made in reference to any litigation. But it must have been made in order to obtain legal advice and, therefore, the relationship of client and legal adviser must exist between the two parties involved. This rule enables individuals to communicate freely and frankly with their legal advisers without the fear of compromising themselves and it is not affected by the curtailment of the right to silence in the Criminal Justice and Public Order Bill.

The Canadian case of *HM The Queen & Niel Rickey, Ministry of the Environment v McCarthy Tetrault Canada Inc. & Donald Stafford* is an interesting illustration concerning documents seized under a search warrant from McCarthy Tetrault, lawyers for Lafarge Canada Inc. It arose from an investigation which Neil Rickey, an investigator with the Ontario Ministry of the Environment, was conducting into alleged spills of wastes at the Lafarge cement plant where Donald Stafford was the Environmental and Process Quality Manager. The applicants asserted in court that the documents in issue were protected from seizure by solicitor–client privilege.

Douglas Thompson, the solicitor at McCarthy responsible for advising Lafarge swore an affidavit stating that, on 29/30 July 1991, he had attended a meeting at the cement plant with Stafford and other senior managers of Lafarge the purpose of which 'was to receive confidential information and provide legal advice concerning the compliance of the plant with environmental laws and policies'. During the meeting discussion took place concerning a potential prosecution in relation to the facility. The affidavit stated that the documents for which privilege was claimed were notes and memoranda prepared by Thompson of confidential communications between him and his client. Against this the prosecution produced a reminder notice circulated prior to the meeting which referred to the meeting as an 'environmental audit' and which referred to Thompson's role as the recorder and keeper of the information developed.

The judge observed that underlying this dispute was the wider controversy within the field of environmental law relating to the status of information and documents generated as part of an environmental audit. He held that characterizing an exercise as an environmental audit does not in itself answer the question whether the information communicated to the solicitor as part of the exercise is privileged; the relevant inquiry is whether the exercise was truly conducted in good faith for the purpose of obtaining legal advice. The judge reviewed the documents which were claimed to be privileged and held that they confirmed the purpose of the meeting to be to obtain legal advice and that the communication was intended to be confidential.

This ruling indicates that the results of environmental audits can be protected from disclosure under the doctrine of legal professional privilege as long as the audit is conducted for the purpose of obtaining legal advice. The issue has yet to be argued before the British courts but it is possible they would apply similar principles to those applied by the Canadian court.

Thus there are two separate, if similar, rules. The first is the privilege against self-incrimination where a witness is required to answer questions or produce documents which would incriminate him or her whether in or out of court. The traditional rule is that the witness is entitled to refuse to answer such questions or produce such documents although, under the changes introduced by the Criminal Justice and Public Order Bill, an inference of guilt may be drawn from the witness's refusal. The second is legal professional privilege protecting communications (verbal or written) between a person and his or her legal adviser as well as communications between a legal adviser and third parties which are undertaken for the purpose of an on-going or prospective litigation. Although there is no English case law on the point it is thought that the records of environmental audits would only be privileged if they could be brought under either of these heads of privilege.

11.1.3 Statutory Limitation of the Privilege

The rule against self-incrimination is a common law rule and is not based on any statutory provision. In recent years statutes, including environmental statutes, have made considerable inroads into the rule. These statutues provide that, under controlled circumstances, a suspect can be compelled to answer questions and produce documents since the right to silence can frustrate attempts to carry out investigations. The power to compel answers and the production of documents has been available to the HSE since the enactment of the Health and Safety at Work etc. Act. It has recently been extended, by ss 17 and 69 of the EPA 1990, to HMIP, local authorities under LAAPC and the waste regulators, but not to the NRA.

These provisions enable inspectors to require a person to answer such questions as the inspector thinks fit and to sign a declaration as to the truth of the answers. The inspector is able also to require the production of records kept in fulfilment of legal requirements. Where the information is recorded in computerized form, extracts may be demanded. No answer given as a result of the exercise of these powers is admissible in evidence against the person in proceedings and the investigator's powers do not compel the production of documents which may be withheld on grounds of legal professional privilege. Despite the Criminal Justice and Public Order Bill, no inference may be drawn from the failure or refusal, on grounds of legal professional privilege, to produce documents. Thus, there is a limited abridgement of the rule against self-incrimination to enable investigations to be conducted without compromising the ability of suspects to defend themselves in subsequent trials.

There is a second statutory limitation of the privilege against self-incrimination. This enables the NRA to serve a written notice under s. 202 of the **Water Resources Act 1991** requiring a person to produce specified information; failure to do so is a criminal offence. The other regulators, including the water companies, have similar powers. This power came up for consideration in *Environment Protection Authority v Caltex Refining Co. Pty Ltd*, an Australian case. Following the commencement of a prosecution against Caltex for alleged contravention of the **New South Wales Clean Water Act 1970**, the State Pollution Control Commission served two notices upon Caltex requiring the production of documents including records relating to effluent from the defendant's refinery on the dates of the alleged offences. Caltex argued that it was not bound to incriminate itself by producing the documents but the High Court held that the privilege against self-incrimination does not extend to corporations. In the UK the privilege has been held to extend to corporations. Therefore it can be argued that the power cannot be used to gather evidence and information for the sole purpose of use in pending criminal proceedings.

In spite of the restrictions on enforcement agencies to compel the production of evidence, many operators choose to provide the information voluntarily, i.e. to 'confess'. Reasons include the desire to cooperate with the agency in finding a solution to the problem, the hope of avoiding a prosecution and the hope of receiving lenient treatment at the hands of the court for showing remorse. Confessions are thus an important feature of the enforcement process.

11.1.4   Admissions

The general rule under common law is that the person best able to give evidence is the person with first-hand knowledge. Therefore, it is not usually admissible for a witness to attempt to prove disputed facts by giving evidence of matters said or written by someone else. Such evidence is known as 'hearsay evidence' (see *R v Harz, R v Power*). This common law rule is known as 'the rule against hearsay'. It is a rule with many exceptions, one of which relates 'admissions', i.e. to statements made by a person which are adverse to his or her case. As an exception to the hearsay rule the court may allow testimony to be given about such admissions by the person who heard them.

In both criminal and civil litigation parties may choose to admit aspects of the opponent's case. Such 'formal admissions' are binding and may not be contested in court. Formal admissions may be made because contesting the facts admitted is hopeless or as a result of bargains struck in the course of negotiations with the opponent. But 'without prejudice' admissions made in the course of contractual negotiations, on the understanding that they are not to be used in evidence, are not admissible in court and can be retracted at any time. A third kind of admission, 'informal admissions', are adverse statements made spontaneously; they are admissible in court but are not binding on the maker who is free to repudiate them or explain them away, leaving it to the court to evaluate them and attach whatever significance to them that circumstances allow (*Halsbury's*, Vol. 11(2)).

Confessions

In criminal litigation the possibility that investigators may be tempted to get an admission by threat or promises has led to specific rules relating to admissions being laid down in the **Police and Criminal Evidence Act 1984** (PACE) and the Code of Practice for the detention, treatment and questioning of persons by police officers which is made under s. 66 of PACE (Home Office, 1991). The Code is relied on by enforcement agencies, including environmental enforcement agencies, since they do not have their own code.

Admissions made in the context of a criminal investigation are known as 'confessions'. Although, as a general principle, the fact that an admission, or a confession, was obtained by threat or promise and in violation of the requirements laid down in PACE and the Code does not render it inadmissible, it seriously undermines the value that may be attached to the confession. Additionally, the judge has the discretion to disallow it if he or she concludes that the failure to comply with these requirements was prejudicial to the accused; the accused's legal representative can be expected to object to the admission of such a confession.

Section 82(1) of PACE defines a confession to include 'any statement wholly or partly adverse to the person who made it, whether made to a person in authority or not or whether made in words or otherwise'. The rule relating to confessions is set out in s. 76(1) which provides that

> in any proceedings a confession made by an accused person may be given in evidence against him in so far as it is relevant to any matter in issue in the proceedings and is not excluded by the court . . .'

Section 76(2) then sets out the two conditions under which the court may exclude the confession, regardless of whether it may be true; i.e. where the confession was or may have been obtained:

1   By oppression or
2   In consequence of anything said or done which was likely to render it unreliable.

To give practical guidance on the requirements of s. 76, a Code of Practice was drawn up under s. 66 of PACE dealing with the questioning of persons by police office. As the court said in *R v Keenan*, the purpose of the Code is to safeguard against the investigator inaccurately recording or inventing words used in questioning a person and also to make it difficult for a person to make unfounded allegations that the investigator had inaccurately recorded or invented an interview. Therefore it is irrelevant whether the form of the interview is formal or informal; the Code applies in either case.

A formal interview is described below while an informal one may be spontaneous. As the court held in *R v Absalom*, a series of questions directed by police to a suspect with a view to obtaining admissions on which proceedings could be founded amounts to an 'interview' to which the Code of Practice applies. The court rejected the argument that, because there was no 'conventional interview', the Code was inapplicable and held that 'this is just the sort of situation in which these provisions are most significant'.

The Interview

The Code states that a person reasonably suspected of an offence must be cautioned before any questions about it (or further questions if it is his earlier answers that provide the grounds for suspicion) are put to him for the purpose of obtaining evidence which may be given to a court in a prosecution. There is no need for a caution if questions are being asked for some other purpose, such as to ascertain his identity. The terms recommended for the caution are 'you do not have to say anything unless you wish to do so, but what you say may be given in evidence'. This is a restatement of the defendant's right to silence under the common law and this caution does no more than remind him of it. It may need to be redrafted in view of the changes introduced by the Criminal Justice and Public Order Bill. The proposed replacement states that 'you do not have to say anything. But if you do not mention now something which you later use in your defence the court may decide that your failure to mention it strengthens the case against you. A record will be made of anything you say and it may be given in evidence if you are brought to trial'. The caution should be recorded.

The investigator is advised to inform the interviewee that he or she has a right to have legal advice during the interview. The Code sets out a number of circumstances where an interview may proceed without a solicitor, as follows:

1   Delay will involve an immediate risk of harm to persons or serious loss of, or damage to, property or

2 Awaiting the solicitor's arrival would cause unreasonable delay to the process of the investigation

3 The solicitor nominated cannot be contacted, has previously indicated that he does not wish to be contacted or has declined to attend.

Third, an accurate record must be made of each interview whether or not the interview takes place at a police station. The record must state the place of the interview, the time it begins and ends, the time the record is made (if different), any breaks in the interview and the names of all those present. The record must be made during the course of the interview, unless this would not be practicable or would interfere with the conduct of the interview, and must constitute either a verbatim record of what has been said or an account of the interview which adequately and accurately summarizes it. If the record is not made at the time of the interview it must be made as soon as practicable after it. The record must be timed and signed by the maker and unless it is impracticable the person interviewed shall be given the opportunity to read the interview record and sign it as correct or to indicate the way in which he or she considers it inaccurate. If the person interviewed refuses to sign it this must be recorded. It would be good practice, although the Code does not say so, for the person interviewed to ask and, if necessary, insist on a copy of the interview record.

The final point to make in relation to confessions is that a corporation cannot be bound by confessions made by an employee unless the employee is authorized to speak on behalf of the corporation. A director or other similarly placed senior officer may be authorized to make statements binding the company. But such a director or other similar officer may be charged in their own right, in which case confessions by them could be given in evidence in their own trial. Additionally, in relation to environmental offences which typically arise due to the actions of employees, interviewing employees is the principal way in which the details of the offence are discovered. Even where the confession itself is not introduced in evidence it may give the investigator 'leads', making a pertinent line of defence unsustainable. The interview is therefore an important stage in the investigation for both the suspect and the enforcement authority.

11.2   Sample Evidence

Enforcement authorities do not have to rely only on interviews to obtain evidence. They gather or require the operator to gather and submit the results of samples of a discharge or emission. Indeed, gathering sample evidence is a principal activity of all enforcement authorities. HMIP and the local authorities (with the exception of the use of the Ringelmann Chart for measuring dark smoke) are free to use whatever sampling equipment they consider appropriate and HMIP's Guidance Notes indicate its preference for automated continuous on-line monitoring and sampling devices. The NRA is in a unique position in that s. 209 of the **Water Resources Act 1991** specifies a particular procedure for collecting samples to be used in court proceedings. The procedure, which is known as the tripartite sampling procedure, is premised on manual, rather than continuous, sampling.

11.2.1   The Tripartite Sampling Procedure

Over the years s. 209 has gained status as an NRA enforcement mechanism in its own right, quite apart from its use to generate data for use in a prosecution. As an enforcement mechanism, tripartite sampling is to be distinguished from routine sampling, which constitutes the normal monitoring procedure to ascertain how dischargers are performing. If the routine sample discloses a breach the discharger is sent a warning letter seeking an explanation and warning that the next sample taken will be a tripartite one, which could lead to a prosecution. This alone will often lead to the discharger correcting the problem. In this way the NRA is able to carry out its enforcement duties without having to take tripartite samples constantly, given that they cost about three times as much as routine samples.

In relation to effluent passing from land to controlled water, s. 209 states that the result of the analysis of any sample taken on behalf of the NRA shall not be admissible in any legal proceedings unless the person who took the sample on doing so, or as soon as practicable thereafter:

1   Notifies the occupier or the owner of the land of his intention to have it analysed
2   There and then divides the sample into three parts and places each part in a container which is sealed and marked and
3   Delivers one part to the occupier or owner, retains one part for future comparison and submits the third part to be analysed.

The section does not prevent pollution offences from being proved in some other way by, for example, calling the testimony of someone who witnessed the act. All it requires is that where reliance is to be placed on the results of the sample evidence taken on behalf of the NRA then this procedure must have been followed if the sample evidence is to be admissible. Notably, if the sample is not being taken on behalf of the NRA then the tripartite procedure need not be followed. Therefore, third parties like environmental pressure groups need not take tripartite samples, although a tripartite sample is likely to carry far greater weight in court than a single one. This raises the question whether samples gathered by the discharger and handed over to the NRA in compliance with consent conditions are 'taken on behalf of the NRA'. This is important because the NRA hopes to rely increasingly on self-monitoring by dischargers and has indicated that charges paid for consents will be reduced proportionately with the extent of self-monitoring undertaken (NRA, 1993).

Although the point has never been tested in court, the draft Urban Waste Water Treatment Regulations have sought to put the matter beyond doubt in relation to discharges from urban waste water treatment plants. They provide that records which a sewerage works operator must provide under his or her consent conditions shall, in water pollution proceedings, be admissible in evidence against the operator. The Regulations provide also that a sample which is taken and analysed by the operator in compliance with a consent condition shall not be treated as being taken on behalf of the NRA. This still leaves the question open in relation to other direct dischargers into watercourses, although the NRA has successfully prosecuted Pasminco (Europe) Smelting Company in a magistrates' court using sample evidence supplied by the company itself (ENDS, 1992).

Finally, in relation to the third part of the sample retained for future comparison, the court in *R v Rechem International Ltd* held that the tripartite procedure is not invalidated where comparison is impossible because the sample has deteriorated. The court took the view that 'for future comparison' is descriptive of the purpose of the act to be done, namely retaining the sample; the validity of the procedure is not dependent on whether future comparison proves possible. The court also rejected the argument that, because the glass container used absorbed sample constituents, it was not a suitable container as required, holding that the statute requires the container to be suitable at the time it is used. This interpretation means that the discharger must immediately send his or her own portion of the sample for analysis, and not rely on future comparison.

11.2.2 Automatic Sampling

The other main issue raised by the tripartite sampling procedure is whether it includes computerized automatic sampling devices. The NRA has developed a number of such devices which are able to monitor twenty-four hours a day, all year round, thus increasing greatly the chances of detecting breaches of consent conditions and other pollution incidents. Two of these devices, known as Merlin and Cyclops, are capable of monitoring discharges, warning the enforcement authority when there is a breach and automatically taking a sample of the effluent (Mumma, 1993). The question these devices raise is whether such remotely controlled automated systems satisfy the requirements of s. 209; how, for instance, is the first condition (notify the owner or occupier 'on taking the sample' of the intention to have it analysed) to be met?

The draft Urban Waste Water Treatment Regulations provide that where, in compliance with a condition, a sample is collected by an automatic sampling apparatus, the sample shall be treated, for the purposes of s. 209, as being taken only at the time when it is removed from the apparatus. This enables the officer who comes to remove the sample to notify the owner or occupier of the intention to have it analysed and comply with the other requirements, and conforms to the practice which the NRA intends to use. In fact, the NRA has secured a conviction in a magistrates' court of a discharger on the basis of sample evidence gathered by Cyclops (Croner, 1993). In this particular case the discharger pleaded guilty and so the question relating to the way the sample had been collected was not considered. It is likely, however, that a court would find that the practice meets the requirements of s. 209.

11.3 The Discretion to Prosecute

The concept of 'discretion' is central to the enforcement process. Discretion is available to all enforcement authorities insofar as the law leaves them a choice between various courses of action. Since full enforcement is, in practice, impossible due to factors such as scarcity of resources and the ambiguity of some legal requirements, enforcement can only be effective if it is guided by the exercise of discretion. Thus, there is no obligation in law for a prosecution to be mounted whenever a breach of the law is detected; the enforcement authority has the discretion to pick and choose, deciding to pursue some and ignore others. The phrase 'technical breach' describes infractions which are normally not to be pursued. In making its choice the authority's mandate is to adopt a course of action which best promotes the objectives of the particular law it seeks to enforce.

11.3.1 Prosecution Policy

The exercise of discretion is far from random and is usually guided by a number of factors, ranging from a 'hunch' to consciously articulated policy guidelines. Empirical studies have highlighted a number of factors as influencing the exercise of discretion, most important of which are the nature of the breach, how it was discovered and the offender's attitude (Richardson, 1982; Hawkins, 1984; Hutter, 1988).

The Nature of the Breach

Breaches are either persistent or isolated. The latter kind is more likely to result in a prosecution not least because the breach resembles the traditional criminal offence; it is an 'incident' for which a punishment can be justified easily. Persistent breaches, on the other hand, arise out of the reality that emissions into environmental media is a normal, legitimate industrial activity for which a licence or authorization will have been issued. Unlike the more traditional areas of criminal conduct, such as theft, compliance with the law requires, not the simple act of refraining from an activity, but a more complex act, usually involving identifying the cause of the breach and rectifying it, sometimes at considerable cost. Further, having achieved compliance, it has to be maintained by the expenditure of effort, time and money in, for instance, ensuring that pollution-abatement equipment works properly. Insistence on instant compliance in this context is often impracticable and can amount to a failure to exercise proper discretion if, for instance, the only way to achieve it is to cease operations by closing down the process.

These factors mean that an enforcement authority faced with a persistent breach usually finds itself cast in the role of a technical expert helping the operator to 'solve the problem'. Prosecution is seen as a last resort when all else has failed, because, for instance, the operator has refused to cooperate sufficiently. This situation can lead to the suspicion that enforcement authorities have been 'captured' by process operators and are failing to achieve their objective of environmental protection. Those who take such a view would prefer to see enforcement authorities act more like police officers, not technical experts. In the early 1990s, the perception that UK pollution control authorities were victims of such a capture led to a shift in the practices of both the NRA and HMIP towards a more arm's-length approach to enforcement and a far more frequent resort to prosecution.

The Discovery of the Incident

The way the incident is discovered may have a bearing on the pursuit of a prosecution. Pollution incidents are discovered either as a result of the enforcement authority's inspections or because third parties have reported them. The latter are more likely to result in a prosecution, precisely because the agency would like to be seen to have done something about the report and a prosecution is an incontrovertible way of demonstrating that it has acted decisively on the report.

Emissions are far too numerous for enforcement authorities to spend time monitoring all operators in the hope of catching them committing an offence red-handed. Therefore, monitoring follows a pattern, concentrating on likely offenders. Factors such as the operator's past record and his or her attitude to compliance become important since they help to prioritize monitoring activities. Targeted monitoring is effective in identifying persistent problems while reports from the public normally relate mainly to highly visible isolated incidents.

The Offender's Attitude

A further factor influencing the exercise of discretion is the attitude of the offender. Enforcement authorities perceive offenders as falling into one of four categories on the basis of their occupation, size, demeanour, and responsiveness. The 'socially responsible' group, usually large, profitable concerns, are viewed as conscientious and law abiding, breaching legal requirements primarily through genuine accidents. They often act quickly to remedy the breach. The 'unfortunate' are those who have compliance problems on account of genuine economic and technical difficulties. The 'careless' are those whose compliance problems arise out of sloppy management, inadequate procedures and untrained labour. The last group, the 'malicious', are those who deliberately breach the law either because they want to avoid the expense entailed in compliance or because they just do not care.

Typically, the malicious are prosecuted while discretion is likely to be exercised in favour of a socially responsible and the unfortunate offender. The careless are likely to face a prosecution.

11.3.2   Policy Guidelines for Enforcement Officers

Environmental protection authorities, in particular the NRA and HMIP, have issued internal guidelines to their officials setting out the principles to be followed in making decisions about which cases to pursue. These guidelines formalize the factors which research has shown influences the exercise of discretion. As a matter of law an enforcement agency cannot fetter its discretion and so it remains free to prosecute any case, even one that does not meet the criteria set out in the guidelines as meriting a prosecution.

HMIP's Guidelines identify five factors: (1) failure to comply with a notice, (2) breach of a condition in an authorization, (3) the company's attitude, (4) the nature of the incident and (5) the objective of the prosecution. They state that HMIP's policy is to prosecute when an offence is caused by non-compliance with a legally issued notice. For a breach of a condition the first consideration is whether there has been any environmental harm, and its extent. The second consideration is whether a nuisance was caused. The company's attitude is to be determined from the events leading to the incident and the company's record in dealing with both HMIP and the public. Regarding the nature of the incident, relevant questions include whether the incident was foreseeable, the steps the company took to avert it and why these failed and the company's response to the failure. The fifth factor relates to what will be gained by the prosecution, i.e. publicly embarrassing the operator, inflicting a financial penalty, seeking to demonstrate publicly HMIP's policy and attitude and seeking to reflect public concern (HMIP, undated).

The NRA's Guidelines are considerably more comprehensive (NRA, 1991). Incidents are placed into three categories. Category 1 are major incidents involving potential or actual persistent effect on water quality or aquatic life; closure of potable water, industrial or agricultural abstraction; extensive death of fish; excessive breaches of consent conditions; extensive remedial measures; or a major effect on amenity value. Category 2 are significant incidents involving notification to abstractors; significant death of fish; a measurable effect on invertebrate life; making water unfit for stock; contamination of a watercourse bed; or a reduced amenity value by odour or appearance to the public, owners or users. The final category, minor incidents, are cases of suspected or probable pollution which on investigation turn out to be difficult to prove or substantiate or to have no notable effect.

Categories 1 and 3 are straightforward; a prosecution is the normal course of action in Category 1 and a warning letter, which simply warns the discharger to mend his or her ways, in Category 3. The question of discretion arises in Category 2 incidents and the NRA has given guidance to officers on the appropriate course of action. Three courses of action are possible depending on the circumstances of the case; a prosecution, a caution, or a warning. Ten factors are identified which, if present either singly or in combination, will result in a prosecution or a caution. The absence of the same factors will mean that only a warning will be issued. The factors are a high risk to abstractions, death of fish, effects on amenity, negligence, a previous history of pollution or breach of consent conditions, poor operational management, an absence of unforeseeable problems, lack of precautions, little or no post-incident remedial work, and a significant breach of consent conditions.

The difficult question relates to whether to prosecute or caution a discharger.

11.3.3 Cautions

According to the NRA's policy document a caution is to be given where it is not appropriate to prosecute but it is clear that an offence was committed. It is appropriate only if the discharger accepts that he or she is guilty; if he does not the proper course of action is to bring a prosecution. The caution is formally given and formally recorded. The NRA wishes to use the caution in subsequent court proceedings for a different offence. Its policy, therefore, is to seek the consent of the discharger to the caution, explaining to him that a record of it will be kept as part of his 'history' for possible subsequent use. Accepting a caution is not therefore risk-free to the discharger since it may subsequently be used to portray the discharger as a 'repeat offender', leading to enhanced penalties in subsequent court proceedings. Its attraction to both the NRA and the discharger is that it offers an apparently easy way out of the difficult cases where neither party can be confident of winning the case in court.

The NRA's procedure where the officer has opted to go for a caution is for the officer to recommend a prosecution subject to the offer of a caution. The caution is a standard form letter sent to the discharger with the request that he or she sign it. The letter states the name of the alleged offender and his address, the date of the offence, the statute contravened and details of the offence. It asks him to admit to the offence, to consent to being cautioned and to confirm that he understands the significance of the caution. It is worth pointing out that even where the discharger opts to accept a caution it is still important to make sure that the details of the offence as stated in the letter of caution are correct before signing it; once signed, the opportunity to 'set the record straight' is lost.

It is interesting that no statute provides for cautions to be issued by any enforcement agency. Cautions originate from an administrative practice of the police to caution alleged offenders and are now relied on by many other agencies. Additionally, it is not clear that cautions would be admissible in court if challenged; so far, they have not been the subject of judicial comment. This uncertainty no doubt makes the decision on whether to go for a caution or to risk a prosecution a more difficult one for the alleged offender.

11.4   The Offences

Environmental and health and safety offences arise under various statutes. These offences can be tried summarily, on indictment or either way. Summary offences (those triable summarily) are tried by magistrates' courts without a jury, indictable offences (those tried on indictment) are tried in the Crown Court with the assistance of a jury and 'either way offences' are those which can be tried in either court depending on the surrounding circumstances, in particular the seriousness of the offence and the maximum penalty for the offence in the magistrates' court.

Summary offences are usually less serious than indictable ones. If an offence is triable either way the magistrates' court in which the charge is laid has to examine the circumstances in order to decide whether to commit the offence for trial in the Crown Court. The procedure for this examination is set out in the **Magistrates Court Act 1980**. A magistrates' court can also try an indictable offence and then send it to the Crown Court for sentencing where it thinks that the magistrates' court sentence is inadequate (Smith and Hogan, 1992).

The sentence may be either a fine or a prison sentence or both. The level of fines which may be imposed are specified in one of three ways; by stating a particular sum of money on the face of the legislation (such as £20 000 in the **Water Resources Act 1991** for an offence under s. 85); by making reference to the 'statutory maximum' (i.e. the offender shall be liable to a fine not exceeding the statutory maximum); or third by making reference to the 'standard scale' (i.e. the offender shall be liable to a fine not exceeding a level, say, level 3 on the standard scale).

The statutory maximum is the maximum penalty specified in s. 32 of the Magistrates' Court Act 1980. This section specifies the penalties which a magistrates' court may impose if it tries an offence which is triable either way. The standard scale of fines is set out in s. 37 of the **Criminal Justice Act 1982** as amended by the **Criminal Justice Act 1991** and currently reads as follows: level 1 (£200); level 2 (£500); level 3 (£1 000); level 4 (£2 500) and level 5 (£5 000). The more serious the offence, the higher is the penalty. The statutory maximum and level 5 on the standard scale are both £5 000.

The Appendix to this book lists the environmental and health and safety offences and the associated fines and prison sentences, where applicable.

11.5   Criminal Liability for Directors and Companies

11.5.1   Personal Liability

A standard feature of environmental legislation is the provision imposing personal criminal liability on directors and other senior officers of companies. These provisions are found in:

1   Section 157 of the EPA
2   Sections 217(1) and 210(1) of the Water Resources Act 1991 and Water Industry Act 1991 respectively
3   Section 37 of the Health and Safety at Work etc. Act 1974.

Typically, the provision states that

> Where a body corporate is guilty of an offence and that offence is proved to have been committed with the consent or connivance of, or to be attributable to any neglect on the part of, any director, manager, secretary or other similar officer of the body corporate or any person who was purporting to act in any such capacity, he as well as the body corporate shall be guilty of that offence and shall be liable to be proceeded against and punished accordingly.

An allied offence normally found in many, but not all, of these statutes states that

> where the commission of an offence is due to the act or default of some other person, that other person may be charged with and convicted of the offence whether or not proceedings for the offence are taken against the first-mentioned person.

This provision is found in s. 158 of the EPA 1990, s. 217(3) of the Water Resources Act 1991 as well as in s. 36(1) of the Health and Safety at Work etc. Act 1974.

Personal liability arises where the director or senior officer (or someone acting in that capacity whether or not duly appointed) consents to, connives in or is neglectful in relation to the commission of the offence. A director 'consents' if he or she is well aware of what is going on and agrees to it; he or she 'connives' if he or she is equally well aware of what is going on but agreement is tacit, not actively encouraging what happens but letting it continue and saying nothing about it; third, an offence is 'attributable to the neglect of' of a director where he or she omits to do something for which he or she is under a duty (*Huckeby v Elliot*).

In recent years the environmental protection and health and safety agencies have started bringing proceedings against individuals in their capacity as directors. It has therefore become important to be able to say precisely what category of company officer can be described as a director or other similar officer.

In *R v Boal* the appellant was the assistant general manager of a bookshop. He was in charge while the general manager was away on a weeks's holiday when an inspection of the shop's premises by the local fire authority showed serious breaches of the fire certificate for the premises. The appellant was charged along with the company with offences against the **Fire Precautions Act 1971** on the basis that he was a 'manager'. The appellant pleaded guilty but then appealed. The Court of Appeal held that the intended scope of the legislation was to fix criminal liability only on those who were in a position of real authority and who were responsible for putting proper procedures in place, i.e. the decision makers in the company who had both the power and the responsibility to decide corporate policy and strategy: 'It is not meant to strike at underlings.' The appellant was only responsible for the day-to-day running of the bookshop rather than enjoying any sort of governing role relating to the affairs of the company; he was not a 'manager'. The appeal was allowed.

In *Woodhouse v Walsall MBC* Mr Woodhouse was employed by Caird Environmental Ltd (CEL) as 'General Manager—Minworth'. Caird carried on the business of providing waste disposal services at Minworth, among other premises. The Minworth site included a vehicle park area which was not part of the area licensed as a waste disposal site. CEL used a trailer parked on the vehicle park for storing controlled waste, an offence for which it was convicted. A prosecution was also brought against Mr Woodhouse on the basis that he was a 'manager' under the provisions of COPA 1974. He was convicted and he appealed. Granting the appeal the court said 'the test of whether someone was a manager of a body corporate was not just whether that person was in a position of real authority but also whether he was a decision maker who had power and responsibility to decide corporate policy and strategy'.

An enforcement authority faced with similar facts (i.e. where the person who caused the offence is not senior enough to be considered as a director) should not charge the person responsible as a director but rather should charge him with the alternative offence, i.e. under the provisions dealing with offences due to the act or default of 'some other person'.

11.5.2 Vicarious Liability

But where the company, rather than the employee, is charged with an offence, the status of the employee responsible for the offence cannot be used as a defence unless some statutory provision makes such a defence possible. This is because a company is responsible vicariously for the acts of its employees. This was the issue in *NRA v McAlpine Homes East Ltd* where the question was whether an offence committed by an employee is an offence committed by the company. The NRA charged McAlpine Homes East Ltd with the offence of polluting a watercourse. The pollution occurred when cement from a contruction site entered the stream, killing fish. The company argued that the site agent and site manager were the ones responsible for letting the pollution occur. Although both were its employees, the company maintained that they were not senior enough to be acting on its behalf and their actions could not be considered as being the company's actions. The magistrates accepted the argument and acquitted the company.

On appeal the court overturned the justices' decision, pointing out that an employer is liable for pollution resulting from its own operations carried out under its essential control. A company can only escape liability in situations such as those where a third party, like a trespasser, breaks the 'chain of causation' or employees 'go on a frolic of their own'. The judge stated further that the question to be asked in all cases where a company is prosecuted under s. 85 of the **Water Resources Act 1991** is whether as a matter of common sense the company, by some active operation or chain of operations, caused the pollution of the stream.

The court distinguished two cases in which the status of the employee directly responsible for the offence has been used successfully by the company as a defence. In *Tesco Ltd v Natrass* the company was charged with an offence under the **Trade Descriptions Act 1968** but raised the defence under s. 24(1) of that Act that the offence was committed by some other person, namely, the manager of the store in question who was not a director of Tesco Ltd or a person in a similar position. The court acquitted Tesco Ltd on the basis that the manager was 'another person'. The *McAlpines* court distinguished the *Tesco case* on the basis that it was concerned with whether the company could invoke a defence section not with whether the company had committed the offence.

Similarly, in *Seaboard Offshore Ltd v Secretary of State for Transport* the court acquitted the company of contravening s. 31(1) of the **Merchant Shipping Act 1988** which made it the duty of the owner of a ship to take all reasonable steps to secure that it was operated in a safe manner. The House of Lords held that the duty is a personal one and the owner is criminally liable if he or she fails personally in the duty but not for the acts or omissions of his or her employees if he has himself taken all such reasonable steps. The *MacAlpine* court pointed out that the duty was not to take all reasonable steps to avoid pollution; rather, it was not to cause pollution.

If convicted the director faces the same penalties stipulated for the offence that the company would face but, additionally, he or she can be sent to prison. Section 2 of the **Company Directors Disqualification Act 1986** a court may also disqualify a person who has been convicted of an indictable offence (i.e. an offence triable either way) from being a director, liquidator, administrator, receiver or manager of a company or otherwise being concerned in the management, formation or promotion of a company. That this power can be used following conviction for an environmental or health and safety offence was shown by the two-year disqualification which Lewes Crown Court imposed on a director convicted of contravening a prohibition notice arising out of unsafe work practices at his company's quarry (*New Law Journal*, 1992).

References

Blunt v Park Lane Hotel Ltd and Briscoe [1942] 2 All ER 187.

Croner, 'Cyclops traps river polluter', *Croner Waste Management Briefing*, Issue 6, No. 6, March (1993).

Environment Protection Authority v Caltex Refining Co. Pty Ltd (1993, unrep.).

ENDS Report No. 211, 'Smelter incriminates itself by reporting illegal discharge', August, 38 (1992).

Halsbury's Laws, 13, 4th edn, para. 1.

Halsbury's Laws, vol. 11(2) paras 1118, 1124 and 1134.

Hawkins, K., *Environment and Enforcement*, Clarendon Press (1984).

HM The Queen & Neil Rickey, Ministry of the Environment v McCarthy Tetrault Canada Inc. & Donald Stafford (1992, unrep.).

Hutter, B., *The Reasonable Arm of the Law*, Clarendon Press (1988).

HMIP, *Guidelines for Prosecution* (undated).

Home Office, *PACE—Codes of Practice*, revised edn, HMSO (1991).

Huckerby v Elliot [1970] 1 All ER 194.

LMELR, *Land Management and Environmental Law Report*, October/November (1991), Issue 5/3, p. 170 and February (1992), Issue 1/4, 23–24.

Mumma, A., 'The use of compliance monitoring data in water pollution prosecutions', *JEL*, 5/2, 191 (1993)

New Law Journal, 1037 (1992).

NRA, *Policy Implementation Guidance Note No. 1: Enforcement and Prosecution with Respect to Pollution Incidents Affecting Controlled Waters*, 1 April (1991, unpublished).

NRA v McAlpine Homes East Ltd, The Independent, 3 February (1994).

NRA, *Charging for Discharging* (1993).

R v Boal [1992] 3 All ER 117.

R v Harz, R v Power [1966] 3 All ER 433.

R v Keenan [1989] 3 All ER 598.

R v Absalom [1989] 88 Cr. App. Rep. 332.

Richardson, G., *et al.*, *Policing Pollution*, Clarendon Press (1982).

R v Rechem International Ltd (1993, unrep.), transcript dated 10 September 1993, ref. 9305622*4*1, Newport Crown Court, Gwent.

Seaboard Offshore Ltd v Secretary of State for Transport [1993] 1 WLR 1025. House of Lords decision—transcript, 23 March 1994.

Smith, J.C. and Hogan, B., *Criminal Law*, 7th edn, 23–24, Butterworths (1992).

Tesco Ltd v Natrass [1972] AC 153.

Triplex Safety Glass Co. Ltd v Lancegaye Safety Glass (1934) Ltd [1939] 2 All ER 613.

Woodhouse v Walsall MBC [1994] Env LR Part 1 30.

12

Civil Law and the Environment

12.1 Background

Increased environmental awareness has led to more frequent action in the civil courts. Typically, the civil action is brought by private parties, although public bodies also occasionally resort to civil action. The private litigant is usually seeking a remedy for a private injury or grievance. Such action can, however, lead to environmentally protective measures being taken to avoid potential liability. Civil liability thus complements the criminal law regime for environmental protection. Indeed, the potential liability associated with ownership or control over contaminated land has raised civil liability to the top of the agenda in the debate on environmental protection mechanisms. The UK, the EC, the Council of Europe and UNEP are all examining the role of the civil liability principles in environmental protection.

The basis of a civil law claim is referred to as a 'cause of action', which arises when an injury occurs to person or property. Where the injury was caused by a public body exercising its public powers, the cause of action is said to be a public law cause of action; otherwise it is a private law cause of action. The public law causes of action are *ultra vires*, natural justice and error of law; these are redressed by *certiorari*, prohibition, *mandamus* and declaration, referred to as remedies. The private law causes of action are trespass, nuisance, the rule in *Rylands v Fletcher* (also known as the strict liability rule) and negligence, redressed by an award of damages, injunction and/or a declaration.

The general rule is that a private person may bring a private law civil action only to redress a private injury, not an injury to the public, such as damage to the environment. Redressing an injury to the public is the function of the Attorney General, representing the Crown. As the court said in *Gouriet v Union of Post Office Workers*,

> ... the jurisdiction of a civil court to grant remedies in private law is confined to the grant of remedies to litigants whose rights in private law have been infringed or are threatened with infringement. To extend that jurisdiction to the grant of remedies

for unlawful conduct which does not infringe any rights of the plaintiff in private law is to move out of the field of private into that of public law with which analogies may be deceptive and where different principles apply (p. 500).

A private individual wishing to bring an action on behalf of the public has to seek the permission of the Attorney General to use the AG's name, in which case the suit is known as a 'relator action'. A private party can, however, bring an action in his or her own name on the basis of an interference with a public right in two situations: where the interference with the public right also interferes with some private right of the person complaining; or where, in the absence of any interference with a private right, he has suffered damage peculiar to himself, over and above that suffered by the rest of the public. *Rose v Miles*, decided in 1815, illustrates this situation. The defendant wrongfully moored his barge across a public navigable creek, obstructing it. The plaintiff who was travelling on the creek was forced to unload his barge and transport his cargo by land at considerable expense. The court held that he had suffered particular damage, enabling him to sue in his own name even though the right to navigate on a public creek is a public, not a private, right.

A public law civil action is used primarily to challenge the legal validity of the decisions and actions of public bodies, a process known as 'judicial review'. Such an action is not a substitute for a private law cause of action. Thus, one may not proceed by way of judicial review simply because the defendant is a public body; the dispute must concern the exercise of public power or a public duty (*Equal Opportunities Commission v Secretary of State for Employment*). It is also not an appeal on the merits of the dispute but, rather, concerns the legality of the act or decision.

12.2 Judicial Review

Judicial review exists both as a statutory and as a common law remedy (Wade and Bradley, 1991). It may be awarded against a public body to:

1   Quash a decision (*certiorari*)
2   Stop it from acting unlawfully (prohibition)
3   Require it to perform its duty (*mandamus*)
4   Declare the legal position of the litigants (declaration)
5   Give monetary compensation or
6   As an injunction before the matter is determined, to hold the position of the parties.

The order is awarded where the public body has acted:

1   Beyond its legal powers (i.e. *ultra vires*)—a decision or an act of a public body may be *ultra vires* for reasons such as the failure to take into account relevant matters or taking into account irrelevant ones

2 Contrary to the principles of natural justice—these require an absence of bias and a fair hearing in decision making or
3 In error of the law.

12.2.1 Judicial Review as a Statutory Remedy

Many statutes make provision for those who are 'aggrieved' with the decision of a public body to challenge the legal validity of the decision by making an application to the courts. There is a short time limit—normally six weeks—within which the application may be made. Typically, the corollary to this right is that, after the expiry of the six weeks, the decision 'shall not be questioned in any legal proceedings whatever'. This mechanism is designed to enable public bodies to implement decisions quickly without risking a legal challenge.

These statutes do not define 'person agggrieved'. Denning LJ said in *A. G. (Gambia) v Njie*

> The words 'person aggrieved' are of wide import and should not be subjected to a restricted interpretation. They do not include, of course, a mere busybody who is interfering in things that do not concern him; but they do include a person who has a genuine grievance because an order has been made which prejudicially affects his interests.

The question arose in *Buxton v Minister of Housing and Local Government* in which the minister's decision to overturn the decision of a local authority refusing planning permission to extract chalk was challenged by neighbouring landowners who feared injury to their land from the development. The court denied the applicants' standing on the ground that the phrase 'person aggrieved' in a statute meant a person who had suffered a legal grievance; since the applicants had no legal rights which had been infringed they were not entitled to challenge the minister's decision.

This interpretation of entitlement, or 'standing', to bring action excluded representative organizations, a point illustrated by *Burke v Minister of Housing and Local Government*. The applicant sought to have a local authority's compulsory purchase orders in respect of certain land and premises quashed. He was not and never had been the owner or occupier of land or premises comprised in the orders but he was the secretary of a tenants' association, to which two persons living in the premises comprised in the orders belonged. He argued that, in these circumstances, he was a 'person aggrieved' by the orders and was entitled to make the application. The court dismissed the application on the ground that the applicant had not suffered a legal grievance and therefore he was not a 'person aggrieved'.

Since these early decisions the trend has been towards a more liberal interpretation which recognizes the right of representative bodies to bring action. In

Turner and Another v Secretary of State for the Environment the chairman and secretary of a local preservation society who had objected to a proposed development and made representations at the local public inquiry were granted standing to challenge the Secretary of State's decision, a challenge they lost because of a legal technicality unrelated to the question of standing. According to Ackner J,

> any person who, in the ordinary sense of the word, was aggrieved by a decision, and certainly any person who had attended and made representations at the inquiry, should have the right to establish in the courts that the decision was bad in law . . .

Organizations representing property owners, or similar interest groups, make judicial review applications to protect a private, not an environmental, interest. Standing for such groups, however, opens up the possibility for other representative groups with an overtly environmental remit, such as the Tidy Britain Group in relation to litter-abatement orders, to bring action to protect the environment. This possibility has been developed particularly in the context of the common law judicial review applications.

12.2.2   Judicial Review as a Common Law Remedy

The procedure for a common law judicial review application is set out in s. 31 of the **Supreme Court Act 1981** and Order 53 of the Rules of the Supreme Court. These require an application to be made to the High Court. As a preliminary step the applicant must seek leave of the court, allowing the application to be made. The need to obtain leave enables the court to filter out deserving from undeserving applications; the latter are dismissed without a hearing.

Leave to apply for judicial review can only be granted if the court considers that the applicant has 'sufficient interest' in the matter to which the application relates. Sufficient interest, or standing, is considered at two stages in the proceedings; at the preliminary stage when the application for leave is made, and again during the hearing of the merits of the application. At the preliminary stage the question is whether the applicant has sufficient interest to apply to the court while, at the main hearing, the question is whether the applicant has sufficient interest to be entitled to a remedy, assuming that the case is made out (*Inland Revenue Commissioners v National Federation of Self-Employed Businesses Ltd*).

Applicants for judicial review may be one of three kinds of person; a local authority, a private individual, or a representative organization. The position of the local authority is the most straightforward. Section 222 of the **Local Government Act 1972** gives local authorities power to bring proceedings in their own name if they 'consider it expedient for the promotion or protection of the interests of the inhabitants of their area'. Private individuals and representative organizations, on the other hand, have to demonstrate sufficient interest.

In *R v Secretary of State for the Environment ex parte Rose Theatre Trust Co.* 'the Theatre Company' was formed to preserve the remains of a historical theatre which was discovered during the development of a site. The company's application for the theatre to be protected under the **Ancient Monuments and Archeological Areas Act 1979** failed and the company sought judicial review of the Secretary of State's decision. Its standing to seek judicial review was challenged on the ground that it did not have 'sufficient interest' in the matter. This challenge succeded on the basis that the company could have no greater claim to standing than its individual members had.

Recently, however, there has been a trend towards granting standing to environmental organizations. In *R v HMIP and MAFF ex parte Greenpeace*, Greenpeace sought judicial review of the decision to grant British Nuclear Fuels Ltd permission to test its nuclear plant at Sellafield. BNFL's challenge of the applicant's standing failed. The court held that Greenpeace was an entirely responsible and respected body with a genuine concern for the environment, 2 500 of whose members lived around the plant. Additionally, Greenpeace had the expertise to mount a well-informed challenge thereby saving the court's time and resources. The judge distinguished the *Rose Theatre case* on the basis that the company had been formed for the exclusive purpose of saving the theatre and no individual member could show any personal interest in the outcome.

Similarly, in *R v Secretary of State for the Environment ex parte Friends of the Earth*, FoE sought judicial review of the Secretary of State's decision not to take enforcement action against two suppliers of public drinking water for their failure to meet the standards prescribed for the pesticide levels in drinking water. The court held that FoE had standing to bring the application since FoE was 'a company of high repute and accepted as having relevant expertise'.

The rationale for granting standing to environmental organizations in the two decisions is the expertise of the relevant organizations, enabling them to conduct an action professionally and thus save the court's time and resources. This is important, particularly in an era when environmental protection has become a complex and professional pursuit involving the interpretation of complex pieces of legislation and sifting through technical and scientific evidence. It is self-evident that an individual would not be able to mount the sort of well-informed challenge that is often necessary.

R v Poole BC ex parte Beebee and Others took this trend further and recognized the overtly environmental agenda of such organizations. The case concerned an application for judicial review of a grant of planning permission for a housing development on land which the Nature Conservancy Council wished to designate as a 'site of special scientific interest'. Two representatives of the Worldwide Fund for Nature (UK) and two members of the British Herpetological Society (BHS) applied for judicial review of the decision.

The BHS had a long-established association with the subject sites and much of its work had been funded by the Nature Conservancy Council. Indeed one of the conditions of the planning permission for the housing estate provided that 'prior to any development starting on the site a full season's notice shall be given to the BHS to enable the catching and relocation of rare species known to inhabit the site'. The position of the WWF was that it had made grants to the BHS since 1971 to assist them in carrying on their work and was an internationally renowned environmental organization. The court held that 'the BHS, with its long association with this site, its financial input into the site and its connection with planning permission by being named therein, had sufficient interest to make the application for judicial review'. The WWF, however, did not, on its own, have sufficient interest.

This case seems to indicate that by close association and active involvement with environmental protection issues, particularly at local levels, an environmental organization can acquire sufficient standing to bring an application whose purpose is the protection of the environment. Fully developed, this would amount to granting standing to an organization to represent environmental interests, the closest one can come to giving the environment standing in its own right.

12.2.3 Costs

The general rule is that the party losing pays the costs of the successful party. These can be considerable and costs are often a deterrent, preventing many individuals and environmental organizations from bringing an application for judicial review.

There is a line of cases indicating that a non-party (such as an environmental organization) who provides financial support for litigation which does not succeed may be held liable for the successful party's costs. In *Singh v Observer Ltd* the court said

> the court would not be helpless to make an order, should it be proved that an action has truly been kept going purely because of outside financing, and thus to have been maintained, without the maintainer having any interest whatsoever in the litigation, and by persons who hope never to be made liable for a penny of the other side's costs, should their action fail.

This restricts the extent to which environmental organizations can resort to the strategy of prompting an individual who has standing to bring the action. The court may order the organization to meet the costs of the action, in spite of the fact that the name of the organization does not appear in the case.

The courts have discretion to waive the general rule as to costs. Increasingly, it is argued that environmental organizations who act out of a genuine concern for the environment, rather than for personal gain, should be encouraged by not being made to pay costs should the action fail. This argument succeeded in *the Greenpeace case* but failed in *the Friends of the Earth case*. The court in the latter case said that 'while there may be something to be said for a subsidy to be given by the tax payer to FoE, this is an inelegant way of achieving that'. Thus, the issue is still unresolved and is likely to vary from case to case.

12.3   Action under Private Law

12.3.1   The Causes of Action

As indicated above, there four private law causes of action: trespass, nuisance, the rule in *Rylands v Fletcher* and negligence.

Trespass

Trespass arises where a person causes physical matter to come into contact with another's land. Trespass, therefore, protects an occupier's right to enjoy his or her land without unjustified interference. It is limited, however, to direct, rather than indirect, interference as illustrated by *Southport Corporation v Esso Petroleum Co. Ltd*. Owing to a defect in its steering gear, an oil tanker belonging to the first defendant became stranded in the estuary of a river. To prevent the tanker from breaking its back, the second defendant, the ship's master, jettisoned 400 tons of oil cargo which was carried by the tide to the foreshore belonging to the plaintiffs, causing damage. The plaintiffs brought action based on trespass, nuisance and negligence. The court dismissed the trespass claim because 'the discharge of oil was not done directly onto their foreshore, but outside in the estuary. It was carried by the tide onto their land, but that was only consequential, not direct. Trespass, therefore, does not lie'.

Nuisance

There are two types of nuisance; public and private. Often the same act gives rise to both types of nuisance simultaneously.

A public nuisance is an interference with the public's reasonable comfort and convenience. A public nuisance is an interference with a public right and is a common law criminal offence. As Denning LJ said in *Attorney General v P.Y.A. Quarries Ltd* 'it is a nuisance which is so widespread in its range and so indiscriminate in its effect that it would not be reasonable to expect one person to take proceedings on his own responsibility to put a stop to it, but that it should be taken on the responsibility of the community at large'. A recent example in the context of environmental law is the prosecution of South West Water Authority in early 1991 for having supplied drinking water that was contaminated with aluminium sulphate to residents of Cornwall.

Private nuisance is an interference with an occupier's use and enjoyment of his or her land. But not all interferences amount to a nuisance; to do so the interference must be unreasonable, causing material and substantial injury to property or unreasonable discomfort to those living on the property. The defendant's responsibility arises from his use of his or some other land in such a way as to injure a neighbouring occupier. In *Southport Corporation v Esso Petroleum Co. Ltd*, discussed above, the court held that 'the discharge of oil was not a private nuisance because it did not involve the use by the defendants of any land, but only of a ship at sea'. Thus, nuisance is intended to govern the way neighbouring occupiers use their respective property. It is for this reason that it is the tort most frequently relied upon in claims relating to pollution and other environmental degradation.

The reasonableness or otherwise of the activity giving rise to the nuisance depends on the locality in which the activity is conducted, a factor of considerable importance in environmental disputes. In *Sturges v Bridgman*, a confectioner had for more than twenty years used a pestle and a mortar in his back premises which abutted on the garden of a physician. The noise and vibration were not felt as a nuisance and were not complained of. But in 1873 the physician erected a consulting room at the end of his garden, and then the noise and vibration became a nuisance to him. His action for an injunction was granted, the Appeal Court holding that

> whether anything is a nuisance or not is a question to be determined, not merely by an abstract consideration of the thing itself, but in reference to its circumstances; what would be a nuisance in Belgrave Square would not necessarily be so in Bermondsey.

Strict Liability: the Rule in Rylands v Fletcher

The rule arose from the eponymous case in which the defendant had constructed a reservoir to collect and hold water for his mill. Under the defendant's land were underground workings of an abandoned coal mine the existence of which he was unaware. After the reservoir had been filled the water escaped down the underground workings through some old shafts, flooding the plaintiff's colliery. The plaintiff sued and the court's decision was that

> the person who for his own purposes brings on his land and collects and keeps there anything likely to do mischief if it escapes must keep it in at his peril, and if he does not do so, is *prima facie* answerable for all the damage which is the natural consequence of the escape.

The case went on appeal to the House of Lords which confirmed this statement of the law, one of the judges adding that the defendant was liable because he had been engaged in a 'non-natural use of his land'.

The case made a landholder strictly liable for the consequences of escapes from his or her property. This cause of action has not been relied upon greatly, partly because the meaning of 'non-natural use' has never been clear, some taking the view that it refers to hazardous uses of land with others arguing that it means no more than bringing onto land things 'not naturally there'.

Negligence

The tort of negligence arises from a failure to exercise the care demanded by the circumstances with the result that the plaintiff suffers an injury. Unlike the three other causes of action, the ability to bring an action for negligence is not based on the occupation of property. A plaintiff needs to show that he or she is owed a 'duty of care' and that the defendant has breached that duty, resulting in damage to the plaintiff.

In *Donoghue v Stevenson*, Lord Atkin stated that the duty of care is owed to 'persons so closely and directly affected by the defendant's act that he ought reasonably to have them in contemplation as being so affected when directing his mind to the acts or omissions which are called in question'. Foreseeability (i.e. could a reasonable person in the defendant's position have foreseen the damage resulting?) is inherent in negligence as a cause of action.

12.3.2 Private Law Remedies

As indicated above there are three private law remedies: damages, injunction, and declaratory judgment. An award of damages is compensation given to a party who has suffered an injury. The sum awarded is determined on the basis that the injured party should be put in the position he or she would have been in if he or she had not been injured. An injunction, on the other hand, is a court order directing a party either to do or to refrain from doing something. It is normally granted to stop a continuing injury or in circumstances where damages would not be adequate compensation. Thus an injunction will not be granted unless the injury is serious.

Typically, the court balances the inconvenience which refusing the injunction would cause the plaintiff against the inconvenience which granting it would cause the defendant, a concept referred to as the 'balance of convenience'. This has been criticized on the ground that forcing a plaintiff to accept monetary compensation because the defendant's activity would suffer greatly if an injunction were granted is comparable to acquiring compulsorily the plaintiff's right to the enjoyment of his or her property. However, the balance of convenience principle applies only where the damage can be adequately compensated monetarily; if not, an injunction will be granted although it may be suspended to give the defendant time to take remedial measures (*Pride of Derby and Derbyshire Angling Association Ltd v British Celanese Ltd*).

Finally, the declaratory judgment is a court's declaration of the rights and duties of parties to an action but without an award of either an injunction or damages. Its value lies in settling a dispute before damage actually occurs. However, as the court stated in *Gouriet v Union of Post Office Workers* 'the jurisdiction of the court is not to declare the law generally or to give advisory opinions; it is confined to declaring contested legal rights, subsisting or future, of the parties represented in the litigation before it and not those of anyone else' (p. 510).

12.3.3 The Riparian Owner's Right to Water

Under common law a land-owner (or occupier) is presumed to own everything on the land 'up to the sky and down to the centre of the earth', a principle now much attenuated by statutory restrictions. Equally important is the common law principle which considers running water, air and light as being 'things the property of which belongs to no person but the use to all' (*Liggins v Inge*). Accordingly, a land-owner has no property in running water, air and light as such; what his or her ownership gives him or her is a 'natural right' to use these elements. The right is incidental to the ownership of land. A riparian owner has, for instance, 'a right to water' (*Stockport Waterworks Company v Potter*).

Riparian owners are land-owners (and occupiers) whose property is contiguous to running water, giving them access to the water. They have a 'a right to water' because they are able, of right, to exercise the right available to all members of the public to use running water; others can only exercise this right under some arrangement with a riparian owner, otherwise they would be committing a trespass in crossing riparian land to get to the water. The right to water is one shared by all riparian owners and so its use must be reasonable. No one owner may use the water in a way which prejudices the right of other riparian owners (*Embrey v Owen*). The corollary to the right to water, air and light is the right to sue under common law against unreasonable and prejudicial use by other riparian owners.

The extent of the riparian owner's right to water and therefore the scope of reasonable use of water is reducible to three rights: a right of access (and navigation), a right to the natural quantity of the water in the watercourse and a right to the natural quality of that water. These three rights are known as 'riparian rights'.

The right to navigate a tidal river belongs to all members of the public but only a riparian owner has a right of access to his or her land, enabling him or her to embark and disembark there (*Lyon v Fishmongers Company*). The riparian owner's right to quantity enables him or her to abstract, divert, obstruct or impound the water, although this is now subject to restrictions under the **Water Resources Act 1991**.

The water abstracted may be used for 'ordinary', i.e. domestic, purposes, such as drinking in which case there is no restriction on the quantity which may be abstracted, even if this exhausts all the water in the river (*McCartney v Londonderry & Lough Swilly Railway*). Water abstracted for 'extraordinary' purposes, such as irrigation, is restricted insofar as it is subject to the rights of other riparian owners; the riparian owner must restrict its use to his or her land and not give it to third parties if this would diminish the quantity available to other riparian owners (*Swindon Waterworks Co. v Wilts & Berks Canal Navigation Co.*). The right to quality entitles the riparian owner to the flow of water past his or her land in its natural state of purity, undeteriorated by noxious matter discharged into it by others (*Jones v Llanrwst UDC*).

12.3.4   The Cambridge Water Company Case

This case, *Cambridge Water Company v Eastern Counties Leather plc*, fought on the basis of the traditional riparian owner's right to quality, illustrates the continuing utility of these common law principles in the context of environmental protection. Eastern Counties Leather (ECL) produced leather at its tannery in Sawston near Cambridge. In the leather tanning process the company used chlorinated solvents, first tricloroethene (TCE) and later perchloroethene (PCE). Until 1976 the solvent was delivered in 40-gallon drums; when solvent was needed a drum was taken by forklift truck and tipped into a tank. After 1976 the use of forklifts was discontinued, the solvent being piped directly. During the period when forklifts were used, regular, but small, spillages of PCE occurred. PCE seeped into the ground beneath ECL's works and made its way into the aquifer below. It was accepted in court that a reasonable supervisor at ECL could not have foreseen, before 1976, that these spillages would enter the aquifer or damage the water there. The only harm that could have been foreseen was that somebody might be overcome by fumes from a spillage.

The Cambridge Water Company (CWC) was set up by statute to supply water in the Cambridge area. In 1976 it purchased a borehole at Sawston Mill, built a new pumping station and in 1979 put it into use. In 1980 the EEC Directive 80/778 relating to the quality of water intended for human consumption was adopted, setting a limit on PCE concentrations in drinking water. In 1980 an analytical chemist discovered that the water supplied in the Cambridge area had PCE concentrations far in excess of the limit set in the Directive. The source of the PCE contamination was traced to the Sawston Mill borehole which was then taken out of use. Investigations led to the conclusion that the PCE contamination had originated from ECL's premises.

CWC brought an action against ECL on grounds of negligence, nuisance and *Rylands v Fletcher*. The High Court dismissed the action on the ground that ECL could not reasonably have foreseen that such damage could occur and that in any case the use of solvent such as PCE was not a non-natural use of land under the rule in *Rylands v Fletcher*. The Court of Appeal allowed CWC's appeal on the ground that an earlier case, *Ballard v Tomlinson*, had held that where the nuisance is an interference with a natural right incident to riparian ownership then the liability is a strict one; accordingly there was no basis for attaching importance to the reasonableness of ECL's inability to foresee the consequence of those spillages. ECL appealed to the House of Lords.

The House of Lords held that there was no rule of law imposing liability for unforeseeable damage simply because the right affected was a natural right: 'The question whether liability may attach in any particular case must depend on the principles governing liability under [nuisance or *Rylands v Fletcher*]'. The court disagreed also with the High Court's view that storage of PCE was not a non-natural use of land, thinking it 'an almost classic case of non-natural use'. However, the court did not clarify the meaning of the phrase beyond stating that the creation of employment is not enough to make a particular use a natural use. Third, the court held that *Rylands v Fletcher* did not create liability any more strict than that created under nuisance; the two differed only insofar as *Rylands v Fletcher* enabled action to be brought in cases of isolated escapes from land. This was a significant development insofar as it had previously been assumed that *Rylands v Fletcher* created liability which was somehow stricter than liability under nuisance, covering activities thought to be ultra-hazardous. The court's stance was that any such liability would have to be imposed expressly by statute.

The court's decision on two other issues were of particular concern to the business community in that the development of civil liability in areas such as contaminated land was seen to be linked to the court's decision in this case. The decision on foreseeability was considered crucial, the argument being that a ruling that foreseeability was not necessary would be tantamount to introducing 'retrospective liability', i.e. liability for damage which could not be foreseen at the time of the relevant act. To the relief of the business community, the court held that 'foreseeability of harm is a prerequisite for the recovery of damages in nuisance and *Rylands v Fletcher*'. The court granted ECL's appeal on the basis of foreseeability, holding that since ECL could not have foreseen the damage they could not be liable. The court thus affirmed the decision in *The Wagon Mound* (No. 2) (1967), the case seen as having imposed the test of foreseeability of damage in nuisance actions.

The other issue concerned whether the basis of liability should be strict liability or fault-based liability, i.e. liability only where fault or negligence could be shown. On this issue the judgment was less pleasing to the business community which favours fault-based liability. The court held that liability in nuisance as well as in *Rylands v Fletcher* is strict liability and not based on any finding of fault: 'The fact that the defendant has taken all reasonable care will not of itself exonerate him from liability'.

This very important decision is likely to consolidate the growing practice of environmental audits to ensure that foreseeable environmental damage is rectified. At a time of growing environmental awareness and standards the defence of unforeseeability will prove difficult to sustain in future. Similarly, as proof of fault is not necessary to sustain a cause of action in both nuisance and *Rylands v Fletcher*, an impetus towards higher standards in the operation of environmentally damaging activities is likely to be created.

12.4 EC and Council of Europe Civil Liability Laws

Civil liability as a mechanism for repairing environmental damage is high on the agenda of several international organizations, including the EC and the Council of Europe. Several proposals have come forward and the Council of Europe has adopted a Convention on the subject.

12.4.1 The Council of Europe Convention on Civil Liability

The Council of Europe Convention on civil liability for damage resulting from activities dangerous to the environment was agreed in March 1993 and opened for signature at Lugano, Switzerland on 21 June 1993. So far, Cyprus, Finland, Greece, Iceland, Ireland, Italy, Liechtenstein, Luxembourg and The Netherlands have signed it. The UK has signalled its intention not to sign it. The European Commission has indicated that it is not seeking the approval of the Council of Ministers for European Union member states to sign it pending the resolution of its own proposals on civil liability. But the Convention needs only three ratifications and so it is likely to come into force soon.

The Convention applies to dangerous activities, defined as activities involving dangerous substances, but not nuclear substances; activities involving genetically modified organisms and micro-organisms; waste handling operations and landfilling operations. It does not apply, however, to carriage unless it is by pipeline or is an integral part of other activities. The Convention makes the operator of the dangerous activity strictly liable for damage (including pure economic loss as well as preventive measures and measures for reinstatement) caused during the period when that operator was exercising control over the activity. The Convention only applies to incidents or continuous occurrences taking place after its entry into force.

If the incident consists of a continuous occurrence all operators successively exercising control during the occurrence shall be jointly and severally liable; an operator shall, however, be liable only for the part of the damage that occurred while he or she was in control. If the damage becomes known after such dangerous activity has ceased the last operator shall be liable unless he or the person who suffered damage proves that all or part of the damage resulted from an incident before he became the operator in which case he shall only be liable for that part of the damage resulting from incidents while he was the operator.

The Convention makes specific and exclusive provision for landfill sites. Essentially, the operator at the time when damage caused by waste becomes known is liable for the damage. If, however, the damage only becomes known after the closure of the site, the last operator will be liable. But if it is proved that only a part of the damage was caused by the landfill operation, the operator will be liable for only that part. An attempt is made to avoid retrospectivity in that the Convention only applies to damage which becomes known after the Convention enters into force, ignoring the date of the incident which actually caused the damage. Further, there is no liability if the site was closed lawfully (rather than abandoned) before the entry into force of the Convention or if the operator proves, where the operation continues after the Convention enters into force, that the damage was caused solely by waste deposited before that entry into force.

The Convention provides that the operator shall not be liable in five situations: (1) to wars and similar situations; (2) acts of a third party; (3) where the damage resulted necessarily from compliance with a specific order or compulsory measure of a public authority; (4) pollution 'at tolerable levels' under local relevant circumstances; and (5) a dangerous activity taken lawfully and reasonably in the interest of the injured party. The Convention requires state parties to ensure that operators conducting a dangerous activity are required to participate in a financial security scheme or to have and maintain an appropriate financial guarantee to cover the liability under the Convention.

The Convention also makes provision for access to information held by public authorities. It provides that the person who suffered damage may request the court to order an operator to provide him with information necessary to establish a claim for compensation under the Convention. An operator against whom a claim is made may also request the court to order another operator to provide him with information necessary to establish the extent of his possible obligation to compensate the person who has suffered the damage, or of his own right to compensation from the other operator. Any operator may, however, refuse to provide information where such information may incriminate him.

There is a three-year limitation period within which actions for compensation must be brought beginning with the date on which the claimant knew, or ought reasonably to have known, of the damage and the identity of the operator. In any case, action cannot be brought after thirty years from the date of the incident which caused the damage. This period runs from the end of the last occurrence in cases of a series of occurrences. In respect of landfills the thirty years run from the date on which the site was closed.

An innovative feature of the Convention is the provision enabling associations whose objective is the protection of the environment to bring an action in an administrative or judicial forum requesting the prohibition of the activity or the taking of preventive, corrective or remedial measures. Before ruling on the request the body with whom the request is lodged may hear the competent public authorities.

12.4.2 Civil Liability for Damage Caused by Waste

This EC proposal for a Directive on civil liability for damage caused by waste (COM (89) 282 final—SYN 217) (OJ No. C 192/6) was submitted by the Commission on 1 September 1989. It was later amended. The proposed directive makes the producer of waste liable under civil law for the damage and impairment of the environment caused by the waste, irrespective of fault. The proposal does not cover nuclear waste or damage by oil regulated under relevant international Conventions. The remedies available shall include an order to reinstate the environment and/or take preventive measures or pay the costs for such measures. The proposal provides that common interest groups or associations whose object is the protection of nature and the environment shall have the right to seek any of the available remedies.

The proposal states that the producer shall not be relieved of liability because he holds a permit issued by the public authorities. It provides a thirty-year limitation period for the right to bring an action. The proposal provides for compulsory insurance cover or other financial security. It also requires the Commission to study the feasibility of a European fund for compensation for damage and impairment of the environment caused by waste.

The proposal also attempts to rule out retrospective effect by stating that it will not apply to damage or impairment of the environment arising from an incident which occurred before the date of implementation. The proposal has not been adopted by the Council of Ministers and the signs are that it has been overtaken by the Green Paper on Civil Liability which the Commission subsequently published.

12.4.3 The Green Paper on Civil Liability

On 14 May 1993 the European Commission published a Green Paper on Remedying Environmental Damage (COM (93) 47 final) for consultation. It considers the usefulness of civil liability as a means of allocating responsibility for the costs of environmental restoration. Its preference appears to be for a strict liability regime. Second, it seeks to investigate the possibility of remedying environmental damage not met by the application of civil liability principles. This arises where damage arises from chronic pollution, authorized pollution and past pollution. It investigates details of existing joint compensation schemes, their problems and limitations. Issues identified as requiring consideration include the need to ensure that environmental restoration is achieved, the allocation of the costs of restoration among responsible sectors of the economy and the need to maintain a preventive effect while sharing responsibility more widely.

The Commission invited comments on the Green Paper by 1 October 1993. On 3 and 4 November a joint hearing of the Commission and Parliament was held in Brussels to discuss this issue further. The Commission has yet to act on the results of the consultation process. Only the UK, Denmark and The Netherlands sent written responses to the consultation paper by the October deadline. The UK took the view that action at EC level was not necessary, a view with which the House of Lords Committee on the European Communities disagreed (House of Lords, 1993). It is thought that the next stage will be a Commission paper setting out firm proposals for action before a draft directive is proposed. An EC directive on this issue is therefore likely to take several years to develop.

12.5 Personal Injuries Claims

There is a growing trend for personal injuries litigation arising out of claims of damage caused by environmental pollution. These claims, two recent examples of which are set out below, have been funded by legal aid which is available under the **Legal Aid Act 1988** in appropriate cases. The principle issue in these cases concerns causation.

Reay and Hope v British Nuclear Fuels concerned a claim that ionizing radiation emitted from the nuclear processing activities carried on by BNFL at Sellafield was the cause of death from leukaemia of the first plaintiff's daughter and of cancer suffered by the second defendant; the plaintiff's case was based, not on the alleged effects of the radiation on themselves, but on paternal preconception irradiation (PPI) causing mutation in the sperm of the plaintiff's fathers and through this means causing a predisposition in the children to these diseases. The case failed because the court held that there was insufficient evidence that PPI could cause these diseases.

A second example concerns a claim against an electricity company by people who developed brain tumours. The claim is based on the allegation that electricity pylons over the plaintiffs' houses created eletromagnetic fields which caused the tumours. The case has yet to come to court and therefore it is not clear whether the plaintiffs will succeed in establishing causation (*Daily Telegraph*, 1994).

Personal injuries claims based on environmental pollution are private law claims and are determined on the principles requiring proof of causation, foreseeability and duty of care. Because the injury is indirect, proof of causation will remain a significant problem for plaintiffs in cases of this kind.

References

A. G. (Gambia) v Njie [1961] 2 All ER 540, 511.
Attorney General v P. Y. A Quarries Ltd [1957] 2 QB 169.

Ballard v Tomlinson [1885] 29 Ch D 115.

Burke v Minister of Housing and Local Government (1957) 8 P & C.R, 25 (digested in 57, 1583).

Buxton v Minister of Housing and Local Government [1961] 1 QB 278.

Cambridge Water Company v Eastern Counties Leather plc [1994] 1 All ER 53.

Daily Telegraph, 'Childhood leukaemia linked to power lines', 9 June 1994.

Donoghue v Stevenson [1932] AC 562.

Embrey v Owen (1851) 6 Exch. 353, 155 ER 579.

Equal Opportunities Commission v Secretary of State for Employment [1994] 1 All ER 910.

Gouriet v Union of Post Office Workers [1978] AC 435.

House of Lords Select Committee on the European Communities, *Remedying Environmental Damage*, 3rd Report, HMSO (1993).

Inland Revenue Commissioners v National Federation of Self-Employed Businesses Ltd [1982] AC 617.

Jones v Llanwrst UDC [1911] 1 CHD 393.

Liggins v Inge (1831) 7 Bing 682, 131 ER 263, 268.

Lyon v Fishmongers Company [1876] 1 App. Cas. 662.

McCartney v Londonderry & Lough Swilley Railway [1904] AC 301.

Overseas Tankship (UK) Ltd. v Marts Dock & Engineering Co. Ltd. (The Wagon Mound) [1967] AC 617.

Pride of Derby and Derbyshire Angling Association v British Celanese Ltd [1953] 1 All ER 179.

R v HMIP and MAFF ex parte Greenpeace, The Independent, 30 September 1993.

R v Secretary of State for the Environment ex parte Friends of the Earth, The Times, 4 April 1994.

R v Secretary of State for the Environment ex parte Rose Theatre Trust Co [1990] 1 QBD 504.

R v Poole BC ex parte Beebee and Others (1991) 3/2 *Journal of Environmental Law*, 293.

Reay and Hope v British Nuclear Fuels (1993, unrep.).

Rose v Miles (1815) 105 ER 773.

Rylands and Fletcher (1886) ER 3 HL 330.

Singh v Observer Ltd [1989] 2 All ER 751, 756.

Southport Corporation v Esso Petroleum Co. Ltd [1954] 2 QBD 182.

Stockport Waterworks Co. v Potter (1864) 3 H & C 300, 159 ER 545.

Sturges v Bridgman (1879) 11 CH D 852.

Swindon Waterworks Co. v Wilks & Berks Canal Navigation Co. (1875) 7 LR 697.

Turner and Another v Secretary of State for the Environment (1973), Vol. 288, *The Estates Gazette*, 32.

Wade, E.L.S. and Bradley, A.W., *Constitutional and Administrative Law*, 11th edn, Chap. 30, Longman (1991).

Appendix: Table of Criminal Offences, Defences and Penalties

Contents

Water Resources Act 1991
(Regulator—NRA)

Statutory provision	Offence	Defences	Penalty	
			Magistrates' court	Crown court
1 S. 85 (1) and (2)	Discharging to controlled waters matter which is poisonous, noxious or polluting	• Discharge made under a consent or authorization (s. 88) • Discharge made in an emergency; reasonable steps taken to minimize effects; and NRA notified (s. 89(1))	£20 000 and/or 3 months in prison	Unlimited fine and/or 2 years in prison
2 S. 85(3) and (4)	Discharging trade or sewage effluent to controlled waters/sea or to land	"	£20 000 and/or 3 months in prison	Unlimited fine and/or 2 years in prison
3 Ss 24 and 25	Abstracting or impounding water from a source of supply	Abstraction/impoundment made under licence Abstraction falls within statutory exception (s. 27)	£5 000	Unlimited fine
4 S. 173 and Sch. 20 para. 7	Obstructing an officer of the NRA exercising a power of entry under ss 169–172	• Obstruction not intentional • Reasonable cause	£1 000	
5 S. 202(4)	Failing to comply with a notice to supply information required in connection with the control of pollution	Failure due to 'reasonable excuse'	£5 000	

Water Industry Act 1991
(Regulators—DWI and sewerage companies)

Statutory provision	Offence	Defences	Penalty Magistrates' court	Crown court
1 S. 70	Supplying water unfit for human consumption	• Did not know that water would be used for human consumption • Took reasonable steps and exercised due diligence to prevent breach	£5 000	Unlimited fine and/or 2 years in prison
2 Ss 84(5) and 168–172	Intentionally obstructing officer exercising power of entry	• Obstruction not intentional • Reasonable excuse	£1 000	
3 S. 85(3) and S. 203(4)	Failure to comply with notice to supply information	Reasonable excuse	£5 000	
4 S. 86(6) and Sch.6 para 12	Failure to comply with duty to give assistance and information required by DWI Inspector	Reasonable excuse	£5 000	
5 S. 109(1)	Obstructing entry by DWI Inspector	• Obstruction not intentional • Reasonable excuse	£1 000	
	Causing a drain or sewer to communicate unlawfully with a public sewer	Communication made with permission of sewerage undertaker	£2 500	
6 S. 111(3)	Putting a prohibited substance into a public sewer or into a drain or sewer	• Substance not a prohibited substance • Consent of sewerage undertaker	£5 000 plus £50 on each day on which offence continues	Unlimited fine and/or 2 years imprisonment
7 SS 118(5) and 121(5)	Discharging trade effluent into public sewer	Discharge made under a consent	£5 000	Unlimited fine

EPA 1990, Part I IPC and LAAPC
(Regulators—HMIP and local authorities)

Statutory provision	Offence	Defences	Penalty	
			Magistrates' court	Crown court
1 S. 23(1)(a)	Carrying on a prescribed process	Process carried on under authorization	£20 000	Unlimited fine and/or 2 years in prison
2 S. 23(1)(b)	Failing to notify authority that authorization has been transferred		£5 000	Unlimited fine and/or 2 years in prison
3 S. 23(1)(c)	Contravening prohibition or enforcement notice		£20 000	Unlimited fine and/or 2 years in prison
4 S. 23(1)(d)	Failing to answer questions or furnish information required by Inspector	Document protected by legal professional privilege (s. 17(10))	£5 000	
5 S. 23(1)(e)	Preventing another from answering Inspector's questions		£5 000	
6 S. 23(1)(f)	Obstructing Inspector	Obstruction not intentional	£5 000	
7 S. 23(1)(g)	Failing to comply with notice to supply information	Reasonable excuse	£5 000	Unlimited fine or 2 years in prison
8 S. 23(1)(h)	Making false statement	Did not know statement was false	£5 000	Unlimited fine or 2 years in prison
9 S. 23(1)(i) and (j)	Making a false entry in records kept under s. 7 or possessing a forgery	Did not know statement was false	£5 000	Unlimited fine or 2 years in prison
10 S. 23(1)(k)	Impersonating an Inspector		£5 000	
11 S. 23(1)(l)	Failure to obey court order to remedy matters		£20 000	Unlimited fine and/or 2 years in prison

Waste Management, Part II of EPA 1990 etc.
(Regulators—WRA)

Statutory provision	Offence	Defences	Penalty	
			Magistrates' court	Crown court
1 S. 33(1)(a) and (b)	Depositing or keeping, treating or disposing of waste	• Activity conducted under a licence/exemption • Took reasonable steps to avoid offence • Instructed by employer and unaware of offence • Acts done in emergency and authority informed	£20 000 and/or 6 months in prison	Unlimited fine and/or 2 years in prison
2 S. 33(5)	Managing special waste	,,	,,	Unlimited fine and/or 5 years in prison
3 S. 1 of the Control of Pollution(Amendment) Act 1989	Transporting waste	,,	£5 000	
4 S. 34 (EPA 1990)	Breach of Duty of Care as respects waste	Took all reasonable measures to avoid breach	£5 000	Unlimited fine
5 S. 69(9)	• Failing to answer Inspector's questions or produce documents • Preventing another from doing so • Obstructing Inspector	Documents covered by legal professional privilege Obstruction not intentional	£5 000	
6 SI 1980 No. 1709	Failing to comply with special waste consignment note requirements	• Took all reasonable steps and exercised due diligence to avoid offence • Acted in emergency and complied as soon as possible	£5 000	Unlimited fine and/or 2 years in prison

Continued overleaf

Waste Management, Part II of EPA 1990 etc. *Concluded* (Regulators—WRA)

Statutory provision	Offence	Defences	Penalty	
			Magistrates' court	Crown court
7 SI 1988 No. 1652	Failure to comply with transfrontier shipment of waste consignment note requirements	"	"	"

Statutory nuisance, Part III of EPA 1990

(Regulator—local authority)

Statutory provision	Offence	Defences	Penalty	
			Magistrates' court	Crown court
1 SS 80(4) and 82(8)	Contravening a statutory nuisance abatement notice	Reasonable excuse	£5000 plus £50 for each day of offence	
2 S. 80(6)	Contravening a statutory nuisance abatement notice on industrial, trade or business premises	• Reasonable excuse • Best practicable means used to prevent or minimize nuisance • In relation to noise, noise covered by consent	£20 000	

Litter, Part IV of EPA 1990
(Regulator—litter authority)

Statutory provision	Offence	Defences	Penalty	
			Magistrates' Court	Crown court
1 S. 87	Leaving litter	• Litter left lawfully • Litter left with consent • of owner/occupier or other responsible person	£2 500	
2 Ss 87 and 88	Leaving litter	"	Fixed penalty of £10 imposed by litter authority officer (not court)	
3 Ss 91(9) and 92(6)	Failure to comply with litter-abatement order		£2 500 plus £125 for each day of offence	
4 S. 94(9)	Failure to comply with a court order requiring compliance with a street litter control notice	Reasonable excuse	£2 500	

GMOs under Part VI of EPA 1990
(Regulators—DoE and HSE)

Statutory provision	Offence	Defences	Penalty	
			Magistrates' court	Crown court
1 S. 118(1)(a)	Importing or acquiring, releasing or marketing GMOs	• Acted under and consent/exemption • Carried out a risk assessment and gave notice to the Secretary of State • Did not know it was a GMO • Took all reasonable precautions and exercised due diligence to avoid offence	£5 000 and/or 6 months in prison	Unlimited fine and/or 5 years in prison
2 S. 118(1)(b)	Failure to carry out a risk assessment and/or give Secretary of State notice and/or information	"	"	"
3 S. 118(1)(c)	Keeping GMOs	• Acted under consent/exemption • Did not know if it was a GMO • Took all reasonable precautions and exercised due diligence to avoid offence	£20 000 and/or 6 months in prison	Unlimited fine and/or 5 years in prison
4 S. 118(1)(d)	• Importing or acquiring GMOs without carrying out risk assessment • Importing or acquiring GMOs despite risk to the environment	• Not required to carry out risk assessment • Acted under consent • Did not know it was a GMO • Took all reasonable precautions and exercised due diligence to avoid offence	"	"

Continued overleaf

GMOs under Part VI of EPA 1990 *Concluded*
(Regulators—DoE and HSE)

Statutory provision	Offence	Defences	Penalty Magistrates' court	Crown court
5 S. 118(1)(d)	• Keeping GMOs without informing himself of possible damage to the environment and identifying risks • Continuing to keep GMOs despite risks • Not using BATNEEC to keep GMOs and prevent damage to the environment	"	"	"
6 S. 118(1)(d)	Releasing or marketing GMOs without informing himself of risks; despite risks; or without using BATNEEC to prevent damage to the environment	"	"	"
7 S. 118(1)(e)	Not keeping a record of risk assessment or giving Secretary of State required information	Reasonable excuse	£5 000 and/or 6 months in prison	Unlimited fine and/or 2 years in prison
8 S. 118(1)(f)	Contravening a prohibition notice	Took reasonable precautions and exercised due diligence to avoid offence	£20 000 and/or 6 months in prison	"
9 S. 118(1)(g)	Failing to answer questions or produce documents or assist Inspector exercising a power of entry	• Reasonable cause • Document protected by legal professional privilege	£5 000 and/or 3 months in prison	

		Offence	Defence		
10	S. 118(1)(h)	Preventing another from appearing before or answering Inspector's questions		"	"
11	S. 118(1)(i)	Obstructing Inspector	Obstruction unintentional	£5 000 and/or 6 months in prison	Unlimited fine and/or 2 years in prison
12	S. 118(1)(j)	Obstructing Inspector from sampling, seizing or destroying GMOS	"	"	"
13	S. 118(1)(k)	Failing to provide relevant information as required under a notice by the Secretary of State	Reasonable excuse	"	"
14	S. 118(1)(l)	Making false/misleading statement	Did not know statement to be false	"	"
15	S. 118(1)(m)	Making false entry in records	Falsehood not intentional	"	"
16	S. 118(1)(n)	Forging or using forged document	No intent to deceive	"	"
17	S. 118(1)(o)	Pretending to be an inspector		£5 000	
18	S. 118(1)(p)	Continuing keeping a GMO without a risk assessment or giving notice to Secretary of State despite conviction of an offence	• Acted under a consent/exemption • Took reasonable precautions and exercised due diligence to avoid offence	£1 000 on each day on which offence continues	

Town and Country Planning Act 1990
(Regulator—local planning authority)

Statutory provision	Offence	Defences	Penalty	
			Magistrates' court	Crown court
1 S. 171D	Failing to comply with a planning contravention notice	Reasonable excuse	£1000	
2 S. 179	Non-compliance with an enforcement notice	• Did everything to secure compliance • Not aware of the existence of enforcement notice	£20 000	Unlimited fine
3 S. 187	Contravening a stop notice		"	"
4 S. 188	Contravening an order under s. 102 requiring discontinuance of use or alteration or removal of buildings or works	Took all reasonable measures and exercised due diligence to avoid offence	£5 000	"

Noise offence under COPA 1974, Part III

(Regulator—local authority)

Statutory provision	Offence	Defences	Penalty	
			Magistrates' court	Crown court
1 S. 60(8)	Contravening a construction site noise control notice	Acted under a s. 61 consent	£5 000 plus £50 for each day on which offence continues	
2 S. 61(10)	Failing to bring consent to the notice of person carrying out construction work	Took all reasonable steps	"	
3 S. 65(5)	Emitting noise exceeding registered level	Acted under consent	"	
4 S. 66(8)	Contravening a noise reduction notice	• Reasonable excuse • If a business or a trade, used best practicable means to prevent/counteract noise	"	

Offences under Health and Safety at Work etc. Act 1974
(Regulator—HSE)

Statutory provision	Offence	Defences	Penalty Magistrates' court	Crown court
1 S. 33(1)(a)	Failing to ensure the health, safety and welfare at work of employees (s. 2(1))	Did everything that was reasonably practicable	£20 000	Unlimited fine
2 "	Failing to prepare and revise a written statement of policy on the health and safety at work of employees (s. 2(3))		"	"
3 "	Conducting undertaking without ensuring that non-employees are not exposed to risk (s. 3(1) and (2))	Did everything that was reasonably practicable	"	"
4 "	Failing to take reasonable measures to ensure that premises are safe and without risk to non-employees (s. 4)	"	"	"
5 "	Failing to prevent emissions of noxious or offensive substances (s. 5)	• Used best practicable means to prevent and render emissions harmless • Process in question is a prescribed process	"	"
6 "	Failing to ensure that article or substance is so designed and constructed as to be safe and without risk to persons at work (s. 6(1)(a) and s. 6(4)(a))	• Did everything reasonably practicable • Not its manufacturer, importer, designer or supplier	"	"

No.	Offence	Defence		
7	Failing to test and examine article or substance (s. 6(1)(6) and s. 6(4)(b))	"	"	
8	Failing to supply necessary information about intended use of article or substance and conditions necessary for its safe and risk-free use and dismantlement (s. 6(1)(c) and s. 6(4)(c))	"	"	
9	Failing to inform persons supplied about risks (s. 6(1)(d) and s. 6(4)(d))	"	"	
10	Failing to research into and eliminate/minimize risk to health and safety by article or substance (s. 6(2) and s. 6(5))	• Not its designer or manufacturer/supplier importer • Did everything reasonably practicable	"	
11	Failing to ensure that an installed article is safe and risk free	• Not the person who installed it or supplied or imported it • Did everything reasonably practicable	"	
12	An employee fails to take reasonable care of his health and safety and of others at work or to cooperate with employer (s. 7)	"	"	
13 S. 33(1)(b)	Interfering with or misusing things provided for health, safety or welfare (s. 8)	Action not intentional and not reckless	£20 000	Unlimited fine and/or 2 years in prison

Continued overleaf

Offences under Health and Safety at Work etc. Act 1974 *Concluded* (Regulator—HSE)

Statutory provision	Offence	Defences	Penalty Magistrates' court	Penalty Crown court
14 S. 33(1)(e)	Failing to answer questions or produce documents or assist Inspector (s. 20)	• Document protected by legal professional privilege • Reasonable excuse	£2 000	
15 S. 33(1)(f)	Preventing another from appearing before and answering questions of Inspector		£2 000	
16 S. 33(1)(g)	Contravening a prohibition/enforcement notice		£20 000 and/or 6 months in prison	Unlimited fine and/or 2 years in prison
17 S. 33(1)(h)	Obstructing customs officer detaining articles or substances	Obstruction not intentional	£2 000	
18 S. 33(1)(i)	Contravening a notice to furnish information to the Health and Safety Commission		£2 000	
19 S. 33(1)(n)	Pretending to be an Inspector		£2 000	
20 S. 33(1)(o)	Failing to comply with a court order to remedy matters		£20 000 and/or fine 6 months in prison	Unlimited fine and/or 2 years in prison
21 S. 33(1)(d)	Contravening a requirement under Health and Safety Regulations		£2 000	
22 S. 33(1)(c)	Contravening requirement or prohibition imposed by Health and Safety Regulations (made under s. 15 of the Act)	Various defences stated on the face of the relevant Regulations	£2 000 or specified in Regulations	Unlimited fine and/or where action contrary to a licence or without a licence, then 2 years in prison; or specified in Regulations

Injurious substances
(Regulator—HSE)

Statutory provision	Offence	Defences	Penalty Magistrates' court	Crown court
1 SI 1993/1643	Contravened restriction on use and/or marketing of cadmium		£5 000	Unlimited fine and/or 2 years in prison
SI 1992/1583 and SI 1992/311	Ugilec 141,121 or 21 and/or DBBT; PCBs and PCTs		,,	,,
SI 1993/1	Lead carbonate and sulphate in paint and mercury components in textiles; PCP		,,	,,
2 SI 1994/232	Contravening prohibition on marketing of certain batteries and/or Secretary of State's notice	Reasonable excuse	£100	
3 1994/199	Importing, loading, unloading, supplying storing non-refrigerant containers contrary to prohibition		£5 000	Unlimited fine and/or 2 years in prison

Control of Pesticides Regulations 1986
(Regulators—DoE/MAFF and local authorities)

Statutory provision	Offence	Defences	Penalty	
			Magistrates' court	Crown court
1 SI 1986/1510 and Food and Environment Protection Act 1985, s. 16(12)	Advertising, selling, supplying, storing or using a pesticide	Action done under approval	£5 000	Unlimited fine

Planning and Hazardous Substances Act 1990

(Regulator—local planning authority)

Statutory provision	Offence	Defences	Penalty	
			Magistrates' court	Crown court
1 S. 23	Having on land a quantity of a hazardous substance above controlled quantity	• Acted with consent • Did not knowingly cause to be on land and/or did not know of presence • Was not in control of land • Took all reasonable precautions and exercised all due diligence to avoid offence • Could only be avoided by breaking statutory duty	£20 000	Unlimited fine

Index